AMERICAN POLITICS:
THE PROMISE OF DISHARMONY

By the same author:

No Easy Choice: Political Participation in Developing Countries
    (with Joan M. Nelson, 1976)

The Crisis of Democracy (with Michel Crozier and Joji Watanuki, 1975)

Authoritarian Politics in Modern Society: The Dynamics of Established
    One-Party Systems (coeditor with Clement H. Moore, 1970)

Political Order in Changing Societies (1968)

Political Power: USA/USSR (with Zbigniew Brzezinski, 1964)

Changing Patterns of Military Politics (editor, 1962)

The Common Defense: Strategic Programs in National Politics (1961)

The Soldier and the State: The Theory and Politics of Civil-Military
    Relations (1957)

American Politics: The Promise of Disharmony

Samuel P. Huntington

THE BELKNAP PRESS

OF HARVARD UNIVERSITY PRESS

Cambridge, Massachusetts, and London, England   1981

Written under the auspices of the Center for International Affairs,
Harvard University

Library of Congress Cataloging in Publication Data

Huntington, Samuel P.
   American politics.

   Includes index.
   1. United States—Politics and government—
Philosophy.   2. Idealism, American.   3. Social
classes—United States.   I. Title.
JK39.H84   320.973   81–10051
ISBN 0–674–03020–6   AACR2

For

Timothy and Nicholas

who inherit the promise

PREFACE

The ultimate origins of this book are to be found in one of my more helpless moments as a young man. At the start of my Ph.D. oral examinations in May 1949, Professor Samuel H. Beer fixed me with a steady eye and asked: "Mr. Huntington, what is the relation between political thought and political institutions?" I did not answer the question then, but I have been grappling with it ever since. This book is an effort to deal in part with this question in the American context. It was written as an extended essay and is meant to be suggestive rather than definitive. Its purpose is to set forth a way of looking at American politics that emphasizes elements that have at times tended to be neglected and to provide a perspective that in some measure explains why America has had both so much political consensus and so much political conflict.

My active work on the relation between American political ideas and political institutions began in 1973 when I was the beneficiary of a Guggenheim Fellowship and a Visiting Fellowship at All Souls College, Oxford. The results of this initial thinking were embodied in an article, "Paradigms of American Politics: Beyond the One, the Two, and the Many," *Political Science Quarterly* 89 (March 1974): 1–26, portions of which are incorporated into this book. I completed first drafts of two chapters before my entry into the government in early 1977, but the bulk of the writing was done after my return to Harvard in the fall of 1978. During this latter period my work was greatly facilitated by grants from the American Enterprise Institute for Public Policy Research and from National Affairs, Inc. Throughout, the Center for International Affairs at

Harvard helped tremendously by furnishing an intellectually and materially supportive environment for research and writing.

The refinement of the ideas in this book was forwarded by the questions and challenges to which those ideas were subjected by the students in my course on American political development. Many people provided invaluable assistance to me in my research; they include John Heine, Kenneth I. Juster, Christopher Leman, Mahmoud Mamdani, Arthur Sanders, and Steven R. Verr. Barbara Talhouni, Cynthia Knuth, and Linda Cohn patiently and expertly typed draft after draft. Aida Donald and Austin Ranney read the manuscript in toto and nicely managed to be both critical and encouraging in their comments.

To all these individuals and institutions—as well as to others not named here—I am deeply grateful for contributions that truly were indispensable to the making of this volume.

CONTENTS

1 The Disharmonic Polity   1
  "Our Practice of Your Principles"   *1*
  The One, the Two, and the Many:
     Structural Paradigms of American Politics   *5*
  Ideals versus Institutions   *10*

2 The American Creed and National Identity   13
  Political Thought in America   *13*
  Sources, Scope, and Stability of the Creed   *14*
  Political Ideas and National Identity   *23*

3 The Gap: The American Creed versus Political
     Authority   31
  Consensus and Instability   *31*
  The Gap in Comparative Perspective   *42*

4 Coping with the Gap   61
  The American Case of Cognitive Dissonance   *61*
  Patterns of Response   *64*
  The Gap and American Political Style   *75*

5 The Politics of Creedal Passion   85
  Creedal Passion Periods in American History   *85*
  The Climate of Creedal Passion   *91*
  Creedal Conflict: The Movement and the Establishment   *105*
  Reform and Its Limits   *112*
  Political Earthquakes and Realignment   *122*

6   The Sources of Creedal Passion   130

Why Creedal Passion Periods? 130
General Sources:
   Comparable Phenomena in Other Societies 131
Specific Sources:
   The Timing of Creedal Passion Periods 138
Original Sources:
   The Roots of It All in the English Revolution 149
The Protestantism of American Politics 154

7   The S&S Years, 1960–1975   167

From the Fifties to the Seventies:
   The Changing Pattern of Response 167
Complacency and the End (?) of Ideology 169
Interlude of Hypocrisy, Surge of Moralism 173
The Mobilization of Protest 180
The Dynamics of Exposure 188
The Legacies 196
Reform and the IvI Gap 197
Institutional Realignment 203
The Misuse and Erosion of Authority 211
Cynicism and the Restoration of Authority 214

8   The Viability of American Ideals and Institutions   221

The Future of the Gap 221
History versus Progress? 222
America versus the World? 236
Power and Liberty: The Myth of American Repression 246
The Promise of Disappointment 259

Notes   265

Index   293

AMERICAN POLITICS:
THE PROMISE OF DISHARMONY

1 THE DISHARMONIC POLITY

"Our Practice of Your Principles"

As is His wont, God did not dare. Although it had showered the night before, the morning of the second Thursday in June 1969 dawned warm and sun-drenched. Steamy vapors rose from the soaking grass and dripping chairs, carefully ordered in their rows in the Yard, promising a hot and humid day for Harvard's 318th commencement. But although the University authorities maintained their usual casual optimism about the cooperation of the Almighty, there was considerable concern that less godly creatures might dare to be less accommodating. Turmoil, protest, and violence were reaching new peaks on American campuses that spring. The previous year, Columbia University had erupted into chaos. In April 1969 had come Harvard's turn, with the seizure of University Hall, the police bust, the student strike, the disruption of classes, and the endless mass meetings and bullhorns, demonstrations and demands, caucuses and resolutions. The night before commencement, prolonged negotiations among university officials, student leaders, and SDS (Students for a Democratic Society) extremists had produced an agreement that the normal order of ceremony would be interrupted to permit one of the SDS revolutionaries to speak briefly to the throng of ten thousand. Before dawn a contingent of younger and presumably somewhat more robust faculty members had been quietly admitted through the locked gates of the Yard and had surrounded and occupied the platform—a pre-emptive measure to head off others with more disruptive intentions.

As it turned out, such precautions were unnecessary. Overt revolutionary challenges to civil and academic authority during the two-hour ceremony were minimal. The SDS speaker "blew it," as one student said, with a tedious, uncompromising monologue which elicited loud boos from the audience. The protest walkout from the ceremonies drew less than two hundred students. The revolutionary impulse was limited to a clenched-fist greeting to university president Nathan Pusey by the graduating seniors, serving along with the clenched fists stenciled on their academic gowns as a lingering reminder of the upheavals earlier in the spring.

The revolutionary challenge to established authority thus fizzled in Harvard Yard, as it has always fizzled in American society. But one major challenge to established authority was posed in the Yard that day, and in traditional American pattern it came not from the fringes but from the mainstream. In appropriate Harvard fashion, it was posed intellectually rather than physically. It was to be found in the English Oration delivered by Meldon E. Levine, a native of Beverly Hills, California, and a graduate student in law. "What is this protest all about?" Levine asked. Addressing himself to the alumni, faculty, and parents and presuming to speak for his fellow students, he answered this question briefly—and accurately. Our protest, he said, is not an effort "to subvert institutions or an attempt to challenge values which have been affirmed for centuries. We are NOT," he emphasized, ". . . conspiring to destroy America. We are attempting to do precisely the reverse: we are affirming the values which you have instilled in us and which you have taught us to respect. You have told us repeatedly that trust and courage were standards to emulate. You have convinced us that equality and justice were inviolable concepts. You have taught us that authority should be guided by reason and tempered by fairness. AND WE HAVE TAKEN YOU SERIOUSLY." We have tried to put into practice your principles, Levine told the older generation, and you have frustrated us and obstructed us. "You have given us our visions and then asked us to curb them." We want to do what you have taught us is right to do, but "you have made us idealists and then told us to go slowly." All we ask is that "you allow us to realize the very values which you have held forth."

Speaking on behalf of the younger generation, Levine did not contemptuously confront his elders with the claim that a youthful European Marxist or African nationalist might have made: We reject your reactionary, traditional, outworn beliefs and instead proclaim our own radical and revolutionary principles. Instead, his plea was a peculiarly American one: We of the younger generation simply want to put into practice those ideals in which you—and we—believe. It is, as he summed it up in the title of his talk, "a conflict of conscience: our practice of your principles." We question your war, your repression, your temporizing, your inaction in the name of your basic values. We do not proclaim a New Truth to challenge the old myths of earlier generations. We instead invoke the Old Truths and charge you, the older generations, with deserting those truths. You are the apostates, not we. You are, in effect, the subversives; we are the loyalists, who proudly reaffirm the principles that you ignore.

Levine's remarks were greeted with a loud, sustained, standing ovation from his classmates, while many parents and alumni, as one reporter put it, "sat stony-faced and silent."[1] As a child of the 1960s (who had been president of the Berkeley student body during the 1964 uprising there), Levine had precisely caught the spirit of that decade. By and large, the struggles of the 1960s did not involve conflicts between partisans of different principles. What the 1960s did involve was a reaffirmation of traditional American ideals and values; they were a time of comparing practice to principle, of reality to ideal, of behavior to belief. Politically the 1960s began with sit-ins, bus boycotts, and civil rights marches, focused on that area of American life where the gap between ideal and reality was most obvious and blatant. Politically this period of idealistic reaffirmation came to a climax in the end of a Presidency in which the gap between practice and principle likewise became morally and politically intolerable. The years between were filled with protests, outraged moral protests, at the failure of political institutions and leaders to perform in the way expected of them, and with escalating exposures of the breadth of the gap between political ideal and political reality. The principal struggles were between those who wanted to reshape reality to conform with the ideal—immediately—and those who were willing to tolerate the gap for varying lengths of time. Many questioned, for instance, the means and the speed with which racial inequities should be remedied, but no one articulated a systematic defense of racial discrimination. Many were reluctant to see a President driven from office, but no one systematically defended dishonesty and dissimulation by public officials. What was at issue was not a matter of principle but the way in which those principles should and could be applied in practice.

This gap between political ideal and political reality is a continuing central phenomenon of American politics in a way that is not true of any other major state. The importance of the gap stems from three distinctive characteristics of American political ideals. First is the *scope* of the agreement on these ideals. In contrast to most European societies, a broad consensus exists and has existed in the United States on basic political values and beliefs. These values and beliefs, which constitute what is often referred to as "the American Creed," have historically served as a distinctive source of American national identity. Second is the *substance* of those ideals. In contrast to the values of most other societies, the values of this Creed are liberal, individualistic, democratic, egalitarian, and hence basically antigovernment and antiauthority in character. Whereas other ideologies legitimate established authority and institutions, the American Creed serves to delegitimate any hierarchical, coercive, authoritarian structures, including American ones. Third is the changing *intensity* with which Americans believe in these basic ideals, an intensity that varies from time to time and from group to group. Historically, American society seems to evolve through periods of creedal passion and of creedal passivity.

As a result of these three characteristics, an ever-present gap exists between American political ideals and American political institutions and practice. This gap has altered during the course of American history, at times narrowing and at other times broadening. These changes reflect both changes in "objective" reality—the distribution of power in American society—and also, of course, changes in the nature of American ideals and in the intensity of commitments that Americans have to those ideals. "Witness the intensity with which" we hold to our—and your—convictions, Levine implored his commencement audience. Other decades have lacked this intensity; the rhetoric of ceremonial addresses has been the same but the passion has been absent. The age of protest of the 1960s, however, was a period of moral reaffirmation, a period in which the best as well as the worst were filled with a passionate intensity focused on the need to realize in practice the central principles and values of the American Creed.

The 1960s thus had much in common with other periods of creedal passion, when the values of the American Creed had been invoked to challenge established institutions and existing practices—periods such as the Revolutionary era of the 1760s and 1770s, the Jacksonian age of the 1820s and 1830s, and the Populist-Progressive years of the 1890s and 1900s. In a sense, the gap between ideal and institution condemns Americans to coexist with a peculiarly American form of cognitive dissonance. At times, this dissonance is latent; at other times, when creedal passion runs high, it is brutally manifest, and at such times, the promise of American politics becomes its central agony.

The One, the Two, and the Many: Structural Paradigms of American Politics

This central characteristic of American politics has received little notice in the traditional theories or paradigms of American politics. Over the years, the prevailing images of American politics have been shaped by three such paradigms.

What is often referred to as the "Progressive" theory emphasizes the continuing conflict between the few who are rich and the many who are poor. It is, indeed, better referred to as the "class-conflict" theory of American politics, since it has been espoused by many others in addition to early-twentieth-century Progressive historians. Federalist thinkers such as John Adams assumed that "there is no special providence for Americans, and their nature is the same with that of others." Consequently, they also assumed that the social divisions that existed elsewhere would be reproduced in America. "The people, in all nations," Adams said, "are naturally divided into two sorts, the gentlemen and the simplemen . . . The great and perpetual distinction in civilized societies has been between the rich, who are few, and the poor, who are many." In similar terms, Alexander Hamilton agreed that "all communities divide themselves into the few and the many."[2] In postulating this image, Hamilton's sympathies were with the rich, while Adams was deeply and equally suspicious of both rich and poor. At the end of the nineteenth century the Progressive historians attacked Federalist politics and identified themselves with the poor, while retaining the Federalist picture of American society. The essence of the Progressive paradigm was well summed up by Vernon Parrington in notes that he wrote for but did not use in *Main Currents of American Thought:*

> From the first we have been divided into two main parties. Names and battle cries and strategies have often changed repeatedly, but the broad party division has remained. On one side has been the party of the current aristocracy—of church, of gentry, of merchant, of slave holder, or manufacturer—and on the other the party of the commonality—of farmer, villager, small tradesman, mechanic, proletariat. The one has persistently sought to check and limit the popular power, to keep the control of the government in the hands of the

few in order to serve special interests, whereas the other has sought to augment the popular power, to make government more responsive to the will of the majority, to further the democratic rather than the republican ideal—let one discover this and new light is shed on our cultural tendencies.[3]

The Progressive interpretation dominated American historical writing until after World War II, when it was displaced by the consensus theory. It was maintained, however, by Marxist analysts and radical sociologists, such as C. Wright Mills, and came back to the fore in the writings of New Left revisionist historians of the 1960s.

The key elements of the Progressive approach, as with that of the Federalists, were, first, a stress on the significance of economic interests, as distinguished from idealistic purposes, as the motive moving men in history, and, second, an emphasis on the extent to which American history (and, for the Federalists, history generally) could be interpreted in terms of the clash between two contenders for wealth and power: the popular party and the elite party. Over time, the particular groups in this conflict might change, but the struggle itself would continue. The Progressives clearly hoped that in due course the popular party would triumph, but there was nothing in their theory to specify why or when this should happen. Until that nebulous point in the distant future did arrive, American history would be an ongoing struggle between the good guys and the bad guys, and, as Louis Hartz pointed out, one of the comforting aspects of their theory was that it "always had an American hero available to match any American villain they found, a Jefferson for every Hamilton."[4]

The consensus theory of American politics posits an image of American politics that is, in many respects, the polar opposite of the Federalist-Progressive approach. According to this theory, the key to understanding American history is not the conflict between two classes but rather the overwhelming predominance of the middle class. For a variety of reasons —the absence of feudalism, the abundance of free land, the shortage of labor, the resulting opportunities for vertical and horizontal mobility, the early introduction of universal manhood suffrage, and the prevalence of a "Lockean" ethos of liberty, equality, individualism—class consciousness and class conflict never developed in the United States as it did in Europe. Instead there was the "pleasing uniformity" that had struck Crèvecoeur and the social and political equality that had so impressed Tocqueville. As a result, class-based ideologies never developed in American politics as they did in European politics. A consensus on middle-class values prevailed, and the conflicts that have existed in American politics have been over relatively narrow issues of economics and personality within the framework of the all-pervading basic consensus.

The consensus theory received its classic statement in the works of Tocqueville. It was reformulated in more nationalistic terms by the "Patriotic" historians in the latter part of the nineteenth century and then reappeared in its most self-conscious and explicit form in the two decades after World War II in the writings of Richard Hofstadter, Daniel Boorstin, Talcott Parsons, David Potter, Daniel Bell, Seymour Martin Lipset, and, most notably, Louis Hartz. The popularity of the theory at this time reflected the success of the New Deal and the failure of social revolution in the 1930s, the general prosperity and abundance of American life, and the emergence of the Cold War as the central feature of American foreign relations.

In contrast to the Progressive theorists, the consensualists tended to place their argument about the United States in a comparative context. For Hartz in particular, comparison with Europe was a central theme. Viewed from a European vantage point, he argued, the dualism that had been the focus of the Progressives shrank almost to insignificance. Unlike Europe, America lacked both feudalism and socialism. The controversies of American history were all among different varieties of liberalism. Widespread liberalism, in turn, reflected the absence of an aristocracy and of a class-conscious proletariat and the dominance of a middle class. In so arguing, Hartz used Marxist categories to arrive at Tocquevillian conclusions. Unchallenged by competing ideologies, however, American liberalism in his view lost its ideological system and rigor; it became immobile, irrational, absolute, and unthinking, at times turning in on and shadowboxing against itself.

A third theory, the pluralist paradigm, holds that the central feature of American politics is the competition among interest groups. The process version of this approach sees politics as a struggle among large numbers of relatively small interest groups. The organization version emphasizes the dominant role of a small number of large, well-organized groups in shaping public policy. Proponents of the process theory tend to be favorably disposed toward that process, seeing a rough approximation of the public interest emerge out of open, competitive struggle in the political free market, where it can be assumed that constitutional and governmental structures do not significantly discriminate among groups in terms of their access to the political process. Proponents of the organization version, on the other hand, usually emphasize the extent to which the established groups control the political process and make meaningless many of the pretensions of the democratic system premised on individual equality. At the extreme, this version of the pluralist approach can have many resemblances to the class-conflict theory.

The pluralist paradigm received its classic statement by James Madison in *The Federalist* (particularly Number 10). It was reformulated by Arthur F. Bentley in the early twentieth century, and it reemerged as the dominant interpretation of American politics among political scientists after World War II. It is, in some measure, quite compatible with the consensus paradigm, since the conflicts among interest groups over particular issues can be conceived of as occurring within the framework of a broad agreement on basic political values. In fact, one paradigm almost implies the existence of the other: they differ in that one stresses the basic agreement and the other the specific issues that are fought over within the context of this agreement.

Each of these three theories has its strengths and its weaknesses. The class-conflict theory points accurately to the existence in America of significant inequalities in wealth and income. It argues inaccurately, however, that these differences have been a principal continuing basis for political cleavage in American society. While American politics has at times been polarized, it has seldom, if ever (the New Deal was the most notable exception), been polarized between rich and poor. More generally, in attempting to sandwich American political struggle into a simple, dualistic framework, the class-conflict theory does scant justice to the complexity and variability of the struggle. For many of the class-conflict theorists, class conflict more accurately describes what they think American politics should be like rather than what it actually has been like over the course of centuries. The consensus theory, on the other hand, rightly acknowledges the absence of European class-based ideologies and the widespread agreement in the United States on liberal, democratic, individualistic, Lockean political values. Particularly in its Hartzian formulation, however, it also tended to suggest that the existence of an ideological consensus meant the absence of any form of significant social conflict. In fact, the United States has had more sociopolitical conflict and violence than many European countries. "Americans," as Hofstadter neatly put it, "do not *need* ideological conflict to shed blood on a large scale."[5] Why this should be the case is ignored by consensus theory. Finally, the plural-

THE DISHARMONIC POLITY 9

ist paradigm—in both its process and organizational versions—clearly describes the way in which American politics functions a good part of the time. It does not, however, anymore than the consensus theory, provide for or explain the passion, upheaval, or moral intensity that at times envelopes the American political scene.

All three paradigms share one important characteristic: each explains politics in terms of social structure. The decisive influences on American politics are not the political values, institutions, and practices or the processes of change and development, but rather the nature of American society. The issue at stake among them is whether American society can best be understood in terms of one consensus, two classes, or many groups. From this structural approach flow two other implications.

First, the structural characteristics of society that shape its politics are held to be relatively permanent. Each theory, as we have seen, has had its own proponents over the years going back to the eighteenth century. The consensus theory acknowledges little or no change in the consensus. The class-conflict theory holds that the particular classes may change (that is, from landowners versus landless to capitalists versus workers), but the division of society between rich and poor—and the conflict between rich and poor—goes on. In similar fashion, the pluralist theory allows for the rise and fall of specific groups in the political process but not in the underlying pluralistic character of society or in the way groups interact in American politics. In its own way, each paradigm sets forth a picture of how American politics functions at any one point in time; none sets forth a picture of how American politics changes over time. Each is essentially static in its approach. How will American society and politics in the future differ from what they have been in the past? According to all three, the answer essentially is more of the same.

Second, all three paradigms posit the predominant role of economic and materialistic interests in politics. The upper and lower classes of the class-conflict theory are divided by their economic differences and they conflict with each other in politics over their respective efforts to maintain and enhance these differences or to reduce and perhaps even eliminate them. The interest groups of pluralist theory can include ethnic groups, but have been conceived primarily in economic terms as regional, occupational, and industrial groups. Lastly, the consensus theory does highlight the importance of political values and ideas, but argues that either the absence of such ideas or the broad agreement on them precludes serious political conflict. That agreement, in turn, rests on the overwhelming predominance of the middle class. Whereas the class-conflict and pluralist theories see American politics dominated by the scrambling of grubby materialistic interests, the consensus theory reduces it all to placid harmony and dullness.

Ideals versus Institutions

The structural paradigms of American politics are not totally wrong, but they are limited. They omit almost entirely the role that political ideas and idealism, moral causes, and creedal passions have played in American politics. Almost everyone agrees that the United States was conceived in terms of certain political ideals and inspired by the promise or dream of liberty and equality. These political ideals are central to American national identity and have played a critical role in shaping American political evolution and development. Yet the pluralist theory of American politics ignores them entirely, the class-conflict theory sees them simply as the ideological weapons of opposing economic classes promoting their own materialistic interests, and the consensus theory suggests, in effect, that because they are universally accepted they are universally irrelevant. Rich fight poor for more of the economic pie, groups squabble over their allocations of the pie, or all relax in their enjoyment of it. That the political ideals and visions which define the existence of the nation might also be central to understanding its politics and might play a crucial role in shaping its political conflicts and political development seems to be an unrecognized possibility. The structural paradigms portray an American politics without purpose, without moral conflict, without passion, without promise, and, most importantly, without guilt. Can class conflict, group process, or consensus fully explain the passions and the intensity of the 1960s, the 1890s, the 1860s, the 1830s, and, most importantly, the 1770s? The structural picture of American politics is not so much Hamlet without the Prince of Denmark as it is Deuteronomy without the vision of the promised land.

When foreigners ask, "What is American politics all about?" it cannot be explained to them simply in terms of a Namier-like struggle of faction and group, or a Marxist-like confrontation of classes, or a complacent consensus. It is, in some measure, all of these things, but it is also much more. To see American politics purely as a reflection of social structure is to miss the teleological—as distinguished from the mechanistic—dimension of that politics. The ways in which individuals, groups, and classes act in politics are decisively shaped not only by their own perceptions of their immediate interests but also by the ideological climate and the common political values and purposes that they all recognize as legitimate. The United States has lacked European-style ideological conflict, yet its politics has been infused with more moral passion than those of any European country. "America," Santayana once observed, "is all one prairie, swept by a universal tornado."[6] The consensus theory posits the uniformity of the prairie but not the fury of the tornado that the prairie's very flatness engenders. In the United States, ideological consensus is the source of political conflict, polarization occurs over moral issues rather than economic ones, and the politics of interest groups is supplemented and at times supplanted by the politics of moralistic reform. America has been spared class conflicts in order to have moral convulsions. It is precisely the central role of moral passion that distinguishes American politics from the politics of most other societies, and it is this characteristic that is most difficult for foreigners to understand.

The importance of political ideas and values in shaping the course of American development has not always been neglected in historical writing, and in part for this reason it tended to become discredited. The progressive realization of American ideals was a familiar theme among nineteenth-century "Patriotic" historians. "The unifying principle" of history for George Bancroft, as Hofstadter points out, "was progress ordained and planned by God—the advance of liberty, justice, and humanity, all of which were peculiarly exemplified in American history, where providential guidance had brought together a singularly fit people and fit institutions . . . American history could be seen as a kind of consummation of all history."[7] The same theme, viewed considerably more ambivalently, was also present in Tocqueville. Common to both was the concept of American history as a gradual but steady unfolding and realization of the ideals of liberty, equality, and democracy.

This interpretation accurately highlighted the extent to which the pursuit of these ideals was central to the American political experience. What it did not highlight, however, was the extent to which the failure to realize those ideals was equally central to that experience. The image of the triumphant realization of the American promise or ideal was an exercise in patriotic unreality at best and hypocrisy at worst. The history of American politics is the repetition of new beginnings and flawed outcomes, promise and disillusion, reform and reaction. American history is the history of the efforts of groups to promote their interests by realizing American ideals. What is important, however, is not that they succeed but that they fail, not that the dream is realized but that it is not and never can be realized completely or satisfactorily. In the American context there will always be those who say that the institutional glass is half-empty and who will spill much passion attempting to fill it to the brim from the spring of idealism. But in the nature of things, particularly in America, it can never be much more than half-full.

This gap between promise and performance creates an inherent disharmony, at times latent, at times manifest, in American society. In a harmonic society, as André Béteille has argued, the existential and normative orders are consistent with each other; in a disharmonic society they are in conflict. "In a harmonic system inequalities not only exist in fact but are also considered legitimate. In a disharmonic system inequalities are no longer invested with legitimacy although they continue to exist in fact." Traditional India with its caste system was a harmonic society because its social inequalities were considered legitimate. The United States, on the other hand, is a disharmonic society because its social and political inequalities "exist in a moral environment which is committed to equality."[8]

Social, economic, and political inequalities may well be more limited and political liberties more extensive in the United States than they are in most other societies. Yet the commitment to equality and liberty and the opposition to hierarchy and authority are so widespread and deep that the incongruity between the normative and existential orders is far greater in the United States than elsewhere. Traditional India was clearly more unequal than modern America, but modern America is clearly more disharmonic than traditional India. The extent to which a society or a political system is harmonic or disharmonic depends as much upon the values of its people as upon the structure of its institutions. Any society, moreover, necessarily involves a certain irreducible minimum of inequality and hierarchy. The variations in attitudes toward inequality, hierarchy, and authority among the peoples of different societies are likely to be at least as great as the variations in actual inequality, hierarchy, and authority among those societies, particularly in the modern world. With its unique consensus on and commitment to liberal, democratic, and egalitarian political values, the United States is the modern disharmonic polity par excellence.

2 THE AMERICAN CREED AND NATIONAL IDENTITY

Political Thought in America

The poverty of political thought in America has been a frequent source of complaint on the part of social critics and political scientists. This complaint is, by and large, justified: political theory has been relatively underdeveloped in the United States in comparison with Europe. Outstanding political philosophers and highly systematized class-based ideologies have been notably absent from the American scene. But it is a mistake to move from this truth to the assumption that political ideas have played a less significant role in the United States than they have in Europe. In fact, just the reverse may be true. In America, political ideas may have been less sophisticated in theory but they have also been more important in impact than in most other societies. They have been a critical element in the definition of national identity and in the delimitation of political authority.

People have been attempting to define American national identity or "national character" ever since national consciousness first emerged in the eighteenth century. Personality traits, social characteristics, geographic and environmental features, behavioral patterns, and historical experiences have all been invoked by one analyst or another. There is no need here to enter into or even to review this continuing debate. Our argument concerns not national character but something much more concrete, identifiable, and measurable: national political values and beliefs. We are concerned not with behavioral or cultural patterns, personality traits, or psychological makeup, but with ideas—specifically political ideas. Our argument is that:

1. Since the late eighteenth or early nineteenth century, there have existed in the United States certain basic political values and ideas that can be thought of as the "American Creed."

2. This Creed has been broadly supported by most elements in American society.

3. Although some modifications of the Creed have occurred over time, its central elements have changed relatively little in the course of two hundred years.

4. In contrast to the situation in most European societies, this Creed has played and continues to play a central role in the definition of American national identity.

Sources, Scope, and Stability of the Creed

What are the values of the American Creed? Innumerable studies have itemized them in various ways, but the same core political values appear in virtually all analyses: liberty, equality, individualism, democracy, and the rule of law under a constitution. These are different and yet related political ideas; they stemmed from several different sources and yet came together so as to reinforce one another in the American mind in the late eighteenth and early nineteenth centuries.

These core ideas are set forth succinctly in the Declaration of Independence. More broadly, they can be thought of as involving several major elements. The oldest is the constitutional strand, with its roots in medieval ideas of fundamental law as a restraint on human behavior. Law, in this sense, was conceived of as something that was beyond human control but not beyond human knowledge. Man discovered law, he did not make it, and this law, whether viewed as divine law, natural law, or customary law, provided the norms for human behavior. In Europe in the seventeenth century, these traditional ideas of law began to be supplanted by new ideas of absolute sovereignty and the power of men—be they absolute monarchs or members of supreme parliaments—to make law as they saw fit. In that same century, however, the older ideas of fundamental law as a restraint on human action were exported to and took root on the American continent.

A second major source of the ideas of the American Creed is seventeenth-century Protestantism, which contributed elements of moralism, millennialism, and individualism to the American political outlook. More particularly, Protestantism stressed the primacy of the individual conscience, the close connection between the spirit of liberty and the spirit of religion, the role of the congregation as a voluntary association, the importance of democracy within the church and its implications for the polity ("no bishop, no king"), and, in due course, the abandonment of religious establishments. The United States is the only country in the world in which a majority of the population has belonged to dissenting Protestant sects. Protestant values reinforced republican and democratic tendencies in the eighteenth century and provided the underlying ethical and moral basis for American ideas on politics and society.

To these strands, the eighteenth century added Lockean and Enlightenment ideas of natural rights, liberty, the social contract, the limited role of government, and the dependence of government upon society. Finally, the idea of equality—set forth boldly in the Declaration of Independence as the basis for organizing society—challenged accepted ideas of the legitimacy of distinctions based on rank, status, and inherited privilege. If all men are created equal, then all must count equally politically, and hence all must have an equal right to vote for their governing officials. The basis was laid for popular sovereignty and the democratization of government in the nineteenth century. The idea of equality, one aspect of the Protestant strand in the American Creed, was thus reinforced by the democratic and revolutionary currents at the end of the eighteenth century.

Ideas of constitutionalism, individualism, liberalism, democracy, and egalitarianism are no monopoly of Americans. In some societies, some people subscribe to many of these ideas and in other societies many people subscribe to some of these ideas. In no other society, however, are all of these ideas so widely adhered to by so many people as they are in the United States.

People sometimes speak of an American "ideology." But in the American mind, these ideas do not take the form of a carefully articulated, systematic ideology in the sense in which this term is used to refer to European belief systems such as traditional conservatism, liberalism, Marxism, social democracy, and Christian democracy. They constitute a complex and amorphous amalgam of goals and values, rather than a scheme for establishing priorities among values and for elaborating ways to realize values. They do not have the key characteristics that distinguish an ideology from other sets of political ideas.[1] They are, for instance, far more diffuse, incoherent, and undeveloped intellectually than Marxism. Some have described these ideas in terms of the "liberal tradition" in America. If one had to apply one adjective to them, "liberal" would be it, but even this term does not convey the full richness and complexity of the amalgam. It thus seems more accurate and appropriate to speak of American political ideas or beliefs in the plural, and in the singular to follow Gunnar Myrdal and others and simply speak of the American Creed.

The unsystematic and unideological character of this Creed is reflected in the fact that no theory exists for ordering these values in relation to one another and for resolving on a theoretical level the conflicts that inherently exist among them. Conflicts easily materialize when any one value is taken to an extreme: majority rule versus minority rights; higher law versus popular sovereignty; liberty versus equality; individualism versus democracy. In other societies, ideologies give priority to one value or the other, but in American society all these values coexist together in theory, even as they may conflict with each other when applied in practice. They coexist, indeed, not only within American society, but also within individual citizens. Though every American may have his own view of the proper balance among these conflicting values, few Americans would unhesitatingly give absolute priority to one value over another. However much one values majority rule, at some point its application is limited by the need to recognize minority rights. However much one believes in individual liberty, at some point individual aggrandizement cannot be permitted to make a mockery of political and moral equality. The checks and balances that exist among the institutions of American politics are paralleled by the checks and balances that exist among the ideas of the American Creed. This political "ideology," as Robert Mc-Closkey noted, is not "a consistent body of dogmas tending in the same direction, but a conglomerate of ideas which may be and often are logically inconsistent." It is "characteristic of the American mind . . . to hold contradictory ideas simultaneously without bothering to resolve the potential conflict between them."[2]

Nowhere is this better illustrated than in the relation between liberty and equality in the American Creed. In Europe these two values are commonly thought to be inherently opposed to each other. From Plato on, political theorists saw the extension of equality as ultimately involving the destruction of liberty, as society becomes homogenized and leveled, paving the way for the rise of the despot. In the eighteenth century, liberty was the aristocratic value and equality the bourgeois democratic value; in the nineteenth century, liberty became the bourgeois value and equality the proletarian value. The expansion of equality thus involved in the eighteenth century the suppression of the rights, liberties, and privileges of estates, orders, and corporations, and in the nineteenth century the restriction of rights of contract and private property. Tocqueville's view of equality in America reflected this European experience. Few Americans have shared his fear that the expansion of equality would signal the death-knell of liberty. The American approach is instead well summed up by Michael Walzer's argument that "liberty and equality are the two chief virtues of social institutions, and they stand best when they stand to-gether."[3] In the United States they did historically move hand-in-hand. They developed in conjunction with, not in opposition to, each other, representing not so much the political values of opposing social classes as the opposing political values of a single middle class. The eighteenth-century value of liberty was quickly joined by the nineteenth-century value of equality. Americans generally give liberty precedence over equality, but different groups assign different weights to each, and virtually all groups give high levels of support to both values.[4] A continuing theme of American political discourse has been the effort to reconcile one with the other, most notably in the economic sphere, where ideas of equality of opportunity coexist with ideas of liberty of achievement. Those who have been concerned with the promotion of one have generally also been concerned with the promotion of the other. "In the United States," Daniel Bell observed, "the tension between liberty and equality, which framed the great philosophical debates in Europe, was dissolved by an individualism which encompassed both." As Herbert Croly put it, "the Land of Freedom became in the course of time also the Land of Equality."[5]

How broad has been the agreement on these ideas? The Americans, said Tocqueville in one of his most quoted remarks, "are unanimous upon the general principles that ought to rule human society." Some foreign and native observers before him and countless numbers after him have reiterated this point. "Americans," Gunnar Myrdal argued, echoing Tocqueville's language one hundred years later, "of all national origins, classes, regions, creeds, and colors, have something in common: a social *ethos,* a political creed."[6] In the mid-twentieth century, the validity of these impressionistic observations was underscored by the overwhelming evidence provided by public opinion poll data. Such data indicated that the key values of the American liberal-democratic Creed commanded the support of well over 75 percent of the population.[7] When the key values and principles of the American Creed are expressed in highly general terms, support for liberty, democracy, majority rule, minority rights, freedom of speech and religion, and, less clearly, equality approaches unanimity from virtually all groups in the American public.[8] As the formulation of values is made more specific and related to concrete applications of these values to particular situations, support drops off considerably and cleavage may become more pronounced than consensus. In such circumstances, those who have more education, who are more active in politics, or who occupy leadership positions in community organizations are more likely to support the values of the Creed.[9] The consensus on the values of the system, in short, is broadest among those most active in the system and who benefit the most from it. Those with higher socioeconomic status also are less likely than those of lower status to perceive major differences between the values of the system and the reality of the system. In terms of overall preferences, however, there would appear to be little doubt that, as one comprehensive analysis in the early 1970s concluded, "the United States has had a high degree of consensus on fundamental political values at the community and regime levels."[10]

The broad agreement that has existed throughout American history on these values is reflected in the fate of potential alternative political value systems. Such systems could only develop where there was some social and economic base to nurture political beliefs different from those that generally prevailed. Three such bases—regional, class, and ethnic—conceivably have existed at one time or another in American history.

The most significant effort to develop an alternative set of political values was that which occurred in the prebellum South. A society based on slavery clearly contradicted virtually all the core values of the American Creed. As a result, as the slave system came under increasing attack after 1830, Southern writers and thinkers developed a highly articulate and systematic conservative defense of the society built on that foundation. Resorting to classic conservative ideas and arguments which historically had been used to defend many other types of societies, they strove to develop an ideological alternative, and the writings of the "Reactionary Enlightenment," to use Hartz's term, constitute an outpouring of political theorizing unique in American history. Conservative ideas were, for them, a weapon to be used to defend their society against the growing economic and demographic preponderance of the North and the intensifying ideological assault of the abolitionists. Their substantive theory, however, remained ambivalent. Wishing to retain what they could of their Jeffersonian heritage, they wavered uncertainly between the philosophies of John Locke and Sir Robert Filmer.[11] In the end, when their society was destroyed in the Civil War, their efforts at alternative political theory died too and were quickly forgotten.

The rapid industrialization that followed the Civil War necessarily involved the creation of an industrial proletariat which, presumably, created the socioeconomic base for a socialist movement comparable to those that were simultaneously emerging in Europe. The failure of such a movement to develop mass political appeal is perhaps the most dramatic evidence of the preponderance of liberal-democratic values in America. The issue of "Why no socialism in the United States?" has been explored at length by a variety of social scientists beginning with Marx and Engels, and various causes have been assigned a variety of weights.[12] The absence of feudalism permitted the unchallenged spread of liberal, bourgeois values and this, in turn, prevented socialism from developing significant appeal: in effect, "no feudalism, no socialism." In addition, the nature of the original settlers (particularly those of the dissenting and separatist religious sects), the abundance of free land, and the opportunities for horizontal and then vertical mobility all promoted the dominance of the middle class. In an agricultural society the basic form of wealth is land, and in most agricultural societies the amount of land is always limited and usually fixed. The population is permanently divided between those who own land and those who do not, or between those who own more land and those who own less. In America, however, no such division of the people could last. The opportunities for land ownership were too real. The resulting failure (outside the plantation South) to develop a system of agricultural classes and the pervasiveness of a "free-farmer society" set the pattern of relative abundance and relative mobility which survived industrialization and urbanization and ensured the widespread adoption of middle-class values and standards.

Although the first working-class parties in the modern world were formed in the United States in the 1830s, industrialization failed to produce a class-conscious working-class movement committed to Marxism or some other form of socialism. This was a result of the prior achievement of universal white male suffrage, the general openness of political institutions, the continuing opportunities for vertical and horizontal mobility, the ethnic diversity and geographic dispersion of the working class, and the preexisting prevalence of the liberal-democratic norms of the American Creed. In some measure, the latter, with their stress on equality and mobility, served indeed as a surrogate form of socialism.[13]

A third possible social base for an alternative to liberal democracy was furnished by the massive influx of poor immigrants with peasant backgrounds from southern and eastern Europe at the end of the nineteenth and the beginning of the twentieth centuries. These immigrants, Hofstadter argued, brought with them an outlook that contrasted dramatically with the prevailing values and moralistic emphases based "upon the indigenous Yankee-Protestant political traditions, and upon middle-class life." This other system,

> founded upon the European backgrounds of the immigrants, upon their unfamiliarity with independent political action, their familiarity with hierarchy and authority, and upon the urgent needs that so often grew out of their migration, took for granted that the political life of the individual would arise out of family needs, interpreted political and civic relations chiefly in terms of personal obligations, and placed strong personal loyalties above allegiance to abstract codes of law or morals. It was chiefly upon this system of values that the political life of the immigrant, the boss, and the urban machine was based.[14]

The interaction between the immigrant ethic and the indigenous ethic provides one way of looking at changes in American politics during the first half of the twentieth century.

The immigrant ethic left its mark upon American political organization and practice, particularly during the New Deal years. But by the early 1960s, the most important development in urban politics was precisely the extent to which the immigrants and their children were replacing their own traditional ethos with that which had been traditional in the United States. "The immigrant lower class has been and is still being absorbed into the middle class at a rapid rate. This has profoundly affected the outlook of the electorate, for the middle class has always held to the Anglo-Saxon Protestant political ideal and those who have joined it have accepted this ideal along with others . . . Increasingly the 'new immigrant' has come to demand candidates who, whatever their origins, have the community-serving ethos and the public virtues that have long been associated with the Protestant elite."[15] The subsequent political events of the 1960s and 1970s confirmed the perspicacity of this analysis. The enhanced significance of ethnic power in American politics was paralleled by the withering of the ethnic ethic in American politics.

No lasting and significant alternatives to the liberal-democratic value system have emerged in the United States. In this respect, the basic proposition of the consensus paradigm is valid. There is, however, still the possibility that the content of the consensus, the mix of values in the liberal-democratic amalgam, may have changed over time. Are the predominant American political values of the late twentieth century basically the same as those of the late eighteenth century? By and large, the classic (that is, Tocquevillian) answer to this question has stressed the continuity in American values: "Two things are surprising in the United States: the mutability of the greater part of human actions, and the singular stability of certain principles. Men are in constant motion; the mind of man appears almost unmoved. When once an opinion has spread over the country and struck root there, it would seem that no power on earth is strong enough to eradicate it . . . Cogent reasons . . . prevent any great change from being easily effected in the principles of a democratic people."[16]

Well over a century later, the judgments of mid-twentieth-century social scientists generally confirmed Tocqueville's conclusion. "Though there were shadings through time," argued Clyde Kluckhohn in 1958, "the central and distinctive aspects of the American value system were remarkably stable from the eighteenth century until the [nineteen] thirties and, in spite of some changes that have occurred and are in process, the characteristic American values remain highly influential in the life of the United States." Five years later Seymour Martin Lipset concluded that "there is more continuity than change with respect to the main elements in the national value system." In 1967 Lloyd Free and Hadley Cantril argued that the Mayflower Compact, John Locke, and the Declaration of Independence "reflect the basic political values that have shaped the American political system for nearly three hundred and fifty years . . . The underlying personal political credos of the majority of Americans have remained substantially intact at the ideological level." An exhaustive survey in 1972 led Donald Devine to affirm in similar language that "the values of Locke, Madison, and the other liberals of the seventeenth and eighteenth centuries represent essentially the same values which comprise the American political culture at the present. Although it has changed, the remarkable phenomenon is that American political culture has survived so unchanged under substantial environmental pressure."[17]

The relative lack of change in American political values is also reflected in the way in which three distinguished European observers summarized the prevailing values at three different points in American history. From Maine to the Floridas, Tocqueville argued,

> and from the Missouri to the Atlantic Ocean, the people are held to be the source of all legitimate power. The same notions are entertained respecting liberty and equality, the liberty of the press, the right of association, the jury, and the responsibility of the agents of government.
> . . . The Anglo-Americans acknowledge the moral authority of the reason of the community as they acknowledge the political authority of the mass of citizens; and they hold that public opinion is the surest arbiter of what is lawful or forbidden, true or false. The majority of them believe that a man by following his own interest, rightly understood, will be led to do what is just and good. They hold that every man is born in possession of the right of self-government, and that no one has the right of constraining his fellow creatures to be happy. They have all a lively faith in the perfectibility of man.[18]

A half-century after Tocqueville, James Bryce summed up the principal elements of the Creed in strikingly similar fashion: (1) the individual has sacred rights; (2) the source of political power is the people; (3) all governments are limited by law and the people; (4) local government is to be preferred to national government; (5) the majority is wiser than the minority; (6) the less government the better. A half-century after Bryce, Gunnar Myrdal argued that Americans had in common a creed of "humanistic liberalism," which developed out of the Enlightenment and which embodied the "ideals of the essential dignity of the individual human being, of the fundamental equality of all men, and of certain inalienable rights to freedom, justice, and a fair opportunity."[19]

All this suggests little change in basic American political values. In the 1950s, however, the thesis was advanced that fundamental changes were taking place in both American national character and American values. The "inner-directed" person was giving way to the "other-directed" person; the group was replacing the individual; the traditional, Puritan, moralistic style and its associated values were being supplanted by a more tolerant, more relativistic, more socially oriented and less achievement-directed style and set of values.[20] If this thesis was valid, it would suggest that substantial changes were under way in the content of the American consensus and that, at least for a time, the consensus would be disrupted along generational and perhaps class lines.

The change thesis was, however, dubious for three reasons. First, a persuasive case was made that the attitudes and values presented by the change thesis as new developments on the American scene had actually figured prominently in descriptions of America by foreign observers since the early nineteenth century.[21] What the change thesis argued was new was, in fact, actually old. Second, the 1960s saw a recrudescence of individualism and moral passion in American politics, as intense as any in American history. What the change thesis argued was passé, in fact turned out to be present a decade later. Finally, the evidence is mixed concerning the extent to which the change thesis holds valid for personal values. Looking at children's reading texts, for example, inner-directed achievement imagery increased during the nineteenth century, then decreased in the twentieth at the same time that other-directed affiliation imagery increased. Surveys of children's ideals (that is, whom they would most like to resemble) during the first six decades of the twentieth century, however, do not show any significant shift away from achievement motivation or any change in aspiration levels.[22] With respect to political values, the evidence overwhelmingly suggests a high level of continuity. Writings purporting to identify peculiarly American traits or values in four different periods of American history (pre-Civil War, 1865–1917, 1918–1933, 1933–1940) showed "no important difference between the traits mentioned by modern observers and those writing in the earlier periods of American history." Traits such as democracy, equality, and freedom were mentioned in all four periods.[23] The verbal symbols in Presidential inaugural addresses also changed little during the first one hundred fifty years of American history.[24] While clearly ideals such as liberty and equality acquire different meanings through their application in new contexts, the core meaning of the value remains. It is, indeed, reaffirmed by being continually reapplied.

Political Ideas and National Identity

For most peoples, national identity is the product of a long process of historical evolution involving common ancestors, common experiences, common ethnic background, common language, common culture, and usually common religion. National identity is thus organic in character. Such, however, is not the case in the United States. American nationalism has been defined in political rather than organic terms. The political ideas of the American Creed have been the basis of national identity.

Thirty years before the battles of Lexington and Concord, the Georgian monarchy had been threatened by another serious challenge much closer to home: in 1745 a Stuart claimant to the throne had raised a Scottish army, broken English rule in Scotland, and advanced to within one hundred twenty miles of London. Separated by only thirty years, these two crises—the '45 and the '75—could hardly have been more dramatically different. One was a traditional conflict involving family, dynasty, nationality, and religion, the other a revolutionary conflict over political principles and legitimacy. In what was truly a novel event in world history, Americans did not assert their independence because their ethnicity, language, culture, or religion differentiated them from their British brethren. The United States came into existence at a particular moment in time—July 4, 1776—and it was the product of a conscious political act based on explicit political principles. "We hold these truths to be self-evident," says the Declaration. Who holds these truths? Americans hold these truths. Who are Americans? People who adhere to these truths. National identity and political principle were inseparable. From the beginning, as Croly noted, the American past was "informed by an idea." And hence there was from the beginning the tendency, as a distinguished English historian put it, "to describe the national identity as allegiance to political principles; to equality, freedom, inalienable rights, and authority derived from the consent of the governed . . . The Americans are a political people. The Revolution, the Declaration of Independence, the constitutions of the states and the Constitution of 1787 explain their national existence." From Crèvecoeur to Tocqueville to Bryce to Brogan to Myrdal, foreign as well as domestic observers have singled out this striking phenomenon. Given all the other variety in American life and the diverse sources and times of people becoming Americans, national identity could be defined in few other ways. The Creed is, indeed, as Myrdal put it, "the cement in the structure of this great and disparate nation."[25] If it were not for the American Creed, what would Americans have in common?

Two hundred years after the Revolution, political factors were still at the heart of American national identity. In the late 1950s, for instance, national samples of the population in five countries, including the United States, were asked: "Speaking generally, what are the things about America that you are most proud of?" In response, 85 percent of Americans mentioned some aspect of the "American government or political tradition—the Constitution, political freedom, democracy, and the like."

Political factors were mentioned by only 46 percent of the British, 30 percent of the Mexicans, 7 percent of the Germans, and 3 percent of the Italians. The Americans, on the other hand, had much less pride than these others in the characteristics of their people, the physical attributes of their country, and the contributions of their country to the arts. They identified their country not with personal, social, geographical, or cultural qualities, but with political values and practices.[26] In this respect, the differences between the American and British responses are probably "indicative of the contractarian aspects of American polity by contrast with the more organic character of British life, for what most strongly joins Americans together is our consciously chosen experiment in liberal democratic politics rather than the totality of our historical culture . . . These data indicate that we *define* the nation politically; what we all have in common is a system of constitutional rights. Beyond this lies a complex cultural sphere, the vast area of private life. A more organic society like Britain does not make such a separation of the areas of life one from another."[27]

The United States thus had its origins in a conscious political act, in the assertion of certain basic political principles, and in adherence to constitutional agreements based on those principles. It is possible to speak of a body of political ideas that constitutes "Americanism" in a sense in which one can never speak of "Britishism," "Frenchism," "Germanism," or "Japanesism." Americanism in this sense is comparable to other ideologies or religions. "Americanism is to the American," Leon Samson has said, "not a tradition or a territory, not what France is to a Frenchman or England to an Englishman, but a doctrine—what socialism is to a socialist." To reject the central ideas of that doctrine is to be un-American. There is no British Creed or French Creed; the Académie Française worries about the purity of the French language, not about the purity of French political ideas. What, indeed, would be an "un-French" political idea? But pre-occupation with "un-American" political ideas and behavior has been a recurring theme in American life. "It has been our fate as a nation," Richard Hofstadter succinctly observed, "not to have ideologies but to be one."[28]

This identification of nationality with political creed or values makes the United States virtually unique. In terms of their nationality and ideological makeup, countries can generally be divided into four categories. Some countries, such as the People's Republic of China, are characterized by monism of both ideology and nationality. In some, such as France,

Germany, and Italy, several ideologies have historically coexisted within the context of a single nationality. In other countries, such as the Soviet Union and Yugoslavia, a single ideology provides the framework for bringing together several distinct nationalities. Still other countries, such as historically the United Kingdom, may be characterized by pluralism of both nationality and ideology.

The United States does not fit neatly into any of these categories. Like communist states, the United States has a single pervasive dominant political creed or ideology, but the relation between political creed and nationality in the United States differs significantly from that in communist societies. In some communist countries, like China, an ideology was superimposed on a single preexisting, well-established nationality. In similar but reverse fashion, it could be removed without destroying the basis of national identity: the Chinese could stop being communist and not stop being Chinese. In the Soviet Union, as in Yugoslavia, on the other hand, communist ideology was used to create a multinational state by superimposing the ideology on several preexisting and clearly identifiable nationalities each with its own language, culture, traditions, and territory. The existence of the Soviet Union, as well as of Yugoslavia, is thus intimately linked to the prevalence of the ideology. If the ideology and its associated political superstructure were removed the nationalities would remain and, in the absence of a new political superstructure, would provide the basis for Russian, Ukrainian, Lithuanian, Uzbekistani, and other political communities out of what had been the Soviet Union, and for Serbian, Slovenian, Croatian, and Macedonian political communities out of what had been Yugoslavia.

The United States, on the other hand, is composed, apart from the Indian tribes, not of nationalities but of ethnic groups. In America, ethnicity exists apart from nationality; ethnic groups make no claims to a separate national identity. During the early years of the Republic, British elements predominated in the population and the British heritage was central to American life. Yet even from the start, ethnic diversity also existed: as a result of the "First Immigration" of the eighteenth century, in 1790 forty percent of the American people were of non-English extraction.[29] The Second and Third Immigrations of the mid-nineteenth century and at the turn of the twentieth century dramatically multiplied the numbers and diversity of the American immigrant population. They also brought to the fore the issue of what it meant to become an American.

There were three possible answers. First, immigrants could conceivably become Americans by being fully assimilated into the culture and community of the white Anglo-Saxon Protestants, who still constituted not only the premier but the largest ethnic entity on the American scene. This, however, quickly turned out to be a result desired by neither group. Second, immigrants could become Americans by participating in a melting pot process of ethnic intermarriage and cultural interpenetration out of which would emerge a new American type reflecting the diverse origins of American immigrants. Ethnic ties and identity, reinforced paradoxically by the openness of American society, made this at best a slow process involving centuries as well as generations. Third, for the immigrants, becoming an American could mean accepting and identifying with American social, economic, and political values and institutions— whose appeal had, of course, been a principal reason for their immigration in the first place. In effect, a bargain was struck: ethnic groups retained so long as they wished their ethnic identity, but they converted to American political values, ideals, and symbols. Adherence to the latter was the test of how "American" one was, and it was perfectly compatible with the maintenance of ethnic culture and traditions. The primordial or organic ties remained in large part ethnic; the political or ideological ties were American. A hyphenated American was thus quite different from a hyphenated non-American. To say that someone is an Anglo-Italian means that he has English and Italian forebears. To say that someone is an Italian-American means that he has Italian forebears but that he has American political values and is a member of the American political community. At times, descendants of earlier immigrants could and did speak contemptuously of "hyphenated Americans," but first- and second-generation Americans were better Americans for being hyphenated. Defining and maintaining an ethnic identity was an essential building block in the process of creating an American national identity.

American political values and ideals thus had their roots primarily in British sources, but American national identity was defined in terms of the former rather than the latter. In the 1830s, Tocqueville could still inaccurately refer to Americans generally as "Anglo-Americans." A century later, the emergence of the term "WASP" marked the final phase in the demotion of the Anglo-American to the status of one ethnic group among many and the end of any effort to define American national identity in ethnic rather than political terms. As a result, in the United States, as in no other society, ideology and nationality are fused and the disappearance of the former would mean the end of the latter.

This identification of political ideas and nationality contrasts dramatically with the historical experience of western Europe. In Europe, political ideology and nationalism crossed each other. Ideologies expressed and shaped the interests of "horizontal" units (social classes), while nationalism, in its various manifestations, expressed and shaped the interests of "vertical" units (ethnic and linguistic communities). In eighteenth-century Europe, the aristocracy played an independent role in politics, and the middle class consequently had to develop a high degree of political consciousness and activity in its struggle to establish its position with respect to the aristocracy. In the course of this struggle, the two sides articulated their distinctive ideologies of liberalism and conservatism. Subsequently the development of the working-class movement produced equally systematic and highly developed socialist ideologies, the most important of which was Marxism. Thus, the high level of class development and the interaction and conflict among the classes produced the ideological trinity of conservatism, liberalism, and socialism.

Each of these ideologies tended to be articulated on a transnational basis. Conservative aristocratic doctrines, historically antinational, received their principal institutional embodiment in the Congress of Vienna in 1815. They reflected the assumption that there was more in common between two aristocrats, one of whom was a foreigner, than between two nationals, one of whom was an aristocrat. Liberal thinkers developed their own internationalism rooted in the ideas of free trade and the harmony of interests. Socialists preached the international unity of the working class. Thus, each ideology competed with nationalism as well as with other ideologies. The ideologies became more systematic and doctrinaire to counter the appeals of nationalism. Nationalism, in turn, became more romantic and mystical in order to overcome class and ideological differences—the "better Hitler than Blum" propensity which at one time or another could be found in most European social groups. Where the class struggle was more intense, as in France and Germany, so also was the nationalism; where the class struggle was more moderate, as in Great Britain, so also were the assertions of nationalism. Politically, nineteenth- and early twentieth-century Europe could be viewed as a grid of crosscutting cleavages, divided vertically by the appeal of *patrie* and nationalism and horizontally by the appeals of class and ideology, with this two-way competition giving a peculiar stridency and intensity to each appeal.

These conflicting pulls of ideology and nationalism have been lacking in the American political experience. Ideology and nationalism reinforced each other, yet the absence of conflict between the two also meant that each in some measure diluted the other. Ideology did not have to be developed in systematic and overt form in order to articulate and justify the appeal of class against class or class against nation. Similarly, nationalism did not have to be developed in such an emotional and irrational way as to justify the appeal of fatherland over class. American "patriotism," as Bryce observed, "is in one aspect stronger than that of Frenchmen or Englishmen because it is less broken by class feeling, but it has ceased to be aggressive."[30] In comparison to European nationalism, American nationalism is in a sense more "intellectualized," since it is defined more in terms of political ideas and principles; in comparison to European ideologies, on the other hand, the American Creed is less systematic and intellectualized because it reflects a national consensus and is identified with American nationalism.

As a result of this identification of the nation with certain political ideals, the American political experience has been quite limited compared to that of other nations. Political ideas and beliefs that cannot be encompassed in the American Creed remain on the fringe of American society and the American consciousness. In western European and other societies, ideological diversity has prevailed within the context of a common national community. Don Camillo and his communist rival are both quintessentially Italian and neither would deny the Italianness of the other. In the United States, on the other hand, where the liberal-democratic ethos of the American Creed has preempted the scene, the American experience with forms of government has been similarly limited. Although significant changes have obviously occurred in American political institutions in the course of two hundred years, the United States has still had only one Constitution and one system of government based on one set of political ideas. Other nations often see constitutions come and go every generation. The Germans have had five very different political systems in this century. Between 1789 and 1979 France had five republics plus six other political systems. Even in Great Britain the constitutional system and ideological makeup were very different in the late twentieth century from what they had been in the late eighteenth century. In such societies, the nation endures while the political system changes. When the national identity and unity of these countries are endangered, it is by ethnic and subnational movements, by Basque, Breton, or Scottish nationalism, not by changes in the political system or the dominant political ideas in the society.

In the United States, in contrast, ethnic cultural identities coexist with a national identity rooted in a particular set of political ideas and institutions. "The American Constitution," Hans Kohn pointed out, "is unlike any other: it represents the lifeblood of the American nation, its supreme symbol and manifestation. It is so intimately welded with the national existence itself that the two have become inseparable."[31] For this reason, American national identity is in a sense very fragile, threatened not by ethnic separatism but by disillusionment with its political ideals or with the effectiveness of its political institutions. Destroy the political system and you destroy the basis of community, eliminating the nation and, in effect, returning its members—in accordance with the theory on which that nation was founded—back to a state of nature. In other countries, one can abrogate the constitution without abrogating the nation. The United States does not have that choice.

American identity thus involves adherence to certain substantive political ideals. "To be an American," Carl Friedrich said, "is an ideal; while to be a Frenchman is a fact."[32] American identity is defined in normative terms, French identity in existential terms. French political behavior, in this sense, is whatever Frenchmen in fact do in politics; American political behavior, on the other hand, is what American political ideals say Americans ought to do in politics. There is an external standard by which to judge what is American apart from what Americans do. Americans may think un-American thoughts, American officials may engage in un-American behavior, and American governments may fight un-American wars. The "religion of the Republic," Sidney Mead said, "is essentially prophetic," and this imposes a noble and chastening destiny because "its ideals and aspirations stand in constant judgment over the passing shenanigans of the people, reminding them of the standards by which their current practices and those of their nation are ever being judged and found wanting."[33] The "ideal national Promise," in Croly's phrase, which distinguishes the United States from other nations, is a source of anxiety and anguish. The promise of the American future is the indictment of the American present.

3 THE GAP: THE AMERICAN CREED VERSUS POLITICAL AUTHORITY

Consensus and Instability

Studies of American politics often point to the widespread consensus on the basic elements of the American Creed as evidence of the stability of the American political system. The assumption is that consensus on values translates into support for institutions. It is, indeed, frequently assumed that the stability of a democracy is particularly dependent upon the existence of a broad agreement on democratic values; democracy cannot work if a substantial portion of the public is basically opposed to it and supports authoritarian movements of the left, right, or center. Deeply felt class divisions over the proper sources of political authority, church-state relations, or the role of the state in the economy clearly can give rise to major instabilities in a democratic political system. When people think about instability, they typically have in mind this cleavage-based instability, and they tend to believe that anything that moderates the polarization, develops cross-cutting cleavages, or furnishes a basis for consensus will also contribute to greater political stability. And in a deeply polarized society, such measures may well enhance stability.

From this analysis, however, it is often implied that because dissension means instability, consensus therefore enhances stability. If people agree on democratic values, the successful functioning of democratic institutions is more or less assured. In fact, this is not necessarily the case. Just as there is an instability that follows from an excess of cleavage, so also there is an instability that follows from an excess of consensus. In comparison with Europe, the United States has had relatively little class warfare and ideological conflict. But it has had its own forms of political instability, which have in large part been rooted in the content of the American political consensus.

Whether or not a consensus on political values contributes to political stability depends on the nature of those values and the relation between them and the political institutions and practices in the society. If the prevailing political values legitimize and sanctify those institutions and practices, they enhance political stability. It is, however, quite conceivable that the core ideals and values of the consensus may provide a basis for challenging the legitimacy of the dominant political institutions and practices. This is precisely the case in the United States, and it is a phenomenon that is characteristic of politics in the United States as of that of no other major society.

The widespread consensus on liberal-democratic values provides the basis for challenging the legitimacy of American political practices and the authority of American political institutions. The consensus constitutes an external standard for judging institutions, and often for judging them harshly. Political institutions and practices never measure up to the ideals and values of the Creed, and hence can be seen as illegitimate. The extent to which this challenge manifests itself overtly depends on the way in which people perceive those institutions and practices. At times, people can look at politics as it is practiced in the United States and be blind to any divergence of this practice from the ideals of the American Creed. At other times, people may also perceive a vast gap between politics as it is in practice and politics as it should be according to the norms of the American Creed. Intense awareness of this gap becomes a driving force for reformation of the political system. These efforts to bring political reality into accord with political principle are the major source of political change in America.

Cleavage in the United States thus does not take the form of idea versus idea, as in Europe, but rather of idea versus fact. The conflict is between two groups who believe in the same political principles: those who find it in their interest to change existing institutions immediately so as to make them comply with those principles, and those who accept the validity of the principles but who perceive existing institutions as being in accord with the principles insofar as this is feasible. Other societies may be more divided than the United States along class lines and over conflicting weltanschauungs, but it is the peculiar fate of Americans that the beliefs that unite them as a nation should also divide them as a people. The same Creed that is the source of national identity is also the source of political instability. Conflict is the child of consensus, and the most passionate and traumatic controversies among Americans derive from the liberal-democratic values on which they so overwhelmingly agree.

The Antipower Ethic

The basic ideas of the American Creed—equality, liberty, individualism, constitutionalism, democracy—clearly do not constitute a systematic ideology, and they do not necessarily have any logical consistency. At some point, liberty and equality may clash, individualism may run counter to constitutionalism, and democracy or majority rule may infringe on both. Precisely because it is not an intellectualized ideology, the American Creed can live with such inconsistencies.

Logically inconsistent as they seem to philosophers, these ideas do have a single common thrust and import for the relations between society and government: all the varying elements in the American Creed unite in imposing limits on power and on the institutions of government. The essence of constitutionalism is the restraint of governmental power through fundamental law. The essence of liberalism is freedom from governmental control—the vindication of liberty against power, as Bernard Bailyn summed up the argument for the American Revolution. The essence of individualism is the right of each person to act in accordance with his own conscience and to control his own destiny free of external restraint, except insofar as such restraint is necessary to ensure comparable rights to others. The essence of egalitarianism is rejection of the idea that one person has the right to exercise power over another. The essence of democracy is popular control over government, directly or through representatives, and the responsiveness of governmental officials to public opinion. In sum, the distinctive aspect of the American Creed is its antigovernment character. Opposition to power, and suspicion of government as the most dangerous embodiment of power, are the central themes of American political thought.

When major inequalities in wealth emerged in the latter part of the nineteenth century, Americans developed a "gospel of wealth" to legitimate them. Great wealth was the reward for great effort, great merit, great risks. They continued to believe that gospel well into the twentieth century. In contrast, Americans have never developed a justification for

but does not have to be anti-gov't.

major inequalities of power. Thus, while Americans may have a gospel of wealth, they have never had—and, in the nature of things, cannot have —a gospel of power. Instead, they have a pervasive antipower ethic.

"If there is one message I have gotten from the Pentagon Papers," Daniel Ellsberg told a cheering crowd of MIT students in the fall of 1971, "it is to distrust authority, distrust the President, distrust the men in power, because power does corrupt, even in America."[1] If there were any who did not get the message from the Pentagon Papers, they almost surely did shortly thereafter from the Watergate tapes. It is an old message, a refrain continually repeated through more than two hundred years of American history. The "first Americans," Charles Hendel argued, "still regarded authority with a jealous eye, wary and fearful of it in any guise. This general attitude became an ingrained habit of American character" and flowered into "an uncritical general philosophy unfavorable to authority in any form . . . The free, responsible, self-governing individual is thought of as self-sufficient."[2]

During the Revolutionary years, this attitude manifested itself in the contraposition of liberty and power. In Europe, as James Madison said, power granted charters to liberty; in America, liberty granted charters to power. The Jacksonians gave renewed emphasis to the dichotomy: the issue, John C. Calhoun said in 1826, was "between power and liberty." More explicitly, government itself, even democratic government, was a threat to liberty. "It is under the word *government*," declared the leading Jacksonian journal, "that the subtle danger lurks. Understood as a central consolidated power, managing and directing the various general interests of the society, all government is evil, and the parent of evil."[3]

The opposition to power and government remained characteristic of the American outlook in the twentieth century. "For as long as polls have been taken, when Americans have been asked about their attitudes toward government *in the abstract,* the attitudes expressed have been preponderantly negative." Compared to other peoples, Americans have relatively high trust in each other, but a much lower trust in government. The American tradition involves "high amounts of community and regime trust together with limited amounts of authority trust . . . The lack of trust mentioned by Dickens, and especially by Bryce, relates to the political authorities and not to the regime and community levels."[4]

Indicative of the American antipathy to power and government is the virtual absence of the concept of "the state" in American thought. In its modern form, the idea of the state originated in the fifteenth and sixteenth centuries and came to full fruition in the age of absolutism that followed. Machiavelli, Hobbes, and Bodin were its prophets, the continental absolute monarchs its creators. The idea of the state implied the concentration of sovereignty in a single, centralized, governmental authority. This concept never took hold among the English North American colonists, who had brought with them an older tradition rooted in medieval constitutionalism and the writings of Sir Thomas Smith, Richard Hooker, and Sir Edward Coke. While seventeenth-century Englishmen disputed the sovereignty of Parliament versus that of the Crown, Americans avoided both. Despite the fulminations of Blackstone that "there is and must be" in all states "a supreme, irresistible, absolute and uncontrolled power, in which the *jura summi imperii,* or rights of sovereignty reside," the Americans stubbornly held to a contrary position throughout the eighteenth century. As a result, the development of constitutional and political ideas in England separated from that in America. Jeremy Bentham and the utilitarians, with their emphasis on centralized authority, rationality, and utility (as against dispersed power, morality, and natural rights), had little impact on American thought. Bentham, indeed, denounced the Declaration of Independence as "a hodge-podge of confusion and absurdity in which the theory to be proved is all along taken for granted."[5]

Only at the end of the nineteenth century, when certain American scholars (among them Woodrow Wilson) studied in Germany, did the state make an appearance in American political thought. Its tenure was limited to a place in academic writing, and a relatively brief one at that. Even during this period, Henry James could comment that the United States had "No State, in the European sense of the word," and European visitors were impressed with the absence of any recognizable concept of the state in America. After his visit to America in 1871, the conservative Austrian aristocrat Baron von Hübner argued that "the liberty of the individual must necessarily be limited by the liberty of all represented by the State . . . You grant too much to the individual and too little to the State. The greater portion of the scandals and abuses which we see in your country arise from that source. The control of the organs of public opinion is insufficient. What is wanting, is the control of an admitted authority recognized by all the world." Two decades later, Bryce declared that the "Americans had no theory of the State and felt no need for one . . . The nation is nothing but so many individuals. The government is nothing but certain representatives and officials." A few years afterward, H. G. Wells similarly commented that "a sense of the state" was missing in the

United States, and G. K. Chesterton argued that "nowhere do they so completely despise the State, nowhere do they so utterly disunite the State, as in what we call the United States."[6] While the powers and functions of government grew tremendously in the twentieth century, they were not matched by any comparable change in the way in which people thought about the authority and autonomy of government. Government was still conceived of as the servant of society; the idea of the state as a legitimizing authoritative entity remained foreign to American thinking and, as a consequence, the European concept of *raison d'état* continued as the discredited polar opposite to American traditions of liberalism, constitutionalism, and natural rights.

The contrast between American and European attitudes toward the state is also manifest in two other areas. Early-nineteenth-century America saw the success of the movement to eliminate what remained of religious establishments and erect a wall of separation between church and state. This development is often cited as evidence of American commitment to freedom of religion. It is also evidence of the American commitment to the limitation of political authority. In Europe, state churches historically performed the function of reinforcing and legitimizing political authority. In America, political authority was stripped of this support and left alone without religious defenses to confront a suspicious liberal society. The differences in American and European attitudes toward political authority are also reflected in the nature of their extremist movements. In Europe, the nationalist or fascist Right and the socialist or communist Left have favored a strong state. In America, in contrast, radicals at both ends of the political spectrum have tended to be more individualistic, antistatist, libertarian, and in favor of decentralization and popular control.[7] They have shared a desire to reduce, not to enhance, political authority. Thus, in each case, what extremist movements carry to an extreme is the prevailing political disposition of their own society.

The deep-rooted American suspicion of government is also dramatically reflected in the way in which changing American views of human nature are related to American attitudes toward power and authority. "The American Government and Constitution," it has been said, "are based on the theory of Calvin and the philosophy of Hobbes."[8] In the seventeenth and eighteenth centuries, there was much truth in this observation. Puritan conceptions of sin and guilt plus Hobbesian ideas of human egotism combined to produce what can only be described as a rather unattractive view of human nature: people pursue their self-

interests in wealth and power, and, at best, wise statesmanship designs
institutions and processes that can produce at least a minimum of public
virtue out of a superfluity of private vices. Nowhere are these basic assumptions about people and society more explicitly spelled out than in the
words of the Founding Fathers in the debates of the Constitutional Convention and in the pages of *The Federalist*. One of the most striking
changes in American political and social thought was that which occurred
in the dominant conception of human nature during the fifty years after
the Constitutional Convention. The image of man as essentially sinful,
evil, and grasping, a being whose dangerous instincts and propensities
had to be controlled by skillfully molded political and social institutions,
gave way to an essentially benign view of human nature. Man came to be
perceived as inherently good and potentially perfectible.

One might have thought that these two widely different views of human
nature would give rise to two widely different views on the role of government in society. In fact, both views were used to justify limitations on
government. The Founding Fathers argued that men in power would be
tempted to do evil and would infringe the rights and liberties of others
unless they were restrained by countervailing power. Hence, government
must be weak because men are evil. Their more optimistic successors, on
the other hand, started with the opposite assumption about man but arrived at a similar conclusion about government. Because men are inherently well intentioned and reasonable, strong government is not necessary to control or direct them: government should be weak because men
are good.

These similar conclusions from differing premises were not necessarily
dictated by pure logic. Starting from assumptions about human nature
similar to those of the framers of the Constitution, Thomas Hobbes arrived at a very different concept of the role of political authority. Starting
from assumptions about the inherent goodness of man similar to those of
nineteenth-century democrats, Jean Jacques Rousseau arrived at very
different views about the scope and role of government in society. What
is striking, in short, is the way in which the American hostility to political
authority led Americans, no matter what their view of human nature,
to favor weak government over strong government.

In somewhat similar fashion, Americans have tended to interpret
those two potentially conflicting values of the American Creed—equality
and social mobility—in such a way as to be compatible with opposition to
authority. In a variety of ways, Cora Du Bois has pointed out, the "Ameri-

can hostility to figures in authority" has operated "to play down status differences" and to produce an informality and familiarity in manners or, in Bryce's term, "equality of estimation." Success is valued, but some forms of success, particularly those that do not involve hierarchical authority relationships, are valued considerably more than others. "Upward mobility is valued as successful activity, but when it reaches a point where it outstrips the premise of equality and the focal value of conformity it borders on *hubris* . . . It is the boss, the politician, the teacher, the 'big shots' who are disvalued figures to the extent that their superordinate position implies authority. It is the movie star and the baseball hero who are valued figures since their pre-eminence connotes no authority but at the same time dramatizes the meteoric rise to fame and popularity through hard work and youthful striving."[9] Winning the race against others is good; exercising power over others is bad. Americans may praise famous men but they do not celebrate powerful ones. Similarly, the man who does achieve, the "self-made man" (itself an American term), "likes to boast of his achievement, to exaggerate the obscurity of his origin, and to point out the 'Horatio Alger' quality of his career." In Europe, on the other hand, the upwardly mobile person more "often prefers to forget his origins if they are in a lower class."[10]

Antipathy to power produces ambivalence toward wealth. "Equality" in American thinking has rarely been interpreted as economic equality in terms of wealth and income, but rather as equality of opportunity. Major social innovations such as free, universal, compulsory public education have been justified in large part by this value. Economic inequalities are legitimate insofar as they are the result of talent, work, achievement. Great wealth also becomes legitimate when it is used for socially beneficent purposes. The American tradition of philanthropy, unique in the world, is the tribute that illiberal concentrations of wealth pay to the norms of a liberal society. More generally, money becomes evil not when it is used to buy goods but when it is used to buy power. Large accumulations of wealth are acceptable until they are transformed into monopolies and trusts, which exercise economic power by dominating the marketplace. The American antitrust mania, unique among industrialized societies, focuses precisely on the point at which wealth becomes power. Similarly, economic inequalities become evil when they are translated into political inequalities. As a result, considerable effort has been invested over the years to exposing and regulating lobbying and political contributions. This outlook also manifests itself in the ambivalent American attitude toward "bigness." In objects it is good; in organizations—which involve the structuring of power—it is bad. Big buildings, big automobiles, big wealth in the sense of individual wealth, have historically been viewed favorably. Big business, big labor, and, most particularly, big government have been viewed unfavorably.

The IvI Gap

In his classic study of race relations in the United States, Gunnar Myrdal brilliantly pinpointed "an American dilemma" that existed between the deep beliefs in the concepts of liberty, equality, and individualism of the American Creed and the actual treatment of black people in American society. He probed, however, only one manifestation (albeit the most dramatic one) of the widespread gap between American political ideals and institutions—referred to here as "the IvI gap." What he termed "an" American dilemma is really "the" American dilemma, the central agony of American politics.

American liberal and democratic ideas form a standing and powerful indictment of almost all political institutions, including American ones. No government can exist without some measure of hierarchy, inequality, arbitrary power, secrecy, deception, and established patterns of superordination and subordination. The American Creed, however, challenges the legitimacy of all these characteristics of government. Its ideas run counter to the nature of government in general. They run counter to the nature of highly bureaucratized and centralized modern government. They run counter to both the original and inherited nature of American government.

Therein lies the dilemma. In the United States, government is legitimate to the extent to which it reflects the basic principles of the American Creed. Government can never, however, reflect those principles perfectly, and it is therefore illegitimate to the extent to which people take seriously the principles of the American Creed. If people try to make government more legitimate by bringing political practice more into accord with political principle, they will weaken government rather than strengthen it. Because of the inherently antigovernment character of the American Creed, government that is strong is illegitimate, government that is legitimate is weak.

In practice, in comparison with European societies, government has always been weak in America. This weakness originally was the product of the fact that no need existed in the United States to centralize power and establish a strong government in order to overthrow feudalism. In this sense, as Tocqueville pointed out, Americans "arrived at a state of democracy without having to endure a democratic revolution, and . . . are born equal instead of becoming so." The absence of feudalism thus eliminated a major negative impetus to strong government. The presence in its place of a pervasive consensus on liberal and democratic values furnished an additional, positive incentive to limit government. In the absence of a consensus, strong government would have been necessary; as Hartz pointed out, it is only because the images that the framers of the Constitution had of American society were erroneous that the system of divided and checked government that they created was able to last.[11] The fact of consensus thus made possible weak political institutions. The content of the consensus reinforced the weakness of those institutions.

Strong government has historically emerged in response to the need either to destroy a traditional society or to fight against foreign enemies. In the seventeenth-century era of state-building in Europe, absolute monarchs engaged in both activities simultaneously and unremittingly. From the start, the United States was spared the need to do the first, and shortly after its birth it was spared the need to do the second in any serious way until well into the twentieth century. The United States was able to maintain national independence and national security without having to create a strong apparatus. When this situation seemed to change in the 1940s and 1950s, many of the instrumentalities of a strong state machinery were created. This development took place, however, only because Americans at that time were relatively unconcerned about realizing their political values in their domestic political practice, however much they might have been concerned about protecting those institutions from foreign threats. In the 1960s, when Americans became concerned about the gap between their political ideals and their political institutions, they began to eviscerate the political and governmental institutions that had been developed to deal with foreign enemies.

In any society, of course, some gap exists between political ideals and political practice. In a society in which the dominant ideology is one of absolute monarchy, and in which theoretically there are no restraints whatsoever on the power of the ruler, political practice will reveal very real limits on the ruler's power. "Unofficial" reality will deviate from "official" ideology. Efforts to bridge this gap will tend to reinforce the power and authority of the existing institution; they will be efforts to make the incomplete absolutism that does exist into the more complete absolutism that should exist. Such efforts will enhance the legitimacy of the state by strengthening the state. Contrast this relationship with that which prevails in the United States. One function of an ideology in a political system is to legitimate rule, to furnish a persuasive and compelling answer to the question: Why obey? The American Creed, however, provides the rationale for restraints on rule. It is a much more fruitful source of reasons for questioning and resisting government than for obedience to government.

Unless Gov't is "democratic"

Political ideas do play a role in America—a purgative role that is not characteristic of other societies. In countries in which there are a variety of ideologies and belief systems, there are a variety of sources of challenge to governmental institutions, accompanied almost invariably by a variety of defenses for these institutions. Tradition and social structure furnish a basis for the legitimacy of some institutions, and particular ideologies and political theories can be used to legitimize individual institutions. Attacks on one set of institutions from the perspective of one ideology generate equally intense defenses from the perspective of other ideologies. In the United States, on the other hand, the consensus is basically antigovernment. What justification is there for government, hierarchy, discipline, secrecy, coercion, and the suppression of the claims of individuals and groups within the American context? In terms of American beliefs, government is supposed to be egalitarian, participatory, open, noncoercive, and responsive to the demands of individuals and groups. Yet no government can be all these things and still remain a government. "Credibility gaps" develop in American politics in part because the American people believe that government ought not do things it must do in order to be a government and that it ought to do things it cannot do without undermining itself as a government.

Can some justify hierarchy & discipline.

Does gov't have to include all these things? Why not?

The ideological challenge to American government thus comes not from abroad but from home, not from imported Marxist doctrines but from homegrown American idealism. The stability of political institutions is threatened not by deep-rooted cleavages but by deeply felt consensus. Americans cannot be themselves unless they believe in the Creed, but they also must be against themselves if they believe in the Creed. The more intensely Americans commit themselves to their national political beliefs, the more hostile or cynical they become about their political institutions. As a result of the IvI gap, the legitimacy of American government varies inversely with belief in American political ideals.

The Gap in Comparative Perspective

A gap between political ideal and political reality exists in all societies, but the United States is unique among countries in the scope and depth of its commitment to liberal, democratic, and egalitarian values. This "atomistic, individualistic ideology," George Lodge observed, truly "constitutes a fundamental aberration from the historically typical norm."[12] Over the years, dozens of systematic studies and hundreds of impressionistic ones have compared American values, political and otherwise, with those of other countries. Almost without exception they show Americans to believe more strongly in liberal, egalitarian, democratic, and individualistic values than people in other societies.[13] The United States differs from some societies, particularly those in Europe, in the extent of its historical consensus on these values. It differs from other societies, including Asian and communist societies, in the substance of that consensus. In most other countries, not only is the political ideology supportive of the state but the formulation and articulation of that ideology is controlled by those who control the state. In the United States the gap between political ideal and political reality is a weapon always available for use by social groups against those who control the state. The dominant political creed constitutes a standing challenge to the power of government and the legitimacy of political institutions. Political authority is vulnerable in America as it is nowhere else.

European Societies

Consider the contrast between the United States and European societies. Most western European societies have inherited patterns of ideological pluralism, giving rise to interclass and interparty ideological conflict. As a result, the political institutions reflect a variety of ideological influences. The adherents of particular ideologies typically have had distinctive and continuing affinities with particular political institutions. Conservatives support the monarchy (if there is one), the executive, the aristocracy, upper houses in the legislature, the courts, and, traditionally, the bureaucracy. Liberalism and republicanism are identified with parliaments and parties. Socialists and Marxists support trade unions, working-class parties, universal suffrage, and, in some circumstances, popularly elected legislatures. As a result, when the legitimacy of an institution is challenged in terms of one ideology, it can usually be defended in terms of another that has significant appeal within the society.

In the French republics, the republicans and the Left historically challenged and the Right defended the power of the executive; their roles were
reversed with respect to the power of the assembly. In Britain a Marxist
attack on the Crown or Parliament will lead to liberal, democratic, socialist, or conservative defenses of these institutions. In America, on the other
hand, if an institution or practice is illegitimate according to the democratic and liberal norms of the American Creed, it has no alternative defenses available in conservative, aristocratic, Marxist, or Christian democratic traditions, as there would be in most western European countries.
There is only one source of legitimacy, and if it is taken seriously much of
what is inherent in any government—including government in the United
States—verges on illegitimacy. Political institutions and practices stand
alone and defenseless before the overpowering liberal consensus.

The ideological pluralism in Europe also means that liberal, democratic,
and egalitarian norms are generally weaker in European countries than
they are in the United States and that nonliberal, nondemocratic norms
stressing hierarchy, authority, and deference are stronger. Comparisons
of. political culture consistently document these differences. From
Crèvecoeur and Tocqueville to the present, almost without exception,
European observers have focused upon egalitarianism, openness, absence
of social hierarchy, suspicion of political authority, and belief in popular
sovereignty as critical characteristics distinguishing American from European politics. In the mid-twentieth century, as Max Beloff summarized it,
the "United States is still essentially, in the things that make it different
from Western Europe or from Britain, the United States that Tocqueville
saw."[14] In comparison with major European countries such as Britain,
Germany, and Italy, the United States has a "participant" political culture.
The "participant orientation in the United States appears better developed
than subject orientation and to some extent dominates it." This imbalance,
Gabriel Almond and Sidney Verba argued, "is the result of American
historical experience with governmental and bureaucratic authority—an
experience that began with distrust and revolution against the British
Crown, and that has been consolidated by the American tendency to subject all governmental institutions, including the judiciary and bureaucracy,
to direct popular control." Similarly, a significantly lower proportion of
Americans than Europeans agreed that "the individual owes his first duty
to the state and only secondarily to his personal welfare."[15] (See Table 1.)

The political values and attitudes of young people reveal differences
between Europe and America comparable to those found in the political

Table 1. Individual freedom versus duty to the state.[a]

	United States	United Kingdom	Germany	Italy	Mexico
Agree	25%	38%	41%	48%	92%
Disagree	68	55	45	32	5
Don't know, etc.	7	7	14	20	3

Source: Donald J. Devine, *The Political Culture of the United States* (Boston: Little, Brown, 1972), p. 193, reporting results of survey included in Almond-Verba study.

a. Statement presented to respondents: "The individual owes his first duty to the state and only secondarily to his personal welfare."

cultures generally. In a study of the attitudes toward democracy of teenagers in the United States, the United Kingdom, Germany, and Italy, the Americans were "more often highest in choosing the democratic options and lowest in choosing the anti-democratic options."[16] Similar results were obtained by Greenstein and Tarrow when they polled American, English, and French schoolchildren as to their reactions to a hypothetical situation in which a policeman stopped the head of state for speeding. The American children were almost twice as likely as the British and French children to imagine that the head of state would be punished (that is, they expected the President to be treated like any other citizen), were much more likely to imagine the head of state approving the action of the policeman (that is, they expected the President himself to adhere to egalitarian norms), and were almost twice as likely to maintain that in this situation "everyone should be equal before the law."[17] In yet another study, American, British, and German schoolchildren were asked to choose individual values and priorities that they would use in organizing a hypothetical island society. The "overall orientation" of the Americans was described as "equalitarian," combining both a commitment to the public good with a stress on "negative freedom," whereas the British were found to be oriented to private interest and the Germans were concerned with rules and obedience.[18]

With its interlocking history and its similar social, economic, political, and geographical characteristics, Canada closely resembles the United States. No other country, except possibly Australia, has political and social values so similar to those of the United States.[19] Yet significant differences exist. Canada has no counterpart to the dynamic drive "to realize the American dream of liberty and justice for all." As a result, its politics has lacked the messianic strand and the extremist movements that have existed in American politics; it has been more relaxed, tolerant, varied, and uninspiring. American political culture is utopian and pragmatic, Canadian political culture only pragmatic.[20]

Canadians have historically been more conservative, more collectivist, more pro-state and respectful of authority, and less egalitarian and individualistic than Americans. "What is clearly absent from Canadian political consciousness, though salient in the American, is the conviction that the state and its apparatus are the natural enemies of freedom."[21] Canadian national character, it has been argued, "tends to be ascriptive, anti-egalitarian, and bureaucratic; the American tends to be egalitarian, achievement-oriented, and entrepreneurial." Canadian conservatism has not been of the same individualistic, antigovernment, laissez-faire variety as American conservatism. In contrast to American politics, Canadian politics encompasses a strong corporatist strand, deferential patterns of authority, and a "quasi-participative" politics. Fundamentally, "the difference is between the American Lockean, individualistic conception of society and an organic, collective view brought initially to Canada by the Empire Loyalists who settled there following the American Revolution."[22] More generally, in contrast to the United States, English Canada is not a "one true myth culture" and the pattern of Canadian development established "the legitimacy of ideological diversity in English Canada."[23]

Bilateral comparisons between the United States and individual European countries underline even more dramatically the American commitment to egalitarian and democratic values, and the differences between ideological homogeneity and ideological pluralism. Since the eighteenth century, the contrast with Britain has been particularly striking. Even allowing for the hyperbole of which he was capable, Edmund Burke still articulated a central aspect of the attitudes of Englishmen toward authority when he declared, "We fear God; we look up with awe to kings; with affection to parliaments; with duty to magistrates; with reverence to priests; and with respect to nobility." Fear, duty, awe, reverence, respect, even affection are not words that one would ever use to describe American attitudes toward sources of authority. The American approach was equally well summed up by Burke when he said that the "fierce spirit of liberty" was stronger among the Americans, "probably, than in any other people of the earth," and that in the American character "a love of freedom is the predominating feature which marks and distinguishes the whole." The Americans "are Protestants, and of that kind which is the

most averse to all implicit submission of mind and opinion . . . The
dissenting interests have sprung up in direct opposition to all the ordinary
powers of the world . . . All Protestantism, even the most cold and passive,
is a sort of dissent. But the religion most prevalent in our northern colonies is a refinement on the principle of resistance: it is the dissidence
of dissent, and the Protestantism of the Protestant religion."[24]

In the following centuries, acute observers, including Tocqueville and
Bagehot, continued to stress the egalitarian and competitive elements in
American political culture in contrast to the deferential and ascriptive
values prevalent in Britain. Deference has historically been characteristic
of both British middle-class and working-class viewpoints.[25] Writing in the
mid-1960s, historian A. P. Thornton concluded that the British people
were "still habituated to authority, and still—despite the satire from the
flanks of the middle class—inclined to that deference to it that Bagehot
had commented on a century before, although more perceptive as to its
nature."[26] Similarly, a study of the personal qualities most admired by
American and English insurance clerks found the Americans much more
likely to admire "un-moral, environment-exploiting qualities," whereas
the English were much more likely to admire "control of anti-social impulses." Young elites in England are more ideologically diverse than those
in the United States, who are overwhelmingly liberal in outlook. The
central theme among the Americans, moreover, "was of a failure to live
up to American ideals, in matters of race, poverty and the use of national
power abroad."[27]

Both the United States and Great Britain are democratic and pluralistic, but the United States is also egalitarian, individualistic, and populist,
whereas Britain is hierarchical and collectivist. "Even when it is distrusted," Edward Shils observed, "the Government, instead of being
looked down upon, as it often is in the United States, is, as such, the
object of deference." These different attitudes toward authority produce
markedly different approaches to government secrecy and individual privacy in England and America, differences that were dramatically revealed
during the McCarthy years of the early 1950s and again during the years
of exposure of the late 1960s. "The United States has been committed to
the principle of publicity since its origin . . . Repugnance for governmental secretiveness was an offspring of the distrust of aristocracy." In
contrast, "the acceptance of hierarchy in British society permits the Government to retain its secrets, with little challenge or resentment."[28]

A major contrast also exists between American attitudes and those that have historically prevailed in Germany. Authoritarianism in the family, in society, and in politics was widely perceived as characteristic of German culture. The state and its authority were central to German political practice and theory. Discipline was much more stringent, authority much more respected, and status differences much more clearly defined and valued in the German military than in the American armed forces. "For the American," Alex Inkeles and Daniel Levinson observed, "precise differences in status are a source of discomfort, since they challenge his conception of himself as an equal, as an individual who will be valued for his personal qualities and on the basis of those alone." In contrast, the Germans manifested "a strong interest in status" and were said to be "most comfortable in relations where status is precisely defined. Correspondingly, status differences are always kept unmistakably distinct in the German military . . . Authority and discipline are infinitely more demanding and rigorous in the German Army, because the American values the self and sees obedience to authority as essentially ego-humbling."[29]

Similar differences existed between German and American children. In the mid-1930s, comparing the status of children in pre-Hitler Germany with their status in the United States, Kurt Lewin observed that "to one who comes from Germany, the degree of freedom and independence of children and adolescents in the United States is very impressive. Especially the lack of servility of the young child toward adults or the student toward his professor is striking. The adults, too, treat the child much more on an equal footing, whereas in Germany it seems to be the natural right of the adult to rule and the duty of the child to obey."[30] These differences undoubtedly narrowed after 1945, but they did not disappear. In the 1966–67 four-country study, for instance, which revealed American schoolchildren most likely to choose democratic options and least likely to choose antidemocratic ones, German schoolchildren were most likely to do just the reverse. (Schoolchildren in the United Kingdom and Italy ranked in the middle.)

In similar fashion, German parents were much more likely than American parents to engage in "parenting behavior," controlling, directing, and associating with their children. For German children, this meant "a prolongation of dependency, postponement of participation in semi-autonomous peer-group activity, and delay in the development of motives for self-directed achievement." Research in the late 1960s found among German adolescents "a docile, dependent, almost childlike attitude towards government authority"—an attitude missing among their English and American peers. In yet another study of Germans and Americans in their late teens, the Americans were found to be more achievement-oriented, more insistent on their individual freedom to choose what they wanted, and more willing to adapt these free choices to group norms. The Germans, on the other hand, found their sense of self by controlling themselves in terms of an idealistic code. "The German starts with 'I must' —a sense of living up to standards expected of him, rather than an 'I want' as the American does. In fact, starting with an 'I want' seems inexcusably selfish to the Germans. 'Wants' need to be suppressed for the good of the whole. Hence the emphasis on will power: 'I must be able to do what I should.' " These differences, in turn, were reflected in the high esteem that government employment had in Germany, compared with its low esteem in the United States.[31]

In the United States, the critical question has always been whether democratic and liberal norms are sufficiently tolerant to accommodate an effective system of government. In Germany, the question has historically been whether traditional authoritarian and hierarchical norms can be sufficiently modified to accommodate a democratic system of government. The gap between political norms and political institutions was too great to permit the Weimar Republic to survive. In West Germany, political institutions have been less democratic and political values less authoritarian than they were in Weimar. Yet even in the early 1960s, the striking passivity of the Germans with respect to politics, the lack of political involvement by a large portion of the population, and their "subject orientation" toward the output-bureaucratic side rather than the input-political side of government all seemed to "indicate a political system in which firmly democratic attitudes are as yet not established." Eighteen years after World War II it could thus still be concluded that "ascriptive, elitist values are far from dead in West Germany." Other studies showed that the themes in German reading texts for children in the 1950s did not different significantly from those in texts written in the 1920s. Consequently it was wrong, at least as of the early 1960s, to think that "the Germans have fundamentally changed" and become "good democrats like the Americans"; the Germans, it was argued, "have a political but not a psychological democracy."[32]

Between the early 1960s and the late 1970s, however, important changes did occur in West German political culture and support for democratic values increased significantly. In 1953, for instance, 50 percent of the West German public favored a democratic system of government; in 1967, 74 percent thought that democracy was the best system for Germany; and in 1972 and 1976, 90 percent said they were satisfied with democracy in West Germany. Other studies and surveys support the conclusion that in the years after 1959 "democratic and participatory norms" became "widespread" in West Germany.[33] This shift in German political values and attitudes was largely a product of generational change, with the generations that emerged on the political scene after 1945 manifesting much greater commitment to democratic values than those who had matured during the Empire, the Weimar Republic, or the Third Reich. In the early 1970s, Karl Dietrich Bracher argued that there still existed within Germany "a continuation of pre-fascist and authoritarian conditions and patterns of behavior," and another scholar could claim that "the state tradition" was "still alive in the German political consciousness."[34] It seemed probable, however, that such tendencies would continue to subside as successive age cohorts were socialized into the democratic political culture of the Federal Republic.

[margin handwritten note: So such drastic change can occur in as short a time as a generation]

These changes in German political culture reduced the differences between the German and American political values. At the end of the 1970s, it was, indeed, claimed that German political culture was, in some respects, closer to the ideal, democratic "civic culture" than either British or American political culture. This broadening support for democratic values in Germany was also associated, at least temporarily, with broader support for and pride in German political institutions. In 1959, for instance, only 7 percent of West Germans mentioned their political institutions as something they could be "most proud of." In 1978, 31 percent of the German public said they were especially proud of their political institutions.[35] In the 1960s and early 1970s, consequently, a mixed political culture, including both authoritarian and democratic elements, gave way to one characterized by a fairly broad consensus on democratic values. During these years, this consensus generated support for and pride in the democratic political institutions of the Federal Republic. It also, however, contained within itself the seeds of a new cleavage similar to that which traditionally existed in the United States. In the early 1950s, the emerging democratic institutions of West Germany were challenged by the significant support that still existed for authoritarian political values. In the late 1970s, the established democratic political institutions of West Germany were criticized because they deviated too far from the democratic political values that had become dominant in the country. Germans

were increasingly "likely to demand that it [their political system] live up
to its ideals . . . The elements most critical of German society in the late
1970s are found among the same groups, the young and the well educated,
that spearheaded the growth of democratic norms during the preceding
three decades."[36] Democratic consensus was generating a German version
of the "American disease" of cognitive dissonance rooted in the gap between political ideals and political reality.

Perhaps the outstanding aspect of French political culture is its dual
character. On the one hand, there is a tradition of elitism, hierarchy, and
sharp class divisions. On the other, there is the French Revolution's
legacy of liberty, equality, and fraternity. The result has been continuing
cleavages and at times polarization in political values. "The ascriptive,
elitist, and particularistic aspects of French values," Lipset observed,
"facilitated the emergence of politics along class lines, while the emphasis
on equalitarianism, universalism, and achievement has led the less privileged strata to sharply resent their position." The attitudinal consequences
of this bifurcated legacy are neatly reflected in a 1960s poll of Grenoble
schoolchildren on the question: "Was the Revolution of 1789 a good or
an evil?" Fifty-five percent of the children said good, 30 percent evil.[37]

Interpretations of French political culture are dominated by what William Schonfeld labeled "two-France theories." At the individual level, this
means that "each Frenchman has two distinct sets of dispositions toward
political authority: he both fears, dislikes, distrusts, and seeks to avoid
submission to authority and concurrently needs, seeks, and depends upon
political authority." The reluctance of the French to resolve problems in
face-to-face negotiations among equals results in both the strengthening
of authority and its centralization. Yet, at the same time, authority has to
be exercised within certain defined constraints and may be subject to sudden disruption. The result, as Stanley Hoffmann suggested, is neither a
democratic nor an authoritarian pattern, but rather "the coexistence of
limited authoritarianism and *potential* insurrection against authority."[38]
In a sense, the authoritarian strand of the French tradition faces an ever-
present potential challenge from the revolutionary strand of that tradition.
The parallel and contrast with the United States are clear: in the United
States the equivalent of the revolutionary tradition is the only tradition in
politics, and there is no authoritarian tradition in government.

Fewer studies have been done comparing political values in the United
States with those in Southern European or Latin American countries. It
seems probable, however, that such comparisons would yield differences

similar to those between the United States and Britain, France, and Germany. It has been observed, for instance, that North Americans most often fear tyranny, oppression, and the abuse of power, whereas Argentinians—and Latin Americans generally—fear disorder and anarchy. Americans feel uneasy when the government is too strong, Argentinians and other Latins when it is too weak. In support of this argument, one study of Mexican and American schoolchildren concerning the concept of respect found that among the Americans "there seems to be a consistent overall pattern of relatively detached give-and-take among equals." The Mexican pattern was "quite different" and tended "to be on the authoritarian mode. Most of the Mexicans think that respect involves a positive duty to obey; and a third of them, unlike most American students, feel that respect means you *have* to obey the respected person, whether you like it or not." Another study found that 94 percent of Mexican students, compared with only 59 percent of American students, agreed with the statement that "obedience and respect for authority are the most important virtues a child should learn."[39] As in other societies, attitudes in Mexico toward authority relations in politics parallel those toward authority relations in the family, the dominant authority of the father going hand-in-hand with his responsibility for the other members of the family.

Major differences have thus existed between American political values, with their stress on individualism, liberty, equality, and opposition to power and authority, and political values in other Western countries where values are more varied and more heavily weighted toward authority and hierarchy. In the 1960s and 1970s support for democracy did become more widespread in West Germany, but liberal, democratic, and anti-government values still did not have in Europe the virtual unanimity of support that they commanded in the United States. Liberty and equality have historically also been more widespread in practice in America than they have been in Europe. Yet the IvI gap has been smaller in Europe than in the United States, and hence European observers have not been sensitive to its existence in America. At least since Tocqueville, they have stressed the relative prevalence of equality and liberty in America without differentiating the normative and existential dimensions. With the notable exception of Gunnar Myrdal, they have focused on the gap that separates American ideals and institutions from European ideals and institutions, glossing over the gap between American ideals and American institutions. They have, consequently, missed the disharmony that is such a central feature of American politics.

Non-Western Societies

The Anglo-American relies upon personal interest to accomplish his ends and gives free scope to the unguided strength and common sense of the people; the Russian centers all the authority of society in a single arm. The principal instrument of the former is freedom; of the latter, servitude.   *Alexis de Tocqueville (1835)*

Their reliance upon order and hierarchy and our faith in freedom and equality are poles apart and it is hard for us to give hierarchy its just due as a possible social mechanism. Japan's confidence in hierarchy is basic in her whole notion of man's relation to his fellow man and of man's relation to the State.   *Ruth Benedict (1946)*

The American cultural perspective, of course, places strong emphasis on the importance of the individual in society, on personal responsibility, and on self-realization. The Chinese emphasis on social interrelatedness, on the basic importance of group life, and on submission of the individual to collective interests, stands out as a fundamental cultural difference.   *Richard H. Solomon (1971)*

The Soviet Union and the major societies of Asia—China, Japan, India—lack the tradition of class-based ideological pluralism that has characterized western European development. Some of them, indeed, have been characterized by a high degree of homogeneity in political values and ideology. In some measure, the Soviet Union, China, and Japan are "consensus" societies like the United States and unlike the societies of western Europe. What distinguishes these societies from the United States is the content of the consensus. In Japan, despite the import of Western democratic, socialist, and Marxist ideologies, a continuity in basic norms of social and political organizations has been maintained from the late feudal Tokugawa era into the modern, post–World War II period. In the Soviet Union, a successful revolutionary party eliminated the liberal tendencies that appeared in the late nineteenth century and imposed ideological homogeneity on a reconstructed society. In China, revolutionary upheaval produced a new political culture combining elements of both revolutionary and traditional (Confucian) political culture. In all three societies, however, as the quotations above suggest, the dominant values and norms of the political culture differ fundamentally from the liberal, democratic, egalitarian, and individualistic values that prevail in the United States. The tradition of middle-class liberalism, which preempts the scene in the Uinted States and shares the stage in western Europe, has been totally absent or has had only a marginal or aborted existence in these non-Western societies. As a result, in all three societies the dominant norms have tended to reinforce and to strengthen political authority, in contrast to the United States, where they tend to limit and weaken that authority.

The Soviet Union resembles the United States in that its identity is defined primarily in political and ideological terms. In terms of its abstract substance, Soviet ideology could also, like that of the United States, pose challenges to political authority. Marxism is, after all, the revolutionary ideology par excellence; it contains substantial humanistic elements; and it posits the withering away of the state in the postrevolutionary transition from socialism to communism. Thus, in both the United States and the Soviet Union, the political system is, in a sense, closeted alone with an ideology that is against authority and against hierarchy, while at the same time favorable to social, economic, and political equality and the dilution of government into society. Yet Marxism, as it exists in the Soviet Union, is not just Marxism, it is Marxism-Leninism, and the latter makes explicit provision for an organ—the communist party—whose functions include both ideological interpretation and political rule. The central tenet of Marxism-Leninism is the dominance of the party; the corresponding tenet of "Americanism" is the dominance of the people. In the Soviet Union, the ideology cannot be used against the system because the ideology holds that those who control the system also control the ideology. Marxism-Leninism thus becomes a tool for the maintenance of the Soviet system and a theoretical framework in terms of which leadership elites may debate political and policy choices, but it cannot become a vehicle for challenging the system.

In the United States, no single group or institution monopolizes the interpretation of American political ideas and principles. Those principles are, in many respects, even more hostile to established authority than those of Marxism, and hence they are regularly used by social forces to limit, constrain, and weaken political authority. Hence, too, the more intensely committed one becomes to American ideals, the more critical one becomes of the structure of authority in American institutions. In the Soviet Union, on the other hand, the more intensely committed one becomes to Marxism-Leninism, the more supportive one becomes of the structure of authority in Soviet institutions. The problem for Soviet leaders is caused by people losing their commitment to the ideology of the leaders and becoming indifferent, passive, and cynical. The problem for American leaders is caused by people intensifying their commitment to the ideology of the leaders and attempting to reform and change institutions, practices, and leaders. Dissidents in the United States often—and successfully— appeal to the values of American liberalism. Dissidents in the Soviet Union typically are driven to appeal against the values of Soviet Marxism-Leninism and to urge that these values be moderated or supplemented by religious, liberal, or humanistic norms.

At the more basic, if less conscious, cultural level, Soviet norms and attitudes toward authority represent a natural evolution out of the Russian past. In the sixteenth century, Ivan the Terrible said that "the rulers of Russia have not been accountable to anyone, but have been free to reward or to chastise their subjects," and this traditionally has been the case. Autocratic rule, the subordination of all to the state, the centralization of political authority, and the necessity for obedience were all continuing elements in the Russian political tradition—elements that were challenged only weakly and transitorily by the liberalism imported from the West in the late nineteenth and early twentieth centuries. "It can be said of the Russians, great or small," the Marquis de Custine observed in the 1830s, that "they are intoxicated with slavery." The "terrified reverence for authority" denoted by the Russian word *strakh* marks a holdover from peasant Russia to communist Russia. In this, as in the broader pattern of "dual Russia"—the existence of a state above and apart from the nation—the political norms and practice of the Soviet system have their roots in the autocracy of the czarist past.[40]

In Soviet Russia, "the demand for obedience" is the central element in the political creed. It is also the first imperative in the upbringing of the Soviet child, self-discipline being the second. In comparison with their American counterparts, Soviet children tend to be less hostile toward adults, less rebellious, less aggressive, and less delinquent. They have "less inclination to engage in anti-social behavior," and less autonomy, reflected in the fact that in the United States, peer group pressures on children typically conflict with adult pressures, while in the Soviet Union they reinforce such pressures.[41] More generally, Russians seem to have a long-standing need for authority and order, and a fear of too much freedom that makes them uncomfortable with a politically free-wheeling, individualistic polity. Even émigrés from the Soviet Union in the 1940s were disturbed by the extent of free speech in the United States and "seemed basically disposed as well to accept the idea of centralized and essentially autocratic determination of national policy." In the late 1970s, a keen observer of the Soviet Union used similar terms: "Deeply rooted values that have prevailed since Czarist times foster a mystical respect for cen-

tral authority, a yearning for order and unanimity, a distaste for disagreement and diversity, a dread of any turmoil of ideas. From this perspective,
American society looks chaotic and frightening."[42]

The dominant social and political norms in Japan also differ sharply
from American values and are much more supportive of existing structures of authority. There are, indeed, many similarities between the historical development of the Japanese and Russian political cultures,
including their stress on collectivism, the state, and hierarchy and their
opposition to individualism, which distinguish them from the American
and other Western traditions.[43] In key respects, the political cultures of
the United States and Japan "are as different from one another as may
well be" and represent "deviant cases, ideal-type extremes in the spectrum of world experience." American ideals of "individualism, equality,
mobility, competition" have little appeal in the Japanese context. "[The
Japanese] ethic is group loyalty, hierarchical subordination redeemed by
human intimacy, disciplined cooperation, a furious concern with the
honor of their role. Their responsibility is not to the universal god or
the singular self but to the social nexus and the particular lord. Their
dogged virtue is in conformity to social demands and in the hard work
that fosters social harmony."[44]

Instead of the egalitarian values prevalent in the United States, "rank
is the social norm on which Japanese life is based." Japanese typically
organize themselves vertically into a hierarchy of unequals rather than
horizontally as an association of equals. "Japanese admit the fact of
inequality; it is given; it is natural." "Ranking consciousness," or what
Ruth Benedict referred to as the Japanese "faith and confidence in hierarchy," is a preeminent characteristic of the Japanese approach to the
relations among individuals, groups, and nations. Each unit must be lo-
cated at its appropriate spot in a hierarchy of superior-subordinate relations. For a country engaged in international relations, it is a question of
"taking one's proper station." As one perceptive Japanese analyst put it,
"the first element" in the problems posed by Japanese psychology in
viewing relations with another nation is "the Japanese tendency to view
their foreign relations hierarchically, in terms of 'high' and 'low' (*jō-ge
kankei*), just as Japanese usually view their personal relations."[45]

In contrast to the individualism of Western societies, the Japanese person tends to be much more group-oriented and to identify with a single
group of heterogeneous individuals who perform a variety of diffuse or
relatively unspecialized roles. Loyalty to the group is emphasized; mo-

bility from one group to another is discouraged; overt disagreement within the group is frowned upon. Japan, as one scholar has observed, "is a collectivistic society." In such a society, the critical need is to avoid competition and disharmony, and hence elaborate consultation within the group is required before a decision can be reached. Americans, on the other hand, are comfortable with open conflict, majority votes, and a more individualistic, "lone ranger" style of leadership.[46]

The preference for hierarchy and collectivity over equality and individualism reinforces the system of authority. At the time the Jacksonian passion for equality was engulfing the United States and impressing Tocqueville, the population of Tokugawa was stratified into classes and the political roles of the lower classes—merchants, artisans, peasants—was "restricted to the provision of loyalty, obedience, and support." The historical "iconic image" in the United States has been "the revolution against power misused . . . From the foundation of the United States there has been an explicit concern for the limitation of power. The history of Japan, on the other hand, is one of anarchic struggle and civil war or authoritarian domination, with nothing between these two extremes, for almost two millennia. How should the Japanese not welcome authority?"[47] After the Meiji Restoration the old system changed, but traditional patterns of deference and respect for authority continued into the late twentieth century. As Chie Nakane described it:

> The preeminence of authority implants in the Japanese a ready submissiveness, alongside fear and hostility. They are afraid to offer open hostility to authority and instead commit themselves to it, while admonishing one another to "wrap yourself up in something long" or "stand in the shadow of a big tree." Obedience in Japan takes the form of total submission. Any criticism of or opposition to authority tends to be seen as heroism . . . And, interestingly enough, such deeds today are labelled as democratic action. Often it is merely opposition for opposition's sake; it is nearer in essence to emotional contradiction, than to the rational resistance from which further reasonable development might be expected.[48]

In the thirty years after World War II, liberal and democratic values gained support in Japan, particularly among younger people. In 1953, for instance, the statement "If a competent political leader is available, it is better to leave things to him instead of discussing them among ordinary citizens" evoked agreement from 43 percent of the Japanese public and disagreement from 38 percent. In 1973, only 23 percent agreed with this statement, while 51 percent disagreed with it. Other indicators suggest, however, that even in the late 1960s, Japanese attitudes toward democracy were ambivalent. In 1973, 43 percent of the Japanese public said that they had a good opinion of democracy, 30 percent said they had a good opinion of liberalism, and 40–50 percent in each case said that their view would depend on the circumstances.[49] Between early 1953 and 1973 the proportion of the population that would follow conscience over custom in a personal decision decreased somewhat (41 percent to 36 percent), while the proportions that would prefer a paternalistic supervisor at work (81 percent) to a nonpaternalistic one (13 percent) and "discipline" (66 percent) over "freedom" (22 percent) in the upbringing of children were virtually unchanged. In the early 1960s, Japanese were also about evenly divided as to whether politics was improved by holding elections from time to time.[50] As of the early 1960s, the dominant value pattern in Japan, it was said,

> has in it substantial elements of the old order which emphasized the family and nation over the individual; discipline, duty, and obligation over freedom; distinction in status over equality; and racial arrogance over egalitarianism. The younger generation and the better educated, however, are slowly moving toward individualism and commitment to "democracy," but the movement is uneven, with strong survivals of ethnocentric, hierarchical, and holistic attitudes.

Authoritarian views—summarized in the phrase *kanson mimpi* (the official respected, the people despised)—remained a significant component in the national outlook.[51]

These traditional values supporting group loyalty, hierarchical ranking, and submission to authority are a product of Japanese history. They have been and will be modified by the impact of imported democratic, liberal, and socialist ideas. It would be a mistake, however, as Nakane warns, to assume that such traditional values are necessarily out of place in a society shaped by modernization and industrialization. Indeed, just the reverse may be true, and here there is a striking paradox in the comparison between the United States and a society like Japan. In some measure, "equality" is a modern, democratic value. In the absence of an aristocratic, feudal, or hierarchical tradition in the United States, this value takes precedence. In Japan as well as in the societies of western Europe, ideas of equality and democracy must compete with norms of social distinction, hierarchy, and inequality. The actual functioning of modern society, particularly a large, industrialized, bureaucratized society, requires, however, some measure of distinction, hierarchy, and inequality. Hence a society like Japan, which preserves into the modern era significant elements of its "traditional" value pattern, may find that these values have new relevance and usefulness. The great strength of the Japanese vertical type of organizational structure, Nakane suggests, "lies in its effectiveness for centralized communication and its capability of efficient and swift mobilization of the collective power of its members. The importance of its contribution to the process of modernization is immeasurable . . . This structure served to underpin Japan's post-war economic growth."[52] Americans and American-influenced Japanese who look upon this structure as feudal or traditional fail to see the extent to which it operates positively rather than negatively in "the interests of modernization."

The contrast between American values and Chinese values is equally striking. As was the case with Japan, Chinese society "stands at the opposite pole from American society. It rests on a fundamentally different ordering of values and principles." Unlike Americans, Chinese traditionally did not exist apart from their group. They had no natural rights or liberties. Instead the emphasis was on the "individual's duties and responsibilities to society and its subcollectivities."[53]

The central characteristics of traditional Chinese political culture were inequality, hierarchy, and absolutism. Absent from such a culture were elections, participation, representation, separation of powers, independent religion, and outside law. Or, as another scholar put it, in Chinese culture "authority was supposed to be absolute, harsh, and even ruthless; yet it was also seen as being subtle, wise, and the source of morality. It was to be feared and distrusted, yet also to be revered and relied upon."[54] Hierarchy, is pervasive. "An equal relationship," John Fairbank argued, "has little precedent in Chinese experience . . . Their solution [to politics] began with the observation that the order of nature is not egalitarian but hierarchic." Hence as Lucian Pye said, "in politics, there are no equals, only superiors and inferiors." Government is of supreme importance in China. In traditional China, there were no significant sources of status, power, or wealth outside of government—a phenomenon that continued into republican China and exists on a reintensified scale in communist China. The contrast with the United States—where wealth and status have traditionally been achieved outside government—is particularly marked. Government itself commands respect and prestige in China on a scale that is

almost unique among societies. The "Chinese never developed," Pye observed, "the concept that governmental authority should be held in check
in order to respect the integrity and the logical necessity of other large-
scale systems of human interrelationships." The Chinese thus place "an
extreme value on political power."[55]

Within traditional Chinese society, the state was seen as above and
autonomous from society, and authority was centralized. "The distinction between ruler and subject, official and citizen, was sharp in both
theory and practice." The emphasis on respect for authority pervaded all
human relationships. It began with "the paramount value of filial piety . . .
No other culture in history has placed such a stress upon filial piety as has
the Chinese." The pervasiveness of authority in the society reinforced that
of the state. In traditional China, the "sense of respect for authority which
Confucian family life sought to instill was seen as basic to the stability of
the dynasty." Or as one eleventh-century Chinese philosopher observed:
"Only recognition of the relationship between superior and subordinate,
between high and low, can insure order and obedience without confusion.
How can people live properly without some means of control?"[56]

The Chinese demand for strong systems of authority, it has been
argued, is related to their fear of the confusion and conflict that will result
from its absence. At the same time, there is the need to maintain not only
respect for authority but distance from authority, in order to avoid its
potentially harsh impact. "People eat people," and hence government is
necessary, but "oppressive government is more terrible than tigers." The
result is a traditional outlook that could best be described as a "sense of
passive impotence before power." It involved "an anxiety before social
authority which produces such behavior as indirection in dealings with
superiors, great reluctance to criticize, and an over-willingness to please
those in power."[57] The concentration of power is the desirable, appropriate, and necessary remedy to the tendencies toward divisiveness and
conflict.

Traditional Chinese culture thus strongly emphasized the value of
hierarchical authority, centralized power, and a strong state. During periods of dynastic breakdown, these features tended to weaken or disappear. A Chinese IvI gap would then open up, precisely the reverse of that
which has typified American politics during periods of creedal passion. In
due course, however, after an interlude of confusion and war, a new ruler
would seize control and establish his possession of the Mandate of
Heaven, and the reality of Chinese government would once more be

brought back into greater accord with its underlying principles. In large measure this is what happened after 1949, when the communists reestablished a strong system of authority throughout China for the first time since the beginnings of the decay of the Ch'ing dynasty in the nineteenth century.

Communist ideology—even, and in some respect particularly, in its Maoist version—clearly differs significantly from the traditional Confucianist creed. There is, as James Townsend summarized it, a stress on collectivism as against the particularism of clan and village, on class struggle as against social harmony, on activism as against passivity, on self-reliance as against dependence, and on egalitarianism as against hierarchy.[58] The weaving of these conflicting strands into an integrated political culture is still under way. On the other hand, Maoism and Chinese traditional political culture both reject any role for political liberty and individualism; both stress the necessity for a strong state and the subordination of society to the state; and, although their ideas as to what constitutes legitimate authority obviously differ, both see the need for respect for authority.

In many societies, principally in Europe, several different ideologies have existed, and the state has therefore not confronted a monolithic challenge. In Germany, a growing consensus on democratic values in the 1960s and 1970s began to create a relation between democratic ideals and existing institutions that had some parallels to that in the United States. Even so, American political culture still differed significantly from German political culture in its individualism, egalitarianism, and antistatism. In non-Western societies, a single belief system reinforces the authority of the existing order. In Europe, the security of the "is" rests on the plurality of "oughts"; in Russia and Asia, it rests on the control of the single "ought" by the single "is." In the United States, in contrast, the single all-pervasive "ought" rampages wildly beyond the control of the "is." The result is a unique and ever-present challenge to authority posed by the gap between the ideals by which the society lives and the institutions by which it functions.

4 COPING WITH THE GAP

The American Case of Cognitive Dissonance

"Men are not corrupted by the exercise of power or debased by the habit of obedience," observed Tocqueville, "but by the exercise of power which they believe to be illegitimate, and by obedience to a rule which they consider to be usurped and oppressive."[1] But what happens when the prevailing beliefs in a society taint almost all forms of power with illegitimacy and question most governmental rules as at least potentially usurped and oppressive? Precisely because of the liberal-democratic values embodied in the American Creed, the opportunities for the corruption of leaders and the debasement of the people are far more widespread in the United States than they are elsewhere. Americans are, in effect, compelled to develop their own distinctive ways of coping with the gap between liberal ideals and political reality and thus making power legitimate and obedience acceptable.

In a less developed society, traditional institutions lose legitimacy when key elements in the elites in those societies (intellectuals, the military) abandon their traditional beliefs and absorb modern values. In ideologically complex societies, existing institutions lose legitimacy as the social groups adhering to one ideology (for example, the working class) rise in importance and as those adhering to another ideology (for example, the land-owning aristocracy) decline in importance. Established institutions lose their legitimacy because of a change in either the substance or the scope of the prevailing political beliefs and attitudes. In the United States, in contrast, established institutions confront an ever-present challenge to their legitimacy. The gap between the real and the ideal poses a distinctive national problem of cognitive dissonance.

The formal theory of cognitive dissonance was devised by Leon Festinger to explain aspects of individual behavior, but it may also help illuminate the dilemmas facing collectivities. The theory postulates that inconsistency or dissonance in a person's beliefs, attitudes, or perceptions will be "psychologically uncomfortable" and "will motivate the person to try to reduce the dissonance and achieve consonance." The person will also "actively avoid situations and information which would likely increase the dissonance."[2] Among other things, the theory predicts that when the beliefs of a person are dissonant with his own observed behavior shaped by external restraints and requirements, he is likely to attempt to reduce this dissonance by altering his beliefs so as to bring them more into accord with his behavior. This would suggest that insofar as Americans perceive the gap between principle and practice (that is, in terms of the theory, insofar as this relationship is "important" to them), there would be strong tendencies for them to reduce their collective dissonance by bringing their beliefs more into line with their behavior. They would tend to moderate, reduce, or abandon their ideals. Is this a realistic way of resolving the national problem of cognitive dissonance?

The problems posed by this question were nicely illustrated by a panel discussion of the New England Political Science Association held in Amherst, Massachusetts, in the early 1950s. The subject of the panel was national security and individual freedom. The participants included two scholars presumably representing liberal and moderate viewpoints. The star of the panel, however, was Professor Willmore Kendall of Yale, who at that time was well known as a leading and controversial political theorist, an intellectual light in the New Conservative movement, and the mentor of William Buckley. Kendall had obviously been selected to present a "conservative" viewpoint in the discussion. The audience and the panel members were braced for a strong defense of Senator Joseph McCarthy, the FBI, the House Un-American Activities Committee, and government crackdown on radicals and dissidents.

Professor Kendall was not two minutes into his speech when it became clear that his audience had totally misjudged his intentions and outlook. He began with an eloquent and learned articulation of the basic American ideals of individual rights and due process of law, of John Locke and Thomas Jefferson, of the Declaration of Independence and the

Bill of Rights, of the American tradition of freedom of conscience and speech, and of the need to protect these rights against abuses by government. Eloquently and forcefully, he then documented the extent to which these traditional principles and liberties had been violated in recent years. There had been congressional witch-hunts, senatorial inquisitions, book burnings, character assassination, blacklisting of people who exercised their constitutional privileges against self-incrimination, attacks on the freedom of the press, and a wide variety of other actions by governmental agencies, popular groups, and self-proclaimed vigilantes—all of which clearly violated the traditional American ideals of individual rights and liberties.

This situation, Professor Kendall said, is clearly intolerable. What can we do to bring our practices and beliefs into accord with each other? At this point he paused, while his audience waited in pleased expectation for the reforms that he would now propose. And then it came: clearly, Kendall said, we must get rid of our obsolete eighteenth-century ideas about individual rights and freedoms. Two hundred political scientists gasped in shock, incredulity, horror, and dismay. They sat in stunned silence throughout the remainder of his talk.

The well-meaning professors could not bring themselves to believe that Kendall believed what he said. And conceivably he did not: he was quite capable of playing games with audiences. But the shocked disbelief that his remarks engendered illustrates dramatically the extent to which Americans are incapable of solving their problem of national cognitive dissonance by substantially abandoning their values. The Kendall Choice, the alternative most generally predicted by the theory of cognitive dissonance, simply will not work in the American case. If, indeed, Americans could so easily resolve their problem by altering or abandoning their values, they would be like the people of any other nation. But they cannot do so. Their political ideals are at the very core of their national identity. Americans cannot abandon them without ceasing to be Americans in the most meaningful sense of the word—without, in short, becoming "un-American." The Kendall Choice may be a real one for quixotic political theorists, but it is not a real one for the American public and it has never played a significant role in American history.

The dissonance—and the dilemma—thus remain. Americans cannot be themselves unless they believe in their Creed, and if they believe in their Creed they must be against themselves. *must they?*

Patterns of Response

What are the ways in which Americans cope with their national cognitive dissonance? Consensus and stability have generally characterized American political values, and the IvI gap is always present. Variations do occur, however, in the intensity with which groups of Americans hold to their beliefs in American political ideals—that is, the level of creedal passion in American society—and in the clarity with which Americans perceive the gap to exist. Differences in these two variables can yield the four major responses set forth in Table 2.

Table 2. American responses to the IvI gap.

Intensity of belief in ideals	Perception of gap	
	Clear	Unclear
High	Moralism (eliminate gap)	Hypocrisy (deny gap)
Low	Cynicism (tolerate gap)	Complacency (ignore gap)

1. *Moralism.* If Americans intensely believe in their ideals and clearly perceive the IvI gap, they moralistically attempt to *eliminate* the gap through reforms that will bring practice and institutions into accord with principles and beliefs.

2. *Cynicism.* If intensity of belief is low and perception of the gap is clear, Americans will resort to a cynical willingness to *tolerate* the gap's existence.

3. *Complacency.* If intensity of belief is low and their perception of the gap is unclear, Americans can attempt to *ignore* the existence of the gap by in effect reducing its cognitive importance to themselves through complacent indifference.

4. *Hypocrisy.* If they are intensely committed to American ideals and yet *deny* the existence of a gap between ideals and reality, they can alter not reality but their perceptions of reality through an immense effort at "patriotic" hypocrisy.*

* Some may observe that the labels I have given these four responses all carry unfavorable connotations—and this is certainly true. One could, perhaps, find euphemisms and talk about morality rather than moralism, realism rather than cynicism, satisfaction rather than complacency, and patriotism rather than hypoc-

At various times social critics, including foreign observers of the American scene, have seized upon one or another of these four responses as *the* typical American response. In fact, however, all four have been present throughout most of American history, interacting with one another in mutually reinforcing and mutually counterbalancing ways.[3] Complacency is probably the most prevalent response, but it is also the least noted and least notable one. The others have all left a definite mark on American culture.

The tolerance of the IvI gap which is the essence of the cynical response is, for instance, a major source of American humor. Comedy depends on incongruity, and the sources of incongruity vary from one society to another. It has been observed that "nearly all the greatest British comedy rests on class differences. From *The Country Wife* to *The Diary of a Nobody,* from P. G. Wodehouse to Anthony Powell, or from Chaucer to Nancy Mitford, few writers have set out to amuse their readers without going straight to the class structure."[4] In America the source of comedy is not the incongruity between classes, but, as Louis Rubin argued, "the incongruity between the ideal and the real . . . [that] lies at the heart of the American experience." This incongruity provides the central theme of most American humor, manifested most notably, perhaps, in the work of that most American of humorists, Mark Twain. "Out of the incongruity between mundane circumstance and heroic ideal," Rubin goes on to observe, "material fact and spiritual hunger. . . . theory of equality and fact of social and economic inequality, the Declaration of Independence and the Prohibition Act, the Gettysburg Address and the Gross National Product, the Battle Hymn of the Republic and Dollar Diplomacy, the Horatio Alger ideal and the New York Social Register—between what men would be and must be, as acted out in American experience, have come a great deal of pathos, no small bit of tragedy, and also a great deal of humor." This was what Robert Penn Warren identified as the "burr under the metaphysical saddle of America," the problem of living in the same house with "a big promise—a great big one: the Declaration of Independence."[5] The gap between how Americans ideally should behave and how they actually behave furnishes an inexhaustible lode for the ridicule of moral pretense. The Americans delight in being "debunked"—

---

risy. Yet these pleasant alternative labels obscure the critical point: that each response is, in some measure, unsatisfactory and cannot be maintained for long by substantial numbers of people. They tend to hide the problem of the gap rather than to highlight it.

"bunk" itself being an American word.[6] Humor becomes one way of coping with the national problem of cognitive dissonance. The promise of American life is transformed into "the great American joke."

Not surprisingly, foreign observers have often pointed to hypocrisy as a distinctive characteristic of American culture. Although there is no reason to assign it a predominant role, there can be little doubt that it occupies a central place in American politics. Americans want to believe that their liberal-democratic ideals are reflected in their institutions. This belief is often expressed to foreigners and engenders the view abroad that Americans are given to hypocritical moralistic cant. As Irving Kristol suggested, this public hypocrisy has its roots in the "deep emotional commitment" of Americans "to the idea that government—all government, everywhere—should be subservient to the citizen's individual life, his personal liberty, and his pursuit of happiness."[7] Americans find it congenial to believe that at least their government and political system meet this standard. In this respect, hypocrisy, defined by the dictionary as the "false pretense of moral excellence," is a product not just of practice deviating from one's principles, but also of asserting principles that cannot be practiced. Americans thus reduce their cognitive dissonance by clouding their perception of the realities of power, inequality, hierarchy, and constraints in American life.

All ruling classes must in some measure be hypocritical. This is especially true of modern liberal democracies, and the eruption of democracy in America during the Jacksonian years led writers such as Nathaniel Hawthorne to seize upon hypocrisy as the pervasive characteristic of American society. In a democracy, leaders such as Lincoln and Franklin Roosevelt are open to "endless accusations of hypocrisy" because they gave "a new vigor to flagging political principles and loyalties" and "raised the level of moral and political expectations," but were unable "to fulfill the standards they had themselves revived."[8] The most distinguished spokesmen of the American Establishment mouth the clichés of American liberalism as if they were realistic descriptions rather than pious aspirations. Ashamed of their power, their ability to wield it is constrained by their felt need to pretend that it does not exist. Yet although Americans may relish the exposure of hypocrisy, they are not comfortable when it is absent in their leaders. People demand high-mindedness in their public figures, and if "you are extraordinarily high-minded in your political pronouncements, you are bound in the nature of things to be more than ordinarily hypocritical."[9]

In the United States, indeed, public figures may be attacked for not being hypocritical enough—a point well illustrated by the reactions of some political figures to the earthy realism, vulgarity, and pathos revealed in the Nixon Watergate tapes. "There's no reference throughout the whole transcription," observed Senator Bob Packwood sanctimoniously, "to what is good for the American people. There are not even any token clichés about what is good for the people." In similar tones, Chairman Robert Strauss of the Democratic Party felt moved to complain: "It's sadder and sicker than I ever imagined. I keep looking for some mention of the American people, some concern for the nation."[10] Along with his other misdoings, Nixon was guilty of not carrying over into his private conversations with his aides the hypocritical clichés demanded of public rhetoric.

No-Guilt of not Caring

In similar fashion, moralism is also often pointed to as a peculiarly American trait. "Americans are eminently prophets," Santayana once observed. "They apply morals to public affairs; they are impatient and enthusiastic . . . They are men of principles, and fond of stating them."[11] Others have noted how this leads to a penchant, almost perverse in European eyes, for self-criticism, and have pointed to this attitude as the distinguishing characteristic of Americans. Gunnar Myrdal, indeed, defended Americans against the charge of hypocrisy and insisted upon their devotion to the moralistic exposure of evil:

> The *popular* explanation of the disparity in America between ideals and actual behavior is that Americans do not have the slightest intention of living up to the ideals which they talk about and put into their Constitution and laws. Many Americans are accustomed to talk loosely and disparagingly about adherence to the American Creed as "lip-service" and even "hypocrisy." Foreigners are even more prone to make such a characterization.
>
> This explanation is too superficial. To begin with, the true hypocrite sins in secret; he conceals his faults. The American, on the contrary, is strongly and sincerely "against sin," even, and not least, his own sins. He investigates his faults, puts them on record, and shouts them from the housetops, adding the most severe recriminations against himself, including the accusation of hypocrisy. If all the world is well informed about the political corruption, organized crime, and faltering system of justice in America, it is primarily not due to its malice but to American publicity about its own imperfections.[12]

Myrdal's statement about the passion of Americans for exposing their sins is perfectly true. But it is equally true that at various times some Americans may tolerate, ignore, or deny their sins. Moralism, cynicism, complacency, and hypocrisy are all familiar ways by which Americans respond to their cognitive dissonance problem. The role and importance of these responses, however, differ from time to time and from group to group.

Response Dynamics

The propensity of American society as a whole to resort to one response or another, or some combination of responses, varies. The national mood can at different times be described as predominantly one of complacency, hypocrisy, moralism, or cynicism. Experience suggests that recourse to one of these responses may generate consequences that encourage recourse to another response. No one response, however, provides a lasting satisfactory solution to the problem of cognitive dissonance. Each is tried for a while and then abandoned in a never-ending search for a way out of the national dilemma. The logical dynamics of such a cyclical pattern of response are as follows.

1. *Moralistic reform (eliminating the gap).* Since cognitive dissonance cannot be eliminated by changing fundamental principles, changes must occur in institutions and behavior. The moralistic response occurs when people feel intensely committed to American political values, clearly perceive the gap between ideals and reality, and attempt to restructure institutions and practices to reflect these ideals. The combination of intensity and perception furnishes the moral motive to reform. "The history of reform," Emerson said, "is always identical; it is the comparison of the idea with the fact."[13] Major groups in American society become obsessed with the facts of inequality, lack of freedom, arbitrary power. They dramatize those facts and force them upon the public consciousness, making it impossible for decision makers and the attentive public to ignore the extent to which the actuality of political life contradicts American beliefs. The moral indignation of the few stimulates public outrage from the many. Institutions and practices that had been accepted as part of the way things are lose their legitimacy. Demands for curtailing power and reforming the system sweep to the top of the political agenda: reality must be made to conform to the ideal. During such creedal passion periods, the latent disharmonic qualities of American society come to the surface.

2. *Cynicism (tolerating the gap).* Large bodies of people can sustain high levels of moral indignation for only limited periods of time. The un-

veiling of evil, which was first the instrument by which moralism laid bare
hypocrisy, later furnishes the vindication of cynicism against moralism.
The perception of the IvI gap remains, but the expectation that anything
can be done to close the gap dwindles. Those who had expounded the
Creed in order to change reality find themselves increasingly divorced
from reality. The exposers of hypocrisy become the exemplars of
hypocrisy.

Reform begins with the assumption that the elimination of evil can be
achieved by the elimination of evil men-in-power. It moves on to the
assumption that some restructuring of institutions is necessary. It comes
to an end with the realization that neither of these will suffice. Some reformers conclude that the "system" itself must be totally changed and
advocate revolution. Others let the intensity of their commitment to
reform values decline and lapse into at least temporary cynical toleration
of the gap. The feeling that the gap must be eliminated is replaced by the
feeling that nothing can be changed. Moral indignation is replaced by
moral helplessness. All politicians are crooks, all institutions corrupt.
The gap must be accepted—and perhaps even enjoyed, as its role in
American humor suggests.

3. *Complacency (ignoring the gap)*. Cynicism is an effort to live with
cognitive dissonance. But just as most people cannot maintain moral
intensity indefinitely, neither can they indefinitely sustain toleration of
the gap between ideal and practice. "Cognitive dissonance is a noxious
state," and the "severity or the intensity of cognitive dissonance varies
with the importance of the cognitions involved and the relative number
of cognitions standing in dissonant relation to one another."[14] Whereas
the escape from creedal passion to cynicism involves a dulling of moral
sensibility, the escape from cynicism to complacency involves a dulling
of perceptual clarity. The importance of the dissonant cognitions is reduced simply by turning attention to other matters. During such periods
of creedal passivity and perceptual opaqueness, Americans may, if compelled to do so, admit the existence of a gap between ideal and reality—
as they did for years with respect to the role of black people in American
life—but then shunt it off into a back corner of their consciousness and
simply not become terribly concerned about it. The dilemma, as Myrdal
argued, exists but it does not trouble people nor lead them to become intensely and passionately concerned with resolving it. Cognitive dissonance
lurks uneasily beneath the surface of conscience but is not sufficiently
commanding to trouble people seriously. There is no intense concern

with American ideals or with the discrepancy between ideal and reality.

4. *Hypocrisy (denying the gap)*. The ideological nature of their national identity means that Americans cannot indefinitely eschew the affirmation of the basic values and principles of the national Creed. Responding to the need to articulate these values, however, they may still be reluctant to acknowledge the existence of the IvI gap. They may then view themselves through filtering lenses. American institutions are seen to be open and democratic; America is the land of opportunity; the equality of man is a fact in American life; the United States is the land of the free and the home of the brave; it is the embodiment of government of the people, by the people, and for the people. During these periods, Americans so shape their perceptions that they cannot see any gap between the unpleasant facts of political institutions and power in the United States and the values of the American Creed. Reality is hailed as the ideal. The discrepancies are strained out and avoided. The United States not only should be the land of liberty, equality, and justice for all; it actually is.

In due course, however, the intense assertion of American ideals leads to renewed perception of the IvI gap. New individuals and groups begin to use the affirmation of the ideals as a means not of glorifying the American way of life but of exposing it. The hypocritical identification of reality with ideal gives way to the moralistic denunciation of reality in terms of the ideal. The way is cleared for another wave of creedal passion directed toward reform.

This sequence of responses is designed as a model and not as a representation of empirical reality. History does not necessarily develop according to logical patterns. Some measure of psychological dissatisfaction is, however, the inevitable result of the IvI gap and some combination of moralism, cynicism, complacency, and hypocrisy is required to reduce that dissatisfaction. Particular phases in American history often tend to be colored more by one response than by the others, and one response often creates conditions favorable to the rise of another. History does not follow a logical model, but neither is the logical model irrelevant to the understanding of history.

Group Propensities

Just as different responses may predominate in different historical phases, so also different groups in society may have propensities toward

different responses. Age and socioeconomic status appear to have a significant effect upon people's choices.

The American educational system, particularly at the elementary-
school level, indoctrinates its students in American ideals and minimizes
the disparity between ideal and reality. As a result, grade-school children
generally have highly positive and benign images of the political system,
the government, and particularly of the President.[15] They are, in short,
educated in the hypocritical response. These attitudes provide the basis
for their subsequent adult acceptance of the legitimacy of the political
system. Secondary-school children have more "realistic" and, in some respects, more cynical attitudes toward politics. There still remains, however, a substantial difference between their views and those of young adults
who have been out of school for several years. In addition, high-school
seniors have considerably lower levels of political cynicism than do their
parents who went to high school. Among those who leave school after
high school, increasing exposure to the unpleasant realities of political
life combines with feelings of limited political efficacy to produce a significantly more cynical approach to the political process. Among those
who go on to college, on the other hand, an increasingly clear perception
of the IvI gap encourages more of a shift toward moralism. The educational system that minimizes the distinction between ideal and reality for
young children maximizes the impact of perceptions of that gap among
college-age youth. "Societies teach youth to adhere to the basic values of
the social system in absolute terms . . . Compromises which are dictated
by contradictory pressures and are justified in the eyes of many adults are
viewed by idealistic youth as violations of basic morality. Young people
tend to be committed to ideals rather than institutions. Hence, events
which point up the gap between ideals and reality often stimulate them to
action, though cynicism and withdrawal occur as well if they see no
appropriate way to act."[16] As people age, however, the intensity of belief
necessary for either hypocrisy or moralism tends to decline, and among
adults a high correlation exists between cynicism and age.[17]

Socioeconomic status plays an even more important role in shaping
response propensities. The available evidence suggests two significant
tendencies. First, almost all groups in American society favor the basic
liberal-democratic values of the American Creed. People who are better
educated, who are of higher socioeconomic status, and who occupy positions of social or political leadership are, however, more likely to support

those values than are other people. That is, the proportion of such groups affirming support for these values may be 85 percent rather than 65 percent or 70 percent.[18] This difference in breadth of support does not necessarily demonstrate anything about the relative intensity of support from these two groups, but it does suggest the probability that intensity of support will be greater among those of higher socioeconomic position. In addition, people with more education and of higher socioeconomic status are more likely to support the application of liberal-democratic values in specific instances than are other people.[19] Such evidence would clearly seem to indicate greater commitment to and intensity of belief in those liberal-democratic values. In short, there is reason to believe that higher-status people are more likely to be hypocritical or moralistic, and lower-status people cynical or complacent.

A second difference among groups according to socioeconomic status is even more clearly documented by the evidence. People who have less income and less education and who do not occupy leadership roles are more likely than others to have a critical view of the political process and to perceive a significant gap between American ideal and American reality. People of higher status, position, and education are less likely to perceive a wide gap between the two. As Table 3 indicates, Herbert McClosky found substantial differences in political cynicism between "political influentials," that is, people who had been delegates or alternates to a national party convention, and a cross-section of the general electorate. Overall, 10.1 percent of the influentials scored "high" on the cynicism scale, compared with 31.3 percent of the general population.[20] Similarly, a study of political ideology is Muskegon, Michigan, found that "the higher their income, the more people believe that the ideology of pluralism accurately describes the way the system works and, as a corollary, the lower their income, the less symmetry people see between normative and actualized aspects of the ideology . . . Higher income strata tend to equate normative and existential statements about political pluralism, while lower income strata tend to deny their symmetry and to support action to make them more congruent."[21] In similar fashion, black children and poor Appalachian children see the President as deviating significantly more from idealistic norms than do white middle-class children.[22] In short, higher-status people are more likely to be hypocritical or complacent, lower-status people to be cynical or moralistic.

These two conclusions on the relation of socioeconomic status to intensity of creedal beliefs and to clarity of perception of the IvI gap com-

Table 3. Responses to statements expressing cynicism toward government and politics.

Statement	Percent of agreement	
	Political influentials (N = 3020)	*General electorate (N = 1484)*
Most politicians are looking out for themselves above all else.	36.3	54.3
Both major parties in this country are controlled by the wealthy and are run for their benefit.	7.9	32.1
The people who really "run" the country do not even get known to the voters.	40.2	60.5
The laws of this country are supposed to benefit all of us equally, but the fact is that they're almost all "rich-man's laws."	8.4	33.3
Most politicians don't seem to me to really mean what they say.	24.7	55.1
There is practically no connection between what a politician says and what he will do once he gets elected.	21.4	54.0
All politics is controlled by political bosses.	15.6	45.9

Source: Herbert McClosky, "Consensus and Ideology in American Politics," *American Political Science Review* 58 (June 1964): 370.

bine to suggest one broad generalization. People of higher socioeconomic status are more likely than people of lower status to believe intensely in the values of the Creed and are less likely to perceive a major gap between those values and political reality. They consequently are likely to have a propensity toward the hypocritical response. People of lower socioeconomic status are less likely to have intense beliefs in the Creed. A large number of lower-status people probably do not concern themselves with politics and hence do not perceive a significant gap between ideal and reality. They are thus likely to have a propensity toward complacency. Insofar as lower-status people become politically aware, however, they will tend toward a cynical response.

This pattern of group propensities underlies the stability of the political system. Those who most intensely believe in the values of the system are less likely to see a gap between those values and political reality. Those who see such a gap are less likely to have the moralistic fervor to do anything about it. Upper-class and upper-middle-class hypocrisy combines with working-class and lower-class cynicism to perpetuate the status quo. At least this seems to be the predominant tendency for much of the time. To be sure, some people within the higher-status groups are ever sensitive to the gap between ideal and reality and regularly attempt to do something about it. Their success, however, is dependent upon their ability to mobilize additional support from those who are either hypocritical or cynical. Change in the system—or, if one views it unfavorably, instability —occurs when those who perceive the gap develop moralistic passion or when those who feel such passion come to perceive the gap. The latter shift, which normally involves significant changes in the perceptions of the upper middle class, has historically been the most important source of change in American political institutions and practices. Shifts in either perceptions or intensity may also affect different groups in the population differently. In the 1960s, for example, higher-status and lower-status groups both developed clearer perceptions of the gap between political ideals and political reality. As a result, higher-status groups became less hypocritical and more moralistic, furnishing the impetus for wide-ranging reforms of institutions and practices; at the same time, lower-status groups became less complacent and more cynical, causing a massive decline in popular trust and confidence in government, as reflected in public opinion polls.

If Americans do not blind themselves to reality, they have a choice between moralism and cynicism. If Americans do not falter in the intensity of their belief in American ideals, they have a choice between moralism and hypocrisy. Moralism is thus the one response that, in some sense, combines both realism and idealism. It involves the effort to remove the fundamental cause of American cognitive dissonance by reducing or eliminating the gap between promise and practice. In this sense it is the most positive American political response. As American history demonstrates, however, it can be not only the reformer but the destroyer of American institutions. Henry Stimson, at the end of an extraordinarily distinguished career of public service, concluded his memoirs with the words: "The only deadly sin I know is cynicism."[23] As a central figure of the American Establishment, Stimson focused on the popular sin of cynicism and did not recognize the Establishment sin of hypocrisy. More important, he also failed to note that in America the only deadly virtue is moralism.

The Gap and American Political Style

The Power Paradox

The coexistence in America of the antipower ethic with inequality in power gives rise to what may be termed the "power paradox": effective power is unnoticed power; power observed is power devalued. At times Americans have gloried in the conspicuous consumption of wealth, but never in the conspicuous employment of power. The architects of power in the United States must create a force that can be felt but not seen. Power remains strong when it remains in the dark; exposed to the sunlight it begins to evaporate.

The power paradox has manifested itself again and again in American political history and public debate. It is well illustrated by two major analyses of the power of that central institution of American politics, the Presidency.

The first, Richard Neustadt's penetrating volume, *Presidential Power,* published in 1960, was designed "to explore the power problem of the man inside the White House." This is "the classic problem of the man on top in any political system: how to be on top in fact as well as name." This is not easy for the President to achieve. *"The same conditions that promote his leadership in form preclude a guarantee of leadership in fact."* The book's basic theme was quite simple: the President does not have much power, or at least he has a lot less power than people assume. He is hemmed in by forces and groups outside his direct control, particularly Congress, the bureaucracy, and public opinion. Except in rare cases, the President does not have the power to command. His is essentially a power to persuade. He has great and diverse resources but has power only insofar as he can employ them in negotiations and bargaining. Neustadt dramatizes his point by quoting the remarks of President Truman on the frustrations awaiting his successor: "He [Eisenhower]'ll sit here, and he'll say, 'Do this! Do that!' *And nothing will happen.* Poor Ike—it won't be a bit like the Army. He'll find it very frustrating."[24] In 1960, Neustadt's picture of the limited, restrained, checked-and-balanced President was quite persuasive.

Thirteen years later, Arthur Schlesinger, Jr., painted an equally persuasive but very different picture in his work *The Imperial Presidency.*

76 AMERICAN POLITICS

Presidential primacy, he argued, has "turned into presidential supremacy." The "constitutional Presidency" had become the "imperial Presidency and threatens to be the revolutionary Presidency." The Presidency had appropriated the power of Congress in both foreign and domestic affairs, particularly in the former. The result was "an unprecedented concentration of power in the White House and an unprecedented attempt to transform the Presidency of the Constitution into a plebiscitary Presidency." The underlying issue confronting the country was "the expansion and abuse of presidential power."[25]

Readers of these two books would be tempted to conclude that the Presidency was weak in the late 1950s and early 1960s, and, following a decade of steady accretion of presidential power, became overwhelmingly strong in the early 1970s. But this conclusion would in many respects be wide of the mark. Due to the power paradox, something close to the opposite is true. The late 1950s and early 1960s represented a peaking of presidential power; by the early 1970s, it had been checked and reduced to its lowest point in at least forty years. Eisenhower and Kennedy represented the zenith.[26] The decline began with Lyndon Johnson and snowballed during the administration of Richard Nixon, reaching a nadir when he became the first American President to be driven from office.

The process of and the reasons for the decline of the Presidency have been set forth elsewhere. What is relevant here is the extent to which these two seminal books on the Presidency reflect the change in its power. Power revealed is power reduced; power concealed is power enhanced. Neustadt's concern over the "power problem" of the President in 1960 reflects the pervasiveness of presidential power. Schlesinger's equally deep concern over the imperial quality of presidential power in 1973 testifies to the waning of that power. In general, if it becomes widely accepted that the Presidency lacks extensive power and that its occupant is readily checked by other officials and groups, this fact in itself is evidence of *support for* presidential power and hence *the existence of* presidential power. If, on the other hand, people believe that the President is extremely powerful, this in itself is evidence (since great power is viewed as wrong) that the President is not so powerful or that his power is declining. When presidential power is really great, public opinion never considers it to be too great; when presidential power is fading, public opinion considers it inordinate.

The Presidency is not the only example of this phenomenon. In 1961, for instance, as he left office Eisenhower issued his famous warning about the "potential for the disastrous rise of misplaced power" and "unwarranted influence" stemming from the existence of the "military-industrial complex." Apart from a few pro forma nods, these words provoked little immediate reaction. But they could not have been more apposite and timely. The power, well placed or misplaced, of the military-industrial complex peaked in the early 1960s. Three days after Eisenhower issued his warning, John F. Kennedy assumed office and almost immediately launched a major increase in military spending which involved a 45 percent increase in the number of army divisions, a 50 percent increase in Polaris submarine construction, a 100 percent increase in Minuteman missile production capability, and a 100 percent increase in the number of nuclear weapons in strategic alert forces. The early 1960s were the high point of the post–World War II investment in major new military weapons systems. A President of the United States warned of the dangers that could arise from this power complex, yet neither Congress, nor the media, nor public opinion, nor scholars were motivated to act.

Ten years later, the situation was totally reversed. The power of the military-industrial complex was clearly on the decline; public priorities had shifted elsewhere; Congress closely scrutinized and at times rejected new weapons proposals; a variety of antimilitary interest groups and lobbies attacked the defense budget; military spending in real dollars, and particularly spending for hardware, declined year after year in the late 1960s and early 1970s; Lockheed teetered on the brink of bankruptcy. At the same time, and as a part of this decline in the power of the military-industrial complex, warnings about its power and attacks on its power escalated through the media and public debate. Eisenhower's remarks, which had been apposite and ignored in 1961, became inapposite and constantly quoted in 1971. In the course of a few years, a flood of volumes issued forth with titles such as *The Economy of Death, Pentagon Capitalism, American Militarism 1970, How to Control the Military, The Weapons Culture, The War Business, Militarism USA*. No issue of a popular journal was complete without an exposé of the machinations and power of the arms-manufacturing companies and their uniformed allies in the Pentagon. All this furor over the supposedly outrageous power of the military-industrial complex was, however, evidence of the very successful effort to reduce that power.

In some measure, this has always been the American pattern. Even as it achieved independence the nation was denouncing George III as a repressive tyrant and at the same time demonstrating how completely ineffective he was in that role. Throughout American history, the exposés of power, whether by the Muckrakers in the 1900s or their descendants in the 1960s, have been part and parcel of the reduction of power. This is not to say that all people and institutions who are identified, and hence criticized, as powerful are necessarily ineffectual. This clearly is not the case. But it does mean that individuals, groups, and institutions whose power is widely recognized and discussed are less powerful than if this were not the case. In other societies, individuals and groups may go to great lengths to call attention to their power. Awareness of power induces respect, obeisance, fear, awe: power breeds power. In the United States, however, awareness of power induces suspicion, hostility, and outrage. Because of the prevalence of the antipower ethic, awareness of power breeds its own reduction and hidden power is more effective. Because power is less legitimate in the United States than in other cultures, greater efforts have to be made to obscure it. It becomes necessary to deny the facts of power in order to preserve those facts. Yet the opportunities and the pressures to expose and publicize power pervade American public life. Consequently, because its visibility is its greatest vulnerability, the most effective exercise of power is the concealment of power; to cover up power becomes the first imperative of power.

The Cover-Up Imperative and Conspiracy Theories

In the American context, the cover-up of power is no easy task. A distinguishing characteristic of American politics is its open, public quality compared with the politics of other democratic (much less authoritarian) societies. Government is supposed to be open and aboveboard; secrecy implies evil. The American tradition, Edward Shils said, is one of "luxuriating publicity." The idea of *raison d'état,* of secrets of state, never took hold in America, any more than did the idea of "the state" itself. The United States is distinguished by "its passion for publicity and the weakness of traditions which would sustain the conventions of governmental privacy that are common in the democracies of western Europe." As a result, the principal institution of publicity, the press, has a status in the United States that is unequaled in Europe. In the United States, in contrast to Britain, one would never speak of "the awe of the press before the majesty of Government" because "the balance of power between Government and the press favors the Government in Great Britain and the press in the United States."[27] Open government is an American ideal that has not been fully achieved in reality but it is also an American reality that has never been approximated by other societies.

Not only is publicity more pervasive, it is also more erosive of power in the United States than in any other society. Hence, greater efforts are required to hide power in order to preserve its reality and its legitimacy. A vicious circle develops: because power is abhorrent, it must be concealed, and because it is concealed, it becomes even more abhorrent. The pervasive threat of publicity to power produces the pervasive need for secrecy and deception about power. Because exposure is more devastating in its consequences in the United States, secrecy becomes more necessary and more difficult to achieve. There is thus, as Shils pointed out many years ago, a close and natural affinity between publicity and secrecy that works to the detriment of privacy. In Great Britain there has historically been some sort of an equilibrium among these three; in the United States the mania for publicity undermines privacy and creates a hypnotic fascination with secrecy. "Secrecy is less fascinating in Great Britain because privacy is better maintained and publicity less rampant." The United States, on the other hand, is characterized by "the preponderance of publicity and its attendant stress on salvationary secrecy over privacy."[28]

In an environment in which secrecy is salvationary, conspiracy theories are heuristically indispensable. Three circumstances affect the prevalence of conspiracy theories concerning the existence of secret power.

First, if power is clearly concentrated in an absolute monarch, a charismatic leader, or a politburo—if, in other words, there is a single open source of power—little incentive exists to develop a conspiracy theory positing a single hidden source of power. If, however, power appears to be widely dispersed among a number of individuals, institutions, and groups, then many people will find reason to believe that this cannot really be the case, that some hidden locus of power must exist behind the apparent dispersion, and that a small group of all-powerful leaders must be manipulating the actions of others.

Second, conspiracy theories are less likely to be prevalent in societies where politics is viewed simply as the struggle for benefits among self-interested individuals and groups. They are much more likely to take root in societies in which it is viewed as having a major moral dimension, involving the conflict between the forces of good and the forces of evil. Conspiracy theory is the logical extension of political moralism, "for if historical movement at every stage is almost exclusively a matter of good will or ill will, freely chosen, those who make a mistake are not just wrong; they are evil. And all our social and political pathologies are the result of deliberate evil-doing. Given the moralistic premise, how else could we account for them? Senator Joseph McCarthy asked: 'How can we account for our present situation unless we believe that men high in this government are concerting to deliver us to disaster?' "[29]

Third, conspiracy theories are less likely to be prevalent in societies in which power is positively valued. On the other hand, in societies with a strong antipower ethic, hostility to power is likely to generate fear and suspicion concerning the existence of concealed power. In addition, in such societies power that is secret is likely to be more "powerful" than power that is public. Hence, there is good reason to be concerned about the possible existence of secret power.

The dispersion of power in America, the moralistic component of American politics, and the pervasive hostility toward power all conspire to make the United States particularly receptive to conspiracy theories. And, in fact, this has been the case, as many native and foreign observers have noted. "In the history of American political controversy," Richard Hofstadter commented, "there is a tradition of conspiratorial accusations which seem to have been sincerely believed."[30] Conspiracy theories were the midwife at the birth of the American republic: the "fear of a comprehensive conspiracy against liberty throughout the English-speaking world —a conspiracy believed to have been nourished in corruption, and of which, it was felt, oppression in America was only the most immediately visible part—lay at the heart of the Revolutionary movement." The fear of conspiracy had deep roots in the political traditions of eighteenth-century Britain and America, encouraged by both the theory of mixed government and the tendency to dichotomize liberty and power. Whereas Americans and English Whigs saw the threat in a ministerial conspiracy —a view "almost universally shared by sympathizers of the American cause"—George III saw the actions of the rebellious colonists as "a seditious and unwarrantable combination" and a "desperate conspiracy."[31] After independence, every generation and almost every decade saw the existence of a secret conspiratorial power, in one form or another—Illuminati, Masons, Catholics, Mormons, bankers, Jews, communists—threatening the vitals of the Republic. The idea that secret power exists comes most naturally to those distant from power. The conspiratorial interpretation is hence peculiarly characteristic of populist move-

ments and of movements infused with creedal passion for exposure and
reform. "There was something about the Populist imagination that loved
the secret plot and the conspiratorial meeting."[32] Concern over conspiracy
did not die with the Populists, however, and Shils could easily observe in
the mid-1950s that "worry about conspiracy has been a constant feature
of American life for half a century at least."[33]

This tendency to be obsessed with conspiracy has a realistic basis in the
prevailing American attitude toward power. If power is of dubious legitimacy, it must be concealed to be effective. Not only this, but the act of
concealment itself must also be concealed. The rewards of conspiratorial
power are thus much greater in the American context than they are in
societies in which public power is not devalued power, and one should
assume that those who wish to wield power will also conspire to keep
that fact secret. In sum, there are more incentives to develop conspiracies
of power in the United States than in other societies, and hence conspiracy
theories about power which appear to be more prevalent in the United
States than in other societies may also be more justifiable. Indeed, if the
effective exercise of power involves the cover-up of its existence, then it
is only a small logical jump to the ultimate conclusion, the *reductio ad
absurdum* of conspiracy theory, that the most persuasive evidence for the
existence of secret power is the total absence of any such evidence.

The Sincerity Test

Secrecy is thus necessary to hide the facts of power, and deception
is necessary to make those facts appear different from what they are. The
latter is the natural extension of the former: secrecy is the shield of power
and deception the cloak of secrecy. Deception becomes an inherent aspect
of the relationship between government and the public, between political
leaders and followers. The hypocrisy that seizes all of the people some of
the time is common coin for some of the people—their leaders—all the
time. Governmental institutions are made to appear more open and more
responsive to public opinion than they are. Political leaders also must
appear to reflect the will of the people more than is actually the case. They
have no choice but to kowtow to the appearances of democracy, however
much they have attempted to avoid the reality of democracy. The increasing demands, beginning in the early nineteenth century, that government
be made more democratic did in fact increase democracy, but they also
multiplied the institutions and practices by which government could be

made to appear more democratic than it actually was. The demands for democracy in government produced both more democracy and more deception. Because people in the United States expect government to be more democratic than it can be, the government must make itself appear more democratic than it is.

These consequences of the IvI gap help explain the central role that the problem of sincerity plays in American politics. Sincerity can only be an important issue when ideals are taken seriously. In a very different way, as Rubashov illustrated, it can also play a critical role in the politics of communist systems. In them, as in the United States, political figures may feel an overwhelming need to assert and to demonstrate their sincere commitment to the political values and goals of their society. The difficulty of doing this, of course, gives rise to cynicism, hypocrisy, and deception. Implicit recognition of their prevalence enhances the concern with and the value of sincerity.

The meaning of sincerity differs from one culture to another. In Asian cultures, sincerity means almost the opposite of what it means in the United States. In Japan, the emphasis is on the anticipation of the interests of a superior. In China, sincerity involves following a general external code: "One demonstrates 'sincerity' by commitment to one's interpersonal obligations, to society, and not to one's inner feelings. Indeed, one is perhaps most sincere when doing the socially correct thing at precisely the time that inner feelings are urging a different course of action."[34] In both China and Japan, the stress is on the relation of the individual to his associates, to his peers, to his superiors, to his group. Sincerity, in a sense, is almost a group characteristic.

In the United States, on the other hand, sincerity involves the relation of the individual to himself and to his beliefs. It has two dimensions. It involves frankness, truthfulness, and openness about oneself and one's feelings—"telling the truth about oneself to oneself and to others," as Lionel Trilling summarized its meaning in French literature. But in the American context, it means something more. A person might wholeheartedly espouse the view that people are universally devious, narrowminded, and mean, but Americans would not normally call such a person sincere. They would call him a cynic, and a "sincere cynic" would, in their view, be a contradiction in terms. Nor would they describe as sincere a politician who said that he loved power for its own sake and for the opportunity it gave him to manipulate and dominate others. The concept of sincerity in American culture (and probably, as Trilling suggested, in English culture as well) simply does not encompass the possibility of being sincerely evil. Sincerity involves a "single-minded commitment" to "dutiful enterprise."[35] It involves a substantive, moral dimension, a dedication to right beliefs. Americans cannot conceive of Hitler or Stalin as sincere men. In the American context, in short, sincerity means commitment to the liberal-democratic, individualistic ideals of the American Creed. Only in a society in which the incentives to hypocrisy are so numerous could the concern with sincerity as a moral virtue be so deep.

The American definition of sincerity often makes it difficult for Americans to understand foreigners. In foreign cultures sincerity may not only be defined differently, but in the American sense it may also be irrelevant. As Margaret Mead pointed out, to the Bolshevik "all acts commanded by the Party are ethical," and hence "the essential virtue consists in being so goal-oriented (*tseleustremenyi*) that no contradiction can arise between behavior demanded by changes in the Line and the individual behavior— in a diplomat or officer on a border—needed to implement the Line." The more flexible Soviet officials are in implementing the Line, the greater their integrity in terms of their ethic. To Americans, however, such behavior is proof of insincerity. "As consistency and sincerity are regarded by Americans as essential to integrity, and as both are lacking in the behavior of the Soviet leadership, there is temptation to continue to apply American standards of judgment and to regard Soviet behavior as insincere, cynical in the American sense, and so without integrity."[36]

In America, political leaders, both foreign and indigenous, must undergo a sincerity test: Do they really believe what they say? Americans ask this question with mixed hope, incredulity, and skepticism, all of which reflects how difficult it is to be sincere in American public life. Supporting in 1978 the admission to the United States of the white Rhodesian leader, Ian Smith, Senator S. I. Hayakawa argued, "I think the American people deserve to see Smith first-hand. If he's patently a fraud, let's find that out. If he's a sincere man, let's find that out, too."[37] The possibility that Smith might sincerely hold views on race relations that would be abhorrent to a vast majority of Americans was not admitted. Sincerity means a real belief in American ideals. For American public figures, the problem is how to square this belief with the knowledge of how imperfectly those ideals are realized in American institutions and practices. Not sincerity but its opposite, hypocrisy, seems almost unavoidable. Only those who become passionate reformers, clearly and unchallengeably committed to bringing institutions and practices into accord with American ideals, are able to escape having their sincerity questioned. No one asked "Is he sincere?" of William Lloyd Garrison. But for others, the sincerity question—How does he reconcile his belief in American values with his perception of American reality?—is inescapable.

5 THE POLITICS
OF CREEDAL PASSION

Creedal Passion Periods in American History

The responses of cynicism, complacency, and hypocrisy to the national problem of cognitive dissonance do not have major direct consequences for the stability and continuity of the political system—although obviously they may have important long-term effects on how it operates. None of these responses challenges the continued existence of the IvI gap. The fourth possible choice, moralism, does attempt to eliminate the gap by bringing reality into accord with the values and ideals of the American Creed. It thus has direct behavioral and institutional consequences for the operation of the political system and involves major efforts to alter institutions and practices. The impetus for these reforms comes from combining the perception that a major gap does exist with the intense belief that it should not exist.

In various periods of American history, the level of creedal passion has increased generally throughout the body politic. New generations deeply concerned with the gap between ideal and practice supplant earlier generations that were less deeply concerned. Those who were previously relatively unconcerned manifest a new passion to bring reality into accord with principle. The values of the Creed come to play a more central role in people's lives; people become aroused, agitated, politicized.

Although the intensity of this concern cannot be shown to vary regularly over time, four periods of creedal passion stand out in American history: the Revolutionary, Jacksonian, and Progressive eras and the years of protest, exposure, and reform of the 1960s and early 1970s.

These periods differ from other times in American history in the extent to which traditional American ideals were articulated and efforts made to bring institutions and practices into accord with those ideals, in the way in which social conflicts cut across the usual lines of class and region, and in the degree to which major realignments occurred between social forces and governmental institutions.

These periods, of course, have not been the only years of change in American politics. They are distinguished by institutional realignment and reform. At other times in American history, significant shifts have taken place in the relative power of social and economic groups. Such changes, indeed, seem to alternate with the changes of creedal passion periods. The early 1800s, for instance, saw the agrarian interests of the South and West displace the Federalist mercantile and commercial groups as the controlling force behind the national government. The 1860s saw the virtual elimination from power in the central government of Southern agrarian interests and the rise to power of Northern business and industrial interests. In the 1930s recent immigrant groups, organized labor, and the urban working class gained enormous political influence. The focus of change in these periods concerns the role and power of social forces; the focus of change during creedal passion periods concerns the structure and character of political institutions and practices.

The four creedal passion periods share a number of specific characteristics that distinguish them from other periods in American history:

1. Discontent was widespread; authority, hierarchy, specialization, and expertise were widely questioned or rejected.

2. Political ideas were taken seriously and played an important role in the controversies of the time.

3. Traditional American values of liberty, individualism, equality, popular control of government, and the openness of government were stressed in public discussion.

4. Moral indignation over the IvI gap was widespread.

5. Politics was characterized by agitation, excitement, commotion, even upheaval—far beyond the usual routine of interest-group conflict.

6. Hostility toward power (the antipower ethic) was intense, with the central issue of politics often being defined as "liberty versus power."

7. The exposure or muckraking of the IvI gap was a central feature of politics.

8. Movements flourished devoted to specific reforms or "causes" (women, minorities, criminal justice, temperance, peace).

9. New media forms appeared, significantly increasing the influence of the media in politics.

10. Political participation expanded, often assuming new forms and often expressed through hitherto unusual channels.

11. The principal political cleavages of the period tended to cut across economic class lines, with some combination of middle- and working-class groups promoting change.

12. Major reforms were attempted in political institutions in order to limit power and reshape institutions in terms of American ideals (some of which were successful and some of which were lasting).

13. A basic realignment occurred in the relations between social forces and political institutions, often including but not limited to the political party system.

14. The prevailing ethos promoting reform in the name of traditional ideals was, in a sense, both forward-looking and backward-looking, progressive and conservative.

The remainder of this chapter elaborates these general aspects of creedal passion periods. First, however, it may be desirable to say a few words as to why one major political event, the American Revolution, can usefully be analyzed as a creedal passion period, and then why another major political event, the New Deal, does not fit into this pattern.

The American Revolution has always posed peculiar problems for historical interpretation. Was it a "real" social revolution, comparable to the English, French, and Russian Revolutions? Was it simply a national war of independence or liberation? Or was it a unique uprising not classifiable into any of the common broader categories of revolution or international conflict—perhaps even essentially conservative in nature? Each of these interpretations may be useful for some analytical purposes. But the Revolution can also be thought of not as a somewhat suspect member of the broader class of social revolutions or as simply a unique historical event, but rather as one—and the first on a national level—of a class of events that have recurred throughout and are unique to American history. The Revolutionary era was the prototypical period of creedal passion. The three later periods represented a rearticulation of the themes of the Revolutionary years and a replay of the features and patterns of Revolutionary politics.

The Revolution was the most dramatic, most sweeping, and most successful of the efforts to articulate and to realize in practice American political values and ideals. This aspect of the Revolution was neatly caught by Benjamin Rush, in his Fourth of July address in Philadelphia in 1787: "There is nothing more common than to confound the terms American Revolution with those of the late American War. The American War is over, but this is far from being the case with the American Revolution. On the contrary but the first act of the great drama is closed."[1] In comparison with other major revolutions, the American Revolution does appear to have a conservative cast. It clearly did not involve a class struggle along Marxist or French Revolutionary lines; no particular social group was destroyed. But it did set loose a radical and revolutionary ideology—that government derived its legitimacy from the consent of the governed—which defined the basis of political legitimacy in America and set forth a new standard of legitimacy for the world. In this sense, the Revolution was "the most creative period in the history of American political thought. Everything that followed assumed and built upon its results."[2] In the context of American history, the Revolution was indeed a revolutionary event and an event of decisive importance not only in terms of its own immediate consequences, but because it was "the first act" of a drama whose subsequent acts would reiterate in a variety of ways its initial themes and plot. In the later creedal passion periods, Americans attempted to reenact with new targets their successful overthrow of the British monarchy in the 1700s.

The Revolutionary era thus saw the first formulation on a national basis of American political ideas and the first effort to reshape political institutions in their image. The purpose of the Revolution, Irving Kristol said, was "to bring our political institutions into a more perfect correspondence with an actual 'American way of life' which no one ever dreamed of challenging." The effect of the Revolution, in turn, was to reshape "political institutions in such a way as to make them more responsive to popular opinion and less capable of encroaching upon the personal liberties of the citizen."[3] In later creedal passion periods, this purpose was reaffirmed, and the effect was, even if in weakening degree, to make political institutions more responsive, more liberal, more democratic. In each of these four periods, people were agitated over the gap between political ideal and political reality, and in each they attempted to reshape their institutions and practices so as to reduce or to eliminate that gap. As a result, in each of these periods politics has been more intense, more "idealistic," more infused with moral passion than it has been at other times when the pragmatic bargaining among interest groups dominates the scene. There are thus two American politics: the politics of movements and causes, of creedal passion and reform, and the politics of interests and groups, of pragmatic bargaining and compromise. In this respect, too, a contrast existed between late-eighteenth-century politics in England and America: the former embodied a politics of family, faction, and interest, whereas "the Namier denigration of ideas and principles is inapplicable for American politics because the American social situation in which ideas operated was very different from that of eighteenth-century England."[4]

Viewing the American Revolution as the first of a series of periods of upheaval and change peculiar to American history helps explain the striking difference in the appeal of the *ideals* of the Revolution and the *experience* of the Revolution. However much it may have differed from other revolutions, the American Revolution "resembled every other major revolution in western history" in that it possessed "comprehensive and utopian revolutionary ideology" which was "just as much a system of ideas for fundamentally reshaping the character of the society as were the ideologies of those other revolutions."[5] This ideology was republicanism. Its ideals, articulated in the Revolution, are universal in their formulation and in their appeal; they have inspired revolutionaries elsewhere; they have been quoted by radicals and reformers across the globe. The experience of the American Revolution—that is, the usefulness of the Revolution as a historical model—has been much more limited. It was, as Hannah Arendt observed, "from the course of the French Revolution, and not from the course of events in America or from the acts of the Founding Fathers, that our present use of the word 'revolution' received its connotations and overtones everywhere, this country not excluded. . . The sad truth of the matter is that the French Revolution, which ended in disaster, made world history, while the American Revolution, so triumphantly successful, has remained an event of little more than local importance."[6] Epitomizing republican and liberal ideals, the American revolutionary ideology has had a wide appeal, even though no other society has been conceived in its image. As a historical model, however, the American revolutionary experience has been ignored. The concepts, phases, and semantics of the revolution, and, most important, the lessons of how to behave in revolutionary situations, have been drawn first from the French and then from the Bolshevik Revolution.

The moralistic intensity of the creedal passion periods clearly has distinguished them from other times of change in American politics, as well as from eras of stalemate and stagnation. There has been, however, at least one period of American history that has often been thought of as a period of major reform and yet did not fit the pattern of a creedal passion period. This was the New Deal. In fact, the New Deal was a very different sort of phenomenon.

First, the primary concern of the New Deal was not the reform of politics but the restoration of prosperity. Unlike most creedal passion periods, the 1930s was a period of economic depression. The overwhelming issue was how to deal with the country's economic problems. As a result, political reform was a distant second to economic recovery as a New Deal goal.

Second, the need to deal with economic problems meant that the emphasis was on how to use governmental power, not how to break it up. Although New Deal rhetoric incorporated Jacksonian and populist criticism of the malefactors of great wealth, the principal imperatives of the New Deal were directed toward the solution of immediate and pressing economic problems, through governmental action if necessary, rather than the reshaping of political and economic institutions to bring them into accord with the ideals of the American Creed. The opposition to "bigness," so characteristic of creedal passion periods, was evident during the New Deal, but it was a subordinate strand. Governmental interventionism and even collectivism rather than traditional individualism set the dominant tone. As Hofstadter pointed out, the New Deal never manifested any sustained and consistent hostility to the two great ogres of the Progressive era, the machines and the trusts.[7]

Third, almost totally absent from the New Deal were the moralism and Puritanism characteristic of creedal passion periods. The hallmark of the New Deal was pragmatism, opportunism, "bold, persistent experimentation," rather than the passionate reaffirmation of moral values. Progressivism had been characterized by "its traffic in moral absolutes, its exalted moral tone. While something akin to this was by no means entirely absent from the New Deal, the later movement showed a strong and candid awareness that what was happening was not so much moral reformation as economic experimentation."[8] Moral indignation, indeed, was more characteristic of its conservative critics than it was of the New Deal itself. The traditional moral virtues of politics did not rate high in the New Deal pantheon. Leading intellectual figures such as Max Lerner and Thurman

Arnold stressed the importance of means, technique, expertise, and organization over individualism, honesty, integrity, and morality. The New Deal outlook was almost entirely future-oriented, in contrast to the Janus-faced moods prevailing during creedal passion periods.

Fourth, during the New Deal, probably more than at any other time in American politics, political cleavages tended to be along economic class lines. Although the alignment was never perfect, the have-nots were gathered into the Roosevelt coalition in the Democratic Party, while the haves, including many former Democrats, rallied to the Republican Party. The basic political cleavage tended to be horizontal, as opposed to the more vertical cleavage characteristic of creedal passion periods.

Finally, in terms of its results, the New Deal produced major new economic policies and programs—a new relation between the government and the economy—without the efforts to cleanse and purify government, to open up government, and to make government more democratic which had been characteristic of the creedal passion periods. The New Deal resulted in a proliferation of governmental activity and an increase in presidential power. Not the reform of government but the expansion of government was the New Deal's legacy to the next generation.

In contrast to the New Deal years, the Revolutionary, Jacksonian, and Progressive eras and the 1960s and 1970s all were characterized by strikingly similar political climates, patterns of conflict and reform, and realignments of social forces and political institutions.

The Climate of Creedal Passion

The political climate of creedal passion periods is distinguished by widespread and intense moral indignation. Political passions are high, existing structures of authority are called into question, democratic and egalitarian impulses are renewed, and political change—anticipated and unanticipated—occurs. In each of America's four creedal passion periods, similar ideas and methods were employed by comparable constellations of social forces to reshape political institutions and practices in terms of the values of the American Creed.

The atmosphere of discontent. All four periods were characterized by a pervasive unhappiness with things as they were. Discontent was the prevailing disposition, manifested in the widespread questioning and rejection of authority, hierarchy, specialization, and expertise. Actions by governmental officials, which earlier would have been accepted without notice or complaint, were noticed, highlighted, and denounced. Americans came to hate themselves because they were not themselves. All four periods were thus in some measure "revolutionary situations," in R. R. Palmer's sense of the word—times "in which confidence in the justice or reasonableness of existing authority is undermined; where old loyalties fade, obligations are felt as impositions, law seems arbitrary, and respect for superiors is felt as a form of humiliation; where existing sources of prestige seem undeserved, hitherto accepted forms of wealth and income seem ill-gained, and government is sensed as distant, apart from the governed and not really 'representing' them." These words, Palmer and Bailyn agree, aptly describe the temper of the 1760s and early 1770s.[9] They are almost equally applicable to the 1830s, and 1900s, and the 1960s.

Emerson's description of the 1830s could also apply to the other periods: "In politics . . . it is easy to see the progress of dissent. The country is full of rebellion; the country is full of kings. Hands off! let there be no control and no interference in the administration of this kingdom of me." Nor was the individualistic rejection of external authority limited to politics. "The same disposition to scrutiny and dissent appears in civil, festive, neighborly, and domestic society. A restless, prying conscientious criticism broke out in unexpected quarters. Who gave me the money with which I bought my coat? Why should professional labor and that of the counting-house be paid so disproportionately to the labor of the porter and woodsawyer?" All established institutions were under challenge: "Christianity, the laws, commerce, schools, the farm, the laboratory; and not a kingdom, town, statute, rite, calling, man, or woman, but is threatened by the new spirit."[10] The "predominant characteristics" of the Revolutionary period, historian Gordon Wood argued, were "fear and frenzy, the exaggerations and the enthusiasm, the general sense of social corruption and disorder out of which would be born a new world of benevolence and harmony where Americans would become the 'eminent examples of every divine and social virtue.' " In similar fashion, Daniel Webster observed that in the 1820s "society is full of excitement," and Theodore Roosevelt spoke of "a condition of excitement and irritation in the public mind" as characteristic of his times.[11]

Each period was a period of agitation, dominated by the questioning of prevailing institutions and authority. Each gave rise, in some sense, to a crisis of legitimacy which people attempted to resolve by reshaping American political institutions and practices to be more in accord with the

New Deal ?

Civil War ?

values of the American Creed. Because of the nature of American society and the widespread consensus on these liberal values, revolution in the familiar European class-oriented sense of the word did not occur. Instead, the very forces that gave rise to the revolutionary situation produced a nonrevolutionary outcome.

Political ideas and moral passion. In all four periods, political ideas—and ideals—were taken seriously. The years immediately before the American Revolution saw the first significant articulation throughout a society of the ideas of equality, liberty, and popular sovereignty. Among the striking features of these years, Bailyn observed, was "the seriousness with which colonial and revolutionary leaders took ideas and the deliberateness of their efforts during the Revolution to reshape institutions in their pattern." The Revolution, in John Adams' words, was effected between 1760 and 1775 in the minds of the people. *"This radical change in the principles, opinions, sentiments, and affections of the people was the real American revolution."* For the first time, authority was challenged and overthrown in the name of universal democratic principles. Each subsequent period of creedal passion witnessed a manifestation of "a new consciousness" (to use Emerson's phrase) of these old principles.[12]

The meanings of liberty, equality, and democracy and the ways to realize them through institutional reform became a focus of public debate, but no great systematic political theories were articulated. The level of political theory during the four periods failed to rise much above that of a Thomas Paine or a Herbert Croly: neither was an original political thinker but each brilliantly reformulated familiar ideas to meet the needs of his times. Although Paine did not set forth new political ideas, he did create the "secular language of revolution, a language in which timeless discontents, millennial aspirations, and popular traditions were expressed in a strikingly new vocabulary."[13] One talks not about the political theory of these periods but about their political ideas, which were in each period rearticulations and reformulations of ideas that were already well known.

Americans have been variously held to be both a highly idealistic people and a highly pragmatic one. During the periods of creedal passion, the idealistic strain became the dominant one. An intense concern with values, principles, rights, and morality pervaded the public arena. Political ideas became important not primarily for intellectual reasons but for moral ones, and moral indignation generated creedal passion and political controversy. There was a rush to moral judgment on the rights and wrongs of politics. The minds of the American revolutionaries were gripped by an

"aroused moral passion" and "meliorative, optimistic, and idealist impulses . . . that led them to condemn as corrupt and oppressive the whole
system by which their world was governed."[14] In a similar manner, the
Jacksonian years were characterized by the prevalence of a "matched set
of attitudes, beliefs, projected actions: a half-formulated moral perspective involving emotional commitment. The community shares many
values; at a given social moment some of these acquire a compelling importance." All the Jacksonians seemed to be "moralizers." The Jacksonian persuasion was "always more a decalogue of moral prohibitions than
an articulate set of social ends and means." So also, the Progressives
tended to talk in "moral rather than economic terms"; they "set impossible standards"; they were "victimized, in brief, by a form of moral absolutism." Theodore Roosevelt always thought of himself as a moralist,
believing that the central issue in American politics was "the fundamental fight for morality."[15] And morality, moralism, and moral absolutism were surely the hallmark of the 1960s, which, among other things,
saw the emergence of what was labeled the "new political morality."

The affirmation of moral values during creedal passion periods is
Janus-faced. The values and ideals that are invoked are traditional ones;
they derive their legitimacy and their appeal from their earlier presence
in American history. At the same time, the affirmation holds out the
promise, the hope, the dream of realizing these values in the not-too-dis-
tant future. The intellectual temper of the age is both backward-looking
and forward-looking, traditional and radical. During the American Revolution, the colonists used the language of Locke and the early-eighteenth-
century Whigs to invoke the traditional rights of Englishmen. As Hartz
said, the remarkable thing about the "spirit of 1776" was "not that it
looked forward to the future but that it worshipped the past as well."[16]
The American mission for the future was to realize the values of the
American past. The ideas of the Jacksonians, the Progressives, and the
protesters of the 1960s were similarly ambivalent, although a widening
gulf opened between the inherited ideals they hoped to realize and the
institutional reality produced by industrialization and global involvement
that they confronted. Like revitalization movements in other societies,
those of American creedal passion periods have thus, in varying degrees,
been both archaistic and futuristic.[17]

The attack on power and hierarchy. In all four periods, democratic
ideals were reaffirmed: liberty, equality, individualism, and popular control of government, and opposition to hierarchy, specialization, bureau-

cracy, and especially power. The antipower theme was a critical aspect of public discourse in all these eras, and the central issue of the time was often defined as "liberty versus power." The Americans of the 1770s were preoccupied, even obsessed, with the problem of power. Power was inherently evil and corrupting. For them the essential characteristic of power was its aggressiveness: "its endlessly propulsive tendency to expand itself beyond legitimate boundaries." Along with the opposition to privilege, opposition to power was the major theme of the American Revolution. The revolutionaries believed

that power is evil, a necessity perhaps but an evil necessity; that it is infinitely corrupting; and that it must be controlled, limited, restricted in every way compatible with a minimum of civil order. Written constitutions; the separation of powers; bills of rights; limitations on executives, on legislatures, and courts; restrictions on the right to coerce and to wage war—all express the profound distrust of power that lies at the ideological heart of the American Revolution and that has remained with us as a permanent legacy ever after.[18]

The same dichotomy between liberty and power came to the fore again in the Jacksonian years. "Money power," for instance, was "damned precisely as a *power,* a user of ill-gotten gains to corrupt and dominate the plain republican order." The Jacksonian onslaught on power, however, did not last. "Between the Jacksonian war on the bank in the 1830s and the Populist-Progressive agitation of the 1880s and 1890s, few political leaders or movements questioned the concentration of private economic power."[19] In the 1890s this questioning was vigorously resumed. It remained an active theme until the country entered into World War I and then subsided, to reappear with equal intensity in the 1960s. In all four eras, institutions of power were summoned to judgment before the ideals of liberty, and the antipower ethic reinvigorated as a guide to political action.

In each period, the power that was perceived as the threat to liberty took a different specific form. In the 1760s and 1770s it was the imperial power of the British Parliament and Crown. In the 1830s the threat came from monopoly, the Bank of the United States, chartered corporations, and the caucus system. At the turn of the century, the attacks were directed against the machines and the trusts. For the Muckrakers, the enemy included "the 'interests,' 'the System,' high or frenzied finance, plutocracy, the industrial aristocracy, the trusts and monopoly . . . The specific agent in the national orgy of corruption was the corporation."[20] In the 1960s the

Only in foreign policy - not domestically.

target was executive power, the Presidency, and the military-industrial complex. In all four periods, the focus was on some combination of economic and political power: imperial power, money power, slave power, corporate power, executive power. The common enemy in all was large-scale organization. At the extremes, the concern over power and organization became a paranoia about conspiracies that threatened to undermine free society and government. The "paranoiac obsession with a diabolical Crown conspiracy" which existed during the Revolution was matched in the 1820s and 1830s by the fantasies and the fervor of the Anti-Masons, who saw their target as "a conspiratorial order of evil, immoral men who sought to control politics and community life," and by the rhetoric and imagery of the Populists in the 1890s.[21]

The common goal in all four periods was the break-up or reduction of organized power, its reform and control, the opening up of the processes of decision making to public participation. The Jacksonians, it has been said, engaged in "a dismantling operation: an effort to pull down the menacing constructions of federal and corporate power, and restore the wholesome rule of 'public opinion and the interests of trade.' "[22] And "dismantling operations" were precisely what all four periods engendered: major efforts to tear down the perceived structures of political and economic power. The Jacksonians "directed popular resentment of closed political corporations against the caucus system, which they branded as a flagrant usurpation of the rights of the people, and spread the conviction that politics and administration must be taken from the hands of a social elite or a body of bureaucratic specialists and opened to mass participation."[23] Earlier, the American revolutionaries had dismantled the existing structures of British imperialism; subsequently, Populists and Progressives energetically attempted to dismantle political machines by introducing primaries, city managers, civil service, and other institutional reforms, and to break up corporate monopolies through antitrust laws and other forms of government regulation. In the 1960s, similar efforts were made to bring to heel the military-industrial complex, the CIA, and presidential power in foreign affairs. but To use 90u'T acti'n domes

In addition to attacks on what were perceived to be the central institutions of power, each period also witnessed a more general challenge to authority, hierarchy, and specialization. The themes of one period reappeared in the next. In each there was a stress on the abilities of the amateur, the common man, the citizen, against those of the specialist or expert. Each was in some measure a period in which distinctions—

whether based on status, occupation, knowledge, or position—were denigrated, in which there was a stress on homogenization, on "the great principle" (in the words of the Jacksonians) "of amalgamating all orders of society." Specialized learning and specialized institutions of learning were attacked. The military profession in particular usually became a target, and the existence of the military academies was called into question. Whereas power was challenged in the name of liberty, other social, economic, and institutional distinctions were attacked in the name of equality. The Jacksonian goals—"political democracy, equality of economic opportunity, and opposition to monopoly and special privilege"— were equally prevalent and intensely held in the other three periods.[24]

Political participation and organization. The promotion of a cause requires participation and organization. Creedal passion periods thus tend to be characterized by intense and widespread political activity. People are mobilized for action in new ways. New forms of voluntary association appear: committees of correspondence, interest associations, new political parties, farmers' and workers' organizations, cause organizations of various types. The peculiar American contribution to achieving the common good, the public-spirited voluntary association, had its roots in the dissenting Protestant sects that gave New England its being, spread throughout the colonies during the Revolutionary years in the form of committees of correspondence, Sons of Liberty, and Minutemen units, and came truly into its own in the multifarious organizations to promote various causes which proliferated in the Jacksonian period. Tocqueville was indeed right in his oft-quoted remark that when something has to be done in France, the government does it; in England, a local magnate or aristocrat does it; while in America, "you are sure to find an association. . . . The Americans make associations to give entertainments, to found seminaries, to build inns, to construct churches, to diffuse books, to send missionaries to the antipodes; in this manner they found hospitals, prisons, and schools."[25] The number and diversity of associations that Tocqueville marveled at was in fact a major way in which Americans attempted to bring their institutions and practices into line with their beliefs and values. The formation of associations during the Jacksonian years was also accompanied by a substantial expansion of voting participation.

In the Progressive period, too, new movements and associations materialized in great number. This represented a second major wave of voluntary association founding, particularly noticeable in the first years of the twentieth century. It was not accompanied by a parallel increase in voting participation rates—which would have been difficult in any event, given the high levels of voting participation in the 1880s—but it was accompanied by a movement for women's suffrage. In the 1960s there was an increase in voting participation among blacks and the young, and a dramatic surge in other forms of political activity, including demonstrations, protests, associations, propagandizing, and lobbying by conscience and so-called public interest groups. This creedal passion period, like earlier ones, saw the proliferation of new forms of social organization, including utopian communities that attracted enthusiastic adherents. In the 1830s, as James Russell Lowell said, "communities were established where everything was to be common but common-sense."[26]

Modern techniques of creating associations date from the Jacksonian period. As one observer then sardonically commented:

> Whatever is started, a national society must at once be got up, which is imposing in its very name; a list of respectable names must be obtained, as members and patrons, which is also imposing and influential; a secretary and an adequate corps of assistants must be appointed and provided for from the first-fruits of collections; a band of popular lecturers must be commissioned, and sent forth as agents on the wide public; the press, with its many-winged messengers, is put in operation; certificates fitted for the purpose are made out, submitted, subscribed, and sworn to; the entire machinery is put in operation; subsidiary societies are multiplied over the length and breadth of the land; the end proposed is manifestly a good one; and how can the community resist the sway of such an influence?[27]

The tactics of the freedom-riders and other reformers of the twentieth century were not dissimilar from those of the abolitionists of the nineteenth; in talents and behavior, William Lloyd Garrison was the forerunner of Ralph Nader. "So thoroughly did these [Jacksonian] crusaders work out the pattern of reform organization and propaganda a hundred years ago," Arthur Schlesinger, Sr., observed in 1950, "that later generations have found little to add beyond taking advantage of new communication devices such as the movies and radio."[28]

The formation of organizations—both evidence of political participation and a means of channeling such participation—is linked with efforts to reduce the IvI gap. Generalizing from the experience of the Jacksonian and Progressive eras, James Q. Wilson suggested:

> Periods of rapid and intense organizational formation are periods in which the salience of purposive incentives has sharply increased.

Organizations become more numerous when ideas become more important. The most obvious fact in support of such a view is that widespread organizing seems always to be accompanied by numerous social movements. During the era of the 1830s and 1840s, for example, both the Antimasonic party and the abolitionist organizations were formed at the same time, and out of many of the same impulses, as the Great Revival of religious fervor. In 1895–1910, there was similarly an outburst of new gospels, many of them this time secular in nature though still evangelical in tone: free silver, prohibition, nativism, suffragism, the social gospel, Marxism, Taylorism, the settlement-house movement, and countless others.[29]

Veterans of the 1960s will attest to the continued validity of the proposition that organizational activity is a function of creedal commitment.

The media and political communications. The dismantling of power requires the exposure of power. In each of the four creedal passion periods, reform efforts were fueled by the uncovering of and publicity given to the facts of privilege hierarchy, inequality, and corruption. Each period also saw the emergence of new forms of the media, which enhanced the ability of the reformers to communicate their facts and their indignation to the public.

During the Revolutionary years, for the first time in Europe and America "a public opinion, as such, took form, and indeed, the very expression, 'public opinion,' dates in several languages from this time." This public opinion consisted of "groups of people habitually interested in public events, subscribing as individuals or in clubs to newspapers and magazines, incipiently political in their outlook . . . in the sense that they were aware of the importance of government and political institutions, and believed that there was something called the public welfare, which depended on the policies of governments and on the enlightened behavior of citizens." These people were concerned about political affairs at both the local and national levels. Their concern was made possible by and fueled by "the phenomenal growth of the press, both of books and of newspapers and magazines." These improvements in communication constituted "one of the fundamental preconditions to the whole revolutionary era" in America and in Europe.[30] In America the increased circulation of petitions and remonstrances, sermons and orations, almanacs, broadsides, and newspapers contributed to the development of revolutionary consciousness. Most characteristic of and central to the new intensity of communication was the pamphlet, "the most effective weapon of political argument" in the colonies and in Britain. The flexible length, timeliness, and *ex parte* quality of the pamphlet made it the ideal vehicle for the polemical argument of revolution. More than four hundred pamphlets relating to the struggle with Britain were published in the colonies between 1750 and 1776, and more than fifteen hundred had appeared by 1783. "Explanatory as well as declarative, and expressive of the beliefs, attitudes, and motivations as well as the professed goals of those who led and supported the Revolution, the pamphlets are the distinctive literature of the Revolution."[31]

The Jacksonian years saw another jump in the scope and intensity of political communication. Public schools, library companies, bookstores, and adult education movements all played their role. Of striking importance was the growth in newspaper circulation, In 1800 there had been two hundred forty-two newspapers in the United States with a circulation of two hundred thousand. By 1829, there were over one thousand newspapers with a circulation of over one million, a rate of increase in circulation more than double that of population.[32] The growth of the press was intimately related to the emergence of political parties (it was, in large part, an overtly partisan press) and, more generally, to the growth of political and civil associations. As Tocqueville recognized, in a democratic society with a widely dispersed pattern of governmental decision making, the newspaper plays an indispensable role in bringing together those who wish to work toward common public goals. There is "a necessary connection between public associations and newspapers: newspapers make associations, and associations make newspapers." Of all countries in the 1830s, the United States had "at the same time the greatest number of associations and of newspapers . . . The power of the newspaper press must therefore increase as the social conditions of men become more equal."[33]

Mass media developments during the Progressive years were comparable to those that occurred during the Revolutionary and Jacksonian eras. If the pamphlet was the distinctive medium of the Revolution, and the penny press of the Jacksonians, the mass popular press and the cheap magazine were the vehicles of Progressive reform. William Randolph Hearst, Joseph Pultizer, and Edward Scripps developed the large-circulation daily, directed to the needs of the urban populace. They promoted human-interest appeals, relished scandal, exposed corruption, created news where it had to be created, and elevated "events, hitherto considered beneath reportorial attention, to the level of news occurrences by clever, emotionally colored reporting." The magazine world, too, changed dramatically. A "magazine revolution" occurred in the last years of the century, with genteel, limited-circulation periodicals such as *The Atlantic Monthly* and *Harper's* being overtaken by mass-circulation, cheap magazines created by businessmen rather than literary men.[34] These magazines took on many of the characteristics of newspapers in developing their circulations and hit the circulation jackpot when, as with *McClure's* and *The American,* they created the muckraking exposé as a distinctive stock in trade. The average monthly circulation of the muckraking magazines was over three million copies. If *The Saturday Evening Post* and *The Ladies Home Journal* are added, their combined circulation came to over five million copies, at a time when there were only twenty million families in the United States. Similarly, the circulation of daily newspapers increased tremendously, reaching 24.2 million in 1909.[35] Without the development of the newspapers and magazines, political reform and, indeed, the Progressive movement generally would hardly have been possible.

[margin note: 1930's — Radio]

In a somewhat similar manner, in the 1960s television emerged as a major political force, reflecting and shaping a new public conscience and extending still further the political impact of the media through the body politic. A new national press also took shape, in which individual newspapers like *The New York Times* and *The Washington Post,* as well as newsmagazines like *Time* and *Newsweek,* became the dominant outlets for the national political community and organs of opinion capable, as in the Pentagon Papers and Watergate, of challenging and defeating the elected leadership of the national government. Coincidentally, earlier norms of "objective" or "impartial" journalism gave way to those of "advocatory" and "adversary" journalism.

[margin note: Thac did?]

Each of the creedal passion periods has thus seen the emergence of new forms of mass media, which serve as the means through which those who challenge the IvI gap bring their case before an ever-widening public. The press in America has a political role different from that of the press in most other societies. As Tocqueville suggested, there is a relationship between the prevalence of associations and the power of the press. There is also a relationship between the existence of a widespread consensus on basic political values and the power and role of the press. In a consensual society, one function of the press is to embody the consensus and to bring individuals and institutions to judgment. In the United States, the press is almost never governmental and rarely overtly partisan; instead, it is or aspires to be societal. The unique power of the press in American society is in part a product of the American liberal consensus. The media are, in effect, the clergy of the liberal society: they act as custodians of its ultimate values; they expose and denounce deviations from those values; they bestow legitimacy on individuals and institutions who reflect those values. In creedal passion periods, the media have no recourse but to challenge and expose the inequities of power.

Muckraking and the politics of exposure. Long before Theodore Roosevelt gave it a label, muckraking had become a distinctive American style of politics. Only in a society with a consensus on basic values can the simple exposure of facts that run counter to those values trigger political change. Muckraking is effective only when there is agreement on what is muck and what is not. Reform, consequently, involves the exposure of facts rather than argument over values. In this respect, the efforts at change in the United States in the early twentieth century, for instance, stand at an opposite extreme from contemporary Russian efforts. "The difference in the two environments is reflected in the differences between Lenin and Steffens and between the contents of *Iskra* and those of *McClure's*. The Bolshevik attacked with the revolutionary manifesto, the American reformer with the Brandeis brief."[36] From Samuel Adams' publication in 1773 of Governor Hutchinson's private letters, which " 'proved' to an outraged public that purpose, not ignorance, neglect, or miscalculation, lay behind the actions of the British government,"[37] to the *New York Times* publication of the Pentagon Papers two hundred years later, American politics, particularly in creedal passion periods, has been a politics of exposure, and the media as the means of exposure have played a far more influential role in American politics than in the politics of any other society. But exposure is effective only where there is a conscience to be outraged.

Each creedal passion period was distinguished not by the elaboration of new political theory, but by the disclosure of new political facts that ran counter to the central tenets of old political theory. At no time was this better illustrated than during the American Revolution. Then, as later, it was not necessary to argue ideas; it was simply necessary to state them and to demonstrate the extent to which the existing situation departed from them. The revolutionaries believed their truths to be "self-evident," and hence all that was required was that the "facts be submitted to a candid world." In a similar vein, the activities of the Jacksonian reformers inspired Emerson's observation that reform stems from the comparison of the idea with the fact. At the turn of the century, the phenomenon surfaced again with the Populists and Progressives and was duly christened by Theodore Roosevelt. The journalistic exposé, so successfully developed by Ida Tarbell, Lincoln Steffens, Upton Sinclair, David Graham Phillips, Ray Stannard Baker, and their associates, furnished the rationale and the impetus for legislative reforms just as the Brandeis brief, arguing from the facts, became the means of promoting social reform through judicial action. The 1960s and 1970s, in turn, saw the appearance of "the new muckrakers" and a new politics of exposure.

During creedal passion periods, the process of exposure and dismantling tends to expand both horizontally and vertically. In the beginning, outrage may focus on a particular individual, institution, or practice, but it rapidly tends to broaden and to affect widening circles of people and organizations. Walter Lippmann observed that in the early 1900s, "as muckraking developed, it began to apply the standards of public life to certain parts of the business world." In somewhat similar fashion, although it was "originally a fight against political privilege," the Jacksonian movement soon "broadened into a fight against economic privilege."[38] What starts as a drive to expose the evils of politics may soon spread to a concern with the evils of corporation, church, school, and association.

The vertical escalation of moral standards obfuscates the distinction between the serious violation of commonly accepted norms and the minor, seeming, or potential violation of such norms. If bribery cannot be proved against a public official, let it be shown that he accepted a gift; if there is no clear evidence that a public official used his position to advance his own private interest, let it be shown that there exists a potential conflict of interest between his public duty and his private gain. "If the facts will not make out a case of moral deficiency by accepted standards, the standards must be escalated to the point where facts can be found that *will* make out a deficiency; and the public must be educated to be horrified by the resulting new sins in substantially the same degree that they were horrified by the old."[39] The higher the actual level of honesty, the greater the push given to the moral escalator.

In the end, intensifying moral indignation gives way to moral exhaustion and cynicism. This process has been commented upon in each of the three most recent creedal passion periods. "The criticism and attack on institutions which we have witnessed," observed Emerson of the Jacksonian reformers, "has made one thing plain, that society gains nothing whilst a man, not himself renovated, attempts to renovate things around him: he has become tediously good in some particular, but negligent or narrow in the rest; and hypocrisy and vanity are often the disgusting result . . . The wave of evil washes all our institutions alike." In a very similar manner, Hubert Humphrey in 1975 commented on one aspect of a decade of moralistic exposure: "Accountability is the cry of the day. A kind of consumerism is in the air, and neither the Congress nor the public is taking the President's or anybody's word for anything. But there comes a time when suspicion can go too far. There comes a time when you have to trust someone."[40]

The most dramatic description of the political consequences of the politics of exposure and of moralistic reform was supplied by Theodore Roosevelt. It is necessary, he said, "that we should not flinch from seeing what is vile and debasing." There are times and places when the muckraker serves a useful purpose. Nonetheless, "the man who never does anything else, who never thinks or speaks or writes save in his feats with the muckrake, speedily becomes, not a help to society, not an incitement to good, but one of the most potent forces for evil." In elaborating this theme, Roosevelt argued that "there are, in the body politic, economic, and social, many and grave evils, and there is urgent necessity for the sternest war upon them. There should be relentless exposure of and attack upon every evil man, whether politician or business man, every evil practice, whether in politics, in business, or in social life." But it is also necessary to avoid "an epidemic of indiscriminate assault" upon the characters of public men. A balance must be maintained. "Expose the crime, and hunt down the criminal; but remember that even in the case of crime, if it is attacked in sensational, lurid, and untruthful fashion, the attack may do more damage to the public mind than the crime itself." The unlicensed exposure of wrong may lead to the corruption of the public conscience and an obliteration of the distinction between right and wrong. "To assail the great and admitted evils of our political and industrial life with such crude and sweeping generalizations as to include decent men in the general condemnation means the searing of the public conscience. There results a general attitude either of cynical belief in and indifference to public corruption or else of a distrustful inability to discriminate between the good and the bad."[41]

In due course, the climate of creedal passion produces a climate of political cynicism.

Creedal Conflict: The Movement and the Establishment

In its day-to-day functioning, conflict in American politics approximates the Madisonian model posited by pluralist theory. Interest-group politics accounts for most of American politics most of the time, but it does not describe all of American politics all of the time. Consensus theory errs in postulating a low level of conflict in American society; Progressive theory errs in focusing on class polarization as the central cleavage; pluralist theory is inadequate in its description of the sources of American political conflict. Conflicts occur over political ideas as well as over economic and communal interests. Opinion polarizes in great debates and constitutional controversies over the ways in which the principles and values of American politics should be realized in political institutions and practices. The actors in American politics include social movements and crusaders as well as pressure groups and lobbyists. Interest-group politics is thus at times supplemented, and even supplanted, by creedal politics. In contrast to interest-group politics, creedal politics tends to be intermittent rather than continuous, passionate rather than pragmatic, idealistic rather than materialistic, reform-minded rather than status-quo oriented, and formulated in terms of right and wrong rather than more or less. The actors in creedal politics are no less self-interested than the actors in interest-group politics, but their interests are set forth in different terms. Interest-group politics gives way to creedal politics when the groups involved (1) define their goals in terms of basic American values and principles, thereby articulating their appeal in universal terms, (2) make demands for structural change and reform of political institutions and practices, and (3) pursue these demands with moral passion and fervor.

The conflicts of the 1770s, 1830s, 1900s, and 1960s involved interest groups, but the depth of the cleavages, the significance of the issues at stake, and the passions of the participants transcended what is normally meant by the term "interest-group politics." At the same time, although economic issues played a role in these conflicts, the principal cleavages were not primarily along economic class lines. As a result, the nature and causes of cleavage in each of these periods have been subject to extensive debate among historians. Just what was the structure of political battle in the Revolutionary, Jacksonian, and Progressive eras? Efforts to explain these cleavages simply in terms of interest groups or economic classes do not wash. During the Revolution, rich and poor, planters and merchants, small farmers and tradesmen were found among both loyalists and revolutionaries. In some cases, of which the Franklins were the most notable, families divided down the middle. During the Jacksonian period, the lines of cleavage cut across class divisions, with farmers, workers, and entrepreneurs on both sides of the battles over party and issues. The well-to-do were as often on the side of reform as they were in opposition to it. During the Progressive period, major elements of the urban middle classes, the working class, and the farmers were both for and against political and economic reform. And in the 1960s middle-class professionals, intellectuals, and students joined with lower-class blacks to oppose other middle-class professionals and businessmen who were allied with major elements of the working class. In all of these periods, the principal lines of cleavage involving the major issues of the day, although not perfectly vertical, were far from being primarily horizontal.

In each of these periods, the impetus for change sprang from the coming together in a parallelism of interest of elements from both the middle class and the less well-off farmers or working class. The common factor that brought together these diverse social and economic groups appears to be the extent to which they were divorced from and felt threatened by the existing political and economic establishment. During the Revolution, insofar as any one factor differentiated revolutionaries and loyalists, it was the extent to which individuals and groups either were involved with, and saw their interests connected to, the British imperial establishment or saw themselves actually or potentially threatened by the future growth in power of that establishment. Some less well-off groups in colonial society, for instance, viewed the British presence as a counterweight to the economically dominant groups in colonial society and hence had good reason to support British power. In the Jacksonian period, group alignments can in large part be explained by the relation of the groups to existing political and economic institutions, such as the Bank of the United States, which the Jacksonians were attempting either to destroy or to open up and penetrate. Similarly, insofar as there was one characteristic that seemed to distinguish Progressives from their opponents, it was the extent to which the Progressives were recruited from groups outside the local political-economic establishment. Since control of the local establishment rested with different groups in different places, the social-economic background of the Progressives also varied from one place to another.[42] Similar criteria would go far toward explaining the cross-cutting vertical cleavages of the 1960s. In each period, the primary cleavage was between those of whatever economic class who see their interests intimately connected with the existing political and economic structures, whatever their nature, and those of whatever economic class who see their interests connected to the opening up or dismantling of those structures. Polarization during creedal passion periods can divide and has divided economic classes, social strata, interest groups, and even families. As a result, the goals of those spearheading change are invariably defined in the liberal, democratic, and antipower terms of the American Creed.

The assertion of these "traditional" values serves two purposes. It provides the unifying goals, arguments, and rhetoric for the diverse middle-class and lower-class groups divorced from the existing establishment. It also defines the limits within which change is possible without disrupting the reforming coalition. Those with more income, wealth, and education typically have broader and deeper commitment than others to the liberal and individualistic values of the American Creed. Those with economically less commitment to the existing order have ideologically less commitment to the Creed. During a creedal passion period, the values of the Creed are largely articulated by middle-class groups. Middle-class hypocrites become moralists and, by articulating those values, attempt to mobilize lower-class indifferents and cynics. This articulation reinvigorates lower-class acceptance of the Creed. Yet the Creed is the only ideological weapon that can be used to challenge the established order. Here, clearly, is the reason why change and reform in America can go only so far and no further. Middle and upper strata may have an ideological commitment to political reform, but they also have an economic interest in not permitting reform to alter significantly the existing distribution of income and wealth. The poorer classes, on the other hand, may have an interest in substantial economic change, but they lack the ideological motivation to make that change a reality, and, indeed, they are mobilized for political action by appeals to values which guarantee that major economic change will not become a reality.

The articulation of the values of the Creed not only unifies reformers but, second, it places their opponents on the ideological defensive. They are, as Bailyn described the loyalists of the Revolution, ideologically disarmed. There are no alternative creeds readily available to counter the demands for change formulated in terms of the liberal-democratic values on which almost everyone agrees. The argument thus often becomes one over the relative desirability of specific means of change and over the speed and timing of change. The basic cleavage in American politics can often be defined "as a matter of tempo. It is a division, essentially, between those who want to move rapidly toward their vision of a good society, even at the risk of errors of commission, and those who would minimize that risk—but in turn risk errors of omission—by moving too slowly."[43] In a creedal passion period, those who want rapid change increase in both numbers and in the intensity with which they put forward their demands. The controversy is between those who want liberal ideals realized immediately and those who are more willing to adopt an incremental, gradualist strategy for dealing with the IvI gap. "Immediatism" was the label aptly applied to the approach of the man who was, perhaps more than anyone else, the prototypical American radical, William Lloyd Garrison, "the most forceful reformer in our history"—and in some respects the most dramatically successful. "Gradualism in theory," in his words, "is perpetuity in practice." Or, as Garrison's contemporaneous reformer on the peace front, William Ladd, expressed it: "It is an incontrovertible axiom, that *everything of a moral nature which ought to be done, can be done.*"[44] No excuse, in short, exists for a gap between ideal and reality. The opposite approach was represented by William Ellery Channing, no less opposed to slavery than Garrison, but firmly against reliance on "excitement and vehemence" to bring it to an end. It "is not true," as he put it, "that God has committed the great work of reforming the world to passion."[45]

In creedal passion periods, politics tends to become polarized between those who are in favor of reform and change and those who are willing to accept existing institutions as they are. The recurring division is thus not between upper class and lower class, or between elite and mass, but rather between reformers and standpatters, between the "Movement" or movements and the "Establishment" or establishments. The latter always exist; the former are more evanescent, and the intensity of the conflict varies with their rise and fall. In creedal passion periods, more people become intensely involved, committed to the realization of ideals, more agitated, more participant. In the language and meaning of the 1960s, they become "radicalized"—that is, alienated from and intensely critical of the existing structures of power and demanding their reform in terms of American liberal and democratic ideals. In such times, the "conscience community" becomes larger, more active, more focused on particular issues. Not the radical right or the radical left, but the radical center emerges as a major force on the political scene. The dichotomy that Progressive historians claim exists in American politics does not exist continuously between upper and lower classes, but rather intermittently between the Movement and the Establishment.

The Movement is a multifaceted thing. Each creedal passion period sees an eruption and proliferation of particular reform causes and social movements. The causes of women, racial minorities, including particularly blacks and Indians, the ill, the mentally retarded, criminals, and consumers became, in one form or another, the subject of intense political action. Crusades also surface on behalf of moral issues, such as temperance and peace. During the Jacksonian years, as James Russell Lowell observed, "every possible form of intellectual and physical dyspepsia brought forth its gospel. Bran has its prophets . . . Plainness of speech was carried to a pitch that would have taken away the breath of George Fox . . . Everybody had a mission (with a capital *M*) to attend to everybody-else's business . . . All stood ready at a moment's notice to reform everything but themselves."[46] In the 1830s, as in the 1960s, there was The Movement, all encompassing, in favor of all good things, and there were lesser, component movements (for peace, women, civil rights) in favor of particular good things. The movement on behalf of women's rights crested in the 1830s, the early 1900s, and again in the 1960s. The abolitionist movement got underway in the 1830s; the rights of blacks were a subordinate theme in the 1900s; but the civil rights movement and black consciousness dominated the scene in the 1960s. The belief that various social ills could be solved through particular institutions, what David Rothman termed "the discovery of the asylum," manifested itself in the 1820s and 1830s with the introduction of insane asylums, prisons, hospitals, and orphanages. In the 1900s there was a new wave of enthusiasm for other types of reform institutions, such as the settlement house. The "peace movement" in the United States had its real origins in 1828 with the founding of the American Peace Society; it came to the fore again in the anti-imperialist surge against the acquisition of colonies following the Spanish-American War; and it reappeared in dramatic and successful fashion in the opposition to the Vietnam War in the 1960s. Consumer activism, which played a minor role in the 1830s, emerged as a major focus in the 1900s, then disappeared from sight, to resurface prominently and successfully in Naderism and related movements in the 1960s.

There is thus considerable *repetition* from one creedal passion period to another: the favorite causes of one era tend to reappear in the next. There is also, within any one period, a high degree of *affinity* between causes: those who are active on behalf of one cause are also likely to become active on behalf of other causes. "In these movements," Emerson observed, "nothing was more remarkble than the discontent they begot in the movers." Some, like Thomas Paine, Wendell Phillips, Upton Sinclair, and Ralph Nader, seemed to be active in everything. Phillips in addition to abolition, "stood for a multitude of causes, demanding equal rights for women, temperance, freedom for Ireland, justice for the American Indian, abolition of capital punishment, kinder treatment of the mentally ill."[47] Sinclair was active on behalf of consumers, women, labor, economic equality, and public ownership of utilities. Other reformers concentrated their energies on one particular cause while expressing their sympathy for others, as Garrison did in connection with equal rights for women.

The relation of one particular movement to other movements is well illustrated by Alan Grimes' discussion of woman suffrage. Before the Civil War, a close connection existed between this movement and the anti-slavery and temperance crusades. "The feminist movement of the nine-teenth century, like the civil rights movement today, sponsored not only immediate reforms benefiting its own group such as the right of women to enter the universities and the professions, to hold property, and to have custody of their children in divorce cases, but also a host of broader reforms such as peace, temperance, abolition of slavery, and the begin-nings of social welfare legislation." This pattern of relationships during the Jacksonian years reappeared during the Progressive period. "The social ethic of woman suffrage conveniently corresponded to the broader social ethic of progressivism itself. Woman suffrage was, like the direct primary, the direct election of the Senate, the initiative, the referendum, and the recall, not only a reform in itself but an instrument for further reform within the prevailing conception of social goals."[48] The 1960s saw similar close relations between the women's movement and the civil rights and antiwar movements. In sum, an individual or group that has a specific concern with one particular reform also usually has a general reformist weltanschauung which induces the individual or group to be favorably disposed to all reforms.

In the American experience, consensus is not an alternative to political conflict but is, rather, a source of political conflict. Interest-group politics is compatible with consensus; creedal politics is a product of consensus. Conflict occurs not when the consensus breaks down but when the con-sensus is activated, when the consensus couchant becomes the consensus rampant, and when efforts are made to embody the values of the con-sensus in the structure and practice of institutions. The conflicts of creedal politics are not simply over how to promote particular interests that divide people, but also over how and to what extent to realize general ideals that unite people. A consensus on basic values can be a very disquieting and unsettling phenomenon, serving as both an incentive to challenge existing institutions and as a weapon that one coalition of groups can use against another. The most significant upheavals in American politics have arisen not from the absence of consensus but from the assertion of consensus, from efforts to return to first principles, from what in China would be called "purification campaigns" to eliminate arbitrary power and special privilege, economic oligarchs and corrupt politicians. Americans become polarized less over the substance of their beliefs than over how seriously to take those beliefs. At times, they disagree fundamentally on how to apply their ideals and principles to their political institutions and structures. Americans divide most sharply over what brings them together.

In the United States, political change and conflict are associated not with the introduction of new ideas but with renewed commitment to old ones. The appearance of new ideologies, such as Marxism, has had only marginal impact on American politics. Conflict and change derive from creedal passion; they stem from efforts to realize the prevailing values rather than from efforts to challenge them. The reaffirmation of these values can achieve a compelling intensity precisely because of what it is: the invocation of old, accepted, familiar, legitimate, widely supported political beliefs. As Hartz pointed out with respect to the abolitionists, "Ironically, the greatest moral crusade in American history produced practically no original political thought. Garrison is not a creator of political ideas; neither is Phillips. Even Channing is not." The abolitionists saw a need for passion but not for philosophy, and hence "they unite with their very passion a strange and uncritical complacency." As Garrison asked, "Argument is demanded—to prove what?"[49] The self-evident truth that all men are created equal? That slavery is therefore wrong?

Political change in the United States, in contrast to change in western Europe, is normally associated with the appearance of new social movements rather than by the rise to power of new political parties. This contrast is particularly sharp with respect to Canada, which, despite many social, political, and geographic similarities, has largely lacked American-style messianic movements of the left and right because it has also lacked a national Creed.[50] Particular reform efforts in the United States often take on a distinctive moralistic quality not present to the same degree in comparable efforts elsewhere. Comparing American and European anti-slavery movements, for instance, Stanley Elkins observed that "the simple harsh moral purity of our own antislavery movement, from the 1830s on, gave it a quality which set it apart from the others." For the American abolitionists, far more than for the others, the end of slavery "was a problem of conscience"; they displayed "that peculiar quality of abstraction which was, and has remained, uniquely American. For them, the question was all *moral*."[51]

The struggle between the activist and the standpatter in American politics has its parallels in the consensus politics of the Soviet Union. In Soviet politics, too, some are committed to realizing the goals of the Party and its ideology while others are indifferent, masking this indifference behind the meaningless reiteration of official rhetoric. In outlook, the indifferent Soviet citizen may not seem to differ much from the indifferent American citizen. But the Soviet arrives at his similar posture from the opposite direction. Their alternatives to indifference have little in common. The American is indifferent to the reform of government, the Russian to the demands of government. In the Soviet Union, the ideological activist is the insider; in the United States he is the outsider. He crusades not for the system but against the system. When the Soviet citizen loses his indifference, he becomes mobilized in support of the government; when the American citizen loses his indifference, he becomes mobilized in opposition to the government. Most important, in the Soviet Union the capacity to mobilize people politically is monopolized by the Communist Party. The ability of the party activists to mobilize people on behalf of the Soviet system, however, appears to decline over time, as the revolution recedes into history. In the United States, on the other hand, social change regularly produces incentives for different social groups to mobilize people politically to change the system. As a result, the relatively inchoate American liberal ideals have a recurring political vitality—they are put to use—while the much more systematic Marxist-Leninist ideology of the Soviet Union becomes formal, ritualized, and sterile.

Reform and Its Limits

Two major types of political change occur during creedal passion periods. *Reform* is the conscious attempt to bring political institutions and practices more into accord with liberal-democratic values and principles. *Realignment* is a general change in the pattern of relationships between social forces and political institutions; it is not the product of conscious design but the result of the rise of some social forces, the decline of others, and changes in the structure and composition of particular political institutions. The processes of reform and realignment are closely intertwined. The changes in the relations between political institutions and political ideals that are reform interact with the changes in the relations between political institutions and social forces that are realignment.

In the way in which they manifest themselves, both these processes are peculiar to the United States. Neither reform nor realignment is typical of an ideologically divided society. The classic European pattern of political change, for instance, can be seen as involving a distinct series of steps. A new self-conscious social force emerges as a result of social and economic change. This new social force articulates a new ideology reflecting its interests in opposition to those of established social forces. The new social force becomes the base of a new political party and identifies itself with particular governmental institutions that "belong" to the old social forces. A period of political struggle and upheaval leads to the conquest of power (or the substantial sharing of power) by the new social force with its distinctive ideology and its particular political institutions. The rise of the middle class, for instance, led to the emergence of liberalism as an ideology, the development of liberal parties, the rise in the power of the governmental institution (the lower house of parliament) associated with middle-class interests, and the decline in power of those parties and governmental institutions (monarchy, upper house) associated with aristocratic interests. The pattern has been one of ideological conflict and change and the displacement of one institution by another.

In the American process of political change, a new social force similarly emerges and becomes self-conscious as a result of social and economic change. This new social force, however, does not advance a new ideology but articulates with heightened intensity the ideals and principles of the old, prevailing ideology. Instead of developing and promoting new political institutions, it demands that existing institutions be reshaped in the light of the core values of that ideology. This is the distinctive American meaning attached to the word "reform." In some measure, of course, every particular "reform" proposal serves the interest of some particular group and is most ardently advanced by that group. But the proposal, if it is to be considered seriously, must also be couched in terms of the universal values and beliefs of the American Creed. It cannot be seen as simply embodying the exclusive interests of a particular class or group.

To campaign for "Black Power" is to go down a dead-end street; to crusade for "equal rights" is to open up—however slowly and creakingly —doors to new opportunities. The legitimacy and persuasiveness of reform depend upon the extent to which its goals can be formulated in terms of the broadly appealing values of the American Creed.

In America, as in Europe, ideas are weapons, and ideology is the handmaiden of political change. Without the articulation of political ideas and the commitment to ideology, political change does not occur. In Europe, however, the ideology that leads to change in the twentieth century is very different from that which led to change in the eighteenth century. In the United States, in contrast, the themes, slogans, and concerns of one creedal passion period strongly resemble those of another. The arguments for reform, reflected in these themes, also are similar, and the values appealed to by one social force in one reform period are reasserted by a different social force in the next.

At the same time that the rising social force seeks to identify its interests with the values of the American Creed, it also seeks to identify its interests with and to further those interests by securing access to established political institutions. It can, of course, attempt to create a new political party or to develop new governmental institutions. Such efforts may briefly contribute to the furtherance of change. But the success of the new social force depends generally on the extent to which it is able to embody its interests in the existing political parties and existing government institutions. This struggle for access typically leads to a shift in the relations between social forces and political institutions, a political realignment, in which institutional constituencies and functions change. This orientation toward existing institutions is encouraged by the distinctive institutional characteristics of American government: federalism, the separation of power, and loosely structured, decentralized political parties. In America, ideological monism and institutional pluralism thus combine to produce a process of political change fundamentally different from that which has historically prevailed in the ideologically divided societies of Europe.

Political change in the United States has usually meant reform—that is, efforts to bring political institutions and practices into line with previously accepted political ideas and values. Reform is possible only within the context of ideological agreement. Its origins as a concept lie deep in the history of the Judeo-Christian tradition, in the ideas of redemption, renewal, resurrection, reformation, and rebirth. It has even been argued

THE POLITICS OF CREEDAL PASSION   115

that the idea of reform itself is "essentially Christian in origin and early development" and that there was "no true equivalent in pre-Christian times." Within early Christianity the idea focused on the reform of the individual, but it was not limited to that. Its essence was "the idea of free, intentional and ever perfectible, multiple, prolonged and ever repeated efforts by man to reassert and augment values pre-existent in the spiritual-material compound of the world."[52] The reform impetus within the Christian church had its ups and downs over the years, but reemerged in its full glory in that greatest of all efforts at reform in the sixteenth and seventeenth centuries. At this time, the idea of reform acquired broader and more radical connotations as the Puritans worked to create a new heaven and new earth. Its essence, however, continued to involve the ideas of purification and a return to first principles. Reform, as Croly defined it several centuries later for American politics, is "a moral protest and awakening, which seeks to enforce the violated laws and to restore the American political and economic system to its pristine purity and vigor . . . Reform means at bottom no more than moral and political purification."[53]

The impetus to reform has peaked at recurring intervals in American history, coinciding with creedal passion periods. Party reform, for instance, has occurred in three major waves: the Jacksonian reforms of 1820–1840, the Progressive reforms of 1890–1920, and the reforms of the 1960s and 1970s.[54] Together with the Revolution, however, these creedal periods are characterized not just by party reform, but by the widespread efforts to reform a variety of political institutions and practices. With the notable exception of the abolition of slavery, virtually all the major political reforms in American history occurred in the context of these periods. Reforms "tend to cluster in highly concentrated and usually quite brief periods of time."[55]

The Revolutionary era was the first, the greatest, and in many respects the most successful period of political reform in America history. It set the political and ideological pattern for subsequent creedal passion periods. The revolutionaries loosed the spirit of reform on the American waters. The "Republic's designers launched a new faith in political engineering that has persisted strongly in American culture ever since. The main articles of that faith still hold that for every problem there is a solution. That it is better to do something about a problem than to do nothing even though that something may be less than perfect. That, above all, if we can figure out and establish the right *institutions*, the right policies are bound to follow." It is precisely this faith that has "animated our history's most powerful political movements," including those of the Jacksonian and Progressive eras.[56]

The Revolution itself, of course, produced major political reforms. The most sweeping and important involved the break with the British Crown and the establishment of a republican government with legitimacy derived from the consent of the governed. In the context of the eighteenth century this was a totally unprecedented and, in one sense, revolutionary step. But it was also a limited step; it did not involve the social and economic upheaval associated with subsequent class-based revolutions. It involved a change in government, not a change in society; it was a political reform, albeit a most far-reaching and innovative one. In the course of bringing about this reform, the "revolutionaries" introduced other and related changes: the abolition of primogeniture, entail, quit-rents, and other vestiges of feudalism; the separation of church and state; the abolition of slavery in northern states; the enactment of bills of rights; some extensions of the suffrage; reform of the penal codes; removal of some restrictions on business enterprise; and, most important and all encompassing, the passionate, eloquent, and learned articulation of the political ideas—and ideals—that would inspire, guide, and serve subsequent generations of political reformers.

The second major cluster of reforms occurred during the Jacksonian decades of 1820s and 1830s. In politics and government these years witnessed: the introduction of universal white male suffrage and a major expansion of political participation; the fading of the congressional caucus, and the formation of national political parties and the first national political party conventions; popular election of presidential electors and the emergence of the President as the "tribune of the people"; the development of lobbyists and lobbies as an additional means of influencing government; high levels of turnover in elected office, particularly marked in the House of Representatives; the partial democratization of the selection of senators as a result of statewide canvasses in connection with legislative elections; a stress on rotation in office and the spoils system in appointments to government; and a proliferation of the number of elected officials, including judges, at the state and local level. Paralleling these changes in political institutions were equally significant ones in the social and economic spheres: the disestablishment of the Bank of the United States and the opening up of state banking systems; the passage of general incorporation laws that changed incorporation from a special privilege into a routine right; the reform and expansion of public elementary education; and the construction for the first time of institutions—penitentiaries, insane asylums, orphanages, reformatories—as the "places of first resort, the preferred solution to the problems of poverty, crime, delinquency, and insanity." The approach of the reformers was well summed up in Rothman's comment: "The asylum was to fulfill a dual purpose for its innovators. It would rehabilitate inmates and then, by virtue of its success, set an example of right action for the larger society. There was a utopian flavor to this first venture, one that looked to reform the deviant and dependent and to serve as a model for others."[57]

The principal reform targets of the Progressive period were the trusts and the machines. The efforts to correct the evils associated with the big corporation and concentrated economic power included the first antitrust laws, regulatory commissions, consumer legislation, and other laws restricting and imposing standards on the ways in which businesses could conduct their business. In a similar vein, the direct primary, the initiative, referendum and recall, direct election of United States senators, and further extension of the electoral principle to state and local offices were designed to limit the machine by expanding the means of popular control. In addition, civil service, scientific management, and business methods were designed to limit the concentrated political power of the machine by expanding the scope of nonpolitical, technical, and merit considerations in government. In the social sphere, the asylum was rediscovered. "Poverty, squalor, and disease," Lawrence Cremin pointed out, "were hardly new in the nineties." What was new was "an awakening of social conscience, a growing belief that this incredible suffering was neither the fault nor the inevitable lot of the sufferers, that it certainly could be alleviated." The result was a proliferation of new institutions—"civic commissions, charity associations, church leagues, and reform societies galore"—of which perhaps the most notable and distinctive was the social settlement. In education, the progressive movement emerged as "one part of a vast humanitarian effort to apply the promise of American life—the ideal of government by, of, and for the people—to the puzzling new urban-industrial civilization that came into being during the latter half of the nineteenth century."[58] What Horace Mann had been to educational reform in the Jacksonian years, John Dewey was in the Progressive era. In the 1960s and early 1970s, the major institutions of American life were again subjected to a plenitude of reforms similar in goals to those of the three earlier creedal passion periods, although less notably in the extent to which they were realized.

The introduction of reforms does not guarantee their success in producing the consequences their proponents desire. "The perpetual bane of the reformer's existence," Lowi observed of the New York City experience, "is the ease with which the party leaders adapt new structures to old purposes."[59] The point is a familiar one. The institutions and procedures that reformers create are seldom disestablished. Their existence is secure but their purposes and functions change. With rare exceptions, the accomplishments of the reformers over time seem to be "twisted," "perverted," "corrupted," to serve ends very different from those of their creators. There seems to be a certain inevitability and universality to the process.

The ways in which the workings of reforms may frustrate the intentions of reformers are well illustrated by the direct primary. Primaries were a favorite party reform both in the Progressive period and in the 1960s and 1970s. In the Progressive period, primaries were introduced in order to take control over nominations away from the party bosses. Yet the bosses were better able than anyone else to mobilize their lower-class, immigrant supporters to the polls in the low turnout primary elections, and hence used the primary to sustain their power against the middle-class reformers who were attempting to displace them. In the1960s, primaries again became a popular reform, this time designed to take power away from upper-middle-class WASPS and broaden the participation in the system of the lower classes and ethnic minorities. Yet little change occurred in the usual pattern: those who vote in primaries "are richer and better educated . . . more interested in politics . . . and more likely to have strong opinions on the issues and personalities of the day."[60] The introduction of primaries did not enhance the power of the middle classes in the first decade of the twentieth century and did not enhance the power of the lower classes in the seventh decade. The same reform in two different periods was designed to achieve two different results and failed to achieve either.

How can these seemingly perverse results be explained? The answer relates to the determinants of voter turnout. Few people vote in primaries. Voter turnout is a function of organization and socioeconomic status. In the Progressive period, the strong party machines turned out the low-income voters and frustrated the wishes of middle-class reformers. In the

1960s and 1970s, the party machines were gone. Hence primary participation tended to reflect socioeconomic status. Hence the reform that was
designed to enhance the influence of the lower classes instead benefited
the middle classes. In each case, the reform failed because it did not affect
the underlying realities of political organization and social class. When
this is the case, the "actual consequences of party reform are, in the
future as in the past, likely often to disappoint their advocates, relieve
their opponents, and surprise a lot of commentators."[61]

Other instances of this phenomenon abound. The principal beneficiaries
of the campaign finance legislation of the 1970s, designed to curb the
influence of money in elections, turned out to be millionaire and incumbent candidates. Sunset laws, designed to curb bureaucratic agencies,
assigned them new functions and provided them with new incentives to
develop strong constituencies. Sunshine laws, designed to open up governmental proceedings, forced the real decisions further back into the
recesses of informal, off-the-record caucuses and conversations. In the
economic arena, regulatory agencies designed originally to protect the interests of consumers and the general public were captured by the indus-
tries they were created to regulate, a process well described in Richard
Olney's famous advice to the railroad president who asked him to help
abolish the Interstate Commerce Commission. "Looking at the matter
from a railroad point of view exclusively," said Olney, this "would not be
a wise thing to undertake . . . The Commission . . . is, or can be made, of
great use to the railroads. It satisfies the popular clamor for a government
supervision of railroads, at the same time that that supervision is almost
entirely nominal. Further, the older such a Commission gets, the more inclined it will be found to take the business and railroad view of things.
It thus becomes a sort of barrier between the railroad corporations and
the people and a sort of protection against hasty and crude legislation
hostile to railroad interests . . . The part of wisdom is not to destroy the
Commission, but to utilize it."[62] In similar fashion, in the social field,
the asylums created to "reform" the indigent, the sick, and the criminal
soon adapted to the achievement of other goals. "The promise of reform
had built up the asylums; the functionalism of custody perpetuated them.
. . . Proposals that promise the most grandiose consequences often
legitimate the most unsatisfactory developments. And one also grows
wary about taking reform programs at face value; arrangements designed for the best of motives may have disastrous results."[63] The
reforms of one generation often produce the vested interests of the next.

Why this should be the case is reasonably clear. The intense moral fervor that gives reformers and the reform movement their political clout cannot be sustained for any length of time. It is one way of attempting to bridge the gap between political ideals and political reality; in due course it exhausts itself and is superseded by some combination of cynicism, complacency, and hypocrisy. Lowi's analysis of reform in New York City describes a general pattern. "The onset of reform is the beginning of a temporary rejection of the system, the establishment of a channel for making innovations in the established order of things." The reformers' rejection of the system "takes the form of direct participation." The "most outstanding feature of the reform movement in New York," however, "has been its short life." It has not lasted; instead, it followed a cyclical pattern. "Each time its onset was widespread, energetic, irresistible." But each time, the components of the movement dispersed, the energy behind it drained, and the reform system itself was never institutionalized.[64] Such is the pattern of reform generally, a direct result of the nature of reform as an effort to bridge the gap between political ideals and political institutions.

In most other countries, periods of change, particularly social and economic innovation, are associated with the centralization of power in the political system. In America, too, there have been some tendencies in this direction. During periods of creedal passion, however, the prevailing thrust in politics has been toward the opening up of the system, the expansion of political participation, the diffusion and popularization of power. In part this is because the stress during creedal passion periods is not just on social and economic changes, but on political reform as well.

The relative openness and permeability of the American political system make reform possible. Groups previously outside the system can mobilize, organize, participate, and inaugurate structural changes in the system. The goals of reform usually involve enhancing these qualities of openness, permeability, "responsiveness." In the longer term, however, the very success of the reformers in achieving these goals helps to defeat reform. The same features of the American political system that make reform possible and that are strengthened by reform also ensure that its victory will be temporary. The changes that reform produces are the product of a temporary mobilization and coalition of groups. The institutions that reformers create reflect one constellation of political interests and purposes. When this constellation fades in significance, those institutions then respond to the changes in the political environment. The

political system, open to reform and further opened by reform, is also
open to counter-reform.

The reform process, moreover, contains its own paradox. Those reforms most easily adopted are presumably those that have the broadest
appeal, that is, those where the gap between existing practice and accepted
ideal adversely affects the largest groups in the population. These reforms
are most clearly seen to be "in the public interest." In a creedal passion
period, public sentiment, consequently, can be quickly aroused and directed toward their enactment. Once enacted, however, these reforms are
also most likely to lack a well-organized constituency to sustain and protect them and to ensure that they are administered and applied so as to
achieve the intended results. Beneficial to everyone, they are guarded by
no one, and hence they are highly vulnerable to efforts of special-interest
groups to twist them to serve their purposes. Those reforms, on the other
hand, that, while legitimized in terms of the values of the American
Creed, also primarily benefit particular interest groups may be more difficult to enact precisely for that reason. Their consequences for the balance of power among groups are easily seen. At the same time, the
existence of an ongoing organized constituency means that such reforms
are more likely to be applied over a longer period of time in a way more
congruent with their original purposes. In short, those reforms that are
most easily introduced to serve the general interest are also most easily
corrupted to serve special interests.

The frustrations of the Burkean conservative in America have been
graphically describe by Louis Hartz. Lacking a feudal tradition, monarchy, aristocracy, an established church, and significant status differences, the American conservative can only find liberal institutions to
conserve. The frustrations of the progressive reformer, on the other hand,
have similar roots in the liberal consensus but assume a different form.
The conservative in America is frustrated by the fact that American
political institutions are modeled on the liberal ideal; the reformer is
frustrated because, despite his best efforts, those institutions always fall
short of the ideal. Creedal passion periods are periods of progressive
reform. Yet the dragons of inequality and concentrated power that are
slain by one band of reformers in one period rise up again to challenge
another band in another period. The British Crown is eliminated but is
replaced by a commercial oligarchy centered in a national bank. The
oligarchy is displaced but a slave-owning aristocracy becomes even more
powerful. The plantation aristocracy is broken in a civil war which heralds

the rise of an industrial plutocracy with wealth and power far transcending that which existed previously. In due course, corporate power is tamed, in part by the expansion of executive power, which then becomes the source of new threats to liberty, equality, and popular control of government. Ralph Nader, Bob Woodward, and Carl Bernstein have to redo in one generation what Upton Sinclair and Lincoln Steffens did in an earlier one. For the reformer, it is, as Michels said, at best a spectacle "simultaneously encouraging and depressing."[65] Through two hundred years and four major periods of reform fervor, the history of progressive reform is, apparently, the history of much reform but modest progress. Reform seems ephemeral, privilege reincarnate, and the realization of the democratic ideal only marginally closer in 1976 than it was in 1776.

Political Earthquakes and Realignment

Creedal passion periods are characterized by an impetus to reform because social forces invoke traditional political ideals in order to advance their own interests by bringing political institutions more into accord with those ideals. Specific institutional reforms may, however, produce unanticipated or contrary consequences. The most sweeping and lasting impact of a creedal passion period is found not in the progressive reforms that it produces, but in the political realignment that accompanies it: the cry is reform, the result is realignment. This realignment involves a fundamental restructuring of the relations between the principal social forces in society and the principal institutions in the political system. It involves changes in the powers, functions, and constituencies of governmental institutions, usually including but certainly not limited to political parties.

A political realignment in this sense is a much more all-encompassing phenomenon than simply a party realignment or what Walter Dean Burnham has termed a "critical realignment"—that is, "a major change rooted in the behavior of critically large minorities of American voters which durably alters electoral coalitions, the shape of election outcomes, and the flow of public policy."[66] Party or critical realignments have occurred at fairly regular intervals in American history, typically culminating in "critical elections" every twenty-eight to thirty-six years: 1800, 1828, 1860, 1896, 1932. These elections signal major and lasting shifts in party power and in the link between particular parties and

particular social forces. In some of these instances, however, the focus
of the realignment was the rise of a new social force: 1800 marked the
ascendancy of the agrarian Republicans over the mercantile Federalists,
1860 the ascendancy of the industrializing North over the plantation
South, and 1932 the ascendancy of the urban working class over the
previously dominant business groups. These elections signaled major
shifts in power among social groups and between the parties that represented them. They did not, however, involve the profound upheaval in
the overall relations between social forces and political institutions that
occurred during the Revolutionary, Jacksonian, and Progressive eras
and in the 1960s and 1970s. The realignments of 1828 and 1896, for
instance, involved shifts not only among and between political parties
and social forces but also more general changes in the structure, power,
and functioning of governmental institutions. In these cases, party realignment was only one aspect of a broader political realignment.

Viewing party realignments in this broader context helps explain
something that perplexed political analysts of the 1960s. According to
the view that party realignments occur every twenty-eight to thirty-six
years, a party realignment should have occurred between 1960 and 1968.
Many of the familiar prerequisites and correlates of such a realignment
were present: increased political participation, a rise of new issues (civil
rights, Vietnam) that cut across the New Deal party division inherited
from the past, third-party movements, and a loosening of party ties among
many groups in the population, particularly the young. Yet no significant
party realignment occurred; it was, as Burnham said, "a kind of waiting
for Godot" on the part of political analysts.[67] The dynamics that had
previously operated with such regularity in American politics for over a
century and a half seemed to have failed. How can this be explained?

One possible explanation is that what was supposed to happen in the
1960s was not a simple party realignment but a more complex political
realignment—which did in fact occur. What distinguished this political
realignment from those of the Progressive and Jacksonian periods was
that political parties were less important in the overall political system in
the 1960s than they had been previously. Consequently the changes in
roles, power, and constituencies that occurred did not have a major impact
on political parties. The political realignment of the 1960s did not involve
a major party realignment because parties were weak, just as the political
realignment of the Revolution did not involve a party realignment because

parties, in a modern organized sense, simply did not then exist. The frustrated political analysts of the 1960s were, in short, simply waiting for the wrong Godot.

Political realignments can occur in creedal passion periods because of two principles that govern the links between social forces and political institutions. These principles were reflected in the frame of government that the Founding Fathers created in the eighteenth century, and were reinforced by the way in which that frame evolved in subsequent centuries. These are the principles of *constituent plurality* and *constituent mutability*. Both represented major innovations in the theory of government. In the eighteenth century, preoccupation with the goal of balanced government usually manifested itself in the concept of mixed government. According to this theory, each branch of government, as in Great Britain, should represent or embody the interests of a particular estate of the realm. This theory was a not a completely inaccurate description of the British Constitution: the crown represented the royal family, the House of Lords the aristocracy, and the House of Commons the gentlemen, burghers, and other property owners qualified to participate in parliamentary elections. Mixed government assumed a more-or-less immutable and exclusive relation between a social force and a political institution. The number and character of the political institutions in government were to reflect the number and character of the social forces in society. A balance among social orders would be reflected in a balance among political organs.

If this were the case, however, what justification would there be for a multiplicity of political institutions in government in the United States? Charles Pinckney raised precisely this question in the discussion of the Senate in the Constitutional Convention. England, he said, had three orders in society and hence three institutions in government. The United States, however, "contains but one order that can be assimilated to the British nation—this is the order of the Commons. They will not surely then attempt to form a Government consisting of three branches, two of which shall have nothing to represent . . . We must . . . suit our Government to the people it is to direct."[68] For a society composed of "one order" and yet also of many interests, a one-on-one theory of representation would have required either a single central governing body or a large number of such bodies to reflect the diverse factions identified by Madison in Number 10 of *The Federalist*.

The framers of the Constitution, however, did not base their structure of government on a theory of representation. With a few exceptions like Gouverneur Morris and John Adams (who did not participate in the Constitutional Convention), they held little brief for the theory of mixed government. Both in the Convention debates and in *The Federalist,* as well as elsewhere, they paid relatively little explicit attention to the relations between the social forces in American society and the political institutions they were creating. They occasionally referred to the Senate in terms suggesting that they thought it would be more reflective of the interests of small states and that it would be the more conservative and restrained of the two houses of the national legislature. This was almost always in the context of their view that the House of Representatives, directly elected by the people, would be more likely to be swept by popular passions. Although they referred at times to the various interests and groups which at that time made up American society, nowhere did they elaborate a systematic theory of what groups would be represented in what way in which institutions of government. They talked a great deal about the *powers* of the different branches of government, but they said little about the *constituencies* of those branches. The stress of the framers was on "the interior structure of the government," not on its external relations to society. And this interior structure was designed to ensure that "its several constituent parts may, by their mutual relations, be the means of keeping each other in their proper places."[69]

In Europe, Latin America, and elsewhere, governmental institutions and political parties tend to be attached indissolubly and often exclusively to particular social forces; when those social forces decline, they carry "their" political institutions with them. In western Europe, each institution has also tended to be associated with a particular sociopolitical ideology. In the United States, however, in a major political innovation matched in modern history only by the creation of the Leninist party, the framers of the Constitution created a system of government that was responsible to society yet also autonomous from it. Each institution of government was not necessarily linked exclusively to a particular social force, nor was it necessarily linked permanently to any combination of social forces. Pluralism and mutability were provided for in the relations between society and government. They ensured the stability of the latter and the access of the former. In the United States, political institutions have become adept in shifting constituencies to reflect the changing power and influence of emerging and declining social forces. Social forces in turn have confronted multiple potential channels of access to government, and if they have not been able to promote their interests effectively through one institution, they have almost always been able to establish links with another.

During the course of American political development, the constituencies of most formal institutions and of the major political parties have changed dramatically. The principal interest groups in American society —agrarian, commercial, industrial, and labor; religious, regional, and ethnic; liberal and conservative—have at one time or another been on each side of the arguments concerning states rights versus national power, Congress versus the President, the power of the judiciary, Republicans versus Democrats. Governmental institutions have been almost entirely free of sustained association with any particular point of view; they are not thought of as being inherently or irremediably liberal or conservative. Institutional ideologies or briefs advanced by one interest group in one generation on behalf of "its" political institution are taken over by another, often competing, interest group in the next generation. The case for presidential leadership, or judicial review, or states rights may be a conservative argument at one time and a liberal argument at another.

This relationship between social forces and political institutions has two consequences for public debate. First, the arguments between social forces over their respective claims on the polity become transmuted into debates over the respective roles of political institutions within the polity. The head-on clash of social force against social force is thus filtered through institutional channels and in part transformed into a struggle of one institution against another. Second, the advocates in the debate over institutional roles are necessarily to some degree restrained by their unconscious knowledge, if not conscious awareness, that the brief they are arguing one day may be the one they challenge on a later day. How many people active in American public life for several decades have consistently favored either presidential power or congressional power, national authority or states rights, judicial activism or judicial quietism?

A high degree of institutional continuity seems to characterize American government. The relations between the Ninety-fourth Congress and the thirty-eighth President in 1976 did not seem to be fundamentally different from those between most of their predecessors. In this sense, the Founding Fathers designed well: their system of checks and balances has provided for the sustained division of power among the different branches and levels of government. The fact that the balance of power they valued has been largely maintained over the years is, however, to a great extent a product of that aspect of the political system to which they devoted relatively little attention—that is, the relations between political institutions and social forces. The balance of power they valued has been maintained because of the ability of political institutions to adapt to changes in the influence and interests of social forces. No major governmental institution and only one early rudimentary political party (the Federalists) has suffered the fate of the Crown, the House of Lords, or the Liberal Party. Institutional continuity has been the product of institutional adaptability. The interests of a group are not connected indefinitely or exclusively with the interests of any particular political institution. The connection between them, which may be intense and politically important while it lasts, is nonetheless a marriage of convenience, a product of the existing political environment, without deep social or ideological roots. When common interests are no longer served, divorce and remarriage to other partners invariably follow.

The framers' concern for maintaining a balance of power within government led them away from the ideas of both mixed government and the separation of processes, and toward the idea of checks and balances. The concept of mixed government assumed a more or less one-to-one relationship between a social force and a political institution. Far from presupposing the autonomy of governmental institutions, it in effect presupposed "captive" institutions, much as Marxist theory sees the state as the captive of the bourgeoisie. The lack of institutional autonomy means that the power of the governmental institutions varies with the power and importance of the social forces to which they are attached. In the eighteenth century in Britain, a rough equilibrium existed among the monarchy, the aristocracy, and the middle class as social forces, which was reflected in the relations among the Crown, Lords, and Commons as institutions. The balance of power in government was the temporary consequence of a balance of power in society. The onset of democracy, however, upset the societal balance, and during the course of the next century the decline of the monarchy and aristocracy transformed the Crown and the House of Lords into dignified institutions and resulted in the supremacy of the Commons. Neither the Crown nor the House of Lords was able to adapt effectively to changes in society.

In different fashion, the separation of processes produces a similar result. Assigning the legislative, executive, and judicial powers to distinct institutions leads to the supremacy of the legislature, since the legislative or law-making power is clearly superior to the law-executing and law-

interpreting powers. If all legislative power is concentrated in one institution, that body will clearly be superior to the executive and judicial
branches. In order to moderate this tendency, the theory of the separation
of processes, as, for instance, it was developed by Jefferson, often postu-
lated the division of the legislature into two branches that could check
each other. This represented a first step away from a pure separation of
processes toward checks and balances, in which the executive and even
the judiciary would have some share in the legislative power.

The checks and balances theory, which was uppermost in the minds
of the framers, alone of the three theories of balanced government ensured
the maintenance of a balance of power in government. This was done in
part by allowing each branch of government to share in the powers of the
other branches. More fundamentally, if implicitly, this result was also
achieved by allowing for flexibility in the relations between governmental
institutions and social forces. On the one hand, no governmental institution was linked indissolubly and exclusively to any single social force (as
would have been the case in the theory of mixed government). On the
other hand, no governmental institution monopolized the law-making
power which would have enabled it to dominate the other institutions of
government (as would have been the case with separation of processes).
Instead, the checks and balances system provided for competition among
governmental institutions and permitted mutability in the relations between governmental institutions and social forces.

Changes in the linkages between social forces and political institutions
are always taking places. They are not limited to creedal passion periods.
Indeed, realignments between social forces and political parties seem to
take place not only as part of more general reconstitutions of the political
system during creedal passion periods, but also at regular intervals between creedal passion periods. In less regular fashion, governmental institutions may shift constituencies through extended periods of time, as the
Supreme Court did in the shift from the Hughes Court to the Warren
Court. Changes in constituency linkages between social forces and political institutions do, however, tend to be more numerous, more rapid, and
more significant during creedal passion periods than at other times in
American history. During these periods, the clumping of linkage changes
produces a reconstitution of the political system. The system that emerged
out of the Revolution was significantly different from that which had
existed previously; the Jacksonian system embodied additional basic
changes in the powers, functions, and constituency linkages of political

institutions; the reconstitution of the system that occurred during the Progressive period, often labeled by political scientists as "the system of 1896," likewise marked a new pattern of politics and institutional relationships which lasted until the 1960s, when a "new American political system" again emerged.

The peculiar genius of the American system is that, more than other major political systems, it allows for this periodic reconstitution of its principal institutional components. This reconstitution is clearly related to changes in the roles of social forces—classes, interest groups, regions—in the society. The external institutional façade remains, so that the reality of change is obscured in appearance and the fundamental principle of autonomous institutions competing with each other is not challenged. Yet major changes do take place in the powers, functions, interrelations, and constituencies of political institutions. This is the way in which a new balance is struck between the political system and society. Stresses and strains develop along the major political fault line between the plate of social forces on the one hand and that of political institutions on the other, until a political earthquake accurs, releases the tension, and produces a new equilibrium between the societal plate and the political one. These periodic realignments are, as Walter Dean Burnham suggested, "America's surrogate for revolution."[70]

In sum, creedal passion periods involve intense efforts by large numbers of Americans to return to first principles. They are characterized by a distinctive type of political cleavage, major efforts at reform, and significant shifts in alignments between political institutions and social forces. Without the absence of moral intensity that characterizes the "normal" pattern of American politics, the American political system could not long endure. Without the moral intensity of creedal passion periods, it could not change and hence avoid stagnation and decay. From time to time the long-term stability of the system requires a moralistic drive to narrow the gap between ideal and reality. In this sense, a creedal passion period is American politics' finest—and most dangerous—hour.

6 THE SOURCES OF CREEDAL PASSION

Why Creedal Passion Periods?

The place of creedal passion in American politics must be explained at two levels. At the most general level, what causes this overall pattern of political continuity and equilibrium, occasionally interrupted by the intrusion of passion, moralism, intensified conflict, reform, and realignment? Why is interest-group politics from time to time displaced by creedal politics? The general causes of this pattern are to be found in the extent and nature of the American liberal consensus. The pattern is distinctive but not unique to American politics, and it remains to be shown how this general American pattern both resembles and differs from similar patterns in other societies characterized by ideological consensus.

At the more specific level, why do particular manifestations of creedal passion appear at particular moments in American history? Does each outburst of creedal passion have its own specific causes? Or are there some recurring factors that can be identified as the common precipitants of creedal passion periods?

In the end, an exploration of the sources of creedal passion, both general and specific, cannot help but lead the analysis back to the historical origins of it all, to the initial causes of both the general pattern and the specific manifestations of that pattern, which are to be found in seventeenth-century England.

General Sources: Comparable Phenomena in Other Societies

Political change in the United States is distinctive in that: (1) it is episodic, tending to be concentrated in periods of creedal passion occurring roughly at sixty-year intervals; (2) it is associated not with a change in ideologies but rather with a reinvocation and reaffirmation of traditional American liberal values and beliefs; and (3) the overriding purpose of reform during periods of change is to bring American political institutions and practices into accord with these values and beliefs. This pattern of change could only occur in a society with an overwhelming consensus on liberal and democratic values. It could not occur and has not occurred in societies with traditions of ideological pluralism, such as most of those of western Europe.

In societies characterized by a nonliberal ideological monism, phenomena comparable, if not similar, to creedal passion periods may occur when efforts are made to reduce the gap between prevailing political reality and the basic values of the ideology. In most cases, this will mean strengthening governmental authority in order to make it correspond more closely to an autocratic or totalitarian ideal. In a political system produced by a major revolution, however, efforts may be made from time to time to renew or to reaffirm revolutionary values. Such values usually involve elements of purification, puritanism, mass participation, egalitarianism, and a renewal of moralistic devotion and commitment to revolutionary principles. In the Soviet Union since the suppression of the Kronshtadt revolt in 1921, such revolutionary values have been subordinated to the goals of bureaucratic centralism and party supremacy. In Communist China, on the other hand, at least in its first quarter-century, periodic efforts were made to give renewed meaning to revolutionary values, of which the most notable was the Great Proletarian Cultural Revolution.

Despite their basic differences, striking similarities exist between the Cultural Revolution in China and the simultaneous outburst of creedal passion in the United States in the 1960s. In one form or another, virtually all of the fourteen characteristics of creedal passion periods set forth in the opening pages of Chapter 5 can be found in Chinese politics during the Cultural Revolution. The purpose of the Cultural Revolution was "not to replace existing authority but to purify it," and the ideology of the revolution hence "may have more in common with restoration or revitalization movements than with rebellion."[1] This pattern had its roots, in many respects, in Confucianism, in which there was an uneasy gap between principle and practice and which consequently provoked periodic demands for reform in the name of the fundamental values of the system.

> Confucian ideology had this potential—to purify the system as well as to justify it. Confucianism coexisted uneasily with imperial and bureaucratic institutions. The high standards of virtue to which Confucius failed to convert even the petty princes of his day were still less reachable for the rulers of a vast empire. What made the ideology vital and the system viable was the ability of the former to hold a critical mirror to the latter. Periodically throughout Chinese history one discovers a kind of Protestant fundamentalism—the mobilization of the ideas of officialdom against established institutions and practices. One finds echos of this in Maoist fundamentalism which, like its Confucian parallels, is based on a highly selective version of the Sacred Canon.[2]

"Protestant fundamentalism," here used to describe a phenomenon in the Chinese tradition, could not be a more apt phrase for American creedal passion periods. During the Cultural Revolution, too, the effort was made to move forward in practice by turning backward in theory, to cleanse existing practice and rectify evils by a reassertion of "traditional" (that is, Maoist or revolutionary) values. "Purification" in Communist China is the functional equivalent of "reform" in liberal America. In a one-ideology society, change cannot be mediated by a shift in the prevailing ideology: instead, there has to be a reinvocation of the underlying or fundamental values of that ideology. This occurred in Confucian China; it has occurred in Communist China; it recurs in liberal America. It could not occur and did not occur in those brief years in the early part of the twentieth century when ideological pluralism prevailed in China and traditional Confucian, republican, regional, and revolutionary movements vied for control.

Anthropologists have analyzed societies in terms of the differences between "shame cultures" and "guilt cultures." It has been argued that shame, as an external sanction, has been the principal means of social control in Asian societies, including both Japan and China. In Western societies, there has been a greater reliance "on a sense of guilt or 'conscience' as an internal sanction."[3] Although some scholars have claimed that guilt has played a significant role in both traditional and modern Chinese society, the weight of scholarly authority has stressed the importance of shame in shaping behavior in China.[4] In some sense, indeed,

American society may be the guilt culture par excellence, whereas Chinese society is the shame culture par excellence. And it is precisely the strength of these two forms of social control that makes these societies similar. In many societies shame and guilt will both be very weak, but in the United States and China at least one of these two forms of social control is strong. Shame or guilt can be an effective means of social control only in societies with explicit and generally agreed-upon standards of morality. China and the United States meet this criterion. More important than the fact that one may rely on guilt and the other on shame is the common intensity with which they are applied in Chinese and American societies. This shared characteristic makes possible creedal passion periods in one and a· Cultural Revolution in the other.

"The widening dissonance between Maoist ideology and Party practice in 1962–66," one scholar argued, "led to the Cultural Revolution," and another social scientist explicitly analyzed the Cultural Revolution in terms of the theory of cognitive dissonance.[5] In the United States, perceptions of the IvI gap and of its immorality and intolerability have tended to surface first in society among social forces and interest groups seeking to preserve or to expand their access to government. In China, on the other hand, the central leadership in the government provided the initiative; the affirmation of "traditional" values and the attack on existing institutions first came from the top down rather than from the bottom up. Mao Tse-tung, as one Red Guard officer put it, "changed his demands" and began to condemn officials "who were doing what they always had done." In the Cultural Revolution, however, as in American creedal passion periods, the more radical members of the protest movement were those who had previously been least connected with the existing establishment.[6] Both the creedal passion of the 1960s and the Cultural Revolution also involved expansion of political participation and diversification in its forms. In China this was, at least initially, a calculated and controlled process designed to serve the ends of the central leadership. Hence, unlike American creedal passion periods, the Cultural Revolution had a fairly well-defined beginning (in November 1965, with Yao Wen-yuan's attack on Wu Han) and an officially announced end almost three years later (in September 1968).

In the United States, the politics of creedal passion has supplemented and supplanted the normal patterns of interest-group politics. In China, too, the politics of the Cultural Revolution differed significantly from the normal pattern. It was not simply a struggle for power between individuals and factions. As Paul Hiniker asked, "If the Cultural Revolution is to be explained solely as a power struggle, how does one account for the passionate displays of ideological ferver?" Similarly, Lowell Dittmer argued that the Cultural Revolution, particularly with respect to the attack on Liu Shao-ch'i, was not a power struggle disguised as a revolution but rather a revolution disguised as a power struggle, in which the attack on Liu was a means to educate the masses and to produce revolutionary upheaval.[7] During the Cultural Revolution, muckraking became a central form of politics. There was an emphasis on willingness to "wash dirty linen in public" and "an almost obsessive Red Guard concern with exposure," this mass criticism serving the functions of both rectification and mass mobilization.[8] The forms and intensity of mass communication multiplied. There was also, as in the America of the 1960s, an intensification of verbal aggression and of symbolic as well as physical violence. "One outstanding phenomenon of the Cultural Revolution was the prevalence of incivil words and deeds on the part of both the elite groups and the masses."[9]

Much of the other activity in the Cultural Revolution will be familiar to Americans who experienced the passion of the 1960s in the United States. As the Cultural Revolution came to its peak, students at Peking's two major universities "took the initiative to press charges against the university faculties, administration, and the party committees." At Peking University, students denounced "the university president and two other officials for enforcing bourgeois ideology in education, which discriminated against proletarian students and at the same time exalted curriculum and academic learning over policy and ideology." Shortly thereafter, the student movement was expanded into the Red Guards. "Ruthlessly attacking power centers and hysterically demanding mass action, the Red Guards were told to disrupt and paralyze the establishment."[10] The goal of the leaders of the revolution involved "rejuvenating the revolutionary spirit by smashing revisionism and of unifying huge masses of people by recapturing power." The central thrust was against bureaucracy, hierarchy, and specialization. The ideas of "populism, anti-bureaucratism, and rebellion" were used to attack officialdom and bureaucratic authority, but not ideological authority. The ideology of the revolution, indeed, emanated from Mao and those about him. The slogans of the revolution included: "Good men and simple government!" "To rebel is justified!" "Down with officials!"—rallying cries that would have been right at home in the American protest movements of the 1960s.[11]

In China, as in other communist states, the Communist Party was the principal institutional source of legitimacy. During the Cultural Revolution, however, the central position of the party was challenged and undermined. "The whole thrust of the Cultural Revolution," as Benjamin Schwartz said, was "to devalue and diminish its significance." The dictatorship of the proletariat was no longer identified with the dictatorship of the party. Following the Cultural Revolution, efforts were made with some difficulty to rebuild the party.

> The crux of the matter is not whether the Party survives in some form but whether it can ever recover its central sacred charter . . . the Cultural Revolution has unmasked many truths which will not be easily forgotten, particularly by the young who have participated in recent events. The Party may not have engaged in all the heinous bureaucratic crimes attributed to it in Red Guard newspapers but its profane nature as simply another bureaucratic organization devoid of any inbuilt proletarian grace or powers of self-redemption now stands revealed. The institutional charisma will not easily be restored.[12]

No institution has occupied a role in American politics comparable to that of the Communist Party in Chinese politics. But the Presidency clearly has come close to performing such a role, and the "whole thrust" of the democratic surge of the 1960s was, in many ways, "to devalue and diminish" presidental authority. Striking parallels exist between the impact of the Cultural Revolution on the Communist Party and the impact of the passion of the 1960s on the Presidency.

Both the Cultural Revolution and the American upheaval of the 1960s manifested a marked hostility toward norms, such as expertise, specialization, and efficiency, that were associated with economic and bureaucratic development. Mao Tse-tung's thought emphasized the predominance of the social-ethical over the economic-technocratic, the victory of Rousseau over Saint-Simon, as Schwartz summarized it. In the Cultural Revolution, Mao demonstrated that he was "bent on achieving the reign of virtue as he understands virtue and remains unprepared to accept any progress of the 'arts and sciences' which is not based on virtue."[13]

The institutional changes or "reforms" of the Cultural Revolution were, in many respects, the Chinese equivalents of the types of reforms introduced in American creedal passion periods. Mao's approach was "hostile toward increased differentiation and specialization in political structure." The Cultural Revolution "reduced the number of central ministries and simplified the central party apparatus; combined state and party functions at the subnational level in the unified structure of the revolutionary committees; dissolved, suspended, or curtailed parts of the political infrastructure (communications media, the old mass organizations, and the democratic parties); and cut back on the overall size of bureaucracy thereby restricting the possibilities for specialization."[14] In similar fashion, it has been argued that many particular reforms advanced during the Cultural Revolution, such as "the open-door rectification process, the transformation of China's educational system, the establishment of May 7 cadre schools, and the extension of direct class representation in China's revolutionary committees" suggested that the Chinese Communists were trying "to build greater responsiveness and accountability into the system." But the Chinese, like the Americans, could not escape the irony of reform. Particularly with respect to their efforts to eliminate the vestiges of capitalism and to expand mass participation, Lucian Pye argued, "the extraordinary paradox appears to be that Maoists will have produced out of the Cultural Revolution the very results that they have been denouncing."[15]

Scholars of political development in Communist China almost invariably speak in terms of cyclical oscillations between phases of "mobilization" and "consolidation." As Michel Oksenberg put it, "They alternate between periods of mobilization, with an emphasis upon social change, unleashed advance, and conflict and periods of consolidation, with an emphasis upon developing institutions, planned advance, and reconciliation." Mobilization phases, another author observed, "have followed the style of the mass movement, relying on political organization and ideological incentives. Consolidation phases have relied more on administrative organs, bureaucratic procedures, and material incentives."[16] In China, the phases themselves are generally brief and the shift from one to the other quite rapid. The principal mobilization periods are often identified as the phase of socialist consolidation (1955–56), the Great Leap Forward (1958–59), and the Cultural Revolution (1965–68).[17] The aftermath of the Cultural Revolution also resembled the aftermath of America's 1960s: a reemphasis on education, specialization, economic goals, and the reconstituting of institutions that had been disrupted during the years of passion.

The rapidity of the oscillations in China contrasts markedly with the longer-term alternation of creedal passion periods in the United States, this contrast being a dramatic consequence of the different sources of power and initiative in the two societies. The rapid oscillation in China is the product of control from the top; the central leadership in the society has the power to define goals and to change them as well as to mobilize the population and then to demobilize and redirect it. In the United States, on the other hand, oscillations in the intensity of creedal passion depend upon changes in the social structure, the shift in generations, the rise and fall of social groups, and the gradual shifts in perceptions by social groups.

The same considerations that made possible frequent changes between mobilization and consolidation in the first decades of communist rule may make them less frequent subsequently. If the initiative must come from the top, the exercise of that initiative depends upon the attitudes and interests of those who are at the top. Chairman Mao placed great value on the periodic renewal of revolutionary ideals and goals: he "stated more than once that new cultural revolutions would be needed every fifteen or twenty years, i.e., every new generation, to rekindle the sinking flames of enthusiasm."[18] Mao was continuously suspicious of the bureaucratic establishment and rejected a simple identification of the interests of the revolution with the interests of the party. Whether his successors— particularly those of postrevolutionary generations who are not products of the Long March and Yenan—will have the same commitment to the renewal of those values appears dubious. In the United States, basic liberal values remain alive and efforts to realize them are a recurring phenom- enon in politics because they can be articulated and used by any social force which finds that to its advantage. In China the top leadership con- trols the articulation of revolutionary values, and it seems likely that as years pass the leadership may find it less and less in its interest to articu- late those values. The revolutionary impulse slackens; consolidation triumphs over mobilization; the interests of the party, state, and military bureaucracies dominate the political scene.

This change in China from a pattern involving regular alternation of moralism and instrumentalism to one in which instrumental values and approaches predominate will dramatically lessen a major source of am- biguity and tension in the political system. The leaders of communist states necessarily have an ambivalent attitude toward the process of modernization. "On the one hand, modernization is positively valued as a social goal, for modernization means economic development and eco- nomic development means national power. On the other hand, however, modernization entails bureaucracy, instrumentalism, and the consequent attenuation and ritual sterilization of ideological principles." Soviet leaders, for a variety of reasons, early gave priority to "the goal of professionalism, to the creation of a rational, highly differentiated bureaucratic apparatus, and to a degree of operational autonomy for 'expert' hierarchies, particularly in the industrial, state-administrative, and military spheres."[19] In contrast, the Chinese placed greater emphasis on populism than on professionalism, an emphasis that manifested itself most dramatically in the Cultural Revolution, a phenomenon unknown to and impossible in the Soviet system. This Cultural Revolution was thus, in some sense, "a revolution against history—that is, against what appears to be the inevitable development of a privileged stratum in the process of economic development, or, even more boldly, against modernization itself."[20] The Cultural Revolution is, for example, widely held to have set Chinese higher education back by more than a decade. In a fundamental sense, once the revolution is in power, revolutionary values work against social development.

In the aftermath of other major revolutions, revolutionary values and goals gradually disappeared from the scene. In China, at least until the 1970s, periodic efforts were made to keep them alive. With the passing of Mao, these efforts are likely to become less frequent, less important, and less successful. After two hundred years, the American political system still retains its capacity for ideological renewal. The Chinese system could well lose its capacity after a quarter of a century. In losing the capacity to reassert revolutionary values, however, it will also lose the impetus to rebel against history.

Specific Sources: The Timing of Creedal Passion Periods

The reasons why an overall pattern of political change through creedal passion exists in the United States are general and clear. The reasons why creedal passion should come to the fore at particular times in American history are not necessarily so evident. Each major manifestation of creedal passion could conceivably have its own particular cause. Undoubtedly, in each creedal passion period, unique factors were at work that gave the period its own distinctive momentum and character. Yet the periods also have much in common in terms of their political moralism, themes, passion, reforms, and consequences. Were common causes in some way at work in the 1770s, the 1830s, the 1900s, and the 1960s to produce these similar results? Why did American politics in these decades share so

many distinctive characteristics? Why should major changes and upheavals—in terms of both political reforms and political realignments—
be concentrated at these particular times in American history?

This chapter will not try to provide definitive answers to these questions, but will discuss three types of explanation that could plausibly
account for the appearance of particular creedal passion periods. These
periods can be explained as: (1) a rational response to objective changes
in the concentration and abuse of power; (2) the product of exogenous
events—social, economic, demographic, or cultural—that arouse people
to passionate political action; and (3) a phase in a recurring generational
or cyclical process of change in which events in one phase in the cycle
generate the conditions leading to the next phase. No one of these explanations is probably sufficient and all three may be necessary to account
for the eruptions of creedal passion at particular points in American
history.

Rational Response

A central characteristic of creedal passion periods is the scope and
intensity of concern with the concentration and abuse of power. That
underlying uneasiness which Americans always have about power comes
to the fore and shapes the definition of political issues and the patterns
of political development. What must be explained, consequently, is a
change in public consciousness, social mood, and ethos.

One obvious explanation—not necessarily wrong for being obvious—
is that this change in public mood and concern is a rational response to
"objective" changes in the distribution and utilization of power. The targets of creedal passion are, in this sense, also its causes. New structures
of power and authority develop; those in power eventually abuse their
power; the gap between liberal ideal and institutional practice broadens;
and the moralism characteristic of creedal passion periods surfaces as an
effort to reform institutions and reduce the IvI gap. The years before the
American Revolution saw the rationalization and extension of British
power in America and new efforts to impose on the colonists some of the
costs of empire. In this sense, the American Revolution was a rational
response, as the Whigs argued, to the usurpation and abuse of authority
by the Crown and its agents. Similarly, the Jacksonians attacked not
only the undemocratic aspects of the existing political system but also,
and most vehemently, the new centers of economic and political power
that had emerged and that seemed to portend monopoly of the economic

future of the country. The Bank of the United States "was a giant, immensely powerful even on the political side, where it was most exposed. Economically, it was the greatest corporation in the country, by far the leading single domestic agency in the currency and credit system, and accordingly in business affairs. Upon its conduct depended the fiscal routine of the national government and, potentially, the national credit." In its symbolic relations to the country, the bank more closely resembled "that of the powerful king to his state than that of the flag to the sentiment of loyalty."[21] The 1890s saw the emergence of national industrial corporations, trusts, and monopolies, and of urban political machines and bosses, on a scale that had not existed previously. In the 1950s and 1960s, the military-industrial complex and the imperial Presidency were undeniable facts that had developed in the aftermath of World War II and in the context of the Cold War and that clearly concentrated unprecedented power in the national executive. Major abuses of authority did, in fact, occur in the late 1960s and early 1970s.

Prior to each creedal passion period there thus existed "objective" tendencies toward the concentration of power and away from the political values of the American Creed. It seems reasonable that each of these developments should produce a response that exposed the concentration of power, denounced its abuse as a deviation from American political values, and promoted political action and reform to instigate remedies. Such "objective" circumstances may be a necessary condition for the emergence of creedal passion, but the question remains as to whether they are a sufficient condition. Can one conclude that a one-to-one cause-and-effect relationship exists between the concentration of power and abuse of authority, and creedal passion movements to limit power and constrain authority?

The answer is no for three reasons.

First, such a conclusion rests on the assumption that variations in outrage about the abuse of power accurately reflect variations in the actual abuse of power. This may be true, but there is no way in which this can be proved, and there are some good reasons to think that it may not be true. Documented exposure of abuses at one point in time simply sets the minimum for that point in time. The abuses exposed vary from period to period, and conceivably the level of abuse varies in the same way. But this is not necessarily the case. There are two other possibilities. The level of exposure and the level of actual abuse could vary quite independently of each other. The only limitation is that presumably the former can never be higher than the latter, although widespread charges and smears may create the impression of more abuse than there actually is. Alternatively, the level of exposure of abuse could vary inversely with the level of actual abuse. Widespread exposures of the abuse of power, as we have seen, demonstrate extensive public concern about the abuse of power and hence may help reduce those abuses. The principal "objective" variation in the abuse of power may be not an increase above the norm before a period of creedal passion, but rather a decrease below the norm during and after such a period. Or, conceivably, public moralism about the abuse of power could in itself be evidence of an already existing low level of actual abuse. Low levels of public immorality might well coincide with high levels of public concern about public immorality.

The problem here, in more generalized form, is the classic one concerning corruption and other forms of illegitimate behavior. Do multiple exposures of the existence of corrupt behavior indicate the greater prevalence of such behavior or greater antagonism toward such behavior? It has been suggested, for instance, that "crime waves" are as likely to be the product of waves of public concern about crime or variations in media attention to crime as they are likely to be the product of variations in the incidence of criminal behavior.[22] "Corruption," Theodore Lowi similarly noted, "is an index of the level of public morality, but *awareness* of corruption may well be the sign of a healthy system." Well-organized competitive party politics is likely to produce more exposures of corruption than loosely structured personal and factional politics. Hence, over the years, New York City may have appeared to be more corrupt than Alabama, while in fact there may have been relatively little difference in the absolute levels.[23] In comparable fashion, variations in a political system, such as a shift from interest-group politics to creedal politics, may lead to more exposures of corruption with little variations in absolute levels. Theories from both sociology and social psychology suggest that variations in people's perceptions of the IvI gap and in the intensity of their feelings about the gap are likely to vary more frequently than the behavior of political leaders, groups, and institutions. In an established consensual system, the facts of power do change, albeit slowly; the intensity of concern about power also changes, often rapidly.

The second reason why the concentration and abuse of power cannot alone account for periods of creedal passion is that such changes in power have dramatically occurred at times in American history without generating full-scale moral outrage. Consider, for example, the conservative commercial-oligarchical reaction that purportedly manifested itself in the Constitutional Convention and the 1790s; the wild corruption and abuse of power with the onslaught of industrial and transportation predators in the 1870s; and the Palmer raids, Teapot Dome, and Wall Street–dominated normalcy of the 1920s. These apparent deviations from the Creed did not go entirely unnoticed or entirely unprotested, but they clearly did not produce outbursts of moralism comparable to those of the creedal passion periods. As Herbert Croly accurately observed of the reaction to the political and economic evils of the 1870s and 1880s, "The average good American refused to take these evils seriously. He was possessed by the idea that American life was a stream, which purified itself in the running, and that reformers and critics were merely men who prevented the stream from running free. He looked upon the first spasmodic and ineffective protests with something like contempt. Reformers he appraised as busy-bodies, who were protesting against the conditions of success in business and politics. He nicknamed them 'mugwumps' and continued to vote the regular tickets of his party."[24] It was not until a quarter of a century later that the passion for reform blossomed forth in full bloom.

The third reason is that moral outrage has erupted in American history without any clearly observable intensification of the abuses toward whose elimination it is directed. Here, surely, the most puzzling case is "the mystery of the 1830s." Why did reform, including but certainly not limited to abolitionism, erupt in that decade, although it failed to manifest itself in the 1790s, the 1880s, or the 1920s? "American antislavery sentiment," Ronald Walters argued, "took a very different turn after 1831. Where early abolitionism accepted a gradual end to slavery, after 1831 immediate emancipation became the goal and abolitionism became a passion driving men and women into life-long reform careers. Yet slavery was not new in 1831—it had been present for nearly two centuries. And slavery did not suddenly become evil in 1831; by abolitionist logic it had been sinful all along."[25] As David Donald put it, "Were there more men of integrity, were there more women of sensitive conscience in the 1830s than in any previous decade? A generation of giants these reformers were indeed, but why was there such a concentration of genius in those ten years from 1830 to 1840? . . . We need to know why so many Americans in the 1830s were predisposed toward a certain kind of reform movement."[26] Clearly, neither the evil of slavery nor the existence of the Puritan conscience nor both together are sufficient to explain what happened.

In somewhat similar fashion in the Progressive era, Walter Lippmann found that the popular appeal of muckraking was not a result of higher levels of corruption and abuse of power, but rather of a shift in public opinion in which a people "notorious for its worship of success" turned "savagely upon those who had achieved it": "The muckrakers spoke to a public willing to recognize as corrupt an incredibly varied assortment of conventional acts." Why did conventional behavior become corrupt behavior? The reasons, Lippmann said, must be sought in broader social changes that produced unhappiness in the public, "new necessities and new expectations," and hence "a distinct prejudice in favor of those who make the accusations." The level of corruption did not go up; public tolerance of corruption simply went down. "A happy husband will endure almost anything, but an unhappy one is capable of flying into a rage if his carpet-slippers are not in the right place."[27]

So also, in the 1970s, "post-Watergate morality" imposed new, more stringent standards on the behavior of public officials than had existed previously. The question is whether the Watergate-type behavior of public officials in the late 1960s and early 1970s differed more significantly from the pre-Watergate behavior of public officials than the post-Watergate criteria for official morality differed from pre-Watergate criteria. In the initial phases of exposure, the assumption was that the Watergate acts differed significantly not only from the model of what the behavior of public officials should be, but also from the normal pattern of what the behavior of public officials actually had been. As the dynamic of exposure worked itself out, however, this assumption gradually faded. Revelations of the Johnson, Kennedy, and Roosevelt administrations showed that no individual or party monopolized the misuse of power. "It Didn't Start with Watergate" was not just the title of a polemical tract; it also stated a historical truth. As a result, public indignation over the immorality of a few politicians was gradually transformed into public cynicism at the immorality of all politicians.

Exogenous Events

Creedal passion, although aimed at the reduction of excessive power, is thus not caused simply by the existence of excessive power. A high level of the abuse of power may exist with little or no protest. A high level of protest may develop with little or no significant increase in the abuse of power. Moral outrage is impossible without some abuse of power, but some abuse of power is always occurring. Other, exogenous factors must consequently play a role in precipitating outbursts of creedal passion. To pursue Lippmann's metaphor, what happens at work to cause the husband to fly into a rage because his slippers are in the wrong place?

Social scientists have found the causes of social unrest and protest movements in societal strains, relative deprivation, the authoritarian personality, the group structure of society, the contradictions of capitalism, and elsewhere.[28] Almost all of these theories attempt to explain the origins of particular social movements composed of particular people; they are not directed toward the general condition of society as a whole. Although certain groups in society have a greater propensity than others toward moralistic reform, in a creedal passion period this propensity pervades society. What distinguishes such a period is not the existence of social movements, utopian communities, or reform organizations, but rather the extent to which the activities and concerns of these groups set the dominant themes for the entire society. Thus, the exogenous events responsible for creedal passion periods will have to be broader and more pervasive than those that explain the rise of particular social protest movements. The question is not why reform causes and protest organizations exist, but why they "catch on" with so many different groups. Why do large numbers of husbands simultaneously fly into rages over the misplacement of their slippers?

At least four types of exogenous developments may cause people in various social groups to become incensed about the concentration and abuse of power.

First, creedal passion periods have normally occurred during times of generally rising prices and relative prosperity. People were able to focus their attention on political and moral issues rather than on bread-and-butter ones. Conceivably, of course, unrest produced by economic hardship could be displaced onto questions concerning the IvI gap, but in the American context economic concerns are normally articulated in fairly explicit and direct fashion. Consequently, a sense of relative economic optimism and well-being would appear to be a necessary condition for moral and political concerns to come to the fore. In addition, the principal actors during creedal passion periods are social movements that, while primarily middle class in makeup, appeal across class lines, so that both the well-off and the poor are caught up in the passion for reform.

Second, although overall economic development may provide the necessary background for widespread manifestations of creedal passion, asymmetries or imbalances in the process of development could provide the more immediate impetus to such outbreaks. Relative deprivation has been widely identified by social scientists as a source of protest, insurrection, and revolution. Such deprivation occurs when a group's perceptions of the way in which it is or will be treated fall short of its aspirations as to how it should be treated. This is likely to occur during periods of rapid social and economic change, when established relationships among groups are disrupted. Some form of political action or social protest is likely when increases in social mobilization—literacy, education, media consumption, urbanization—outpace increases in the economic wherewithal to meet the escalating aspirations produced by this mobilization.[29] In this sense, the new forms of the media and of political organization that are associated with creedal passion periods may, in part, themselves be exogenous events contributing to the characteristic politics of such periods. In the history of most societies, rapid economic and social change enhances the role of ideology in politics. In European politics, this historically meant the sharpening of class-based ideologies; in American politics, it means renewed commitment to traditional consensual values.

Third, changes in the relative social and economic status of particular groups may motivate those groups to focus on the IvI gap and to attempt to bring about reforms in political institutions and practices. For reasons elaborated by Tocqueville, increased prosperity for all may become intolerable to those who share less fully in it than others. The American Creed, moreover, is an effective and legitimate weapon for a group to use in attempting to promote its entry into the existing establishment. A group would, presumably, be particularly likely to use this weapon if it had improved itself socially and economically but still felt excluded from important centers of decision making. It might also resort to creedal passion under exactly the opposite circumstances—that is, if it felt that it was on the verge of suffering a relative decline in its position in the power structure. This possibility is the central theme of the "status anxiety" interpretations which David Donald applied to the abolitionists of the 1830s and Richard Hofstadter to the Progressives.[30] A creedal passion period may result when social change is so intense and pervasive that some established social groups have reason to fear an imminent "changed pattern in the distribution of deference and power" *and* when other social groups have reason to think they can and should bring about such a change. In these circumstances, "status politics"—or, better, "cultural politics"—may provide an explanation for "a wide range of behavior for which the economic interpretation of politics seems to be inadequate or misleading or altogether irrelevant."[31]

Fourth, young people appear to have a relatively high group propensity toward moralistic behavior. The extent to which society as a whole seems to become consumed in creedal passion could thus vary with the number of and political influence of youth in the society, which in turn are affected by exogenous events such as wars and economic crises. Much historical evidence suggests that young people have, throughout history, played leading roles in revolutionary movements and political upheavals, and that the appearance of these movements and upheavals may be related to rapid increases in the population between the ages of about fifteen and thirty.[32] The 1960s were distinguished by just such an increase. In 1960, young men between fifteen and twenty-nine made up 19.5 percent of the total male population; in 1970 they made up 24.4 percent of the total, an increase unprecedented in demographic records. The absolute increase—13.8 million—in the youthful population (ages fourteen to twenty-four) during the 1960s was greater than the total increase in the youthful population—12.5 million—during the seventy years prior to 1960.

The available statistics also suggest that the youthful proportion of the population increased significantly, although not nearly as dramatically, between 1880 and 1910. This period, too, was characterized by relatively high levels of protest among college students.[33] The critical demographic factors relating youth to politics could be the absolute size of the youth cohort, its size relative to the rest of the population, or, more likely, its size relative to the immediately preceding cohort. An increase in the number of youth, for instance, is likely to increase interactions within that age cohort and reduce the participation of youth in age-heterogeneous groups. Hence, "societal conditions that intensify age-grading (such as a sudden increase in the size of one age stratum or the prolongation of education with a consequent delay in labor force entry) can thus contribute to potential polarization of the age strata." In a similar vein, James Kurth argued that a significant increase in the size of one cohort relative to that of its predecessor is likely to create a "near-peer bottleneck," in which institutions accustomed to handling a certain number of young people are overwhelmed by dramatic increases in those numbers. The inability of these institutions to deal with this flow could, in turn, encourage youth to turn to social and political protest.[34]

Consciousness Cycle

A cycle is a set of regularly recurring patterns of interactions among variables, in which the interaction pattern at time t_1 is necessary and sufficient to produce the interaction pattern at time t_2, and in which the interaction pattern at time t_n is necessary and sufficient to reproduce the pattern that prevailed at time t_1. A cycle thus involves both regular recurrence and internal self-sufficiency. Major manifestations of creedal passion in American history have occurred at fairly regular intervals of sixty to seventy years. At about the midpoint of these intervals, other significant changes have occurred in political power among major economic interests. The instances are limited but the suggestion of periodicity is strong, and the pattern may well antedate the American Revolution.

No one of the four possible responses to the IvI gap can long be sustained by substantial numbers of people. Recourse to one response tends to generate psychological conditions favorable to the emergence of a different response: moralism eventually elicits cynicism, cynicism produces complacency, complacency leads to hypocrisy, and hypocrisy in due course reinvigorates moralism. Given the regularity in the major manifestations of creedal passion plus the logic of a changing response pattern, one can hypothesize that these manifestations may be a result, at least in part, of a cycle in the workings of American public consciousness.

Although it has not been demonstrated that the *logical* sequence of response describes any *historical* sequence of response, the possible validity of such a hypothesis is reinforced by the frequency with which cycles seem to occur in American politics. Cycles have not generally been characteristic of the ideologically pluralistic, class-based politics of western Europe. In the modern world, they are more likely to be observed in postrevolutionary societies characterized by high levels of ideological consensus. This fundamental consensus defines the limits of change, and the search for change within those basic limits swings from one pole to the other. Post-1949 China, as we noted, was marked by swings back and forth between mobilization and efficiency, the Red Guard and the expert. Somewhat similarly, postrevolutionary Mexican politics since the 1930s has been marked by a very conscious and deliberate alternation of more economically conservative and more socially radical presidencies.

As the consensual society par excellence, American society and its politics have been particularly prone to cyclical interpretations. The American party battle has been interpreted as involving the regular cycle of a critical election, party realignment, the emergence of new majority ("sun") and minority ("moon") parties, establishment of an equilibrium, the gradual undermining of that equilibrium by the emergence of new issues inadequately dealt with by the existing party system, a weakening of established party ties among individuals and groups, and a critical or realigning election that starts the process over again. "American political development in general and political party development in particular," as William Chambers summed it up, "have tended to follow a roughly cyclic pattern."[35] Various observers have also noted the existence of a different, but not necessarily entirely unrelated, reform cycle in American politics at both the local and national level, as well as a cycle in Supreme Court behavior between judicial activism and judicial quietism.[36] Somewhat similarly, Arthur Schlesinger, Sr., perceived "tides" in American politics involving the alternation of liberal and conservative eras, averaging about sixteen years each, while another scholar portrayed a twelve-year cycle of conflict, conscience, and conciliation in the politics of presidential elections.[37] The case has also been made that in America "the history of value change is neither progressive nor regressive, but basically cyclical," with shifts occurring in both long-term cycles of one hundred forty-eight years and short-term cycles of forty-eight years. In another notable study, Frank L. Klingberg persuasively demonstrated the existence of a cycle of introversion and extroversion in American foreign policy.[38] It has also been argued that no significant long-term secular trends exist toward either the opening or the closing of avenues of vertical mobility in the United States, but that instead there have been "substantial, relatively short-term, largely cyclical changes in recruitment" to top leadership positions. Incorporating both foreign and domestic politics, David McClelland suggested that a cycle of reform and war is produced by recurring shifts in the American public's psychological need for Power and the need for Affiliation.[39]

To cite these theories is not necessarily to subscribe to them. What is striking about them, however, is not only that they often seem to have a high degree of "fit" in terms of past historical development but that they may produce reasonably accurate forecasts of the future of American politics. Writing in 1939, for instance, Arthur Schlesinger, Sr., predicted that the post–World War II "recession from liberalism" would end about 1962 "with a possible margin of a year or two in either direction." He also predicted that the "next conservative epoch" in American politics would begin in 1978. Written in 1973, Namenwirth's analysis of his forty-eight-year cycle pointed to the peaking of a parochial value concern with wealth and economic problems in 1980. Writing in 1952, Frank Klingberg confidently and accurately pooh-poohed contemporary fears that the United States would withdraw into isolation in that decade. He also predicted that the twenty-seven-year extroversion phase that had begun in 1940 would come to an end in the mid-1960s, which indeed it did, right on schedule.[40] Not even Lyndon Johnson could break the Klingberg cycle.

Political change in the United States can thus often be usefully and accurately interpreted in cyclical terms, and the existence of a moralism-cynicism-complacency-hypocrisy cycle in American public consciousness would be quite in keeping with these other cyclical patterns found in American politics.

Original Sources:
The Roots of It All in the English Revolution

The Revolutionary experience of the 1770s was the first large-scale, organized assertion of American political principles on a national basis. Sixty to seventy years earlier, however, in the last years of the seventeenth and the first years of the eighteenth century, there had been widespread upheaval and unrest in the British settlements in America. These were the years when English colonies were transformed into American provinces. Underlying this transition was a marked increase in social instability deriving from social mobility and status anxiety—"the downright anxiety of all colonials, regardless of the social and economic position they had attained, as they faced an unsettled present and a thoroughly unpredictable future."[41] The situation was characterized by the emergence of new sources of wealth and power, a new flood of immigrants, efforts by the British government to rationalize and strengthen its control over the North American settlements, and the reactions of the colonists to those efforts. In the north, for instance, the effect of the British attempt to create the Dominion of New England and then of its overthrow "was shattering." In its wake the "vast inclusive framework of the New England mind," which had given order to the seventeenth century, "disintegrated speedily after 1690, and by 1730 was virtually dead."[42]

The shift from colony to province "placed a serious strain upon peoples and institutions. On occasion the strain was great enough to bring about rebellions—in most cases short-lived—and nonviolent but dramatic changes that bordered on revolution."[43] Thirteen of eighteen major uprisings during the colonial period, all of them examples of a "pervasive antiauthoritarianism in colonial America," occurred during the last decades of the seventeenth century "among them the crucial Bacon's, Culpeper's, Leisler's, anti-Andros, and Coode's rebellions." This was an age "when men were not content to let sleeping dogs lie. Fears and suspicions were easily aroused; hatred and anger cut deep into men's souls; and trifling incidents were sufficient to arouse doubt and mistrust. Colonial society at this time was in a ferment and quick to respond to outside forces. . . . During the years from 1676 to 1690 insurrections broke out in nearly all the colonies."⁴⁴

Several of the rebellions were associated with the Glorious Revolution of 1688, but others stemmed from a variety of causes. Most produced or reflected changes in the distribution of power in the colonies, either between the Crown and a colonial elite or from one elite to another. Their aim was "to alter the tight distribution of power and profit from what it had been under the arbitrary claims of the oligarchies during the reigns of Charles and James." As in subsequent creedal passion periods, there were at least two objects of attack: "popery" (the threat of Catholic conspiracy) and "slavery" (the abuses of "arbitrary government"), which ran counter to the inherited rights and liberties of Englishmen. The rebellions of 1688–89 involved the well-off as well as the poor and, as in subsequent periods, the revolutionaries were looking both backward and forward.⁴⁵ Underlying the instability and the efforts at reform was the realization of second- and third-generation Americans that the English social structure from which they were detached was not to be replicated in the New World. All in all, the reconstitution of the colonial societies that took place at the end of the seventeenth century bears many striking resemblances to the realignments of social forces and political institutions that took place in subsequent creedal passion periods. The last years of the seventeenth century were, as Richard Maxwell Brown said, "the first American revolutionary period."⁴⁶

They were not, however, the first revolutionary period. Pursuing the sixty-to-seventy-year periodicity thesis back from the end of the seventeenth century brings us, interestingly enough, precisely to the beginning of the first true revolution of modern times. As Michael Walzer argued, the politics of "power, faction, intrigue" is universal in history, even as the politics of interest groups is ubiquitous in American history. With the rise of Calvinism, however, there appeared for the first time a "politics of party organization and methodical activity, opposition and reform, radical ideology and revolution."[47] At this point the history of reform and revolution begins. The desire to reconstitute political and social institutions, to remake society in the image of the ideal, appears on the scene.

In more extreme, dramatic, and revolutionary form, the English Revolution furnished the model for the subsequent manifestations of creedal passion in American politics. The immediate causes of that revolution are found in the efforts of the Crown between 1629 and 1640 to reestablish its power and that of the Church. The issues that were at stake between Crown and Parliament, Episcopacy and Puritans, William Laud and John Pym were not primarily economic and social but rather political, ideological, constitutional, and religious. "The fiscal policies of the 1630s caused formidable opposition, not because royal taxation was particularly oppressive to any class of society—indeed it was quite certainly lighter than anywhere else in Europe—but because the money was levied in an unconstitutional and arbitrary manner, and was used for purposes which many taxpayers regarded as immoral."[48]

In the 1630s, as in creedal passion periods in America, efforts were made to centralize and rationalize authority and to increase the efficiency of government and its ability to penetrate and direct society. The gentry and peers who had exercised influence under the Tudors and even during the reign of James I found their access to power increasingly curtailed. As in the subsequent periods, these developments provoked a reaction. The components for this reaction had, in turn, been produced by and strengthened by previous processes of economic development and social change; the general growth in discrepancies in access to status, power, and wealth; the expansion of literacy and of higher education; the availability of the Bible in English; and the overproduction of educated men in relation to available jobs.[49]

The English Revolution was thus in some measure both a rational response to the attempt by Charles I and Archbishop Laud to strengthen the Crown and the Church and also a product of exogenous economic, social, and cultural developments. It had many other characteristics of a creedal passion period. Since the primary issues at stake were basically political and religious, not social and economic, the lines of cleavage did not divide society along economic class lines, but rather along lines of religion, age, and political access. "Every order of society, every kind of occupation, was represented in considerable numbers on both sides," noted Austin Woolrych. "Puritanism was not just a religion of townsmen, for it ramified through every order of society. It enjoyed wide support among the landed gentry, from affluent knights down to depressed squireens, and its converts were certainly not restricted to the minority of landowners who shared in the entrepreneurial activities of the merchants. At least a fifth of the peers were Puritan in 1640, and so, at the other end of the scale, were thousands of small craftsmen and work-people who were not so much the exploiters of rising capitalism as its victims."[50] When it came to arms, the English Revolution, like the American, "did not merely fissure the landed classes right down the middle, it also split families apart, father against son and brother against brother: one in every seven peerage families was fragmented by war."[51] As in later creedal passion periods, the moral onslaught was directed at twin targets: first the bishops, and then the court and the Crown. The vision of the reformer was also Janus-faced—looking forward, in apocalyptic terms, to "the planting," in Stephen Marshall's words, "of a new heaven and new earth among us" and also to the reconstitution of traditional rights and privileges.

Of central importance to the revolution was the word and the passion behind the word. This derived from the Puritan emphasis on the primacy of the individual conscience and hence on the need to communicate to and guide that conscience on the road to salvation. Puritanism was a preaching religion; the Puritan divines "conceived of themselves as a ministry dedicated to preaching the Word of God, rather than as a priesthood whose prime function was to celebrate the sacraments."[52] As in subsequent creedal passion periods, the reach of the media expanded immensely and took new forms, most notably the widespread circulation of the English Bible, the delivery of sermons and their circulation along with other statements in pamphlet form, and the appearance of weekly newsletters produced by "the first professional journalists." Puritanism was, as Lawrence Stone suggested, something of a cultural revolution and a revolution in which the ideas and doctrines were pressed with passion. Intense moralism was the essence of Puritanism. "The quintessential quality of a Puritan was not the acceptance of any given body of doctrine, but a driving enthusiasm for moral improvement in every aspect of life, 'a holy violence in the performing of all duties.' "[53] The theological and political ideas of the Puritans were not necessarily either terribly sophisticated or terribly original, but although they "may (or may not) be second-hand," as Christopher Hill put it, "the passion behind them is not." When creedal passion reached its peak in the late 1640s, there was a great overturning, questioning, revaluing, of everything in England. Old institutions, old beliefs, old values came in question. Men moved easily from one critical group to another, and a Quaker of the early 1650s had far more in common with a Leveller, a Digger or a Ranter than with a modern member of the Society of Friends. . . . There was a period of glorious flux and intellectual excitement, when, as Gerrard Winstanley put it, 'the old world . . . is running up like parchment in the fire.' Literally everything seemed possible; not only were the values of the old hierarchical society called in question but also the new values, the protestant ethic itself. . . . What was new in the seventeenth century was the idea that the world might be *permanently* turned upside down.[54]

The English Revolution ended with a restoration. The king, Crown, Lords, court, bishops, and Anglicanism reappeared in full splendor on English soil. "Milton's nation of prophets became a nation of shop-keepers."[55] Puritanism, which had appealed to people in all strata of society before the revolution, came to have a restricted appeal to a much narrower segment of society after the revolution. The nonconformist strand of the English political-religious tradition went through various Methodist, Radical, and Labour reincarnations in the following centuries, but the radicalism it inherited from the English Revolution was bottled up, contained, limited to particular classes, regions, and sects. In America, on the other hand, Puritan radicalism spread and diffused to become the core of a credo for a new society. England had a Puritan revolution without creating a Puritan society; America created a Puritan society without enduring a Puritan revolution. England became a society of stable cleavage; America one of unstable consensus, where the gap between the "city upon a hill" and the city in the valley recreated the conditions for further efforts to realize the Puritan goals of the English Revolution.

The Puritan Revolution was a unique event in English history, but it was also a prototypical event for American history. The anguish, the moralism, the passion, the reform conscience, and the exhilaration of that revolution were manifested again and again on American soil in the upheavals in the colonies at the end of the seventeenth century, in the American Revolution, and in the subsequent creedal passion periods of American history. In 1641, for instance, a Puritan minister, Thomas Case, preaching before the Commons articulated the reform spirit as follows:

> Reformation must be universal . . . Reform all places, all persons and callings; reform the benches of judgment, the inferior magis-

trates . . . Reform the universities, reform the cities, reform the countries, reform inferior schools of learning, reform the Sabbath, reform the ordinances, the worship of God . . . You have more work to do than I can speak . . . Every plant which my heavenly father hath not planted shall be rooted up.[56]

Compare this with Emerson's summary precisely two hundred years later of the reform spirit sweeping America in 1841:

In the history of the world the doctrine of Reform had never such scope as at the present hour. Lutherans, Hernhutters, Jesuits, Monks, Quakers, Knox, Wesley, Swedenborg, Bentham, in their accusations of society, all respected something—church or state, literature or history, domestic usages, the market town, the dinnertable, coined money. But now all these and all things else hear the trumpet, and must rush to judgment,—Christianity, the laws, commerce, schools, the farm, the laboratory; and not a kingdom, town, statute, rite, calling, man, or woman, but is threatened by the new spirit.[57]

The spirit of Thomas Case, the Puritan legacy of the English Revolution, is permanently lodged deep in the American consciousness. Periodically, once every second generation, it reemerges to implant its mark of conscience on the otherwise placid and materialistic surface of American politics. At these times, the American nation of shopkeepers again becomes a nation of prophets. The origins of American politics are to be found in the English Puritan Revolution. That revolution is, in fact, the single most important formative event of American political history.

The Protestantism of American Politics

The Intermingling of Religion and Politics

As the decisive religious and political event of the early seventeenth century, the Puritan Revolution was the original source both of the close intermingling of religion and politics that characterized subsequent American history and of the moral passion that has powered the engines of political change in America. Not only was America born equal and hence did not have to become so, but it was also born Protestant and hence did not have to become so. In America, wrote the German theologian Philip Schaff in 1853, "everything had a Protestant beginning."[58] American Protestantism consequently was "constructive Protestantism," in the sense that it was devoted not to the dismantling of Catholicism but to the construction of a new, unspoiled, Protestant society in a virgin land, which, Puritans believed, God had saved from European discovery until they were ready to use it for His purposes.[59]

These origins also explain both the pluralism of religious bodies and the pervasiveness of religious beliefs in America. In the early colonies, church and state were often closely linked. The multiplication of colonies and of churches, however, precluded the creation of a national religious establishment; eventually the identity between church and state broke down, even in the Massachusetts Bay Puritan theocracy. By the nineteenth century, established churches had given way to the separation of church and state and to the continuing proliferation of churches, sects, denominations, and other religious bodies. This proliferation was the product of the nature of Protestantism as a movement. American Protestantism produced no significant theologian between Jonathan Edwards and Reinhold Niebuhr, but it renewed itself continually. America is unique in the world in the number of religious bodies to which it has given birth since the early seventeenth century. This religious fecundity is a product of the extent to which American society has been overwhelmingly Protestant. New churches and movements were founded to dissent from or to protest against those that had been founded earlier. "Protestantism in its many varieties is not the product or carrier of a single protest against one order of religious and political life; it represents rather a whole series of protests directed against many successive orders of Christian faith and against their political guarantors."[60] Each generation saw the formation of new groups and a reordering of groups according to their size. In this context, the Catholic church was not an established presence that Protestants challenged, but rather came "in afterwards as one sect among others, and has always remained subordinate."[61]

The multiplicity of religious groups has been matched by the pervasiveness of religious beliefs among Americans. The widespread practice of religion and of adherence to religious beliefs has been noted by foreign observers since the eighteenth century and is also attested to by the available figures on church membership and attendance. "There is no country in the world," Tocqueville observed, "where the Christian religion retains a greater influence over the souls of men than in America."[62] In the late twentieth century, this judgment still held true. Although figures suggest that the level of religious involvement and the extent of religious practice (such as church attendance) may vary from time to time, until the late twentieth century they did not show any long-term decline in religious commitment among the American public. Americans generally manifested a significantly higher level of religious commitment than did other peoples. Members of religious bodies in America appeared to attend church more frequently than members of the same bodies elsewhere. Twice as many Americans said that their religious beliefs were very important to them as did people in most other industrialized societies. Ninety-four percent of Americans said that they believed in God—a considerably higher proportion than in other societies. (See Table 4.)

Table 4. Religious commitment in the 1970s.

	Religious beliefs very important[a]	Believe in God[b]	Believe in life after death[c]
United States	58%	94%	71%
Canada	36	89	54
Italy	36	88	46
Benelux	26	78	48
Australia	25	80	48
United Kingdom	23	76	43
France	22	72	39
West Germany	17	72	33
Scandinavia	17	65	35
Japan	14	44	18

Source: Surveys in 1974–75 by Gallup International Research Institute for non-U.S. countries and in 1978 by the American Institute of Public Opinion (Gallup), Princeton Religion Research Center, and the Gallup Organization, Inc., for the United States. Reported in *Public Opinion* 2 (March/May 1979): 38–39.
   a. Question asked: "How important are your religious beliefs—very important, fairly important, not too important, or not at all important?"
   b. Question asked: "Do you believe in God or a universal spirit?"
   c. Question asked: "Do you believe in life after death? Do you believe that there is life after death?"

A substantial consensus thus exists among Americans on a few core religious beliefs comparable to that which exists among Americans on the core political ideas of the American Creed. Why should Americans, almost uniquely among modern peoples, manifest such a commitment to religion? The sources lie, in large part, in the nature of the original Protestant religious inheritance. The plurality of sects and the resulting separation of state and church significantly weakened the state but strengthened religion. As a voluntary association, each church and sect had no alternative but to enlist all the energies of its members in its development and expansion. Most of the Protestant sects were committed to active preaching and proselytizing. They had a missionary mission aimed at conversion and regeneration. "Free and powerful in its own sphere, satisfied with the place reserved for it, religion never more surely establishes its empire than when it reigns in the hearts of men unsupported by aught besides its native strength."[63] The ease with which new sects could be founded, moreover, meant that church organization, doctrine, ritual, and functions could be almost infinitely varied to meet the needs of particular ethnic, social, economic, and geographic groups. Each sect thus tended to have its own constituency, and hence the vigorous *pursuit of* members did not translate into equally intense *competition for* members. Instead, almost all sects shared a general commitment to basic Protestant moral values and good works and emphasized the central role of morality in their preaching, causing Tocqueville to marvel at the extent to which ministers of one church often preached in other churches. The explanation, he found, was that in Protestant churches, "you will hear morality preached, of dogma not a word . . . The different preachers, treating only the common ground of morality, cannot do each other any harm."[64] The Protestant emphasis on morality and good works rather than on theology and doctrine made it easier for people to adhere to a generalized religious code, without necessarily, if they did not wish to, becoming committed to the deeper and more esoteric doctrines and practices of particular creeds.

The plurality of religious organizations and the pervasiveness of religious beliefs led to a distinctive relation between religion and politics. In Europe, a single universal church historically coexisted with a plurality of nations. During the Reformation, many of these nations established their own national churches. In America, however, a single universal nation has coexisted with a plurality of churches. From the start, the religious aims of the churches overlapped with and reinforced the political aims of the emerging nation. American revolutionaries of 1776 did not have to react against and challenge an established church supporting the established political order. Hence, unlike the French revolutionaries of 1789, they did not need a secular religion. All could adhere to a generalized religious religion, to the extent that "even the atheists in America speak in a religious key."[65]

The plurality of religious organizations and the pervasiveness of religious belief produced three forms of intermingling between religion and politics.

First, seventeenth-century Protestantism was the source of many of the ideas in the Creed, particularly those related to the central role of the individual conscience. The generalized religious values that were shared first by the Protestant sects, then by Catholic and Protestant churches, and still later by Jewish and Orthodox churches, easily fused with the national political beliefs. In the nineteenth century, "secular life was suffused with a pan-Protestant ideology that claimed to be civic and universal. Pledged to leave private beliefs undisturbed, it was vague enough so that increasing numbers of Jews and Catholics could embrace it. But it infused a generalized piety in school textbooks and civic oratory."[66] The congruence of religious and political values was most notable in the extent to which both reinforced the commitment to democracy and the primacy of the individual conscience. Protestantism in America was "a democratic and republican religion," and this contributed powerfully to "the establishment of a republic and democracy in public affairs." Religious influences have played key roles in shaping the ideas and the semantics of American politics, as shown by the prevalence of such terms as "dirty politics," "the good man," "the moral issue," the "change of heart," and "the crusade."[67]

Second, the absence of any particular established state or national religion opened the way for the direct incorporation of many of the ideas and symbols of generalized religion into American political behavior. Just as the national flag is a symbol found in almost all American churches, so is God found in almost all American national rites and ceremonies. The declaration of their birth assures Americans that they are endowed by their Creator with unalienable rights; Americans pledge their allegiance to one nation "under God"; they proclaim their trust in God on their currency; they are told by their Supreme Court justices that their institutions presuppose a Supreme Being; their public ceremonies invariably begin with an invocation by a clergyman from one religion and end with a benediction by a clergyman from another. Nowhere else in the world are church and state more firmly separated institutionally and religious and political ideas and symbols more closely interwoven in national beliefs.

Third, because national identity is defined in terms of a set of political ideals, the national Creed and the political practices related to it also perform some religious functions. The plurality of sects ensured that all sects would be particularistic and that none could plausibly serve as the instrument for realizing God's purposes on earth. In the absence of a national church, the nation and its political Creed came to serve as a civil religion. Americans bestowed on the nation "a catholicity of destiny similar to that which theology attributes to the universal church" and came to view it as "the primary agent of God's meaningful activity in history."[68]

The result was to give the nation many of the attributes and functions of a church. The United States is, indeed, as G. K. Chesterton said, "a nation with the soul of a church." Fifty years later another European observer could also observe, "You don't have a country over there, you have a huge church."[69] The point is well taken. Just as Americanism as an ideology is a substitute for socialism, at the same time that it incorporates some socialist values, so Americanism as a creed constitutes a national civil religion. The United States, Chesterton said, "is founded on a creed" that "is set forth with dogmatic and theological lucidity in the Declaration of Independence." The Declaration and the Constitution constitute the holy scripture of the American civil religion. Their basic messages have been elaborated and extended in the addresses and sayings of American leaders. The essence of the Creed was succinctly summarized in the "American's Creed" in obvious imitation of that of the Apostles:

> I believe in the United States of America as a Government of the people, by the people, for the people; whose just powers are derived from the consent of the governed; a democracy in a republic; a sovereign Nation of many sovereign States; a perfect union, one and inseparable; established upon those principles of freedom, equality, justice, and humanity for which American patriots sacrified their lives and fortunes. I therefore believe it is my duty to my country to love it; to support its Constitution; to obey its laws; to respect its flag, and to defend it against all enemies.

Little wonder that D. W. Brogan should comment wonderingly on the use of this Creed in the schools in early-twentieth-century America: "Little boys and girls, in a school from which religion in the old sense is barred, solemnly rising each morning and reciting together the 'American's Creed' are performing a religious exercise as truly as if they began the day with "I believe in God the Father Almighty' or asserted that 'There is no God but God.' "[70] Like other religions, the American civil religion has its hymns and its sacred ceremonies, its prophets and its martyrs. It also has its mission: to create "a city on a hill," "the last best hope of earth," and to bring about a "new heaven and new earth" through its "errand in the wilderness" of the world. The "religion of the Republic," Sidney Mead said, "is essentially prophetic,"[71] and it is this Protestant sense of mission that has furnished the dynamic motive force of American politics.

Great Awakenings and Creedal Passion

The Puritan Revolution bequeathed to the American people the belief that they were engaged in a righteous effort to ensure the triumph of good over evil and thus to realize God's will on earth. "No truth is more patent in American history than the fact that this nation is an Old Testament people."[72] Religion was the source of the morality that required the saving of souls on the one hand and the regeneration of society on the other. Each was possible; both were necessary. Passive acceptance of the gap between what should be and what is is intolerable for both the individual and the community. The gap is evil; to condone it is sinful; duty demands moral action to eliminate it. Throughout American history, the principal efforts to achieve these goals have taken the form of religious and political revivals—great awakenings and creedal passion periods.

In the Puritan Revolution, religion and politics were inseparable. In subsequent American history, the religious and political manifestations of the Puritan passion took distinct forms. Yet it surely cannot be a coincidence that the four major creedal passion periods in American political history have been matched by what historians of religion have identified as the four great awakenings of the religious spirit. In addition, while great awakenings are no more subject to precise dating than creedal passion periods, it does appear that each great awakening began a decade or more before the flame-up of creedal passion and then often overlapped with it. The First Great Awakening swept through the colonies in the 1730s and 1740s; the second began in the first years of the nineteenth century and lasted until about 1830; the third began about 1890 and continued into the first decade of the twentieth century; the fourth originated in the late 1950s.[73] Distinct though they may be, the expressions of religious fervor and of creedal passion share similar characteristics and stem from similar sources. As the chronology suggests, they may also be linked to one another in a causal pattern, in which the passion for reform is first directed to the conversion of the individual and then to the reformation of society.

The parallels between great awakenings and creedal passion periods are striking and have not gone unnoted. An awakening or major religious revival can only occur in situations where large numbers of people have previously committed themselves to religious beliefs and in which "backsliding" from those beliefs has become evident. Awakenings are "a *revitalizing* of religion, a repeat performance . . . They do not introduce religon into a region . . . It is simply impossible to have a revival unless there is some institutional and ideational framework that has provided a meaningful context for the revival in the first place."[74] The great awakenings, as a leading scholar put it, occurred when "by the standards of our culture core and the experiences of daily life, our society deviated too far from the moral and religious understandings that legitimized authority in church and state." They were ways "to overcome jarring disjunctions between norms and experience, old beliefs and new realities, dying patterns and emerging patterns of behavior." The awakenings resulted in drastic "restructuring" of "social, political, and economic institutions" and propelled Americans into wars "to speed up the fulfillment of their manifest destiny."[75] The dynamics of the First Great Awakening involved "a public rhetoric able to exploit subconscious feelings of guilt and dependency that were weakly defended against by a hedonistic indifference in the young, or that were easily reactivated in older persons who had externally committed themselves to the evangelical framework but had grown conventional in their piety." The awakening thus required a society in which a gap existed between "religious norms and authority" that had been internalized and "ordinary behavior" that "did not match the accepted injunctions."[76] Revivals were thus one way of dealing with cognitive dissonance at the individual level, securing the forgiveness of past sins, and recommitting errant wanderers to the way of the Lord.

In this respect, awakenings served the same function for Americans individually that creedal passion periods did for Americans collectively. Efforts to reform masses of individuals and efforts to reform society as a whole have similar effects. The American Revolution "was not so much the result of reasoned thought as an emotional outburst similar to a religious revival." It involved an "evangelical Revolutionary impulse, like that of the Great Awakening."[77] In attempting to portray its true significance in American history, one historian has described the Great Awakening of the 1740s as resembling "the civil rights demonstrations, the campus disturbances, and the urban riots of the 1960s combined. All together these may approach, though certainly not surpass, the Awakening in their impact on national life." This was seconded by another religious historian who, in reverse direction, characterized the 1960s "as another Great Awakening which also left the human landscape profoundly changed. In the realm where values, hopes, fears, and cosmological attitudes are shaped, the period was profoundly disturbing."[78]

The immediate sources of great awakenings are similar to and as diverse as those of creedal passion periods. At least five major explanations have been advanced for the First Great Awakening—rapid social change, ideological polarization, western expansion, increased British influence, and class conflict—all of which can, in some sense, be subsumed under the general heading of "changing structures of authority and power."[79] Areas of rapid economic change were often centers of religious revival. During almost half a century of rapid economic development in eastern Connecticut, for instance, land and money were avidly pursued. This generated high levels of "personal instability" and guilt, which then made the area a major center of the First Great Awakening. That awakening was the response of the evangelical mind "to the emergence in colonial America of disparities of wealth, as well as ways of life unknown to earlier, and presumably purer, generations."[80]

In somewhat similar fashion, the intense manifestation of the Second Great Awakening in the "burned-over" district of western New York has been attributed to the broad-gauged economic development of that region, the central feature of which was the building of the Erie Canal. Religious enthusiasm was most intense in those areas of the district in which economic growth had leveled off and stabilized and which had reached "a stage of economy either of full or of closely approaching agrarian maturity."[81] More generally, the Second Great Awakening has been interpreted as a result of the intensification of social strains and dislocations caused by economic development and geographic expansion. The "explosion of religious energy in 1800 was an overt expression of social discontent and political aspiration."[82] The Third and Fourth Great Awakenings, too, followed periods of intense economic development which produced social strains, status insecurity among many groups, and new perceptions of massive deviations in individual behavior from the straight and narrow path.

The awakenings furnished the means of relieving psychological stresses and strains through the experience of conversion. Just as the moralism of creedal passion periods derived from the desire to return to the basic ideals of the American Creed, so the religious fervor of the awakenings derived from the desire to return to the basic teachings of the Bible. People who had internalized highly demanding religious norms came to bear an increasing burden of guilt as their behavior deviated from those norms. The preachers of the awakenings forced people to confront their sinfulness and inevitable damnation. "This confrontation of guilt, the first part of conversion, drove men to despair," as one account of the First

Great Awakening described it, "but the revivalists did not leave their hearers there to suffer. By publicly identifying the sources of guilt and condemning them, the preachers also helped to heal the wounds they first inflicted. Converts were persuaded that by acknowledging and repudiating their old sins, they were no longer culpable. The reborn man was as joyful and loving when the process was completed as he was miserable at its start."[83] Young people were, the revivalists argued, particularly susceptible to the appeals of this process and hence played disproportionate roles in the First Great Awakening as well as in its successors.[84] The "political radicalization" of creedal passion periods is the secular equivalent of the conversion experience that people go through in the awakenings.

Each great awakening witnessed the polarization between those who had seen the light and those who had not. The division in the First Great Awakening between New Side and Old Side Presbyterians and between New Light and Old Light Congregationalists was repeated in later awakenings, paralleling the division in creedal passion periods between "the Movement" and "the Establishment." As in creedal passion periods, those within each denomination who experienced the religious awakening were drawn from diverse sources. In the First Great Awakening "people from all ranks of society, of all ages, and from every section underwent the new birth. In New England virtually every congregation was touched."[85] The division cut across the usual lines of class and status. "The parties and debates of eighteenth-century American religion simply will not yield to the categories of Marx and Beard, for the reason that the fundamental post-Awakening division was an intellectual one—one more aesthetic, in fact, than economic or social . . . What distinguished Americans, so far as the 'great debate' of the eighteenth century was concerned, were differences not of income but, in substance, of taste."[86] And differences in taste corresponded sociologically only with differences in age. Just as the success of reform has often been dependent upon reformers with powerful personalities, so has conversion been the product of powerful revivalists: George Whitefield, Charles Grandison Finney, Billy Sunday, and Billy Graham, to mention only the most outstanding preacher of each awakening.

Each great awakening involved mass proselytizing, often, as in creedal passion periods, accompanied by widespread reliance on new forms of mass communication and persuasion. The great evangelists were also great innovators in the techniques of mass mobilization. Before the mid-eighteenth century, religion was a local phenomenon, rooted in the small community of minister, church, congregation, and parish. The First Great Awakening, however, was marked by the key role played by itinerant preachers, who made religion more universal and more individualistic and less of a community phenomenon.[87] The oral techniques and rhetorical styles of the awakening were then adapted to extend to the masses the revolutionary appeals of the 1770s.[88] In the Second Great Awakening, Finney and others expanded and refined the techniques of the camp meeting and the use of "vigorous advertising methods" to arouse interest and participation. At the end of the century, Dwight Moody became the first revivalist to make extensive use of newspapers and billboards, to organize and train "ushers, choir, counselors, and prayer meeting leaders," and to develop the methods of mass solicitation necessary to fund these efforts. These techniques were more fully developed and expanded in the Fourth Great Awakening, but the decisive factor in that awakening, reaching tens of millions of Americans, was skillful exploitation, most notably by Billy Graham, of the new medium of television. The awakening and television developed simultaneously during the 1950s.[89]

The awakenings were also characterized by mass organizing. Between 1740 and 1760, one hundred fifty new churches were founded in New England and between thirty thousand and forty thousand new church members were added to the rolls. In the Second Great Awakening, the success of the Methodists and Baptists were due primarily not to their theology or doctrine but to the means they developed and employed for mobilizing and organizing people. The legacy of the Second Great Awakening in Oneida County, New York, for instance, consisted of the "Mormon Church, several Adventist denominations, two species of Methodism, and a sprinkling of spiritualist groups."[90] Each awakening gave a new impulse to the proliferation of religious organizations. New sects were formed. Old ones divided and became stronger as a result of the division. As H. Richard Niebuhr suggested, the development of American Protestantism can be interpreted in terms of successive waves of protest against the existing establishment—waves that make church history "one of many reformations" and that reach their peak in the formation of new churches during the years of the awakenings. These waves of "reformation, regeneration, awakening, and renewal" are directed "not against the authority of the old, but against its acceptance and establishment of a mediocre form of men's moral and religious existence."[91]

In theory, success in the reform of the individual could remove any need for the collective, purposeful reform of society, and several great evangelists opposed social and political reforms precisely on the ground that they were not directed to the regeneration of the individual soul.[92] In fact, however, the great awakenings did not just resemble creedal passion periods; they also preceded them, overlapped with them, and, particularly in the earlier years, contributed to them ideas, techniques, people, and passion. In the eighteenth and nineteenth centuries, the religious enthusiasm of the awakenings was easily converted into the political enthusiasm for reform. The ideological and political roots of the American Revolution lay at least as much in the evangelical Calvinism of the First Great Awakening as in the liberal rationalism of the Enlightenment. "What the colonies had awakened to in 1740," Alan Heimert said, "was none other than independence and rebellion." Another scholar wrote that "the roots of the Revolution as a political movement were so deeply imbedded in the soil of the First Great Awakening forty years earlier that it can be truly said that the Revolution was the natural outgrowth of that profound and widespread religious movement."[93] The Second Great Awakening has been called the American "Revolution at work in religion" and the "second American revolution, inward and spiritual . . . evangelical and revivalist."[94] The great reform surges of the Jacksonian years, most notably the temperance and abolitionist movements, were, in turn, religion at work in politics. Throughout the nineteenth century, revivalism was a major source of social reform.[95] By the end of the century, however, the connection between the Third Great Awakening and the reform drives of the Progressive era had become more tenuous than it had been in previous outbreaks of religious and political passion. The Puritan ethic was a significant factor in the movements for woman suffrage and prohibition, but neither of these reforms reflected the interests of the growing masses of urban workers.[96] The roads to individual salvation and societal reform began to diverge.

This divergence became even clearer in the 1950s and 1960s. Many similarities exist between the religious revival of the 1950s and 1960s and the creedal passion of the 1960s and 1970s, and religious leaders and religious groups—most notably in Martin Luther King and the Southern Christian Leadership Conference—played a central role in the development and the success of the civil rights movement. Yet clearly the main thrust of the fourth awakening was not in the direction of the social and political reforms that came to the top of the political agenda. The similarities between Billy Graham and Ralph Nader are clear; the direct connection between them is not. They do nonetheless have common roots in the same Protestant moral passion, which will not tolerate a gap between the ideals of what ought to be and the realities that are.

In America, the ideas of liberty and equality are compatible in a way that contrasts with their stormy opposition in European history. So also in America, religion and politics, religious campaigns and political crusades, have historically reinforced each other despite, and perhaps in part because of, the constitutional and institutional separation of church and state. The passion of the Puritan Revolution has reappeared in periodic religious and political surges that interact with one another, stemming from the same sources, taking comparable forms, mobilizing similar groups, and producing parallel consequences. People aroused about the need to reform themselves are also easily aroused about the need to reform society. And during the periods of great awakening and creedal passion, neither the individual nor the institution that falls short of the prescribed norms can expect to escape their holy terror. In America, the common sources of religious and political belief give political relevance to religion and add religious passion to politics.

7 THE S&S YEARS, 1960–1975

From the Fifties to the Seventies: The Changing Pattern of Response

The high points of historical eras are usually clearly visible. Any historian will feel relatively comfortable in identifying the years when the Renaissance was at its peak, or the Age of Absolutism, or the Victorian era. The starting and ending points of eras, however, are often lost in the complexity, ambiguity, and incrementalism of history. So is it also with the "era of sixes and sevens," or the "S&S Years," which constitute America's fourth major creedal passion period since independence.* The high point of that era was clearly between 1968 and 1971. But when did

---

* The problem of what to call this period is a difficult one. People often refer to "the sixties," but the era also extended well into the seventies. One could speak of "the early sixties to the mid-seventies," but that is unusably cumbersome. Alternatively, we could call it the age of protest, or of outrage, or of exposure, but each of these catches only one aspect of the period and each aspect was also characteristic of other creedal passion periods. If one accepts the argument of this book, one could label 1960–1975 simply "the Fourth Period." That, however, suggests the closing moments of an athletic contest, and, more importantly, it denies these years an independent label and identity of their own (comparable to the labels "Revolutionary," "Jacksonian," and "Progressive") apart from their being one in a series of similar phases. In an effort to come up with a succinct name that will accommodate these various considerations, I have opted for "the era of sixes and sevens" or, more briefly, "the S&S Years," for both numerological and characterological reasons. First, this name does suggest the sixties and seventies. Second, according to *The Oxford English Dictionary*, "sixes and sevens" refers to "the creation or existence of, or neglect to remove, confusion, disorder or disagreement"—a not unreasonable summary of what happened during these years.

it begin and when did it end? Sometime in the late fifties or early sixties? Sometime in the middle or late seventies? Any particular starting and terminal points can serve only symbolic purposes. Yet it is also useful and potentially enlightening for such purposes to be served, and appropriate symbolic starting and ending points for the fourth creedal passion period can be identified with some precision.

The S&S Years began February 1, 1960, when four black college freshmen entered a Woolworth's in Greensboro, North Carolina, sat down at the lunch counter, asked for coffee, were refused service, and stayed seated. The Fourth Period ended almost exactly sixteen years later on January 29, 1976, when the House of Representatives voted 246 to 124 not to release the report of its Select Committee on Intelligence until that report had been cleared by the White House. The Greensboro sit-in began the politics of protest that constituted the first part of the S&S Years; the House vote marked the end of the politics of exposure that dominated the last part. The period began in that area of American life where the gap between democratic ideals and behavioral reality was most marked, and it achieved its most dramatic public policy result in effectively ending government sponsorship and toleration of racial discrimination in America. The dominant tone of the period was set in the late sixties and early seventies in the pervasive, unrelenting questioning of and opposition to authority in almost any form, reaching a peak in August 1974 with the "killing of the king"—the deposition of the central authority figure in American politics, who had been elected to office less than two years earlier by an overwhelming popular vote. It concluded many months later with the exposure of the workings of the country's intelligence agencies, where the contrast between American values of openness and democratic control and the requirements of secrecy and deception was most marked. The desegregation of a society, the resignation of a President, and the dismantling of an intelligence system stand as eloquent testimony to the at least partial effectiveness of the period's assault on inequality, authority, hierarchy, and secrecy.

Between 1960 and 1976 American politics was characterized by an intensity and emotionalism found only in earlier phases of creedal passion. During these years most of the major actors on the political scene were largely, if not entirely, moralistically responding to the dissonance produced by the IvI gap in American politics. Yet complacency, hypocrisy, and cynicism also had their roles to play. The relative importance of each of these responses changed over time, due to changes in people's perceptions of the extent of the IvI gap and to changes in the intensity of their commitment to American ideals. From the mid-1950s to the late-1970s, American responses to the IvI gap moved through the cycle that we earlier identified as the logical pattern for them to follow. This progression can also be related to changing dominant attitudes toward governmental authority and toward governmental action to solve problems. (See Table 5.) The S&S Years thus began in complacency and ended in cynicism. In

Table 5. The sequence of responses in the S&S Years.

Prevalent attitude toward governmental action	Prevalent attitude toward governmental authority	
	Con	Pro
Pro	Mid-sixties to mid-seventies moralism	Early sixties hypocrisy
Con	Late seventies cynicism	Mid-late fifties complacency

between they were dominated by intense moralism. Almost all of the characteristic features found in American creedal passion periods manifested themselves, leaving consequences for the operation of the American political system that would be felt for years into the future.

Complacency and the End (?) of Ideology

The middle and late 1950s were predominantly years of complacency. After the bitter divisions over McCarthyism and the Korean War in the early 1950s, Eisenhower achieved in actuality what he said he wanted to achieve: "an atmosphere of greater serenity and mutual confidence."[1] Americans at that time were generally supportive of governmental authority and also saw little or no reason for either more government or more active government. The prevailing atmosphere was one of contentment and satisfaction. Until the very end of the decade, the gap between ideals and institutions was not clearly perceived and people did not feel intensely committed to the realization of American political values. Those values were, as Daniel Boorstin put it in the mid-1950s, "given by certain facts of geography or history peculiar to us." Americans historically tended "to confound the 'ought' and the 'is,' " and American values were implicit in American institutions. "What one could build on this continent tended to become the criterion of what one ought to build here."[2] In Boorstin's view, environment, institutions, and values were all part of one seamless web: a dramatic and violent contrast between institutions and ideals was precisely what American history lacked.

Concerns about the concentration and abuse of power were at the far margins of American consciousness during these years of creedal passivity in the 1950s. The prevailing image of American politics combined the consensus and organizational pluralism paradigms. Consensus existed and was good. Power existed in a plurality of large organizations—veto groups —that at times made governmental action difficult but also made the serious abuse of governmental power extremely unlikely. What is more, in a brief but notable inversion of the traditional American approach, thinkers in the 1950s became intrigued with the idea that large organization in itself could be good. Big business was more responsible, more enlightened, more likely to act in the public interest than small business. Small businessmen, indeed, were much more likely than big businessmen to be narrow-minded, prejudiced, avaricious, and supporters of Senator Joseph McCarthy. Large-scale organization was not merely accepted; it was defended and justified, and many of its most significant apologists were veterans of the New Deal. "The growth of large organizations," Seymour Martin Lipset suggested, may "actually have the more important consequences of providing new sources of continued freedom and more opportunity to innovate."[3] Opposition to large-scale organization, big corporations, concentrated power, and militarism was relegated to the extreme left and right of the political spectrum. A scholar like C. Wright Mills could publish an eloquent and passionate exposé titled *The Power Elite,* but it would have to wait for another decade before it found its audience. In the meantime, Americans believed in consensus and pluralism as both facts and values.

Reflecting this complacency, political alienation in America reached a low point in the 1950s. The responses of the public with respect to three key questions designed to measure alienation showed significantly less alienation in 1956 than in 1952 and less in 1960 than in 1956. From 1960 on, however, the trend reversed itself, with alienation increasing steadily during the 1960s and early 1970s.[4] The end of the fifties, in short, witnessed the peak of Americans' satisfaction with and identification of their political system. It is hardly surprising that when asked in 1960 of what aspects of their country they felt proud, some 85 percent of the American public mentioned their governmental and political institutions.

The atmosphere of the 1950s prompted intellectuals to argue that the decline or end of ideology was occurring. This idea, stimulated originally by post–World War II developments in Western Europe, became the conventional wisdom of the Western intellectual world following a major conference in 1955 of intellectual and political figures from democratic countries. The outstanding discovery of the conference was that the differences between the left and the right had narrowed and that the two had much in common, particularly when confronted by the challenge posed by Soviet communism. Ideology and ideological combat were seen to be disappearing from democratic politics as a result of "the fact that the fundamental political problems of the industrial revolution have been solved: the workers have achieved industrial and political citizenship; the conservatives have accepted the welfare state; and the democratic left has recognized that an increase in over-all state power carries with it more dangers to freedom than solutions for economic problems."[5] More specifically, the phrase "the end—or decline—of ideology" was used to refer to: (1) the elimination of both fascism (through defeat in war) and, less conclusively, communism (by its identification with the Soviet Union) as viable options in a democratic society; (2) the general decline in intellectual and public discussion of broad ideological alternatives, political theories, far-reaching goals, and utopias; (3) the narrowing of the political distance—in terms of policies and programs—between the major parties in democratic societies; and (4) the weakening of the correlation between socioeconomic class and voting behavior.

For the end-of-ideology theorists, the basic cause for these developments was the steadily expanding economic prosperity of Western society. This clearly proved Marx wrong, made it easier for the industrial working class to be incorportaed as full participants into the economic, social, and political system, greatly expanded the middle class, and made possible the state provision of social security and welfare benefits that competitive democratic politics demanded. As a result, politics would be reduced, in John Kennedy's words, from "basic clashes of philosophy and ideology ... to ways and means of reaching common goals."[6]

Given the seeming success of the mixed economy, democratic politics, and the welfare state, end-of-ideology proponents implicitly and at times explicitly suggested that the trend they described was both *universal* in its applicability to advanced industrial societies and *irreversible* in that it reflected the needs of a new stage of economic development. As so stated, however, the end-of-ideology thesis was not to be borne out by events.

In the first place, it did not take sufficient account of the basic differences in historical development between American and European societies. The thesis was propounded at the same time that Louis Hartz and others were emphasizing the differences between the liberal consensual politics of the United States and the class-based ideological politics typical of Europe. Given these differences, the same phenomenon—sustained economic growth and prosperity—could and did have different consequences. In Europe, affluence created the base for the moderation of class conflict, the reduction in the policy differences between major parties, and the at least temporary cooling of grand ideological debate. Affluence in the United States, on the other hand, produced not the end of ideology (which had never existed in a European sense anyway) but the economic precondition for the rebirth of American moralism. What was taken to be the same thing in Europe and America was, in fact, two quite different things: the long-term easing of class conflict in Europe and short-term prevalence of creedal complacency in America.

Second, in 1962 John Kennedy suggested that as a result of the economic and social changes that had occurred in the United States, there would be no further need for "the great sort of 'passionate movements' which have stirred this country so often in the past."[7] He could not have been more wrong. Equally wrong, however, were those European intellectuals who subsequently saw the failure of the end-of-ideology thesis as proof of the end of American consensus and "the beginning of political doctrine" and conflict among those doctrines: "Ex unibus plures!"[8] What was erroneously interpreted as the beginning of ideological conflict and political doctrines was only the renaissance of political moralism produced by the American consensus. In the 1960s, the American consensus on basic values did not come apart; it came alive.

This awakening produced a politics from the mid-sixties to the mid-seventies that makes those years a clearly identifiable period in American political history. The agenda of politics, the tone of politics, the issues, the intensity, the cleavages, the actors, the forms of political activity—all took on distinctive characteristics. The politics of the S&S Years thus differed significantly from that of the late 1950s and from that of the late 1970s. The distinctive profile of politics from 1960 to 1976 is dramatically revealed in the horseshoe bulge that recurs during these years in a variety of important quantitative indicators of political activity. Predominant were forms of political action—protest, exposure, and reform—that are common in creedal passion periods but of secondary importance in the more normal years of American politics. As a result of what happened during these years, the politics of the late 1970s also differed significantly from that of the late 1950s. More specifically, during the S&S Years major changes occurred in the substance of political attitudes and in the structure and power of political institutions. These changes represent the lasting legacy of creedal passion for American politics during the final quarter of the twentieth century.

Interlude of Hypocrisy, Surge of Moralism

Complacency began to deteriorate at the end of the fifties, particularly in the wake of the successful Soviet launching of the first sputnik in 1958 and the concerns that aroused. There was a renewed feeling of the need to rededicate the nation to American values, reflected in President Eisenhower's creation of a Commission on National Goals. The increasing concern with and commitment to American liberal values was eloquently epitomized in the Kennedy candidacy and the Kennedy Presidency. During the 1960 campaign, Kennedy caught the mood of the times perfectly in stressing the importance of asserting those values in the face of the Soviet threat and the need "to get this country moving again." The dominant views of the times remained highly supportive of governmental authority and strongly in favor of vigorous governmental action in the international field. The largest peacetime increase in military spending up to that time occurred in the Kennedy administration. The prevailing response was perfectly articulated in Kennedy's inaugural address, devoted as it was almost entirely to the projection of American values abroad rather than to their realization within American society. Apart from the slowly growing civil rights movement, Americans paid relatively little attention to the gap between American ideals and institutions at home. One could hardly rally Americans to defend freedom abroad while at the same time pointing to either its absence or the threats to it at home. Consequently, for some people the shift from complacency to moralism was mediated by a brief and partial engagement with hypocrisy. At the same time, others were making the shift from passivity to intense commitment to reform directly, without the foreign detour: the antiwar demonstrations of the late 1960s included veterans of both the Peace Corps and the civil rights marches of the early sixties. While the Kennedys were clearly the master practitioners of cool pragmatic politics, they also, perhaps for that very reason, articulated and capitalized upon the desire of Americans to feel intensely committed to some higher purposes. As John Steinbeck observed in 1960, there existed in the country "a nervous restlessness, a thirst, a yearning for something unknown—perhaps morality."[9]

The willingness to "pay any price, bear any burden" to defend freedom throughout the world did not remain the dominant theme for long. At first, Kennedy had consciously subordinated domestic policy and had gone along with the civil rights movement only to the extent that it was politically necessary, but in 1963 he began to listen to the voices of outrage. The moralistic passion that the struggle for civil rights engendered among both black and white activists spread to other areas, most notably in the opposition to U.S. involvement in the war in Vietnam. Outward-directed patriotic fervor was replaced by inward-directed moralistic indignation. The images that elites and public opinion generally had of American political institutions changed drastically; American politics began to seem radically different from what they thought it ought to be. Respect for authority declined precipitously at the same time that demands increased for governmental action to remedy the IvI gap. Intense moralism surged to the fore among significant politically active groups.

Intensity of commitment cannot be measured easily by any quantitative yardstick. But the fact that commitment increased in the 1960s is surely unquestionable. These were the years, as I have argued elsewhere, that

> witnessed a dramatic renewal of the democratic spirit in America . . . The spirit of protest, the spirit of equality, the impulse to expose and correct inequities were abroad in the land. The themes of the 1960s were those of the Jacksonian Democracy and the muckraking Progressives; they embodied ideas and beliefs which were deep in the American tradition but which usually do not command the passionate intensity of commitment that they did in the 1960s. That decade bore testimony to the vitality of the democratic idea. It was a decade of democratic surge, of the reassertion of democratic egalitarianism.[10]

The classic values of the American Creed—equality, democracy, liberty, individual rights, the limitation of power—were rearticulated with an intensity and fervor fully equal to that of any previous outbreak of creedal passion.

The shift from complacency to commitment was paralleled and, to some extent, followed by changes in the images that Americans had of their political system. These changes are quantitatively visible in public opinion polls. The public's perception of government shifted dramatically between the early 1960s and the early 1970s. The trends in response to five key questions are set forth in Figure 1. In 1964, 64 percent of the public thought the government was run for the benefit of all the people, and 29 percent thought it was run by a few big interests looking out for themselves. By 1974, opinion was almost exactly reversed: 66 percent thought that government was run for a few big interests; 25 percent thought it was run for the benefit of all. Similar shifts occurred in the extent to which people thought government could be trusted to do what is right, wasted tax money, and was run by smart people or crooks. Major changes also occurred in the degree to which people perceived government to be responsive to their views. In 1960, for instance, 73 percent of the public disagreed with the statement that public officials did not "care much what people like me think," while 25 percent agreed with it. By 1974, a quarter of the public had changed its mind: 50 percent believed that officials did not care what they thought, while 46 percent believed that they did.[11]

Changes in public perceptions were not limited to perceptions of government. During the late 1960s and early 1970s, the public's confidence in many other institutions in American society plummeted. Between 1966 and 1976, the proportion of the public that had "a great deal of confidence" in the leadership of the executive branch of the federal government went from 41 percent to 11 percent, of Congress from 42 percent to 9 percent, and of the Supreme Court from 51 percent to 22 percent. During the same ten-year period, drastic reductions also occurred in the proportion of the public that had great confidence in the leaders of medicine (73 percent to 42 percent), higher education (61 percent to 31 percent), the military (62 percent to 23 percent), major companies (55 percent to 16 percent), organized religion (41 percent to 24 percent), and organized labor (22 percent to 10 percent). Among the major institutions of American society, the only one whose leaders commanded greater confidence in 1976 (28 percent) than in 1966 (25 percent) was television news.[12]

Increased commitment to liberal, democratic values, combined with increasingly unfavorable perceptions of governmental and other institutions, necessarily made moralism and opposition to authority the dominant theme of politics. Outrage and protest, together with their sometime children, invective and violence, set the tone for the politics of the late sixties and early seventies. The issues of politics concerned not questions of more or less or of competence versus incompetence, but rather ques-

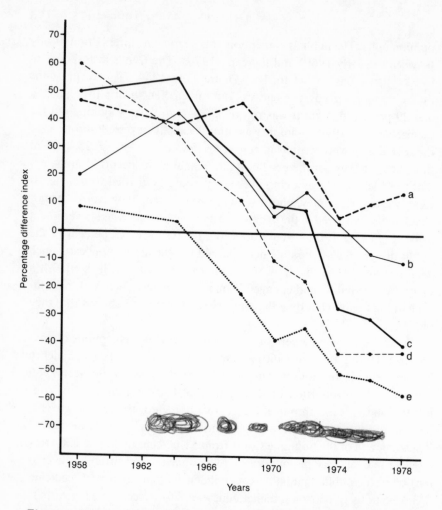

Figure 1. Percentage Difference Index (PDI) for five measures of trust in government. The PDI is the difference obtained by subtracting that portion of the population expressing less trust in government from that portion expressing greater trust in government. (*Source:* Based on data in Warren E. Miller, Arthur H. Miller, and Edward J. Schneider, *American National Election Studies Sourcebook, 1952–1978* [Cambridge, Mass.: Harvard University Press, 1980], pp. 257–259.)

a. "Do you think that quite a few of the people running the government are a little crooked, not very many are, or do you think hardly any of them are crooked at all?" PDI = "hardly any" and "not many" minus "quite a lot."

b. "Do you feel that almost all of the people running the government are smart people who usually know what they are doing, or do you think that quite a few of them don't seem to know what they're doing?" PDI = "know what they're doing" minus "don't know what they're doing."

(Figure 1 continued)

c. "How much of the time do you think you can trust the government in Washington to do what is right—just about always, most of the time, or only some of the time?" PDI = "always" and "most of the time" minus "some or none of the time."

d. "Would you say the government is pretty much run by a few big interests looking out for themselves or that it is run for the benefit of all the people?" PDI = "benefit of all" minus "a few big interests." (Note: In 1958 the question was worded differently from the way it was worded in other years.)

e. "Do you think that people in government waste a lot of money we pay in taxes, waste some of it, or don't waste very much of it?" PDI = "not much" and "some" minus "a lot."

tions of right and wrong. The heart of the S&S Years is, indeed, very neatly defined by the disappearance of economic issues from the top of the political agenda. From 1950 through 1959, an average of 23.6 percent of the American public rated an economic issue as "most important question confronting the country"; in 1971–72, an average of 21.5 percent of the American public singled out economic issues as of critical importance; and from 1973 to 1979, the percentage skyrocketed to 71.7 percent. Between 1960 and 1970, however, only a bare 11.1 percent of the public identified an economic question as the most important problem facing the country: civil rights, foreign policy, the Vietnam War, crime and disorder, and honesty in government supplanted economics in the public's concerns.[13]

The difference between creedal politics and "normal" politics generally was reflected more specifically in the differences between the New Left and the Old Left. The Old Left had been shaped by the economic trauma of the 1930s—the classic struggles for labor union recognition, collective bargaining, jobs, pay, social security, and related benefits. During the 1930s the major issues were economic issues and people divided along class lines with respect to those issues.[14] The Old Left was clearly identified with the working class and the labor union movement and shaped its thinking in Marxist or semi-Marxist terms. In the 1960s, on the other hand, the New Left eschewed the working class and stressed moralism rather than ideology. As the first president of Students for a Democratic Society explained in the early 1960s, "Revolution and the crude Marxian dynamics of the class struggle are rejected or highly modified"; the New Left "begins from moral values which are held as absolute." Similarly, other early New Left activists argued that the movement had to stress "moral issues in place of ideology" or that "the trademark of the new radicals is a primitive moral ideology."[15] Even more explicitly, the purpose of the New Left was concretely defined as the realization in practice of fundamental American political values. "The origins of the New Left," as one SDS statement put it in the mid-1960s, "are not based on ideological (class) confrontation but, on the contrary, emanate from a serious commitment to certain features of the dominant American ideology. The denial of civil rights to the black population was the first issue that led to the emergence of the New Left. The exposure of this denial directly contradicted the dominant rhetoric of equal opportunity and democratic rights."[16]

The difference between the Old Left and the New Left was thus the difference between class politics and economic concerns on the one hand, and creedal politics and moralistic concerns on the other. In somewhat comparable fashion, the mainstream manifestation of the political spirit of the times, the New Politics, differed from the Old Politics because it wished to reform existing institutions to embody more fully American values rather than simply to work within those institutions to achieve materialistic benefits.

The shift in political attitudes was also more broadly reflected in "the way in which the public conceptualized politics." During the central years of the Fourth Period the public was both "more likely to evaluate candidates and parties in terms of issue positions and ideology" and also more likely to develop consistent and coherent positions on political issues. As a result, the proportion of the public that evaluated presidential candidates in ideological terms was much higher in the 1964, 1968, and 1972 elections than it was in the preceding elections or in the 1976 election.[17] (See Figure 2.)

When asked in the early 1970s about the state of morality in America, Alexander Bickel is reported to have replied, "It threatens to engulf us."[18] He was guilty of understatement; it did. But the moralism of the S&S Years was also peculiarly public in nature. With respect to individual personal behavior in a private setting, the old standards of morality were challenged, discredited, and often thrown away with purposeful abandon. With respect to public behavior, however, the old standards of morality were reinvigorated, reasserted, and often applied with relentless conscientiousness. The target of this moralism was almost invariably some form of established authority. The arrogance of power was superseded by the arrogance of morality, and for more than a decade authority—in

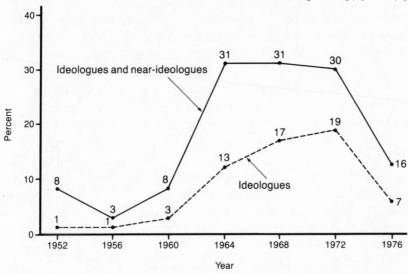

Figure 2. Ideological evaluation of presidential candidates, 1952–1976. (*Source:* Norman H. Nie, Sidney Verba, and John R. Petrocik, *The Changing American Voter,* enl. ed. [Cambridge, Mass.: Harvard University Press, 1980], p. 367.)

government, business, education, religion, the family, and elsewhere— was called into question and often effectively undermined. Politics focused on the evils of hierarchy and officialdom: arbitrary power, unresponsiveness, secrecy, deception.[19] As a result, people no longer felt obligated to obey those whom they had previously considered superior to themselves in age, rank, status, expertise, character, or talents. Within most organizations, discipline eased and differences in status became blurred. Each group claimed its right to participate equally—and perhaps more than equally—in the decisions that affected it.

In American society, authority had commonly been based on organizational position, economic wealth, specialized expertise, legal competence, and electoral representativeness. Authority based on hierarchy, expertise, and wealth all obviously ran counter to the democratic and egalitarian temper of the times, and during the 1960s all three came under heavy attack. In universities, students, who lacked expertise, came to participate in the decision-making process on many important issues. In government, organizational hierarchy weakened, and organizational subordinates acted more readily to ignore, criticize, or defeat the wishes of their superiors. In politics generally, the authority of wealth was challenged and reforms were introduced to expose and limit its influence. Authority derived from legal and electoral sources did not necessarily run counter to the spirit of the times, but when it did, it too was challenged and restricted. The decisions of judges and the actions of legislatures were legitimate to the extent that they promoted, as they often did, egalitarian and participatory goals. "Civil disobedience," after all, was the claim to be morally right in disobeying a law that was morally wrong. It implied that the moral value of law-abiding behavior in a society depended upon the content of the laws, not on the process by which they were enacted. Electoral legitimacy was, obviously, most congruent with the democratic surge, but even so, it too at times was questioned, as the value of "categorical" representativeness was elevated to challenge the principle of electoral representativeness.

The legitimacy of institutions in America derives from liberal, democratic, individualistic values. If institutions are seen, as they were in the Fourth Period, to deviate from those values, they are to that extent illegitimate.[20] This perception, in turn, then releases the constraints on a wide variety of behavior not normally a part of conventional politics. "Take but degree away, Untune that string, And hark! what discord follows," succinctly summarizes the course of American politics during the sixties and seventies. Or, as Daniel Patrick Moynihan warned President-Elect Nixon in 1968, "The sense of institutions being legitimate— especially the institutions of government—is the glue that holds society together. When it weakens, things come unstuck."[21] In the late 1960s, much of America came unstuck.

The Mobilization of Protest

The politics of the S&S Years, like that of other creedal passion periods, was characterized by protest and exposure on behalf of reform. These three forms of politics do not appear only during creedal passion periods, but they do tend to dominate the politics of such periods, while other forms of politics, such as party, electoral, and interest group politics, tend to decline in significance. Moralistic indignation generates passionate drives to expose evil, to protest evil, and to reform evil.

The early years of the Fourth Period were marked by significant changes in political participation and by the mobilization of protest focused largely on civil rights and the Vietnam War. In the United States, much more so than in most other industrialized democracies, political participation rates tend to correlate with socioeconomic status. This overall correlation was not reversed during the S&S Years. Yet the composition of those most active in politics did change significantly. Before 1960, blacks and youth were among the least participant groups in American society. These groups were, however, far more sensitive than others to the gap between American ideals and the realities of racial discrimination and foreign war. During the 1960s, consequently, the participation of these groups in politics increased dramatically; they became, indeed, among the most politically active groups—the political shock troops, as it were, of the American conscience constituency.

For the three presidential elections between 1952 and 1960, the electoral participation index for the American public averaged 13.3; for the four elections between 1964 and 1976, it averaged 17.3. This increase was entirely accounted for by the rise in black electoral participation. The index for whites was 18.7 for the first three elections and 19.3 for the succeeding four. The black electoral participation index, in contrast, zoomed upward from a level of −35.7 for the earlier elections to 7.5 for the four later ones.[22] The increase in political participation among blacks was clearly greater than that which might have been predicted by their slowly improving socioeconomic status. In the 1952 and 1956 elections, black campaign activity was significantly below that which would have been expected on the basis of their educational status. Between 1960 and the 1970s, black campaign acts significantly exceeded the level predicted by education. White campaign acts, in contrast, continued at a relatively constant level slightly above that predicted by education. By the late 1960s, overall political participation rates for blacks were much more equal to those of whites than they had been previously, and blacks were usually more active in politics than whites of similar socioeconomic status. It seems reasonable to conclude that this increased participation by blacks was the result of heightened group consciousness related to the salience of civil rights issues.[23]

As people age, they usually become more politically active, until they reach their fifties when their activity begins to decline; if socioeconomic status is held constant, the decline sets in when people are in their late sixties. Those under age 26 participate less than any other age group.[24] In the late 1960s and early 1970s, however, this generally prevailing pattern did not hold. Young people who were roughly 18 years old in 1965 engaged in an average of 2.1 political activities between 1965 and

1973, compared to an average of 1.7 for their parents. Young adults (21–29 years old) were significantly more active in the 1968 and 1972 elections than those a generation older (44–64 years old). In sum, "young adults in the late 1960s and early 1970s were indeed exceptional in their political participation. The young participated at higher rates than did the young in other years, and they were more active than mature adults during this period. Both patterns were unusual and unexpected."[25] In addition, during these years, liberals of any age tended to be more politically active than conservatives of the same age. The young also tended to be much more liberal than those who were more elderly, and this reinforced their propensity for political action.

The 1960s and the early 1970s are generally thought to be a period of great political controversy and activity in which large masses of citizens became passionately involved in politics in a variety of ways. Yet this impression contrasts rather markedly with the extent to which people engaged in the most widespread form of political participation: voting in elections. Voting participation rates increased significantly during the 1950s, peaked in 1960, and then declined steadily thereafter through 1980, with the sharpest drop coming between 1968 and 1972. If the 1960s were the decade of political action, how can this seeming anomaly be explained?

The answer lies in the purposes of political action in the 1960s. In a creedal passion period, the primary purpose of politics is protest. Political protest is the expression through collective action of opposition to particular conditions, policies, or officials. It can be legal or illegal, peaceful or violent, diffuse or focused. It can take the form of direct action and civil disobedience; it can include meetings, demonstrations, teach-ins, riots, picketing, marches, sit-ins, strikes. In some circumstances, voting itself can be a means of protest, but so also can not-voting. In addition, there are many other more effective and more satisfying ways of registering protest. During the 1960s, all age groups increasingly disagreed with the statement: "Voting is the only way that people like me can have any say about how the government runs things." In 1952, however, virtually the same proportions of those in their twenties and those over sixty agreed with this statement. In 1960, a small generational gap appeared, with 69 percent of those in their twenties and 78 percent of those over sixty agreeing with the statement. By 1968, a wide chasm had opened up, with 37 percent of the younger and 62 percent of the older group agreeing with the statement.[26] Young people, blacks, and other constituencies became disillusioned with voting and ready to engage in a variety of other forms of political action.

As a result, as in previous creedal passion periods, the tactics and arenas of political participation multiplied outside conventional channels. New organizations designed to make political practice conform to political principle proliferated in number and intensified in activity. These included radical and protest organizations, as well as more moderate, reform organizations. A survey of some eighty-three "public interest" organizations in 1972–73, for instance, found that fifty-two (63 percent) had been formed after 1959.[27] People also became mobilized to new levels of activity within the confines of more specialized, supposedly "nonpolitical" institutions: students participated in decision making within universities; stockholders challenged corporation managements; soldiers asserted the right to unionize and bargain collectively; government lawyers organized to protest decisions by the attorney general; priests asserted their claims against bishops. Stimulated in part by the success of the civil rights movement but also in larger part by the ethos of the times, many other sectors of American society—women, Indians, Chicanos, homosexuals, white ethnic groups—developed new levels of group consciousness and engaged in much more intense forms of political activity. In addition, as in previous creedal passion periods, organizations became active on behalf of those unable to help themselves: children, the handicapped, the insane, prisoners, animals.

Americans are known throughout the world as a litigious people. During creedal passion periods this propensity increases markedly. Between 1970 and 1976, for instance, the number of civil rights employment cases initiated in federal courts increased from 344 to 5,321; the number of private antitrust cases rose from 877 to 1,504. In increasing numbers, Americans attempted to use judicial processes to right perceived social wrongs. As one so-called public interest group urged citizens: "Sue them! Sue the IRS! Sue Congress! Take federal agencies to court! Even sue the President himself! You can, you know."[28] During the S&S Years to use Emerson's phrase, a "restless, prying, conscientious criticism" prevailed throughout the land, as people actively asserted and attempted to realize rights that they had previously disregarded.

Even as political participation expanded in a horizontal sense, to new forms and channels, it also escalated in a vertical sense, with a marked increase in the intensity of the protests mounted by the Movement or movements against the established order. Particular expressions of protest, although individually limited in time, occur in clumps, particularly in creedal passion periods. In a liberal environment, moreover, protest can be used to generate protest, by provoking the authorities to react by coercion or violence that in itself is perceived to violate the Creed and serves to mobilize new participants unmoved by the original issue. In the politics of exposure, the most appealing issue is the effort by authority to cover up evil; in the politics of protest, the most appealing issue is the effort by authority coercively to suppress protest against evil. In each case, the creedal immorality of the counteraction by authority provides the basis for a broader appeal. In a liberal society, particular issues appeal to particular groups, but opposition to the misuse of authority appeals to almost all groups.

During the 1960s, protest was of crucial importance in mobilizing public opinion concerning racial discrimination and the Vietnam War. Sit-ins, freedom rides, civil rights marches, and the responses of Southern authorities to them, particularly as revealed through the mass media, helped generate the public support necessary for the enactment of the mid-1960s civil rights legislation. The tactics of protest were perfectly suited for exploitation by the media. Similar tactics were used in the teach-ins, peace marches, and demonstrations that played a key role in mobilizing opposition to the war in Vietnam. The very fact that protest tactics were used commanded the attention of both public and leaders and underlined the intensity of the commitment of those who were marching. Without recourse to the tactics of protest, neither opposition to discrimination nor opposition to the war would have achieved its goals.

Those who became more active politically in the S&S Years also tended to resort to the more intense forms of protest. Eighteen-year-olds in 1965 were six times as likely as their parents to engage in protests or demonstrations during the following eight years, with one out of every six in the younger group participating in such action. Blacks, too, were more willing than other groups in the population to endorse demonstrations as a form of political action, with those blacks who were young and middle class more inclined to do so than other blacks.[29] The role of protest as the characteristic form of political participation in the S&S Years is graphically revealed in the relative frequency of protest demonstrations and riots from the 1950s to the 1970s. (See Figure 3.) From 1948 to 1959, the United States averaged 5 major protest demonstrations annually; from 1960 to 1972, the annual average was 144. In 1973 the number of demonstrations dropped precipitously, averaging 57 annually during

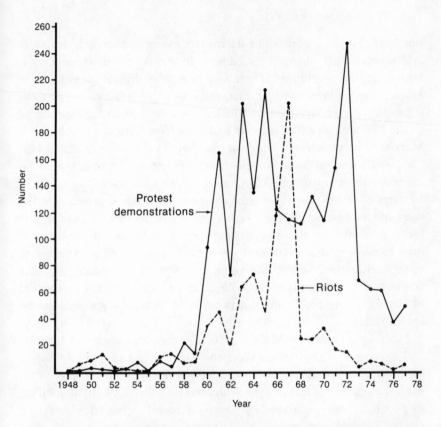

Figure 3. Frequency of protest demonstrations and riots, 1948–1977. (*Source:* Based on data in Charles Lewis Taylor and Michael C. Hudson, *World Handbook of Political and Social Indicators,* 2nd ed. [New Haven: Yale University Press, 1972], pp. 88–89, 94–95, and Charles Lewis Taylor and David A. Jodice, *World Handbook of Political and Social Indicators III* [New Haven: Yale University Press, forthcoming, 1981].)

the next 5 years. The distribution of riots followed a similar pattern: very few in the 1950s, a sharp increase in 1960 that continued to 1967, a tremendous drop-off to an average of 22 for the next five years, followed by a still further drop to single-digit figures in 1973. The curves portrayed by this data dramatically highlight the silhouette of the age of protest.

Many Americans engage in protest during creedal passion periods. The more intense forms of protest are, however, the characteristic political tactic of radicalism. Reform involves efforts to make American political institutions and practices conform to American ideals and values. Revolution is the effort to overthrow both political ideals and political institutions and to replace them with different (for example, Marxist) ideals and institutions. What, then, is radicalism? In the American context, is it reform or is it revolution? These two categories do not seem to leave much room between them. In fact, the essence of American radicalism is precisely its ambivalence on this issue. In the United States, radicals on the Left are those who respond to the question "Are you a liberal or a Marxist?" by answering "both" or "neither." For various reasons (see Chapter 8), radicalism in America is able to encompass both those who are trying to improve the system and those who are trying to destroy it. In terms of tactics, both can agree on the central role of protest. On the one hand, protest eschews violence as a preferred instrument and violence for its own sake. On the other hand, protest goes beyond the pallid confines of conventional politics. It involves moving out of the committee room, legislative chamber, and voting booth "into the streets" for mass action, which may not in itself be illegal but which contains the potential of illegality, and which if illegal may not be violent but which could easily spawn violence.

Liberal reformer and Marxist revolutionary can thus blend together and cooperate in the mobilization and organization of protest. As the data in Figure 3 suggest, however, the more intense forms of protest do not last long. Protest has an ever-decreasing half-life. Substantial numbers of people cannot maintain high levels of moral outrage for sustained periods of time and hence must seek new ways of coping with their dissonance. They may come to feel that their protest has been substantially successful and subside into a more complacent outlook and reliance on more conventional forms of political action to achieve particular legislative goals. They may feel that their protest has been unsuccessful, conclude that no effort of theirs can succeed, and hence lapse into cynicism. Or they may come to reject the entire system—both ideals and institutions —and turn to revolutionary activities to destroy and replace it.

In the late 1950s and early 1960s both New Left organizations—most notably SDS—and black organizations—most notably CORE (Congress of Racial Equality) and SNCC (Student Nonviolent Coordinating Committee)—pursued reformist goals with radical tactics. SDS, like other radical coalitions, stretched "from moderates to Maoists"; the Port Huron statement of 1962 was a statement of general radical reform goals, well within the broad limits of the American radical tradition. "Until 1964," one historian said, "the New Left, in fact, was decidedly reformist and convinced that American institutions could be made to reflect proclaimed ideals."[30] After 1964, however, the appeal of reformism began to subside. In 1965, SDS dropped the anticommunist clause from its constitution and opened its membership to all those on the Left.[31] Parallel changes occurred in its organization, as the needs of central bureaucratic control eclipsed the values of participatory democracy. Marxism, which had been rejected a few years earlier as the out-of-date ideology of the Old Left, was now embraced. Following the 1968 election, SDS was drained still further by factional conflict and began to reject the tactics of protest for those of violence. In 1969, the Weathermen made SDS into a revolutionary organization which, after the failure of the Chicago "Days of Rage" of violent protest in October, went underground at the end of the year. In March 1970, the symbolic end of the transition from protest to revolution came when three Weathermen accidentally blew themselves up making bombs in a house on New York's West Eleventh Street. SDS had always been radical, but the sense in which it was radical changed drastically between Port Huron and Eleventh Street. In its early years it was a radical reform organization because it wanted to realize American liberal values; at the end it was a radical revolutionary organization because it wanted to destroy American liberal institutions. But as a radical protest organization, it could not last: inevitably, its leaders were driven either to making bombs (like Kathy Boudin) or running for Congress (like Tom Hayden).

The leading protest organizations in the civil rights movement went through a similar metamorphosis. In 1960–61, tens of thousands of people participated in hundreds of sit-ins to desegregate lunch-counters and other commercial facilities; blacks and whites cooperated together in the Student Nonviolent Coordinating Committee and in the Southern Christian Leadership Conference; a quarter of a million people participated in the civil rights march on Washington in 1963. The successful mobilization of support, made easier by the seemingly ruthless opposition to desegregation by some elements in the South, created the political environment for the passage of the Civil Rights Acts of 1964 and 1965. In achieving this, some black leaders became absorbed into the electoral and bureaucratic politics of the Establishment, shifting "from protest to politics."[32] Others, however, felt that the civil rights organizations should move in a more radical direction. In 1965–66, SNCC shifted course, substituted the slogan "black power" for "freedom," segregated and then expelled its white workers, and came out against the Vietnam War and in favor of resistance to the draft. At the same time, CORE broke with its nonviolent tradition and endorsed black power and a community organizing strategy in the North.[33]

The general pattern in these organizations involved a shift from protest to violence, from a broad base to a narrow one, and from ideals derived from the American Creed to ones rooted in Marxist or other revolutionary ideology. Perhaps most notable was the shift from shared goals to particularistic goals, reflected most clearly in demands for "black power," "student power," and "workers' power." In American politics, when a group makes the acquisition of power its explicitly articulated goal, it is confessing its inability to achieve that goal. A slogan like "black power" embodies two negative symbols. First, power in general is distrusted and any group that proclaims power as its goal is immediately suspect. Second, "black power" implies power for one group at the expense of others. By so defining its goal, the group sharply limits its appeal. Whites feel compelled by the American Creed to support civil rights for blacks; they are under no such compulsion to support black power. In the American context, the former is in the end irresistible; the latter is from the start self-defeating.

The Dynamics of Exposure

Government in the United States has always been more open than government in other societies, including democratic societies. This has been one result of the absence in America of a "state" in the European sense. The business of government is the business of the public, and consequently it should be conducted in public. This proposition, totally foreign to most cultures, is a basic component of the American Creed. It is reflected in the constitutional guarantees of freedom of speech and of the press, in the penetration of journalists into governmental precincts and processes, in the absence of an Official Secrets Act on the British model, and in the looseness of libel laws. As a result, government in America is subject to much more constant and pervasive exposure to its people than is government in other societies.

Exposure takes two forms. Investigatory exposure is designed to reveal wrongdoing; it is normally the product of particular efforts by investigatory agencies—journalists, congressional committees, law enforcement agencies—aimed at particular targets. Regulatory exposure, on the other hand, is designed primarily to prevent wrongdoing by requiring publicity or permitting publicity for certain types of action. Often the product of exposés produced by investigatory exposure, it takes the form of sunshine laws, the Freedom of Information Act, and legislation requiring reports of lobbying expenditures and campaign contributions. Both investigatory and regulatory exposure are far more prevalent in the United States than in other societies.

Publicity is always present, but it tends to peak during periods of creedal passion. The exposure to which political authority in the United States was subjected in the late 1960s and the early 1970s was unique in modern history, aside from the investigations by revolutionary regimes of their predecessors. During the 1960s various liberal and radical groups and publications intensified their efforts to expose the operations of those in authority, particularly with respect to foreign policy and the Vietnam War. The great age of exposure did not begin, however, until 1971, when Daniel Ellsberg found a newspaper outlet for the Pentagon Papers. This was followed by further revelations concerning the conduct of the war and, in the summer of 1972, by the beginnings of Watergate, which slowly gained momentum and dominated the national media for the next two years. (Watergate was a front-page story in *The New York Times* every day except three during May, June, and July of 1973.)[34] The expanding revelations of the web of involvement in Watergate provided what seemed to be an irresistible lure and a promising career for scores of journalists. In due course, also, the gradual release of the Nixon tapes dramatically revealed the casualness and banality, meanness of motive and narrowness of purpose, that may characterize political leaders at work.

In the fall of 1973, Watergate was supplemented by the revelations and prosecution that led to the resignation of Vice-President Agnew. The resignation of President Nixon the following summer substantially closed down the Watergate exposures, but throughout the fall of 1974 the media were able to continue in the same vein and strip away much of the mystery that had surrounded the wealth, lifestyle, and political operations of Nelson Rockefeller, who had been nominated for vice-president. In December 1974, *The New York Times* broke the story of the domestic intelligence operations of the CIA; during the following year, the press, three governmental investigatory bodies, and sundry individuals competed and cooperated in revelations concerning U.S. intelligence and internal security agencies. Surveillance activities; assassination plans; interception of mail and cable traffic; use of missionaries, businessmen, and journalists as agents; support and financing of political parties, media, and political leaders in other countries; disinformation operations; the names of agents; efforts to overthrow or weaken foreign governments—all these were laid bare in what could only be viewed and was viewed by incredulous foreign officials and publics as a peculiarly virulent form of American madness. In the spring of 1976, the exposure momentum slackened, but for roughly five years the American public was provided with unprecedented revelations of the inner workings of government and the behind-the-scenes actions of public officials.

The great exposés were thus concentrated in the latter part of the S&S Years. On the surface, this seems puzzling. One might think that during a creedal passion period, exposure of injustice and wrongdoing would come first. The veils of rhetoric and official cover-ups would be ripped away, exposing the brutal—and un-American—reality of American politics. This, in turn, would lead to a swelling mass of protest, which would generate reforms to eliminate the evils. The comparison of the ideal and the fact is normally the indispensable prerequisite to reform. How can this apparently perverse appearance of exposure at the end of the process be explained? Two factors are relevant.

First, both protest and reform could precede exposure because the principal evils to which protest and reform were directed—racial discrimination and foreign war—were obvious and blatant. Little or no exposure efforts were necessary to uncover them. What was necessary was to communicate these facts to the public, and this the national media —particularly television—did, with tremendous impact on American politics. As was the case during other creedal passion periods, the media played a central role in the politics of the S&S Years. In the 1960s, that role was played largely by television, which transmitted instantly and vividly to the people images of what was happening in the American South and in South Vietnam. In the 1970s, the critical role was played by the print media, which revealed the malfeasance and misfeasance of public officials in Washington. The electronic media had its impact through the communication of public events, the print media through the revelation of secret events. As a result of the former, protest and reform could and did occur on a major scale before the process of exposure reached its peak.

Second, exposure could not occur until the authority of the executive branch—that is, the plausible targets of exposure—had been weakened, and it could not occur until the power of the press and Congress—that is, the necessary agents of exposure—had been enhanced. The exposure of governmental evil requires the weakening of governmental authority because of the nature of the exposure process. Protest requires the mobilization of outsiders against political authority; exposure requires the disaffection of insiders from political authority. It becomes possible when the lines of authority and control in government and other institutions begin to break down and people within those institutions lose their sense of loyalty to and their belief in the legitimacy of their leaders. A major exposé requires a Daniel Ellsberg or a Deep Throat, and the appearance of such informants in the early 1970s testified to the breakdown of authority in the Pentagon, the White House, and the Department of Justice. Those who are exposed in American politics are not those who are evil and powerful but those who are evil and weak. Exposure produces evidence of villainy; it is itself evidence of weakness, and in turn contributes to this weakness.

On occasion in American history, congressional committees and newspapers have undertaken to investigate military defeats, intelligence failures, and other gross deficiencies or breakdowns in the process of government that are the product of poor judgment, bad communications, insufficient foresight, sloppy administration, or simple stupidity. Such exposures, however, rarely occur during creedal passion periods, because the target at such times is not the incompetence of leadership but its villainy. Exposure is directed toward corruption, bribery, deception, lying, obstruction of justice, nepotism, cronyism, extortion—actions that clearly violate legal or ethical standards. In a different atmosphere, for instance, congressional committees investigating the CIA might have been curious as to why the agency failed so miserably in its efforts to assassinate Lumumba and Castro. But in 1975 no one was interested in the inability of the agency to do what it was told to do, but only in the immorality of what it was told to do. For this type of exposure to occur, there must be a broader climate of opinion which makes people willing to believe evil of their leaders and passionately eager to find such evil.

The weakening of governmental authority was a preeminent characteristic of the politics of the 1960s and the necessary prerequisite to the exposures of the 1970s. Few Presidents came into office with more important enemies and potential enemies than did Richard Nixon. Congress, the national media, the eastern Establishment, the federal bureaucracy, and the aroused protest and reform organizations of the 1960s were all seen—correctly—as enemies of the new administration. In connection with the media, for instance, commentator John Chancellor accurately observed that "other Administrations have had a love-hate relationship with the press. The Nixon Administration has a hate-hate relationship."[35]

In similar terms, Nixon and other members of his administration spoke feelingly and accurately about their isolated and vulnerable position at the peak of power in the federal executive. The weakness of the Nixon administration was revealed in the readiness of informants in the executive branch to cooperate with journalists and congressmen. This erosion of its authority also stimulated the administration to misuse its authority, thereby providing more behavior to be exposed.

A somewhat similar process also made the CIA and FBI into attractive targets. Public unhappiness with the Vietnam War did not become widespread until 1969, whereupon the way was prepared for the revelation of the Pentagon Papers in 1971 and for the subsequent investigations of the CIA in 1975. When the United States was finally driven out of Vietnam in the spring of 1975, congressional committees did not investigate why the United States had lost the war and did not attempt to apportion responsibility among civilian and military officials for this outcome. Congress wanted to pursue evil rather than failure, and to do this it had to find a weak target. The opposition to foreign involvement, going back to the early 1960s, made conditions favorable for an assault on U.S. intelligence agencies. Again, the question of timing was crucial. In early 1967, for instance, a radical employee of the National Student Association learned of the long-standing CIA funding of certain NSA international activities. Three articles detailing these revelations were published in a radical San Francisco magazine, and *The New York Times* and other newspapers wrote stories of possible CIA funding of other programs through foundation channels. The national media, did not, however, rush to exploit this information for their own purposes, and congressional leaders moved not to exploit but to support the actions of the CIA. President Johnson appointed a cabinet-level committee to review quietly CIA covert funding practices; no major congressional investigation was launched.[36] In 1974–75, on the other hand, the initial revelations about the CIA came not from *Ramparts* but from *The New York Times;* Congress and the media rushed in to follow up on these leads; and President Ford's appointment of a commission to investigate alleged CIA misbehavior stimulated the House and Senate to launch their own parallel and competing probes. Investigative reporters and congressional staff members kept the stream of revelations going for an entire year.

Once a favorable climate exists for exposure of the abuses of authority, the process of exposure develops its own characteristics and dynamics. First, the agents of exposure multiply. In the American system, exposure typically requires the participation of three types of people: informants, journalists, and congressmen and their staffs. At the beginning, the informant in the executive decides that the public or his personal interest requires him to bring into the open some information so as to affect either the substance of policy or the identity of the policy makers. Since the informant normally does not wish to reveal his own role in the exposure process, he seeks out someone in the media or in Congress to whom he can in confidence transmit the information and who then assumes responsibility for making it public. As in the case of Ellsberg and the Pentagon Papers, this process may take a while. In terms of securing the timely revelation of his information, Ellsberg undoubtedly made a mistake in going first to the chairman of the Senate Foreign Relations Committee. Newsmen are likely to have fewer inhibitions and greater interest in quick action than congressmen. The informant will, in most cases, wish to transmit the information to a journalist in the national media, where its exposure will receive the attention of those involved in the making of national policy. Once the information is out in the media, appropriate congressmen then move to investigate the charges or revelations. Once a congressional investigation is launched, congressional committee staff members normally establish a symbiotic relationship with the journalists covering the revelations, feeding one another information and tips and promoting their joint interests in continuing the process as long as possible.

An informant who successfully leaks to the press or to Congress evidence of the abuse of authority both encourages others who wish to expose the same target and provokes other informants to retaliate against other targets. Consequently, as the history of both the Pentagon Papers and Watergate exposés illustrates, a scoop by one journalist promotes vigorous competition from others: a "muck race" develops as newsmen pursue old clues and scurry after new leads, in an intense competition to see whose revelation will dominate the next day's headlines. Congressional committees, normally at least one in each house, compete in comparable fashion.

Second, the targets of exposure multiply. Initially, the focus is usually on the presumed wrongdoing of a few officials. The process of exposing those officials, however, uncovers wrongdoing by other officials. In addition, as Watergate again illustrates, the process of exposure may lead officials to take counteractions to coverup their wrongdoing, which in turn provide additional behavior to expose. There is, moreover, a finite limit on the amount of wrongdoing any one official can undertake, and consequently once the machinery of exposure gets moving, it will, in due course, exhaust one target and move on to others. Journalists made every effort to duplicate Watergate in a succession of follow-on "gates": Korea-gate, Lancegate, Billygate. The exposure of some targets stimulates counterexposure efforts of other targets. Thus, the revelations of the abuse of authority by President Nixon generated revelations of seemingly comparable abuses of authority by Presidents Johnson, Kennedy, and Roosevelt. Exposure agents who have scored successfully with one target will attempt to duplicate their success with other targets; the scourgers of the Nixon White House became the purveyors of petty gossip concerning the Burger Supreme Court.

Third, as this last example suggests, the process of exposure very quickly begins to produce decreasing marginal returns, which, however, are as likely to increase as to decrease the intensity of the efforts of the exposure agents. The impact of Watergate, and particularly the final exposure in July 1974 of the tapes that precipitated the President's resignation, gave additional appeal to what Michael Kinsley and Arthur Lubow called "the smoking-gun fallacy"—that is, the belief that "important truths will emerge from this process of sending reporters out to dig up little clues, which will lead to big clues, which will lead to THE TRUTH."[37] This proclivity is rooted in American conspiracy theories that contend that something important is hidden beneath the surface of politics, and that great efforts are necessary to strip away the various layers of deception and reveal the rotten reality of official behavior. In fact, however, just the reverse is true. The longer investigations go on, the less likely they are to uncover major new scandals. The significance of what is exposed varies inversely with the effort required to expose it. The major violations of the American Creed—concentrations of power and wealth, abuses of authority, denials of equal justice and individual rights, discrimination and inequalities—are not easily hidden. The evidence is there for those who wish to see it, appropriate it, and use it. Once started, however, the exposure process, in the effort to uncover major new evils, moves from the momentous to the trivial. It is, consequently, hardly surprising that the wave of exposures in the early 1970s, which had focused on the conduct of a major foreign war, ended in the later 1970s with a focus on the sexual peccadillos of live congressmen and dead presidents.

Fourth, the exposure process requires the multiplication of exposable activity—that is, the multiplication of secrets. To some degree, the credibility of a fact becomes dependent upon how secret it is. An action viewed as evil in itself becomes more evil if it is done in secrecy. Consequently, facts that are not secret often have to be portrayed as secret in order to increase the public's indignation and to enhance the informants' contributions: they become not merely the communicators of the knowledge of evil, but the exposers of the existence of evil. Perhaps the most notable example of the manufacture of a secret concerned the Nixon administration's bombing of Cambodia in 1969 and 1970. The President made the decision to do so on March 16, 1969; the first bombing attack occurred two days later. To avoid embarrassing Prince Sihanouk and complicating peace negotiations with the North Vietnamese, no public announcement was made. On May 9, *The New York Times* ran a long front-page article describing the bombing, which the news magazines and other media followed up in the subsequent weeks. The bombing, which continued for another year, was public knowledge for over ninety percent of the time it was conducted. In subsequent years, however, the "secret" bombing of Cambodia became one of the most frequent and passionately invoked counts in the indictment of the Nixon administration. A "secret" that almost immediately became an "unsecret" continued to be described as a secret for years afterward.* What this incident demonstrates, however, is, first, the inability of the American government to keep a secret, and second, the need for the exposers of secrets to label as "secret" things that are in fact very public.

The multiplication of exposure agents and targets was not limited to the national level of the U.S. government. The success of exposures at

* Typical of these efforts to manufacture a secret was that of *New Republic* columnist TRB in 1974: "Two months after Nixon took office, in March 1969, he started the bombing of the neutral country. He didn't tell Congress or the public. He kept it up for four years. The alleged justification of protecting Prince Sihanouk from embarrassment clearly ceased when Sihanouk was overthrown in March 1970. Nixon kept up the bombing as Commander-in-Chief, orchestrating the conspiracy of silence to keep the lid on the antiwar movement. The Pentagon knew it, the Cambodians knew it, the enemy knew it, the Americans didn't know it" (*The New Republic*, September 7, 1974, p. 2). If Americans read their newspapers, however, they obviously knew about the bombing. In this instance, it should be noted, the critics of President Nixon ate their cake and had it, too. The administration reacted to the rash of news stories about the bombing by tapping the phones of several newsmen and subordinate officials in an (unsuccessful) effort to find the source of the leak. Critics vehemently denounced the administration for doing this, while at the same time continuing to denounce the administration for carrying on a secret bombing which could have been secret only if the leak had not occurred.

that level stimulated new waves of "investigative reporting" at the state and local levels, as local and regional media attempted to duplicate on their level the success of *The New York Times* and *The Washington Post* at the national level. In some instances, this occurred very directly, as when U.S. congressional investigating committees uncovered evidence of corrupt relations between American corporations and officials of foreign governments. The unveiling and purifying effect of American creedal passion led to the exposure and disgrace of the prime minister of Japan, the premier of Italy, and the prince of the Netherlands. In an age of economic interdependence, efforts to reform American political practice thus produced effects in the politics of other countries that would never, in all likelihood, have been produced by the indigenous political processes of those countries.

Pressures for publicity are continuingly present in the American system, but during a creedal passion period they take new and more intense forms. The process of exposure acquires its own momentum, which gives it an existence quite apart from the dynamics of protest and reform. During the S&S Years, exposure peaked in the early 1970s as the momentum of protest began rapidly to fade away. Exposure, in turn, produced extraordinary revelations of the use and abuse of authority in the presidency, intelligence and security agencies, foreign policy establishment, Congress, regulatory agencies, and elsewhere. It also contributed marginally to reform, primarily through the removal of some people from office and their replacement by others. The escalating exposure also, however, hastened and made more pervasive the shift from outraged moralism to jaundiced cynicism in the prevailing public mood. In that way it sounded the death knell of reform and of the S&S Years.

The Legacies

The politics of creedal passion—of moralism and protest, outrage and exposure, ideals and reform—came to an end in the mid-1970s. Like the English in the 1650s, a nation of prophets again became a nation of shopkeepers. A phase in U.S. political life had come and passed, and the politics of the late 1970s did not, at least on the surface, appear to differ that much from the politics of the late 1950s. Indeed, as Russell Baker perceptively suggested, a Rip Van Winkle who had gone to sleep in 1957 and awakened in 1977 would find it hard to believe that the country had been through more than a decade "of assassination and Asian war, of bizarre political plots and impeachment, of men walking on the moon, of snapshots taken of Mars, of burning cities and massive demonstrations." During this period, Baker observed, the American people had passed "through an extraordinary cycle of public emotion" that "began with elation (the New Frontier), changed abruptly to horror (assassination), then to rage (Vietnam), then to shock (Watergate) which turned into disgust as the age of investigation revealed a depth and span of political corruption inconceivable in 1957." Yet, in the end, public life seemed about back where it had been twenty years before, with President Carter delivering homilies on virtue more correct in syntax but little different in substance from those President Eisenhower had delivered twenty years before. "If the streets once swarmed with a citizenry passionately engaged in great political controversies and campuses once catered to miniature revolutions,," wrote Baker in 1977, "the citizenry today, as in 1957, yawns at the smallest suggestion of politics, and campus debates, as in 1957, center on which career may lead to the most comfortable retirement."[38]

History does not, however, return to its starting point. The politics of the late 1970s differed greatly from that of the late 1960s, but it also had to differ significantly from that of the late 1950s if only because the S&S Years had intervened. The political attitudes, practices, and institutions of the late 1970s were inevitably shaped by what happened during that period of creedal passion. The issue is: What were the consequences of creedal passion and how profoundly and permanently did they change American politics?

The most significant legacies of the S&S Years can be seen in: the different impact of reform in narrowing the IvI gap; the realignment of political institutions; the depletion of political authority; and the changes in public attitudes.

Reform and the IvI Gap

As is typical of creedal passion periods, reform efforts during the S&S Years were directed at a wide variety of institutions and practices— political, social, economic, cultural. These included areas of public policy such as consumer and environmental affairs. The principal foci of reform during the S&S Years, however, were civil rights, foreign-military policy, and the political process. To what extent did the reform efforts in these areas achieve their goals?

No meaningful and precise balance sheet can be compiled. Yet even an impressionistic assessment can yield the conclusion that, in terms of the goals of the reformers, the reforms were usually incomplete, often temporary, and at times self-defeating. The degree of success of the reforms was influenced by: (1) the saliency of the evils to be corrected and of the changes proposed to the basic values of the American Creed; (2) the extent to which reforms could be put into effect by essentially one-shot, readily implemented, and hence irreversible decisions; (3) where this condition did not prevail, the extent to which implementation of the reforms was supported by politically effective, permanently organized interest groups; and (4) the extent to which the behavior to be changed by the reforms was rooted in institutions and practices subject to political control within the context of the American Creed, rather than in factors outside such control such as the international environment, the fundamentals of the private enterprise economic system, or the unchangeable irrascibility of human nature. These factors produced a differential pattern of success among the three areas of greatest concern to the reformers.

The most dramatic and far-reaching reform of the S&S Years clearly was sweeping away the structure of legally sanctioned racial segregation and discrimination in the South. By any standard for judging social change, this was no mean achievement. It required the combination of authoritative action from above by the federal courts, Congress, and the federal bureaucracy, plus widespread mobilization and intense activity on the part of blacks and white civil rights workers from below. In hardly more than a decade, basic and essentially irreversible changes occurred in southern politics, government, and education. Prior to the passage of the Voting Rights Act of 1965, 29 percent of eligible blacks in seven southern states were registered to vote, compared with 73 percent of eligible whites. By 1972 one million blacks had been added to the voting rolls: 56 percent of blacks registered, compared with 67 percent of whites. On a national basis, in 1956 the percentage of whites who said they voted was forty-two percentage points higher than that of blacks who said they voted (77 percent versus 35 percent). By 1976 this difference had been reduced to eight percentage points (73 percent versus 65 percent). In the mid-1950s perhaps 100 to 200 blacks held elective office nationwide; by 1979 about 4,500 blacks—including 17 congressmen and the mayors of Detroit, Los Angeles, Atlanta, and New Orleans—held elective office, although this still constituted only about 1 percent of all elected officials.[39]

In somewhat comparable fashion, levels of education achieved by blacks and whites narrowed significantly. The results on school desegregation, on the other hand, were not as impressive. In the South, dramatic changes occurred once the federal government began vigorous enforcement of the Supreme Court's decision in *Brown* v. *Board of Education:* in 1964, ten years after *Brown,* 98.2 percent of southern black schoolchildren still attended all-black schools; by 1972, the number had declined to 8.7 percent. In the North, on the other hand, school desegregation moved more slowly and spottily, reflecting residential patterns, white flight to the suburbs, increasingly active local resistance to busing, and the less than vigorous support of school desegregation by the Nixon administration. Finally, with respect to more strictly economic issues, shifts in previous patterns were least marked. The median family income of blacks increased from about 54 percent of white family income in the early 1960s to 62 percent in 1975, and more blacks moved into higher-status and better-paying types of jobs. At the end of the 1970s, however, substantial economic differences still existed, particularly in unemployment rates, and residential desegregation had made little progress.[40] One careful observer summed up the situation in 1978: "black inequality" still remained a "major problem in American society," yet the gains of the previous two decades had "placed blacks in general much closer to equality—however defined—than ever before in our history." More important, because blacks were a self-conscious, well-organized group with a special interest in preventing backsliding, the reforms that had been made would not be easily reversed. The United States, it was argued in 1978, "cannot return to the conditions which prevailed before the 1960s: blacks are too conscious, civil rights legislation barring overt discrimination is too much a part of our practice, and blacks have achieved enough of a political foothold to prevent a return to a not terribly benign neglect."[41] The S&S Years reduced substantially and permanently the IvI gap with respect to Myrdal's American dilemma.

The efforts in the S&S Years to secure more equal rights for other groups of Americans—Indians, Asians, women, homosexuals—were less clearcut in their results. This resulted in part from the fact that the violations of the civil rights of these groups did not appear to be as blatant as those suffered by blacks in the South, and in part from the fact that efforts to promote civil rights for these groups in considerable measure followed in the train of the campaign for black civil rights. As a result, less time existed to produce comparable results before the moralistic passion for reform began to subside and countercurrents to develop. In the most obvious case, the Equal Rights Amendment almost became part of the Constitution in the mid-1970s, having been approved by Congress and ratified by thirty-five states. At that point, however, the opposition mobilized and it became stalemated.

Reform efforts in the area of foreign and military policy took three forms. First and most immediately successful were the efforts to compel the United States to reduce and then end its participation in the Vietnam War. Opposition to the war was gradually fueled by increasingly massive protests between 1965 and 1968; the war clearly played a major role in the election of Nixon; and by 1969 a majority of the American public opposed U.S. involvement. The new administration almost immediately began the gradual reduction of U.S. troops in Vietnam. The invasion of Cambodia in 1970, however, reactivated massive opposition, and in due course resulted in U.S. agreement to an armistice and disengagement from the conflict. In 1973 it also produced an act of Congress prohibiting U.S. involvement in military action in the Indochinese peninsula, thereby removing the sanction underpinning the armistice agreement completed the previous January. Second, reformers moved to reduce the resources, autonomy, and influence of the major U.S. agencies—the military and intelligence services—involved in overseas operations. For the first time after World War II, Congress refused to approve and drastically reduced funds for major weapons programs. In real terms, military spending declined every year from 1969 through 1975. The personnel strength of the armed forces was reduced to a level significantly below that which existed before the Vietnam buildup. Intelligence budgets were similarly slashed. Covert operations for purposes other than intelligence-gathering were prohibited except with the express approval of the President reported to congressional foreign relations committees. Finally, congressional reformers also moved to rectify what they saw as the excessive power of the President in foreign relations. A War Powers Act attempted to limit his ability to commit the armed forces to military action. Many other actions also contributed to a significant reallocation of authority over foreign affairs between the executive and legislative branches.

The actions designed to produce U.S. withdrawal from the Vietnam War were clearly successful. Whether designed to have that effect or not, they made it much easier for North Vietnam to establish its control over the entire country in 1975. The actions reducing and weakening the military and intelligence services had a major impact that lasted at least through the following decade. By the end of the 1970s, however, people's perceptions of the nature of the threats to national security, coupled with their perceptions of the relative decline of American power, drastically changed public and congressional attitudes on these matters. Military spending became highly popular; restrictions on intelligence and military operations were loosened; the so-called "intelligence charter" originally designed to prevent abuses of power by intelligence agencies became stalemated in Congress, joining the ERA as one of the unconsummated reforms of the S&S Years. Finally, the balance of authority between legislature and executive slowly began to shift back toward the the latter.

The third major set of reforms was directed at the political processes through which public officials were selected and government decisions were made. The major targets at both state and national levels were political parties and elections, legislatures, and the bureaucracy. In all these areas, many reforms were proposed and a considerable number were made. These included the removal or relaxation of restrictions on voting (poll taxes, literacy tests, age requirements, residency requirements); expanded use of the initiative and referendum; the campaign finance laws of 1971 and 1974; and changes in internal party processes to promote greater representativeness of party leaders and, most notably, to expand the use of presidential primaries from seventeen states in 1968 to thirty-seven states in 1980. Reforms in Congress were directed toward weakening the seniority system, expanding congressional staff, multiplying leadership opportunities within Congress, enhancing congressional control over the budget process, opening up committee hearings and meetings to the public, and enacting "ethics" codes designed to minimize potential conflicts of interest. With respect to the bureaucracy, "sunshine laws"— the most notable of which were the Freedom of Information Acts of 1966 and 1974—attempted to open bureaucratic proceedings and records to public scrutiny, while "sunset laws" attempted to place terminal dates on the existence of bureaucratic agencies. In general these reforms in the electoral, party, legislative, and executive processes were designed to make political decision making more public, less susceptible to the influence of money and "special interests," and more open to popular participation and control, and to make decision makers more representative of the people to whom they were presumably responsible.

The extent to which individual reforms achieved the goals of their proponents varied greatly. The overall record of process reforms is mixed at best, and in some cases downright perverse. The removal of restrictions on voting was accompanied by a steady decline from 1960 to 1980 in the proportion of the population exercising the suffrage. The initiative and referendum that had been proposed primarily by populist and liberal advocates in the 1960s became, in the 1970s, the great weapon of conservatives who wanted to cut back taxes and governmental spending. As interpreted by the Supreme Court, the campaign finance laws strengthened the positions of incumbents and millionaires, while at the same time very likely contributing to the decline in voting participation. The proliferation of presidential primaries gave major advantages to out-of-office candidates and to the voters of Iowa and New Hampshire. The efforts to secure more representative national conventions in terms of sociological composition produced national conventions unrepresentative of party voters in terms of political outlook. The diffusion of power in Congress made it increasingly difficult to enact any major legislative program, including one directed toward the goals of reform. The limits on outside earned income enhanced the importance of outside unearned income and, as the Abscam investigation suggested, may have made congressmen more rather than less susceptible to bribery. The growth in congressional staffs created new sources of power no more likely than executive staffs to be responsible to the public. The requirements for publicity drove real decision making back into more informal and unrecorded channels. The Freedom of Information Acts produced a significant expansion in bureaucratic personnel to respond to requests, the bulk of which came from business corporations and lobbyists rather than from the media, public interest groups, or the general public. Sunset laws imposed new responsibilities on bureaucratic agencies and provided them with additional incentives to develop supportive political constituencies to ensure their continued existence.

In the other two major areas of reforms, reformers could point to major accomplishments in racial desegregation and U.S. withdrawal from Vietnam. In the political process area, however, no such dramatic achievements were clearly visible, and the consequences of reform were often quite contrary to the intentions of the reformers. Even the overall record of lasting reform achievements in all three areas was, apart from desegregation, a rather limited one at best, testifying to the resiliency of the gap between ideal and practice and justifying Tom Hayden's perplexed query from the vantage point of the late 1970s: "We ended a war, toppled two Presidents, desegregated the South, broke other barriers of discrimination. How could we accomplish so much and have so little in the end?"[42]

Institutional Realignment

The realignment of political institutions during the 1960s and early 1970s involved shifts in the structures, functions, power, and constituencies of major political institutions similar to those that occurred during the Revolutionary, Jacksonian, and Progressive eras. By the late 1970s, as Anthony King and his colleagues argued, "a substantially new political system" had emerged compared to that which existed in 1960. In key respects, such as presidential nominations, the system that existed in 1960 bore closer resemblance to that of 1932 or even 1912 than it did to that of 1976.[43] The scope and depth of the institutional changes that occurred during the S&S Years have been explored elsewhere and cannot be elaborated here.[44]

Four major changes in institutional roles do, however, warrant mention, both because they involved the central political institutions of society and because they were representative of the type of changes that occurred during the S&S Years. These were the increase in the functions and power of the media and Congress and the decline in the power and functions of the political parties and the Presidency. These changes were not simply a zero-sum reallocation of power. The new importance of the media contributed to the decline of political parties, but this decline had causes that went considerably beyond the rise of television. Similarly, the assertiveness of Congress was only one key factor among many that contributed to the decline of the Presidency.

These shifts were peculiarly significant in their overall implications for the workings of the political system. Historically, the Presidency and the political parties were the two major institutions primarily concerned with integrating diverse interests into effectively functioning electoral and governing coalitions. Congress and the media are ill-equipped to play such integrating roles and are much more capable of playing critical, investigatory, checking, and controlling roles. As we have seen, the relative increase in their power was a prerequisite for the emergence of exposure politics in the early 1970s. As a result of these changes in institutional power, the American political system of the 1970s was less well-equipped to integrate interests into coalitions and to combine policy preferences into legislative programs than the political system that existed prior to 1960.

Technological developments, social trends, and political needs produced four major changes in the position of the press in American politics. First, there was the emergence in the 1950s and 1960s of a truly national printed press, the major elements of which were the national weekly newsmagazines and the major newspapers with a national reach, such as *The New York Times, The Washington Post* and, in due course, *The Wall Street Journal*. These media, together with others, formed the core of a national press establishment that carved out a relationship for itself with the President and other agents of national authority comparable to that which local newspapers had long held with mayors and local authorities in major American cities. To a substantial degree, the journalists associated with these national media determined what was news and set the model for how it should be covered and interpreted. Second, the emergence of television had tremendous impact on how people got their news and, perhaps even more important, on who got the news. The nightly network newsbroadcasts reached an audience far larger than that which had followed printed sources of news. In addition, the television camera affected what was considered news and the making of news. In the beginning, television covered the news; soon, news was produced for television. Third, the increased size and the changed role of the press had its impact on recruitment into journalism. Careers in the media came to attract larger numbers of college graduates, particularly graduates of the better and more prestigious liberal arts colleges. This produced more confident and more vigorous reporters, and more penetrating and extensive news stories. Finally, the combination of these three developments laid the basis for a redefinition of the role of the press, from that of the passive observer and recorder of events to that of the "adversary" of government. Appropriately enough, the highest function of the press came to be defined as "investigative reporting," a multisyllabic label for what a previous creedal passion period had termed "muckraking."

These developments gave the press more power during the S&S Years than it had in the 1950s. Professional students of politics have two principal ways of judging power. One is the reputational technique, which involves asking a cross-section of the relevant public who they think has power. The second is through the analysis of contested decisions to see whose side won. By both these measures, the press did well in the S&S Years. In annual polls from 1974 to 1980, for instance, several hundred leading Americans ranked television on the average as second only to the White House in influence on national policy; in 1974 they ranked it the most influential institution in the country, markedly ahead of the White House. In these polls newspapers always ranked among the dozen most influential institutions, also achieving their top position in 1974 in fourth place behind television, the White House, and the Supreme Court.[45] General public confidence in the leadership of most institutions declined by 15–30 percent between 1966 and 1973; in contrast, confidence in television rose by 16 percent and in the press by 1 percent during these years.[46]

The media, and particularly television, also played major roles in disseminating the images that mobilized public opinion to bring about the passage of civil rights legislation in 1964 and 1965 and U.S. withdrawal from Vietnam at the end of the decade. Television's images of the civil rights struggle in the South were, as Michael Robinson argued, "unusually vivid" and were to a significant degree responsible for the change over a few months in 1963 from 4 percent to 52 percent in that proportion of the American public believing civil rights to be the most important problem confronting the country.[47] With respect to Vietnam, "the greatest emotional force against the war was television news film coverage. As we cannot forget, television showed endless film clips of American troops being killed and injured . . . The contrasts in the treatment of American defeats and alleged defeats (Bataan, Kasserine Pass, the Bulge, compared with *Tet*) or of atrocities (which went essentially unreported in World War II) should stimulate thoughtful people to ask searching questions."[48] Or, as the dean of American newspapermen observed on the last day of the war: "Maybe the historians will agree that the reporters and the cameras were decisive in the end. They brought the issue of the war to the people, before the Congress or the courts, and forced the withdrawal of American power from Vietnam."[49] In the most dramatic institutional confrontations of the Nixon administration, *The New York Times* and Daniel Ellsberg defeated the administration in the Pentagon Papers cases, and *The Washington Post* successfully exposed and eventually brought down the administration in the contretemps sparked by the Watergate burglary. As the *Post*'s executive editor succinctly put it: "The press won in Watergate."[50] In other battles over institutional privileges—the confidentiality of sources, access to judicial proceedings, the law of libel—the press also scored notable victories.

The decline of political parties was an oft-noted phenomenon of the 1960s and 1970s, with many informed observers agreeing with Austin Ranney that the United States was approaching a "no-party system."[51] The decline in party could be seen in the extent to which functions traditionally performed by political parties were increasingly discharged through other means and by other institutions. With the expansion of the primary system, the central function of *nominating candidates for public office* was less and less subject to the control of party organizations and party leaders. The *conduct of political campaigns,* including the raising of funds, was increasingly taken over by the personal organizations of candidates and by professional campaign managers, polling organizations, and political consultants (who could work for a Democratic candidate in one state and a Republican candidate in a neighboring one). Direct mail organizations moved into key positions in fund-raising. In presidential contests, public finance also came to play a role. The central role of television in reaching the voters meant that much less effort was devoted to mobilizing local campaign workers and attempting to reach voters through personal contact.

A third function of political parties had been to *provide a guide to people for voting.* During the 1960s, however, straight-ticket voting in any one election and consistency in party voting from one election to the next both declined precipitously. In the 1940s and 1950s independents made up 20–23 percent of the electorates; in the early 1960s, this proportion began to rise, leveling off at about 37–38 percent in the late 1960s, with 45–50 percent of the new age cohorts entering the electorate in the late 1960s and 1970s refusing to identify themselves with either major party. People no longer relied primarily on party as their guide to a choice among candidates. Issue voting increased in salience as party voting declined. In the 1976 presidential election, issue voting declined somewhat and party staged a modest comeback.[52] The significance of party still remained, however, far below what it had been in the 1950s, with the personal qualities of the candidates and their positions on issues being most important in shaping the average American's vote.

A fourth function of party historically was to provide the channels and means for *recruiting appointed officials in government.* In some measure, parties continued to play this role in the late 1970s. A change in administration in either a state capital or in Washington normally involved a significant change in the higher levels of the executive branch of government. This relationship, however, had already been eroded by the extension of civil service earlier in the century, and it was further reduced in mid-century by the rise of "issue networks" of experts concerned with particular issues and from whose ranks appointments to key positions in the executive branch and on legislative staffs were increasingly made.[53]

Finally, political parties have played a role in the *formulation and implementation of public policy.* Historically this role has been less important in the United States than in other societies, apart from certain exceptional periods such as Woodrow Wilson's first term. In the 1960s, those most active in the two political parties increasingly came to embody two polarized views with respect to public policy. This development made it difficult for the political party to play an integrating function, in terms of creating an electoral coalition, while at the same time the diffusion of authority within both the executive branch and Congress inhibited its ability to decide upon and put through a coherent legislative program. In some respects, as in modifications of the seniority rule by the party caucus, party did become more important in shaping public policy. But these developments did not effectively counterbalance the impact of the major trends toward the further weakening of party.

A variety of different factors contributed to the decline of political parties. Higher levels of education and affluence among voters enhanced the tendencies toward issue voting and toward the development of overall ideological positions on issues. The ease with which candidates (who had the money) could reach voters through television reduced the importance of party organizations and party workers. Many of the reforms introduced during the 1960s and 1970s had the effect (if not the intent) of further undermining the role of party. And, finally, the increasing complexity of issues required increasing expertise and professionalization, which party organizations were generally ill-equipped to provide.

The increase in the power of Congress during the S&S Years had its roots in a natural reaction against the long period of presidential dominance, beginning with the New Deal and reinforced during World War II and the Cold War. It also derived from the changing make-up of Congress —with the influx of younger, more liberal, better educated, and more policy-oriented representatives and senators in the late 1950s and early 1960s. For most of the twentieth century, liberals viewed the Presidency as the principal source of enlightened leadership and progressive legislation and Congress as a bastion of conservatism dominated by southern Democrats and Republicans. In the 1960s and 1970s, both the image and the reality changed. Liberals became fearful of presidential power and entranced with the opportunities for progressive reform through Congress. In the S&S Years, Congress became the institutional channel through which liberal forces attempted to promote changes in American government, American society, and, most notably, American foreign policy.

The shift of power toward Congress was also encouraged by reforms within Congress that reduced reliance on seniority, opened up choice committee assignments to younger members, and multiplied subcommittee chairmanships. The resulting diffusion of power *within* Congress enhanced the power *of* Congress, reducing the ability of any single leader or small group of leaders to "deliver" Congress in negotiations with the President or other outside officials. The ability of Congress to play a more active and positive role in shaping public policy was also significantly strengthened by the growth in congressional staff support during the S&S Years. Two new staff support agencies, the Office of Technology Assessment and the Congressional Budget Office, were created in 1972 and 1974 respectively, and the staffs of the existing agencies, the Congressional Research Service and the General Accounting Office, were significantly expanded. Committee staffs almost tripled in size between 1957 and 1975, and the personal staffs of congressmen more than doubled.[54]

The reforms that groups powerful in Congress wanted to make in foreign-military policy required, as we have noted, a reallocation of power between President and Congress and the extension of congressional control over executive branch activities. In foreign policy, Congress moved to curtail presidential discretion and to compel the executive to be more accountable to Congress. In the 1950s Senator Richard Russell had remarked, "God help the American people if Congress starts legislating military strategy." In the 1970s Congress did just exactly that. In 1970 it imposed deadlines on the withdrawal of U.S. ground forces from Cambodia. In 1973 it prohibited all U.S. "combat activities in or over or off the shores of Cambodia, Laos, North Vietnam, or South Vietnam." The same year it passed the War Powers Resolution prescribing the circumstances under which the President could commit U.S. forces to combat, requiring the prompt reporting to Congress of any such commitment, and limiting the duration of such commitment without express congressional approval. In 1975 Congress prohibited covert U.S. aid to the insurgent forces in Angola opposing the Cuban-supported MPLA. In 1974 and 1975 congressional action seriously affected U.S. relations with the Soviet Union and Turkey by imposing conditions for the granting of "most favored nation" status to the former and the continuation of military assistance to the latter. Throughout the late 1960s and early 1970s Congress displayed a new assertiveness in considering military programs and the defense budget, not hesitating to arrive at its own judgments concerning the merits of the former or to cut significantly the latter.

In 1974 Congress also passed the Budget Control and Impoundment

Act, which restricted the control of the President over the expenditure of appropriated funds and which strengthened the ability of Congress, through new budget committees and the Congressional Budget Office, to exercise overall control over the scope and purposes of government spending. In the same year, Congress required that the director of the Office of Management and Budget and his deputies in the Executive Office of the President be subject to senatorial confirmation. During the S&S Years, Congress also greatly multiplied its use of the legislative veto as a device for controlling executive action. A 1976 survey identified thirty-seven laws, ranging from the Amtrack Improvement Act to the Foreign Military Sales Act, that provided for the use of the veto, the overwhelming majority of which had been passed during the previous decade.[55] Other legislative provisions greatly expanded the range of reports that the executive was required to submit to Congress. At the same time, Congress further asserted its control over the executive branch through its investigations of Watergate, intelligence activities, and other matters.

During the S&S Years, Congress thus enacted a rash of "Presidency-curbing legislation."[56] The overall waning of Presidential power during these years was, however, also rooted in other factors. The reaction against an active role for the United States in the world scene implied a diminished role for the President in the U.S. political scene. The decline of the political parties reduced the importance of the President as party leader and, as a consequence, reduced the certainty that he could secure renomination.[57] Four-year presidential terms became the mean between 1961 and 1981, with one President assassinated, one forced to resign, one induced not to run for reelection, and two defeated at the polls when they did run. In any political system, longevity breeds power, and the contrast between the brief term of Presidents and the Washington durability of senators, representatives, Supreme Court justices, bureaucrats, lobbyists, and journalists necessarily redounded to the disadvantage of the President. In addition, as we have also pointed out, presidential weakness was marked in relation to the press and to the bureaucracy. Every President during the S&S Years expressed his frustration over his inability to secure prompt, active, and responsive compliance with his directives from the bureaucracy.

More generally, during the S&S Years it became clear that a person could become President by creating an effective electoral coalition, but that did not give him the means to govern the country. Election conferred legitimacy but not power, and both were necessary for the exercise of authority. Creating power required the creation of a governing coalition, which became increasingly difficult if not impossible to do as power itself became diffused throughout society. As a result, Presidents increasingly felt a sense of helplessness, an inability to find the levers to be pulled by which to produce the results they felt they had been mandated to achieve. Lyndon Johnson, elected by one of the largest majorities in American history, ruminated as to how essential it was for him to get "the support of the media . . . the Easterners . . . the intellectuals," because "without that support I would have had absolutely no chance of governing the country." He lost much of that support. His successor had almost none; four months after also winning election by one of the largest majorities in American history, he concluded in exasperation, "Nobody is a friend of ours. Let's face it." Neatly expressing the siege mentality of the White House, a senior White House aide advised a young recruit, "One thing you should realize early on, we are practically an island here;" the highest calling was to "protect the President" against the hostile forces surrounding the island. At the end of the 1970s, Gerald Ford could with some legitimacy argue that far from having an imperial Presidency, the United States in fact had "an imperiled presidency."[58]

The four shifts in institutional power that have been noted as major features of the new American political system seem to peak toward the end of the S&S Years. In the later 1970s the public standing of the media declined somewhat, with perhaps some slight moderation of its political clout. With the expenditure of great time and effort, President Carter was able to secure narrow congressional approval for his major foreign policy initiatives, although he was notably less successful in domestic policy. At the beginning of the 1980s, both the capability and will of Congress to challenge the President were less than they had been a decade earlier. The decline of political parties, on the other hand, seemed to continue through the seventies although the Republican Party made something of an organizational comeback, using the federal funds available to the national parties to play an active role in congressional elections. At the beginning of the 1980s, the modest ebbing of the trends that had prevailed earlier was still very far from erasing the basic changes that occurred in American politics after 1960. The Presidency was significantly weaker than it had been then; the parties were shadows of their former selves; Congress was institutionalizing its new power; and the media, particularly the national press and television, played central roles in shaping both elite and popular political attitudes and behavior.

The Misuse and Erosion of Authority

Political authority—that is, the legitimate exercise of power by public officials—can become deficient in two ways. The misuse of authority involves the exercise of power by public officials in ways other than those which have been thought legitimate by the prevailing opinion in society; the realm of power expands beyond the realm of legitimacy. The erosion of authority, on the other hand, involves the shrinkage of the realm of legitimacy within the realm of power. Ways of exercising power previously accepted as legitimate cease to be so considered. The misuse of authority entails a change in the behavior of officials; the erosion of authority entails a change in the substance of or the commitment to the norms of society. Through different means, each produces a disjunction between legitimacy and power in which the exercise of the latter falls outside the sanction of the former. In complex ways, too, each can feed on the other. In some measure, each is unavoidable in any society, and each, carried to an extreme, can disrupt the functioning of society. In the United States, the misuse of authority is more blatant but also more curable; the erosion of authority is less obvious and also less tractable.

During the S&S Years political authority became deficient in both ways. The misuse of authority by officials of the national government was dramatically revealed in 1973 and 1974. Conspiracy to obstruct justice, kickbacks, illegal campaign contributions, burglary, bribery, violation of the civil rights of citizens—the list of alleged crimes by those in high office was a lengthy one. The list of those accused or convicted of those crimes was even more impressive: the President, the Vice-President, three cabinet secretaries, almost a dozen White House staff members, and a variety of other federal officials. The record reveals the misuse and abuse of authority in incredible richness, and strongly suggests the extent to which one abuse of authority breeds another.

The record also demonstrates something else. It is persuasive evidence of the relative effectiveness of the American political system in dealing with the misuse of authority. A primary motive of the framers of the Constitution was to create a system of government that would prevent the abuse of authority and, if that failed, one that would expose abuse, provide the means of ending it, and ensure the bringing to justice those who were guilty of that abuse. To provide security against the concentration of power, as Madison put it, "ambition must be made to counteract ambition. The interest of the man must be connected with the constitutional rights of the place." Hence, the system of checks and balances. Hence also "dependence on the people," which is "the primary control on the government." In the years since 1787, the constitutional checks have multiplied and been institutionalized; government has become more dependent on the people, at least in the sense of being more dependent on choice through popular elections; and other extraconstitutional checks, such as a vigorous and independent press, have served the constitutional purposes of preventing and curbing the abuse of authority. In the history of the world, the government of no other major state is or has been subjected to such an extensive network of controls and checks. In exposing the abuses of authority in the early 1970s, the constitutional system and the political system functioned effectively and precisely in the way in which the framers wanted them to function.

During the 1960s and 1970s, however, authority was not only abused, it was also eroded, and, in some respects and at times, almost eliminated. The range of activity by governmental officials accepted as legitimate by predominant opinion shrank significantly in the S&S Years. Behavior of public officials that had previously induced acquiescence now provoked outrage. The authority of government declined as people ceased to see it as dedicated to the public interest. This erosion was, of course, dramatically reflected in the declining trust and confidence that people had in governmental institutions and leadership. These changes in public attitudes were only one index of a deeper challenge to governmental authority which manifested itself in a variety of other ways.

It would, undoubtedly, be comforting if one could believe that this erosion of authority were simply a product of the misuse of authority. In some respects, the decline of public confidence in government did speed up in the late 1960s and early 1970s, and this phenomenon was undoubtedly in part the result of the revelations of wrongdoing in high places. But it would be totally erroneous to believe that this was the principal causal sequence. The erosion of authority went on independently of the abuse of authority and was not primarily a product of that abuse. As we have seen, in many respects the erosion of authority antedated the misuse of authority, or, more exactly, it antedated the principal revelations of the misuse of authority. The former first manifested itself significantly in the early 1960s; the latter did not appear until the late 1960s and early 1970s. In addition, the questioning of authority was not limited to politics and government, but was part of a much broader challenging of authority in almost all areas of society: the family, schools, universities, churches, businesses, private associations, the military. The erosion of authority, in short, stemmed from both earlier and more general causes than the misuse of authority.

The misuse of authority, on the other hand, may have been in part a product of the erosion of authority. First, the decline in the authority of public officials and, in particular, changes in their own perceptions of their power and legitimacy can stimulate officials to abuse their authority in an effort to restore their authority. The White House under both Johnson and Nixon became pervaded by a sense of political paranoia, as the President and his men confronted an increasingly critical Congress, hostile press, and resistant bureaucracy. In some instances, as with the leaks of the Pentagon Papers and the Cambodian bombing stories, a cause-and-effect relationship between the attack on authority and the abuse of authority was clearly evident. Second, and more important, is the extent to which the erosion of authority leads not simply to an increase in the actual abuses of authority, but rather a change in the public's attitude toward those abuses. In the American context, as we have suggested, increased exposures of official misbehavior are as likely to be a product of increased public concern about such misbehavior as a product of increased misbehavior. There are, indeed, good psychological grounds alone for thinking that variations in the intensity of public attitudes are likely to occur more frequently than variations in the behavior of public officials. Hence, behavior that went quite unremarked at one point in time may well a few years later become the subject of intense indignation and criticism. In 1969, for instance, to take a minor but representative example, various organs of the national press reported at some length on the public expenditures being made to create a "Western White House" at San Clemente. The overwhelming reaction was one of approbation: nothing was too much to ensure the safety and well-being of the President. Five years later the media rediscovered these expenditures and "exposed" them as the improper use of public funds for private purposes. And everyone waxed indignant over such a gross abuse of power. What had changed, however, was not the behavior of the public official but the perception of that behavior by public opinion. Outrage was not a product of changed behavior; the changed perception of the behavior was a product of outrage. People turn against political authority; they challenge and question authority; and this, in turn, produces revelations of the abuse of authority. Indignation is not the consequence of the exposure of wrongdoing; rather, indignation is the motive for exposure, and, in due course, cynicism is the consequence. Indignation, in short, colors the perception, and the perception then legitimates the indignation. In this way, public knowledge of the abuse of authority is a product of the breakdown of authority.

There was significant erosion of authority in the 1960s, and, partly as a result of this erosion, evidence became available in the late 1960s and early 1970s of the existence of significant abuses of authority. But were these abuses of authority more or less horrendous than the abuses that occurred prior to the 1970s? The opportunities and incentives to abuse authority change over time, but they are not likely to fluctuate widely. Some individuals may be more prone to misbehavior than others. But all public officials violate moral and legal norms at some point in their career. Why are some pursued, exposed, and prosecuted for actions that are ignored when they are done by other politicians? The answer for the S&S Years, as for other creedal passion periods, lies not so much in the behavior of officials as in the temper of their times and the extent to which the American psyche becomes possessed by moralistic demons outraged at the gap between ideal and practice. In these circumstances, authority drains away before the flood of moralism. The American political system, which is so superbly designed to prevent and to rectify abuses of authority is very poorly equipped to reverse the erosion of authority.

Cynicism and the Restoration of Authority

In the early 1960s the rise of moralistic outrage generated protests at the gap between American ideals and American practices. These protests led to some reforms in those practices and they were accompanied by significant changes in the power and functions of key political institutions. These shifts, in turn, facilitated a politics of exposure, which produced ever-widening revelations of further gaps between ideal and practice. In the end, rampant exposure helped undermine the impetus to reform and caused people to adapt to the pervasiveness and inevitability of the existing patterns of behavior. In the dynamics of the S&S Years, in short, moralism produced protest, protest against obvious evils yielded to exposure of hidden evils, and exposure produced cynicism which eliminated the motivation for both protest and exposure. The forces it generated brought the creedal passion period to an end.

In the mid-1960s the American people developed highly unfavorable views of the responsiveness and trustworthiness of their government. At the end of the 1970s these attitudes were as strong as or stronger than they had ever been before. In early 1980, 84 percent of the American public felt that special interests obtained more from the government than the people did, 78 percent that the rich were getting richer and the poor poorer, 70 percent that the people in Washington were out of touch with the rest of the country, 64 percent that what they thought didn't count very much anymore, and 50 percent that the people running the country did not really care what happened to them.[59]

In the 1960s, attitudes such as these were accompanied by feelings of outrage, and efforts were made to correct these perceived deficiencies in government. In the late 1970s, the unfavorable perceptions of government remained, but the impulse to take corrective action had disappeared. Like other creedal passion periods, the S&S Years left a stratum of organizations—public interest lobbies, environmental groups, women's groups, minority organizations, and the like—that in some measure institutionalized higher levels of political consciousness and activity than had existed before the 1960s. In the 1970s, however, the intensity and breadth of appeal of these organizations declined from the peaks they had reached a few years earlier. Indignation exhausted itself. The impetus for exposure and reform waned. Political participation and interest in politics subsided. Illustrative of the shift was the fact that whereas 58 percent of college freshmen in 1966 said that "keeping up to date with political affairs" was "essential" or "very important" to them, in 1978 only 37 percent responded similarly.[60] The political efficacy of the American people—that is, their confidence in their ability to influence the political process—went down. Alienation plus apathy yielded cynicism.

By the late 1970s people were disillusioned with the possibility of society reforming government. They had also become disillusioned about the possibility of government improving society. The shift in the mood of the country in 1976 was caught by Jimmy Carter in his campaign with his emphasis on morality, honesty, and integrity on the one hand (which appealed to the lingering elements of moralism in the public mood) and his emphasis on the limits of governmental action on the other (which reflected the rising currents of cynicism and indifference). This country deserves, Carter said, "a government as good as its people" (and, implicitly, as good as its people think it *ought* to be), yet at the same time he foresaw a government that would not and could not do much good for the people. "Lowered expectations" were the keynote of the times.

The political climate of the late 1970s was distinguished by the increasing ascendancy of conservative, antigovernment attitudes among the public at large and of conservative, antigovernment ideas among the intellectual elite. This shift to the right was first marked in the 1976 election results, as Carter defeated his liberal opponents for the Democratic nomination and Ronald Reagan almost unseated an incumbent Republican President. It was marked again in 1978 by the defeat of liberal candidates for state and local office and the victory of conservative, antitaxation referenda in several states. It continued in 1980 with the primary victories of Carter and Reagan, the defeat of Carter in the November election, and the unseating of a number of liberal Democratic senators. Americans were not only distrustful of governmental authority, they were also hostile to governmental activity. In 1959, for instance, when asked to identify which was "the biggest threat to the country in the future," only 14 percent of the public picked "big government," compared to 41 percent who picked "big labor" and 15 percent who chose "big business." In 1978, in contrast, 47 percent of the public picked big government for this honor, compared to 19 percent each for big business and big labor. Similarly, in 1964 only 43 percent of the American public thought the government in Washington was "too big"; by 1976 over 58 percent of the public believed this, and in both 1972 and 1976, 50 percent or more of those identifying themselves as liberals, moderates, and conservatives held this view.[61] During the S&S Years, in sum, the latent antigovernmentalism of the American Creed surged to the forefront of public consciousness.

The immediate legacy of the S&S Years with respect to public attitudes was thus high levels of distrust in government and relatively deep beliefs that little could be done to correct that situation. So long as Americans perceived their government to have deviated far from their ideals as to what government should be, they were, perforce, driven to either a moralistic or cynical response. So long as they remained morally exhausted by the passions of the S&S Years, they were, perforce, inclined to cynicism.

Yet human beings also want leadership, direction, and authority, and in the last years of the 1970s this desire began to emerge. Political commentators and social critics began to criticize the operation of the separation of powers and other constitutional mechanisms for dividing and limiting power. There was a growing feeling that the President then in office had failed them in not providing such a lead. Jimmy Carter had been elected President in 1976 in part because he appealed to the need of

Americans at that point for someone who was personally irreproachable and who was divorced from what had been going on in Washington. He was defeated for reelection in 1980 in part because people then wanted a President who not only was virtuous but also forceful and decisive. We have been "gasping for a lead," as one young congressman said in 1980, but the "hungry sheep looked up and were not fed."[62]

The diminished power of the Presidency became a major cause of concern. In some cases, the shift was remarkably quick. On March 13, 1975, for instance, Joseph Kraft published a column titled "Meddling by Congress in Foreign Affairs Works after All"—a headline that perfectly reflected the fear of presidential power that had prevailed during the previous half-decade. Eighteen months later, he published another column under the heading "It's Time to End 'Congressional Foreign Policy,' " which neatly mirrored the shift in informed public opinion that occurred in the course of a few brief months.[63] In 1978 and 1979 expressions of concern multiplied about the weakness of the Presidency and the need for presidential leadership. Less than a decade after the outpourings of outrage over the "imperial Presidency," Washington analysts were making the case for presidential "majesty."[64] As I argued earlier, these arguments as to the weakness of presidential power were, in fact, evidence of the revival of presidential power.

These signs suggested the possibility of continued movement in the cycle of public responses to the gap between ideal and reality in American politics: from cynicism coupled with distrust of governmental authority and hostility to governmental activity, to complacency marked by acceptance of both governmental authority and existing levels of governmental activity. A shift in public attitudes toward authority cannot in itself, however, bring about the restoration of authority. The latter requires not only a subjective yearning for leadership but also the objective conditions that make leadership possible. These include, first, a change in either the role or the influence of those institutions and groups that most strenuously resist authority, and, second, a reconstitution of the fragmented structures of authority below the national level.

During the S&S Years the media were the institution whose power expanded most significantly and that posed the most serious challenges to governmental authority. The national press was more hostile to political authority than the local press, and national television seemed more critical of such authority than the national press. In part this reflected the attitudes of the people involved in the national media, who, in addition to being liberal on policy issues, also tended to be antigovernment on institutional issues. "Most newsmen," Walter Cronkite said, ". . . come to feel very little allegiance to the established order. I think they are inclined to side with humanity rather than with authority and institutions."[65] The antiauthority attitude of the media also reflected their choice of an adversarial relationship with government. "The media have become the nation's critics," Roger Mudd commented. "As critics, no political administration, regardless of how hard it tries, will satisfy them." A leading print journalist came to the same conclusion: "The national media," said Theodore H. White, "have put themselves into the role of permanent critical opposition to any government which does not instantly clean up the unfinished business of our time." Hence, "no government will satisfy them."[66] The negative impact of the media on the legitimacy of political institutions led one analyst to formulate an "iron law" to the effect that "in nations where news is produced commercially and independently, the level (or branch) of government which receives the greatest emphasis will, in the long run, also experience the greatest public disdain."[67]

With its stress on what was sensational, simple, and controversial, television played a particularly strong role in undermining authority. "Although it has been only recently and partially documented, network journalism tends to be more 'anti-establishment' than print journalism, especially compared to the non-prestige newspapers."[68] In 1963, early in the S&S era, the major networks inaugurated half-hour nightly news broadcasts, which greatly increased popular dependence on television as a source of news and greatly expanded the size of the audience for news. In the late 1960s, greater reliance on television for news was associated with low political efficacy, social distrust, cynicism, weak party loyalty, and low political efficacy. By the mid-1970s, these characteristics had become so widespread among the electorate that the correlation with reliance on television had virtually disappeared.[69] During the S&S Years the overall impact of the media, particularly of television, was to undermine the legitimacy of government. "The messages received by ordinary people during the past fifteen years," Stanley Rothman observed in 1979, "have tended to give the impression that the country's institutions are corrupt and that modern technology is leading us into a cul-de-sac."[70]

"How can we rebuild confidence in the credibility of our institutions?" asked a *Washington Post* editor in the midst of the Watergate tumult.[71]

One way presumably would be for media giants like *The Washington Post*
to stop undermining the credibility of American institutions. That is, the
media could again redefine their role, this time from an adversarial one
to a supportive one. The alternative means of changing the media's impact
on governmental authority would be to reduce their influence on public
attitudes and behavior. At the end of the 1970s some evidence existed that
this might be underway. One significant indication was the extent to
which the power of the press itself became a subject of debate, with 40
percent of the American public in 1979 thinking that the existing curbs
on the press were "not enough."[72] The courts shifted toward a more re-
strictive position concerning press powers, rejecting claims that First
Amendment rights took automatic precedence over other rights, denying
arguments as to the special "protected position" of the press under that
amendment, and broadening the applicability of the law of libel. By the
end of the 1970s the power of the media seemed to be subsiding somewhat from the peaks it had reached at the beginning of the decade.

The broadest, most pervasive, and most fundamental consequence of
the turmoil of the S&S Years was its impact on authority structures
throughout American society. The surge of participatory democracy and
egalitarianism gravely weakened, where it did not demolish, the likelihood
that anyone in any institution could give an order to someone else and
have it promptly obeyed. In this situation, support for a stronger Presidency could not automatically translate into the fact of a stronger Presidency. In practice, a stronger Presidency could emerge only with the
restoration of authority within other institutions and by the reconstitution
of the complex matrices of personal relations and obligations among
leaders. A President can exercise leadership at the national level only if
there are institutional, bureaucratic, associational, and local leaders with
whom he can deal at the subnational level. It is through such a system
rather than through broad appeals to public opinion that Presidents
achieve the policy results they desire. Vigorous and responsible national
leadership requires a network of petty tyrants. The protests, exposure,
reforms, and realignment of the S&S Years substantially shredded that
network. Creating another such network is a complex and drawn-out
process. Until that happens, the gap between the leadership that people
desire and the leadership that the system permits will further discredit
those in leadership positions and, in a vicious circle, make it still more
difficult for them to act.

The S&S Years thus left the United States with a more equitable society, a more open politics, a more cynical public, and a less authoritative and effective government. They left the American people confronting foreign and domestic challenges that required the exercise of power, yet still unwilling to legitimize power.

8 THE VIABILITY OF AMERICAN IDEALS AND INSTITUTIONS

The Future of the Gap

American political ideals and values—the core of American national identity—have been continuously and overwhelmingly liberal, individualistic, democratic. American political institutions have reflected these values but have always fallen short of realizing them in a satisfactory manner. The resulting IvI gap has been a persistent source of tension and cognitive dissonance, which Americans have attempted to relieve through various combinations of moralism, cynicism, complacency, and hypocrisy. The "burr under the saddle," as Robert Penn Warren called it, and the efforts to remove that burr have been central features of American politics, defining its dynamics and shape, since at least the eighteenth century and perhaps before. The question now is: Will the IvI gap and the responses to it continue to play the same role in American politics in the future that they have in the past? Or are there changes taking place or likely to take place in American political ideals, political institutions, and the relation between them that will make their future significantly different from their past?

Three possibilities exist. The relation between ideals and institutions, first, could continue essentially unchanged; second, it could be altered by developments within American society; and, third, it could be altered by developments outside American society and by American foreign involvements. Domestic developments within American society or changes in the international environment could alter the relation between American political ideals and institutions in four ways: the content of the ideals could change; the scope of agreement on the ideals could change; the nature of American political institutions could more closely approximate American ideals, thereby reducing the gap between them; and American political institutions could be significantly altered in an illiberal, undemocratic, anti-individualistic direction; or some combination of these developments could take place.

History versus Progress?

Americans have historically attempted to eliminate or reduce the IvI gap by moralistic efforts to reform institutions and practices in creedal passion periods. These periods have had much in common, and almost always the proponents of reform have failed to realize their goals completely. The relative success of reform however, has varied significantly: in particular, the goals of reform have tended to be more widely achieved in the early periods than in the later ones. In the earlier periods, the affirmation of the goals of liberty, equality, democracy, and popular sovereignty was directed at the destruction or modification of traditional political and economic institutions; in the later periods, it was directed at the elimination or modification of modern political and economic institutions that had emerged in the course of historical development. In the earlier periods, in short, history and progress (in the sense of realizing American ideals) went hand in hand; in the later periods, the achievement of American ideals involved more the restoration of the past than the realization of the future, and progress and history worked increasingly at cross purposes.

The revolutionaries of the 1770s were the first to articulate the American Creed on a national basis and were generally successful in effecting major changes in American institutions: the overthrow of British imperial power, the end of monarchy, the widespread acceptance of government based on popular consent, some extensions of the suffrage, an end to what remained of feudal practices and privileges, and the substitution of a politics of opinion for a politics of status. In part, the articulation of their goals was conservative; the rights asserted were justified by reference to common law and the rights of Englishmen. But the formulation and public proclamation of those rights was also a revolutionary event in terms of political theory and political debate.

In the Jacksonian years, the American ideology was still new, fresh, and directed toward the elimination of the political restrictions on democracy, the broadening of popular participation in government, the abolition of status and the weakening of specialization—that is, of both ascriptive and achievement norms—in the public service, and the destruction of the Bank of the United States and other manifestations of the "money power," so as to open wide the doors of economic opportunity. "Originally a fight against political privilege, the Jacksonian movement . . . broadened into a fight against economic privilege, rallying to its support a host of 'rural capitalists and village entrepreneurs.' "[1] Except for the South and the role of blacks in American society, the Jacksonian reforms did complete the virtual elimination of traditional institutions and practices, inherited from a colonial past or concocted by the Federalist commercial oligarchy, which deviated from liberal-democratic values. All this was progressive in the broad sense, but it too carried with it elements of conservatism. The paradox of the Jacksonians was that even as they cleared away obstacles to the development of laissez-faire capitalism, they also looked back politically to ideals of rural republican simplicity.[2] Restoration, not revolution, was their message.

The institutional changes of the Jacksonian years did not, of course, bring political reality fully into accord with Jacksonian principle. Neither property nor power was equally distributed. In the major cities a small number of very wealthy people, most of whom had inherited their position, controlled large amounts of property.[3] As is generally the case, however, income was much more equally distributed than wealth, and both wealth and income were far more evenly distributed in the rural areas, where 90 percent of the population lived, than in the urban areas. In addition, there were high levels of social and political equality, which never failed to impress European visitors, whether critical or sympathetic. All in all, money, status, and power were probably more equally distributed among white males in Jacksonian America than at any other time before or since. The other central values of the American Creed—liberty, individualism, democracy—were in many respects even more markedly embodied in American institutions at that time.

For these reasons, Gordon Wood argued, the Jacksonian generation "has often seemed to be the most 'American' of all generations." This "Middle Period" in American history has been appropriately labeled because

many of the developments of the first two centuries of our history seem to be anticipations of this period, while many of the subsequent developments taking us to the present seem to be recessions from it. In the traditional sense of what it has meant to be distinctly American, this Middle Period of 1820–1860 marks the apogee in the overall trajectory of American history. Americans in that era of individualism, institutional weakness, and boundlessness experienced "freedom" as they rarely have since; power, whether expressed economically, socially, or politically, was as fragmented and diffused as at any time in our history.[4]

After the democratization of government and before the development of industry, the Middle Period is the time when the United States could least well be characterized as a disharmonic society. It was a period when Americans themselves believed that they had "fulfilled the main principles of liberty" and hence were exempt from "further epochal change."[5] All that was needed was to remain true to the achievements of the past.

In the Middle Period, in short, American dream and American reality came close to joining hands even though they were shortly to be parted. The gap between American ideals and institutions was clearly present in Jacksonian America but, outside the South, probably less so than at any other time in American history. The inequality of social hierarchy and political aristocracy had faded; the inequality of industrial wealth and organizational hierarchy had yet to emerge. Primogeniture was gone; universal (white male) suffrage had arrived; the Standard Oil trust was still in the future.

In the Middle Period and the years following, the only major institutional legacy that was grossly contradictory to the American Creed was slavery and the heritage of slavery, the remnants of which were still being removed a hundred years after the Civil War. With respect to the role of blacks, the Creed played a continuingly progressive role, furnishing the basis for challenging the patterns of racial discrimination and segregation that ran so blatantly against the proposition that "all men are created equal." Hence, in analyzing the American dilemma in the 1930s, Gunnar Myrdal could take an essentially optimistic attitude toward its eventual resolution. He could see hope in America because his attention was focused on the one area of inequality in American life that was clearly an anachronistic holdover from the past.

More generally, the Middle Period marked a turning point in the nature of progress in America. Prior to that time, "progress" in terms of the realization of American ideals of liberty and equality did not conflict with "historical development" in terms of the improvement of economic well-being and security. After the Middle Period, however, progress and history began to diverge. Progress in terms of the "realization of the democratic ideal," in Croly's phrase, often ran counter to historical trends toward large-scale organization, hierarchy, specialization, and inequality in power and wealth that seemed essential to material improvement. Political progress involves a return to first principles; politically Americans move forward by looking backward, reconsecrating themselves to the ideals of the past as guidelines for the future. Historical development involves pragmatic responses to the increasing scale and complexity of society and economy, and demands increasing interaction, both cooperative and competitive, with other societies.

This distinctive character of the Middle Period and its inappropriateness as a foretaste of things to come are well reflected in the observations of the most celebrated foreign observer of the Jacksonian scene. Tocqueville was, in a sense, half right and half wrong in the two overarching empirical propositions (one static, one dynamic) that he advanced about equality in America. The most distinctive aspect of American society, he argued, is "the general equality of condition among the people." This "is the fundamental fact from which all others seem to be derived and the central point at which all my observations constantly terminated." Second, the tendency toward equality in American and European society constitutes an "irresistible revolution"; the "gradual development of the principle of equality" is a "providential fact"; it is "lasting, it constantly eludes all human interference, and all events as well as all men contribute to its progress."[6] Like other European observers before and since, Tocqueville tended to confuse the values and ideals of Americans with social and political reality. His descriptive hypothesis, nonetheless, still rings true. By and large, American society of the Middle Period was characterized by a widespread equality of condition, particularly in comparison to conditions in Europe. Tocqueville's historical projection, in contrast, clearly does not hold up in terms of the distribution of wealth and only in limited respects in terms of the distribution of political power.

In attempting to sum up the diversity and yet common purpose of the Jacksonian age, Joseph L. Blau employs a striking metaphor: "As one drives out of any large city on a major highway, he is bound to see a large signpost, with arrows pointing him to many possible destinations. These arrows have but one thing in common; all alike point away from the city he has just left. Let this stand as a symbol of Jacksonians. Though they pointed to many different possible American futures, all alike pointed away from an America of privilege and monopoly."[7] The Jacksonians were, however, more accurate in pointing to where America should go in terms of its democratic values and ideals than they were in pointing to the actual direction of economic and political development. Industrialization following the Civil War brought into existence new inequalities in wealth, more blatant corruptions of the political process, and new forms of "privilege and monopoly" undreamed of in the Jacksonian years. This divorce of history from progress had two consequences for the reaffirmation of American political values in the Progressive period.

First, during both the Revolutionary and Jacksonian years, the articulation of American political ideals was couched to some degree in conservative and backward-looking terms, as a reaffirmation of rights which had previously existed and as an effort to reorder political life in terms of principles whose legitimacy had been previously established. During the Progressive era, the backward-looking characteristics of the ideals and vision that were invoked stood out much more sharply. As Hofstadter suggested, the Founding Fathers "dreamed of and planned for a long-term future," the Middle Period generations were absorbed with the present, and the Progressives consciously and explicitly looked to the past: "Beginning with the time of Bryan, the dominant American ideal has been steadily fixed on bygone institutions and conditions. In early twentieth-century progressivism this backward-looking vision reached the dimensions of a major paradox. Such heroes of the progressive revival as Bryan, La Follette, and Wilson proclaimed that they were trying to undo the mischief of the past forty years and re-create the old nation of limited and decentralized power, genuine competition, democratic opportunity, and enterprise."[8] The Progressives were reaffirming the old ideals in opposition to large-scale new organizations—economic and political—which were organizing and giving shape to the twentieth century. This was most manifest in William Jennings Bryan, who was, as Croly said, basically "a Democrat of the Middle Period." Bryan, according to Walter Lippmann, "thought he was fighting the plutocracy" but in actuality "was fighting something much deeper than that; he was fighting the larger scale of human life." Bryan was thus a "genuine conservative" who stood for "the popular tradition of America," whereas his enemies were trying to destroy that tradition.[9] But he was also a radical attempting to apply and to realize the ideals of the American Revolution. Bryan was, in fact, just as radical as Garrison, but Garrison was moving with history and Bryan against it. In a similar vein, Woodrow Wilson also reacted to the growth of large-scale economic organization with the call to "restore" American politics to their former pristine, individualistic strength and vigor. To achieve this goal Wilson was willing to employ governmental power, thereby, as Lippmann pointed out, creating the inner contradiction that was at the heart of the Progressive outlook. Among the Progressives, Theodore Roosevelt was most explicit in arguing that large-scale economic organizations had to be accepted; nonetheless he, too, held to much of the older ideal; his argument was couched in pragmatic rather than ideological terms: "This is the age of combination, and any effort to prevent all combination will be not only useless, but in the end vicious, because of the contempt for the law which the failure to enforce law inevitably produces."[10]

Second, the reaffirmation of American ideals at the turn of the century could not be as effective as the Revolutionary and Jacksonian affirmations in realizing those ideals in practice. At the extreme, Bryan became the Don Quixote of American politics, battling for a vision of American society that could never be realized again. In the Revolutionary and Jacksonian periods, the institutional reforms had been substantial and effective. In the Progressive period, both economic and political reforms could, at best, be described as only partly successful. The antitrust laws and other efforts to curb the power of big business made a difference in the development of American business—as any comparison with Europe will demonstrate—but they clearly did not stop or reverse the tendencies toward combination and oligopoly. In the political sphere, the introduction of primaries did not bring an end to political machines and bossism, and, according to some, may even have strengthened them. In Congress, the attack on "Czar" Joseph Cannon established the dominance of the seniority system; paternalistic autocracy, in effect, gave way to gerontocratic oligarchy. The efforts to make government more responsible encouraged the growth of presidential power. That institutional changes were made is indisputable, but so is the fact that, by and large, they were substantially less successful than the changes of the Revolutionary and Jacksonian years in realizing the hopes and goals of their proponents.

The passion of the 1960s and 1970s was, in some respects, ideologically purer than the theories of the Progressives. Perhaps for this reason, it was also somewhat more effective in eroding political authority. Yet outside of race relations, its more specific reforms were little more successful than those of the Progressives. Economic power was assaulted but remained concentrated. Presidential authority was weakened but rebounded. The military and intelligence agencies declined in money, matériel, and morale in the 1970s but were reestablishing themselves on all three fronts by the early 1980s. It seemed likely that the institutional structure and the distribution of power in American society and politics in 1985 would not differ greatly from what they had been in 1960. With the important exception of race relations, the IvI gap of the early eighties duplicated that of the early sixties.

This changing record of success from one creedal passion period to the next reflected the changing nature of reform. In the earlier periods, reform generally involved the "dismantling" of social, political, and economic institutions responsible for the IvI gap. The disharmony of American politics was thought to be—and in considerable measure was—man-made. Remove the artificial restraints, and society and politics would naturally move in the direction in which they morally should move. In later creedal passion periods, beginning with the Progressive era, this assumption of *natural* congruence of ideal and reality was displaced by the idea of *contrived* congruence. Consciously designed governmental policy and action was necessary to reduce the gap. In the post–World War II period, for instance, "for the first time in American history, equality became a major object of governmental policy."[11] The Progressives created antitrust offices and regulatory commissions to combat monopoly power and promote competition. The reformers of the 1960s brought into existence an "imperial judiciary" in order to eliminate racial segregation and inequalities. To a much greater degree than in the earlier periods, in order to realize American values the reformers of the later periods had to create institutional mechanisms that threatened those values.

In a broader context, the actual course of institutional development is the product of the complex interaction of social, political, economic, and ideological forces. In the United States, any centralization of power produced by the expansion of governmental bureaucracy is mitigated by pluralistic forces that disperse power among bureaucratic agencies, congressional committees, and interest groups and that undermine efforts to subordinate lower-ranking executive officials to higher-ranking ones. Yet an increasingly sophisticated economy and active involvement in world affairs seem likely to create stronger needs for hierarchy, bureaucracy, centralization of power, expertise, big government specifically, and big organizations generally. In some way or another, society will respond to these needs, while still attempting to realize the values of the American Creed to which they are so contradictory. If history is against progress, for how long will progress resist history?

Acute tension between the requisites of development and the norms of ideology played a central role in the evolution of communist China during its first quarter century. China can avoid this conflict for as long as its leaders agree on the priority of development over revolution. In the United States, in contrast, no group of leaders can suppress by fiat the liberal values that have defined the nation's identity. The conflict between developmental need and ideological norm that characterized Mao's China in the 1960s and 1970s is likely to be duplicated in the American future unless other forces change, dilute, or eliminate the central ideals of the American Creed.

What is the probability of this happening? Do such forces exist? Several possibilities suggest themselves.

First, the core values of the Creed are products of the seventeenth and eighteenth centuries. Their roots lie in the English and American revolutionary experiences, in seventeenth-century Protestant moralism and eighteenth-century liberal rationalism. The historical dynamism and appeal of these ideals could naturally begin to fade after two centuries, particularly as those ideals come to be seen as increasingly irrelevant in a complex modern economy and a threatening international environment. In addition, to the extent that those ideals derive from Protestant sources, they must also be weakened by secular trends toward secularism that exist even in the United States. The four great awakenings that preceded and were associated with outbursts of creedal passion successively played less central roles in American society, that of the 1950s being very marginal in its impact compared to that of the 1740s. As religious passion weakens, how likely is the United States to sustain a firm commitment to its traditional values? Would an America without its Protestant core still be America?

Second, the social, economic, and cultural changes associated with the transition from industrial to postindustrial society could also give rise to new political values that would displace the traditional liberal values associated with bourgeois society and the rise of industrialism. In the 1960s and 1970s in both Europe and America, social scientists found evidence of the increasing prevalence of "postbourgeois" or "postmaterialist" values, particularly among younger cohorts. In somewhat similar vein, George

Lodge foresaw the displacement of Lockean, individualistic ideology in the United States by a "communitarian" ideology, resembling in many aspects the traditional Japanese collectivist approach.[12]

Third, as Hofstadter and others argued, the early twentieth-century immigration of Catholics, Orthodox, and Jews from central, eastern, and southern Europe introduced a different "ethic" into American cities. In the late twentieth century, the United States experienced its third major wave of postindependence immigration, composed largely of Puerto Ricans, Mexicans, Cubans, and others from Latin America and the Caribbean. Like their predecessors, the more recent immigrants could well introduce into American society political and social values markedly in contrast with those of Lockean liberalism. In these circumstances, the consensus on the latter could very likely be either disrupted or diluted.

Fourth, the historical function of the Creed in defining national identity could conceivably become less significant, and widespread belief in that Creed could consequently become less essential to the continued existence of the United States as a nation. Having been in existence as a functioning national society and political entity for over two hundred years, the United States may have less need of these ideals to define its national identity in the future. History, tradition, custom, culture, and a sense of shared experience such as other major nations have developed over the centuries could also come to define American identity, and the role of abstract ideals and values might be reduced. The *ideational* basis of national identity would be replaced by an *organic* one. "American exceptionalism" would wither. The United States would cease to be "a nation with the soul of a church" and would become a nation with the soul of a nation.

Some or all of these four factors could alter American political values so as to reduce the gap between these values and the reality of American institutional practice. Yet the likelihood of this occurring does not seem very high. Despite their seventeenth- and eighteenth-century origins, American values and ideals have demonstrated tremendous persistence and resiliency in the twentieth century. Defined vaguely and abstractly, these ideals have been relatively easily adapted to the needs of successive generations. The constant social change in the United States, indeed, underlies their permanence. Rising social, economic, and ethnic groups need to reinvoke and to reinvigorate those values in order to promote their own access to the rewards of American society. The shift in emphasis among values manifested by younger cohorts in the 1960s and 1970s does not necessarily mean the end of the traditional pattern. In many respects, the articulation of these values was, as it had been in the past, a protest against the perceived emergence of new centers of power. The yearning for "belonging and intellectual and esthetic self-fulfillment" found to exist among the younger cohorts of the 1960s and 1970s,[13] could, in fact, be interpreted as "a romantic, Luddite reaction against the bureaucratic and technological tendencies of postindustrialism." This confrontation between ideology and institutions easily fits into the well-established American pattern. Indeed, insofar as "the postindustrial society is more highly educated and more participant than American society in the past and insofar as American political institutions will be more bureaucratic and hierarchical than before, the conflict between ideology and institutions could be more intense than it has ever been."[14]

Similarly, the broader and longer-term impact of the Latin immigration of the 1950s, 1960s, and 1970s could reinforce the central role of the American Creed both as a way of legitimizing claims to political, economic, and social equality and also as the indispensable element in defining national identity. The children and grandchildren of the European immigrants of the early twentieth century in due course became ardent adherents to traditional American middle-class values. In addition, the more culturally pluralistic the nation becomes, particularly if cultural pluralism encompasses linguistic pluralism, the more essential the political values of the Creed become in defining what it is that Americans have in common. At some point, traditional American ideals—liberty, equality, individualism, democracy—may lose their appeal and join the ideas of racial inequality, the divine right of kings, and the dictatorship of the proletariat on the ideological scrap heap of history. There is, however, little to suggest that this will be a twentieth-century happening.

If the IvI gap remains a central feature of American politics, the question then becomes: What changes, if any, may occur in the traditional pattern of responses to this gap? Three broad possibilities exist.

First, the previous pattern of response could continue. If the periodicity of the past prevails, a major sustained creedal passion period will occur in the second and third decades of the twenty-first century. In the interim, moralism, cynicism, complacency, and hypocrisy will all be invoked by different Americans in different ways in their efforts to live with the gap. The tensions resulting from the gap will remain and perhaps increase in intensity, but their consequences will not be significantly more serious than they have been in the past.

Second, the cycle of response could stabilize to a greater degree than it has in the past. Americans could acquire a greater understanding of their case of cognitive dissonance and through this understanding come to live with their dilemma on somewhat easier terms than they have in the past, in due course evolving a more complex but also more coherent and constant response to this problem.

Third, the oscillations among the responses could intensify in such a way as to threaten to destroy both ideals and institutions.

In terms of the future stability of the American political system, the first possibility may be the most likely and the second the most hopeful, but the third is clearly the most dangerous. Let us focus on the third.

Lacking any concept of the state, lacking for most of its history both the centralized authority and the bureaucratic apparatus of the European state, the American polity has historically been a weak polity. It was designed to be so, and traditional inheritance and social environment combined for years to support the framers' intentions. In the twentieth century, foreign threats and domestic economic and social needs have generated pressures to develop stronger, more authoritative decision-making and decision-implementing institutions. Yet the continued presence of deeply felt moralistic sentiments among major groups in American society could continue to ensure weak and divided government, devoid of authority and unable to deal satisfactorily with the economic, social, and foreign challenges confronting the nation. Intensification of this conflict between history and progress could give rise to increasing frustration and increasingly violent oscillations between moralism and cynicism. American moralism ensures that government will never be truly efficacious; the realities of power ensure that government will never be truly democratic.

This situation could lead to a two-phase dialectic involving intensified efforts to reform government, followed by intensified frustration when those efforts produce not progress in a liberal-democratic direction, but obstacles to meeting perceived functional needs. The weakening of government in an effort to reform it could lead eventually to strong demands for the replacement of the weakened and ineffective institutions by more authoritarian structures more effectively designed to meet historical needs. Given the perversity of reform, moralistic extremism in the pursuit of liberal democracy could generate a strong tide toward authoritarian efficiency. "The truth is that," as Plato observed, "in the constitution of society . . . any excess brings about an equally violent reaction. So the only outcome of too much freedom is likely to be excessive subjection, in the state or in the individual; which means that the culmination of liberty in democracy is precisely what prepares the way for the cruelest extreme of servitude under a despot."[15]

American political ideals are a useful instrument not only for those who wish to improve American political institutions but also for those who wish to destroy them. Liberal reformers, because they believe in the ideals, attempt to change institutions to approximate those ideals more closely. The enemies of liberalism, because they oppose both liberal ideals and liberal institutions, attempt to use the former to undermine the latter. For them, the IvI gap is a made-to-order opportunity. The effectiveness of liberal-democratic institutions can be discredited by highlighting their shortcomings compared to the ideals on which they are supposedly modeled. This is a common response of critical foreigners to the American polity, but this approach is not limited to liberalism's foreign enemies. The leading theorists of the Southern Enlightenment, for instance, took great delight in describing the inequality and repression of the Northern "wage slave" system not because they believed in equality and liberty for all workers but because they wished to discredit the economy that was threatening the future of Southern slavery. "Their obvious purpose [was] to belabor the North rather than to redeem it."[16]

Those who have battered liberal institutions with the stick of liberal ideals have, however, more often been on the Left than on the Right. There is a reason for this, which is well illustrated by the attitudes of conservatives, liberals, and revolutionaries toward political equality. The traditional conservative opposes equality. He may perceive American political institutions as embodying more equality than he thinks desirable. In this case, he normally opts out of American society in favor of either internal or external emigration. The traditional conservative may also perceive and take comfort in the realities of power and inequality that exist in the United States behind the façade and rhetoric of equality. The liberal defender of American institutions embraces the hypocritical response: he believes that inequality doesn't exist and that it shouldn't exist. Both the perceptive conservative and the liberal hypocrite are thus, in some sense, standpatters, satisfied with the status quo, but only because they have very different perceptions of what that status quo is and very different views as to whether equality is good or bad. The ability of the traditional conservative and the liberal hypocrite to cooperate in defense of the status quo is hence very limited: neither will buy the other's arguments. In addition, articulate traditional conservatives have been few and far between on the American political landscape, in large part because their values are so contrary to those of the American Creed. (See Table 6.)

Table 6. Political beliefs and political equality.

| | Traditional conservative | Liberal | | Marxist revolutionary |
		Hypocrite	Moralist	
Perception of political equality	Doesn't exist	Does exist	Doesn't exist	Doesn't exist
Judgment on political equality	Bad	Good	Good	Good
		Standpatters		Radicals	

On the other side of the political spectrum, a very different situation exists. Like the hypocritical liberal, the moralist liberal believes that inequality is bad. Unlike the hypocrite, however, he perceives that inequality exists in American institutions and hence he vigorously devotes himself to reform in an effort to eliminate it. To his left, however, the Marxist revolutionary has views and beliefs that, on the surface at least, coincide with those of the moralistic liberal. The Marxist revolutionary holds inequality to be bad, sees it as pervasively present in existing institutions, and attacks it and them vigorously. At a deeper and more philosophical level, the Marxist revolutionary may believe in the necessity of the violent overthrow of the capitalist order, the dictatorship of the proletariat, and a disciplined Leninist party as the revolutionary vanguard. If he blatantly articulates these beliefs, he is relegated to the outermost fringes of American politics and foreswears any meaningful ideological or political influence. It is, moreover, in the best Leninist tradition to see reform as the potential catalyst of revolution.[17] Consequently, major incentives exist for the Marxist revolutionary to emphasize not what divides him from the liberal consensus but what unites him with liberal reformers, that is, his perception of inequality and his belief in equality. With this common commitment to reform, liberal moralist and Marxist revolutionary can cooperate in their attack on existing institutions, even though in the long run one wants to make them work better and the other wants to overthrow them.

The role of Marxism in the consensus society of America thus differs significantly from its role in the ideologically pluralistic societies of western Europe. There the differences between liberal and Marxist goals and appeals are sharply delineated, the two philosophies are embraced by different constituencies and parties, and the conflict between them is unceasing. In the United States, the prevalence of liberalism means a consensus on the standards by which the institutions of society should be judged, and Marxism has no choice but to employ those standards in its own cause. Philosophical differences are blurred as reform liberalism and revolutionary Marxism blend into a nondescript but politically relevant radicalism that serves the immediate interests of both. This convergence, moreover, exists at the individual as well as the societal level: particular individuals bring together in their own minds elements of both liberal reformism and revolutionary Marxism. American radicals easily perceive the gap between American ideals and American institutions; they do not easily perceive the conflict between reform liberalism and revolutionary Marxism. With shared immediate goals, these two sets of philosophically distinct ideas often coexist in the same mind.

This common ground of liberal reformer and revolutionary Marxist in favor of radical change contrasts with the distance between the liberal hypocrite and the traditional conservative. The hypocrite can defend American institutions only by claiming they are something that they are not. The conservative can defend them only by articulating values that most Americans abhore. The Marxist subscribes to the liberal consensus in order to subvert liberal institutions; the conservative rejects the liberal consensus in order to defend those institutions. The combined effect of both is to strengthen the attack on the established order. For, paradoxically, the conservative who defends American institutions with conservative arguments (that they are good because they institutionalize political inequality) weakens those institutions at least as much as the radical who attacks them for the same reason. The net impact of the difficulties and divisions among the standpatters and the converging unity of the liberal and Marxist radicals is to enhance the threat to American political institutions posed by those political ideas whose continued vitality is indispensable to their survival.

Two things are thus clear. American political institutions are more open, liberal, and democratic than those of any other major society now or in the past. If Americans ever abandon or destroy these institutions, they are likely to do so in the name of their liberal democratic ideals. Inoculated against the appeal of foreign ideas, America has only to fear her own.

America versus the World?

The IvI gap poses two significant issues with respect to the relations between the United States and the rest of the world. First, what are the implications of the gap for American institutions and processes concerned with foreign relations and national security? To what extent should those institutions and processes conform to American liberal, individualistic, democratic values? Second, what are the implications of the gap for American policy toward other societies? To what extent should the United States attempt to make the institutions and policies of other societies conform to American values? For much of its history when it was relatively isolated from the rest of the world, as it was between 1815 and 1914, the United States did not have to grapple seriously with these problems. In the mid-twentieth century, however, the United States became deeply, complexly, and seemingly inextricably involved with the other countries of the world. That involvement brought to the fore and gave new significance and urgency to these two long-standing and closely related issues. These issues are closely related because efforts to reduce the IvI gap in the institutions and processes of American foreign relations reduce the ability of the United States to exercise power in international affairs, including its ability to reduce that gap between American values and foreign institutions and policies. Conversely, efforts to encourage foreign institutions and practices to conform to American ideals require the expansion of American power and thus make it more difficult for American institutions and policies to conform to those ideals.

Foreign-Policy Institutions

The relation of its institutions and processes concerned with foreign relations to the ideals and values of its political ideology is a more serious problem for the United States than for most other societies. The differences between the United States and western Europe in this respect are particularly marked. First, the ideological pluralism of western European societies does not provide a single set of political principles by which to judge foreign-policy institutions and practices. Those, as well as other institutions and practices, benefit in terms of legitimacy as a result of the varied strands of conservative, liberal, Christian Democratic, and Marxist political thought that have existed in western European societies. Second, and more important, in most European societies at least an embryonic national community and, in large measure, a national state existed before the emergence of ideologies. So also did the need to conduct foreign relations and to protect the security of the national community and the state. National security bureaucracies, military forces, foreign offices, intelligence services, internal security and police systems were all givens when ideologies emerged in the eighteenth and nineteenth centuries. Although the ideologies undoubtedly had some implications for and posed some demands on these institutions, their proponents tended to recognize the prior claims of these institutions reflecting the needs of the national community in a world of competing national communities. European democratic regimes thus accept a security apparatus that exists, in large part, outside the normal processes of democratic politics, and that represents and defends the continuing interests of the community and the state irrespective of the ideologies that may from one time to another dominate its politics.

In Europe ideology—or rather, ideologies—thus followed upon and developed within the context of a previously existing national community and state. In America, ideology in the form of the principles of the American Creed existed before the formation of a national community and political system. These principles defined the identity of the community when there were no institutions for dealing with the other countries of the world. It was assumed that the foreign-policy institutions, like other political institutions, would reflect the basic values of the preexisting and overwhelmingly preponderant ideology. Yet precisely these institutions— foreign and intelligence services, military and police forces—have functional imperatives that conflict most sharply and dramatically with the liberal-democratic values of the American Creed. The essence of the Creed is opposition to power and to concentrated authority. This leads to efforts to minimize the resources of power, such as arms, to restrict the effectiveness of specialized bureaucratic hierarchies, and to limit the authority of the executive over foreign policy. This conflict manifests itself dramatically in the perennial issue concerning the role of standing armies and professional military forces in a liberal society. For much of its history, the United States was able to avoid the full implications of this conflict because its geographic position permitted it to follow a policy of "extirpation"—that is, almost abolishing military forces and relegating those that did exist to the distant social and geographic extremities of society.[18] Similarly, the United States did not seem to need and did not have an intelligence service, a professional foreign service, or a national police force.

In the twentieth century the impossibility of sustained isolation led the United States to develop all these institutions. Much more so than those in western Europe, however, these institutions have existed in uneasy and fundamentally incompatible coexistence with the values of the prevailing ideology. This incompatibility became acute after World War II when the country's global role and responsibilities made it necessary for the government to develop and to maintain such institutions on a large scale and to accord them a central role in its foreign policy. During the 1950s and early 1960s Americans tended to be blissfully complacent and to ignore the broad IvI gap that this created in the foreign-policy and defense sectors of their national life. At the same time, various theories—such as Kennan's ideal of the detached professional diplomat and Huntington's concept of "objective civilian control"—were developed to justify the insulation of these institutions from the political demands of a liberal society.[19] In the end, however, the liberal imperatives could not be avoided, and the late 1960s and 1970s saw overwhelming political pressure to make foreign-policy and security institutions conform to the requirements of the liberal ideology. In a powerful outburst of creedal passion, Americans embarked on crusades against the CIA and FBI, defense spending, the use of military force abroad, the military-industrial complex, and the imperial Presidency, attempting to expose, weaken, dismantle, or abolish the institutions that protected their liberal society against foreign threats. They reacted with outraged moralistic self-criticism to their government engaging in the type of activities—deception, violence, abuse of individual rights—to protect their society that other countries accept as a matter of course. *And it's good that they did.*

This penchant of Americans for challenging and undermining the authority of their political institutions, including those concerned with the foreign relations and security of the country, produces mixed and confused reactions on the part of Europeans and other non-Americans. Their initial reaction to a Pentagon Papers case, Watergate, or investigation of CIA is often one of surprise, amazement, bewilderment. "What are you Americans up to and why are you doing this to yourselves?" A second reaction, which often follows the first, is grudging admiration for a society that takes its principles so seriously and has such effective procedures for attempting to realize them. This is often accompanied by somewhat envious and wistful comments on the contrast between this situation and the paramountcy of state authority in their own country. Finally, a third reaction often follows, expressing deep concern about the impact that the creedal upheaval will have on the ability of the United States to conduct its foreign policy and to protect its friends and allies.

This last concern over whether its liberal values will permit the United States to maintain the material resources, governmental institutions, and political will to defend its interests in the world becomes more relevant, not just as a result of the inextricable involvement of the United States in world affairs but also because of the changes in the countries with which the United States will be primarily involved. During the first part of the twentieth century, American external relations were largely focused on western Europe, where in most countries significant political groups held political values similar to American values. Even more important, lodged deeply in the consciousness of western European statesmen and intellectuals was the thought, impregnated there by Tocqueville if by no one else, that American political values in some measure embodied the wave of the future, that what America believed in would at some point be what the entire civilized world would believe in. This sympathy, partial or latent as it may have been, nonetheless gave the United States a diplomatic resource of some significance. European societies might resent American moral or moralistic loftiness, but they knew and the Americans knew that the moral values Americans set forth (sincerely or hypocritically) would have a resonance in their own societies and could at times be linked up with social and political movements in their societies that would be impossible for them to ignore.

In the mid-twentieth century the widespread belief in democratic values among younger Germans and, to a lesser degree, younger Japanese provided some support for the convergence thesis. At a more general level, however, the sense that America was the future of Europe weakened considerably. More important, in the late twentieth century, the countries with which the United States was having increasing interactions, both competitive and cooperative, were the Soviet Union, China, and Japan. The partial sense of identification and of future convergence that existed between the United States and Europe are absent in American relations with these three countries. Like the United States, these countries have a substantial degree of consensus or homogeneity in social and political values and ideology. The contents of their consensuses, however, differ significantly from that of the United States. In all three societies, the stress, in one form or another, is on the pervasiveness of inequality in human relationships, the "sanctity of authority"[20] the subordination of the individual to the group and the state, the dubious legitimacy of dissent or challenges to the powers that be. Japan, to be sure, developed a working democracy after World War II, but its long-standing values stressing hierarchy, vertical ranking, and submissiveness leave some degree of "disharmony" that has resemblances to, but is just the reverse of, what prevails in American society. The dominant ideas in all three countries stand in dramatic contrast to American ideas of openness, liberalism, equality, individual rights, and freedom to dissent. In the Soviet Union, China, and Japan, the prevailing political values and social norms reinforce the authority of the central political institutions of society and enhance their ability to compete with other societies. In the United States the prevailing norms, insofar as Americans take them seriously, undermine and weaken the power and authority of government and detract, at times seriously, from its ability to compete internationally. In the small world of the West, Americans were beguiling cousins; in the larger world that includes the East, Americans often seem naïve strangers. Given the "disharmonic" element in the American political system—the continuing challenge, latent or overt, which lies in the American mind to the authority of American government—how well will the United States be able to conduct its affairs in this league of powers to whose historical traditions basic American values are almost entirely alien?

Foreign-Policy Goals

In the eyes of Americans, not only should their foreign-policy institutions be structured and function so as to reflect liberal values, but American foreign policy should also be substantively directed to the promotion of those values in the external environment. This gives a distinctive cast to the American role in the world. In a famous phrase, Viscount Palmerston once said that Britain did not have permanent friends or enemies, it only had permanent interests. Like Britain and other countries, the United States also has interests, defined in terms of power, wealth, and security, some of which are sufficiently enduring as to be thought of as permanent. As a founded society, however, the United States also has distinctive political principles and values that define its national identity. These principles provide a second set of goals and a second set of standards—in addition to those of national interest—by which to shape the goals and judge the success of American foreign policy.

This heritage, this transposition of the IvI gap into foreign policy, again distinguishes the United States from other societies. Western European states clearly do not reject the relevance of morality and political ideology to the conduct of foreign policy. They do, however, see the goal of foreign policy as the advancement of the major and continuing security and economic interests of their state. Political principles provide limits and parameters to foreign policy but not its goals. As a result, European public debate over morality versus power in foreign policy has, except in rare instances, not played the role that it has in the United States. That issue does come up with the foreign policy of communist states and has been discussed at length, in terms of the conflict of ideology and national interest, in analyses of Soviet foreign policy. The conflict has been less significant there than in the United States for three reasons. First, an authoritarian political system precludes public discussion of the issue. Since the 1920s debate of Trotsky versus Stalin over permanent revolution, there has been no overt domestic criticism of Soviet foreign policy as at one time being too power-oriented or at another time being too ideologically oriented. Second, Marxist-Leninist ideology distinguishes between basic doctrine, on the one hand, and strategy and tactics, on the other. The former does not change; the latter is adapted to specific historical circumstances. The twists and turns in the party line can always be justified as ideologically necessary at that particular point in time to achieve the long-run goals of communism, even though they may in fact be motivated primarily by national interests. American political values, on the other hand, are usually thought of as universally valid, and pragmatism is seen not as a means of implementing them in particular circumstances but rather as a means of abandoning them. Third, Soviet leaders and the leaders of other communist states that pursue their own foreign policies can and do, when they wish, simply ignore ideology when they desire to pursue particular national interest goals.

For Americans, however, foreign-policy goals should reflect not only the security interests of the nation and the economic interests of key groups within the nation but also the political values and principles that define American identity. If these values do define foreign-policy goals, then that policy is morally justified, the opponents of that policy at home and abroad are morally illegitimate, and all efforts must be directed toward overcoming the opponents and achieving the goals. The prevailing American approach to foreign policy thus has not been that of Stephen Decatur ("Our country, right or wrong!") but that of Carl Schurz ("Our country, right or wrong! When right, to be kept right; when wrong, to be put right!"). To Americans, achieving this convergence between self-interest and morality has appeared as no easy task. Hence, the recurring tendencies in American history either to retreat to minimum relations with the rest of the world and thus avoid the problem of reconciling the pursuit of self-interest with the adherence to principle in a corrupt and hostile environment, or the opposite solution, to set forth on a "crusade" to purify the world, to bring it into accordance with American principles and, in the process, to expand American power and thus protect the national interest.

This practice of judging the behavior of one's country and one's government by external standards of right and wrong has been responsible for the often substantial opposition to the wars in which the United States has engaged. The United States will only respond with unanimity to a war in which both national security and political principle are clearly at stake. In the two hundred years after the Revolution, only one war, World War II, met this criterion, and this was the only war to which there was no significant domestic opposition articulated in terms of the extent to which the goals of the war and the way in which it was conducted deviated from the basic principles of the American Creed. In this sense, World War II was, for the United States, the "perfect war"; every other war has been an imperfect war in that elements of the American people have objected to it because it did not seem to accord with American principles. As strange as it may seem to people of other societies, Americans have had no trouble conceiving of their government fighting an "un-American" war.

The extent to which the American liberal creed prevails over power considerations can lead to hypocritical and rather absolutist positions on policy. As Seymour Martin Lipset pointed out, if wars should only be fought for moral purposes, then the opponents against which they are fought must be morally evil and hence total war must be waged against them and unconditional surrender exacted from them. If a war is not morally legitimate, then the leaders conducting it must be morally evil and opposition to it, in virtually any form, is not only morally justified but morally obligatory. It is no coincidence that the country that has most tended to think of wars as crusades is also the country with the strongest record of conscientious objection to war.[21]

The effort to use American foreign policy to promote American values abroad raises a central issue. There is a clear difference between political action to make American political practices conform to American political values, and political action to make *foreign* political practices conform to American values. Americans can legitimately attempt to reduce the gap between American institutions and American values, but in terms of their values can they legitimately attempt to reduce the gap between other people's institutions and American values? The answer is not self-evident.

The argument for a negative response to this question can be made on at least four grounds. First, it is morally wrong for the United States to attempt to shape the institutions of other societies. Those institutions should reflect the values and behavior of the people in those societies. To intrude from outside is imperialism or colonialism, which also violates American values. Second, it is practically difficult and in most cases impossible for the United States to influence significantly the institutional development of other societies. The task is simply beyond American knowledge, skill, and resources. To attempt to do so will often be counterproductive. Third, any effort to shape the domestic institutions of other societies needlessly irritates and antagonizes other governments and hence will complicate and often endanger the achievement of other, more important foreign-policy goals, particularly in the areas of national security and economic well-being. Fourth, to influence the political development of other societies would require an enormous expansion of the military power and economic resources of the American government. This, in turn, would pose dangers to the operation of democratic government within the United States.

A "yes" answer to this question can, on the other hand, also be justified on four grounds. First, if other people's institutions pose direct threats to the viability of American institutions and values in the United States, an American effort to change those institutions would be justifiable in terms of self-defense. Whether or not foreign institutions do pose such a direct threat in any given circumstance is, however, no easy question to answer. Even in the case of Nazi Germany in 1940, there were widely differing opinions in the United States. After World War II opinion was also divided as to whether Soviet institutions, as distinct from Soviet policies, threatened the United States.

Second, the direct-threat argument can be generalized to the proposition that authoritarian regimes in any form and on any continent pose a potential threat to the viability of liberal institutions and values in the United States. A liberal-democratic system, it can be argued, can only be secure in a world system of similarly constituted states. In the past this argument did not play a central role because of the extent to which the United States was geographically isolated from differently constituted states. The world is, however, becoming smaller. Given the increasing interactions among societies and the emergence of transnational institutions operating in many societies, the pressures toward convergence among political systems are likely to become more intense. Interdependence may be incompatible with coexistence. In this case, the world, like the United States in the nineteenth century or western Europe in the twentieth century, will not be able to exist half-slave and half-free. Hence, the survival of democratic institutions and values at home will depend upon their adoption abroad.

Third, American efforts to make other people's institutions conform to American values would be justified to the extent that the other people supported those values. Such support has historically been much more prevalent in western Europe and Latin America than it has in Asia and Africa, but some support undoubtedly exists in almost every society for liberty, equality, democracy, and the rights of the individual. Americans could well feel justified in supporting and helping those individuals, groups, and institutions in other societies who share their belief in these values. At the same time, it would also be appropriate for them to be aware that those values could be realized in other societies through institutions significantly different from those that exist in the United States.

Fourth, American efforts to make other people's institutions conform to American values could be justified on the grounds that those values are universally valid and universally applicable, whether or not most people in other societies believe in them. For Americans not to believe in the universal validity of American values could, indeed, lead to a moral relativism: liberty and democracy are not inherently better than any other political values; they just happen to be those that for historical and cultural reasons prevail in America. This relativistic position runs counter to the strong elements of moral absolutism and messianism that are part of American history and culture, and hence the argument for moral relativism may not wash in the United States for relativistic reasons. In addition, the argument can be made that some element of belief in the universal validity of a set of political ideals is necessary to arouse the energy, support, and passion to defend those ideals and the institutions modeled on them in American society.

Historically, Americans have generally believed in the universal validity of their values. At the end of World War II, when Americans forced Germany and Japan to be free, they did not stop to ask if liberty and democracy were what the German and Japanese people wanted. Americans implicitly assumed that their values were valid and applicable and that they would, at the very least, be morally negligent if they did not insist that Germany and Japan adopt political institutions reflecting those values. Belief in the universal validity of those values obviously reinforces and reflects those hypocritical elements of the American tradition that stress its role as a redeemer nation and lead it to attempt to impose its values and, often, its institutions on other societies. These tendencies may, however, be constrained by a recognition that although American values may be universally valid, they need not be universally and totally applicable at all times and in all places.

Americans expect their institutions and policies devoted to external relations to reflect liberal standards and principles. So also, in large measure, do non-Americans. Both American citizens and others hold the United States to standards that they do not generally apply to other countries. People expect France, for instance, to pursue its national self-interests, economic, military, and political, with cold disregard for ideologies and values. But their expectations with respect to the United States are very different: people accept with a shrug behavior on the part of France that would generate surprise, consternation, and outrage if perpetrated by the United States. "Europe accepts the idea that America is a country with a difference, from whom it is reasonable to demand an exceptionally altruistic standard of behaviour; it feels perfectly justified in pouring obloquy on shortcomings from this ideal; and also, perhaps inevitably, it seems to enjoy every example of a fall from grace which contemporary America provides."[22]

This double standard is implicit acknowledgment of the seriousness with which Americans attempt to translate their principles into practice. It also provides a ready weapon to foreign critics of the United States just as it does to domestic ones. For much of its history, racial injustice, economic inequality, and political and religious intolerance were familiar elements in the American landscape, and the contrast between them and the articulated ideals of the American Creed furnished abundant ammunition to generations of European critics. "Anti-Americanism is in this form a protest, not against Americanism, but against its apparent failure."[23] This may be true on the surface. But it is also possible that failure —that is, the persistence of the IvI gap in American institutions and policies—furnishes the excuse and the opportunity for hostile foreign protest, and that the true target of the protest is Americanism itself.

Power and Liberty: The Myth of American Repression

The pattern of American involvement in the world has often been interpreted as the outcome of these conflicting pulls of national interest and power on the one hand, and political morality and principles on the other. Various scholars have phrased the dichotomy in various ways: self-interest versus ideals, power versus morality, realism versus utopianism, pragmatism versus principle, historical realism versus rationalist idealism, Washington versus Wilson.[24] Almost all, however, have assumed the dichotomy to be real and have traced the relative importance over the years of national interest and morality in shaping American foreign policy. It is, for instance, argued that during the Federalist years, realism or power considerations were generally preponderant, whereas during the first four decades of the twentieth century moral considerations and principles came to be uppermost in the minds of American policy makers. After World War II, a significant group of writers and thinkers on foreign policy—including Reinhold Niebuhr, George Kennan, Hans Morgenthau, Walter Lippmann, and Robert Osgood—expounded a "new realism" and criticized the moralistic, legalistic, "utopian," Wilsonian approaches, which they claimed had previously prevailed in the conduct of American foreign relations. The new realism reached its apotheosis in the central role played by the balance of power in the theory and practice of Henry Kissinger. Foreign policy, he said, "should be directed toward affecting the foreign policy" of other societies; it should not be "the principal goal of American foreign policy to transform the domestic structures of societies with which we deal."[25]

In the 1970s, however, the new realism of the 1950s and 1960s was challenged by a "new moralism." The pendulum that had swung in one direction after World War II swung far over to the other side. This shift was one of the most significant consequences of Vietnam, Watergate, and the democratic surge and creedal passion of the 1960s. It represented the displacement onto the external world of the moralism that had been earlier directed inward against American institutions. It thus represented the first signs of a return to the hypocritical response to the gap between American values and American institutions. The new moralism manifested itself first in congressional action, with the addition to the foreign assistance act of Title IX in 1966 and human rights conditions in the early 1970s. In 1976 Jimmy Carter vigorously criticized President Ford for believing "that there is little room for morality in foreign affairs, and that we must put self-interest above principle."[26] As President, Carter moved human rights to a central position in American foreign relations.

The lines between the moralists and the realists were thus clearly drawn but on one point they were agreed: they both believed that the conflict between morality and self-interest, or ideals and realism, was a real one. In some respects it was. In other respects, particularly when it was formulated in terms of a conflict between liberty and power, it was not. As so defined, the dichotomy was false. It did not reflect an accurate understanding of the real choices confronting American policy makers in dealing with the external world. It derived rather from the transposition of the assumptions of the antipower ethic to American relations with the rest of the world. From the earliest years of their society, Americans have perceived a conflict between imperatives of governmental power and the liberty and rights of the individual. Because power and liberty are antithetical at home, they are also assumed to be antithetical abroad. Hence, the pursuit of power by the American government abroad must threaten liberty abroad even as a similar pursuit of power at home would threaten liberty there. The contradiction in American society between American power and American liberty at home is projected into a contradiction between American power and foreign liberty abroad.

During the 1960s and 1970s this belief led many intellectuals to propagate what can perhaps best be termed "the myth of American repression" —that is, the view that American involvement in the politics of other societies is almost invariably hostile to liberty and supportive of repression in those societies. The United States, as Hans Morgenthau put it, is "repression's friend": "With unfailing consistency, we have since the end of the Second World War intervened on behalf of conservative and fascist repression against revolution and radical reform. In an age when societies are in a revolutionary or prerevolutionary stage, we have become the foremost counterrevolutionary status quo power on earth. Such a policy can only lead to moral and political disaster."[27] This statement, like the arguments generally of those intellectuals supporting the myth of American repression, suffers from two basic deficiencies.

First, it confuses support for the left with opposition to repression. In this respect, it represents another manifestation of the extent to which similarity in immediate objectives can blur the line between liberals and revolutionaries. Yet those who support "revolution and radical reform" in other countries seldom have any greater concern for liberty and human dignity than those who support "conservative and fascist repression." In fact, if it is a choice between rightist and communist dictatorships, there are at least three good reasons in terms of liberty to prefer the former to the latter. (1) The suppression of liberty in right-wing authoritarian regimes is almost always less pervasive than it is in left-wing totalitarian ones. In the 1960s and 1970s, for instance, infringements of human rights in South Korea received extensive coverage in the American media, in part because there were in South Korea journalists, church groups, intellectuals, and opposition political leaders who could call attention to those infringements. The absence of comparable reports about the infringements of human rights in North Korea was evidence not of the absence of repression in that country but of its totality. (2) Right-wing dictatorships are, the record shows, less permanent than left-wing dictatorships; Portugal, Spain, and Greece are but three examples of right-wing dictatorships that were replaced by democratic regimes. As of 1980, however, no communist system had been replaced by a democratic regime. (3) As a result of the global competition between the United States and the Soviet Union, right-wing regimes are normally more susceptible to American and other Western influence than left-wing dictatorships, and such influence is overwhelmingly on the side of liberty.

This latter point goes to the other central fallacy of the myth of American repression as elaborated by Morgenthau and others. Their picture of the world of the 1960s and 1970s was dominated by the image of an America that was overwhelmingly powerful and overwhelmingly repressive. In effect, they held an updated belief in the "illusion of American omnipotence" that attributed the evil in other societies to the machinations of the Pentagon, the CIA, and American business. Their image of America was, however, defective in both dimensions. During the 1960s and 1970s American power relative to that of other governments and societies declined significantly. By the mid-seventies the ability of the United States to influence what was going on in other societies was but a pale shadow of what it had been a quarter-century earlier. When it had an effect, however, the overall effect of American power on other societies was to further liberty, pluralism, and democracy. The conflict between American power and American principles virtually disappears when it is applied to the American impact on other societies. In that case, the very factors that give rise to the consciousness of a gap between ideal and reality also limit in practice the extent of that gap. The United States is, in practice, the freest, most liberal, most democratic country in the world with far better institutionalized protections for the rights of its citizens than any other society. As a consequence, any increase in the power or influence of the United States in world affairs generally results—not inevitably, but far more often than not—in the promotion of liberty and human rights in the world. The expansion of American power is not synonymous with the expansion of liberty, but a significant correlation exists between the rise and fall of American power in the world and the rise and fall of liberty and democracy in the world.

The single biggest extension of democratic liberties in the history of the world came at the end of World War II, when stable democratic regimes were inaugurated in defeated Axis countries: Germany, Japan, Italy, and, as a former part of Germany, Austria. In the early 1980s these countries had a population of over two hundred million, and included the third and fourth largest economies in the world. The imposition of democracy on these countries was almost entirely the work of the United States. In Germany and Japan, in particular, the United States government played a major role in designing democratic institutions. As a result of American determination and power, the former Axis countries were "forced to be free."[28] Conversely, the modest steps taken toward democracy and liberty in Poland, Czechoslovakia, and Hungary were quickly reversed and Stalinist repression instituted, once it became clear that the United States was not able to project its power into eastern Europe. If World War II had ended in something less than total victory, or if the United States had played a less significant role in bringing about that victory (as was, indeed, the case east of the Elbe) these transitions to democracy in central Europe and eastern Asia would not have occurred. But—with the partial exception of South Korea—where American armies marched, democracy followed in their train.

The stability of democracy in these countries during the quarter-century after World War II reflected, in large part, the extent to which the institutions and practices imposed by the United States found a favorable social and political climate in which to take root. The continued American political, economic, and military presence in western Europe and eastern Asia was, however, also indispensable to this democratic success. At any time after World War II the withdrawal of American military guarantees and military forces from these areas would have had a most unsettling and perhaps devastating effect on the future of democracy in central Europe and Japan.

In the early years of the Cold War, American influence was employed to ensure the continuation of democratic government in Italy and to promote free elections in Greece. In both cases, the United States had twin interests in the domestic politics of these countries: to create a system of stable democratic government and to ensure the exclusion of communist parties from power. Since in both cases the communist parties did not have the support of anything remotely resembling a majority of the population, the problem of what to do if a party committed to abolishing democracy gains power through democratic means was happily avoided. With American support, democracy survived in Italy and was sustained for a time in Greece. In addition, the American victory in World War II provided the stimulus in Turkey for one of the rarest events in political history: the peaceful self-transformation of an authoritarian, one-party system into a democratic, competitive party system.

In Latin America, the rise and fall of democratic regimes also coincided with the rise and fall of American influence. In the second and third decades of this century, American intervention in Nicaragua, Haiti, and the Dominican Republic produced the freest elections and the most open political competition in the history of those countries. In these countries, as in others in Central America and the Caribbean, American influence in support of free elections was usually exerted in response to the protests of opposition groups against the repressive actions of their own governments and as a result of American fears that revolution or civil war would occur if significant political and social forces were denied equal opportunity to participate in the political process. The American aim, as Theodore Wright made clear in his comprehensive study, was to "promote political stability by supporting free elections" rather than strengthening military dictatorships. In its interventions in eight Caribbean and Central American countries between 1900 and 1933, the United States acted on the assumption that "the only way both to prevent revolutions and to determine whether they are justified if they do break out, is to guarantee free elections."[29] In Cuba, the effect of the Platt Amendment and American interventions was "to pluralize the Cuban political system" by fostering "the rise and entrenchment of opposition groups" and by multiplying "the sources of political power so that no single group, not even the government, could impose its will on society or the economy for very long . . . The spirit and practices of liberalism—competitive and unregulated political, economic, religious, and social life—overwhelmed a pluralized Cuba."[30] The interventions by United States Marines in Haiti, Nicaragua, the Dominican Republic, and elsewhere in these years often bore striking resemblances to the interventions by Federal marshals in the conduct of elections in the American South in the 1960s: registering voters, protecting against electoral violence, ensuring a free vote and an honest count.

Direct intervention by the American government in Central America and the Caribbean came to at least a temporary end in the early 1930s. Without exception, the result was a shift in the direction of more dictatorial regimes. It had taken American power to impose even the most modest aspects of democracy in these societies. When American intervention ended, democracy ended. For the Caribbean and Central America, the era of the Good Neighbor was also the era of the bad tyrant. The efforts of the United States to be the former give a variety of unsavory local characters—Trujillo, Somoza, Batista—the opportunity to be the latter.

In the years after World War II, American attention and activity were primarily directed toward Europe and Asia. Latin America was, by and large, neglected. This situation began to change toward the late 1950s, and it dramatically shifted after Castro's seizure of power in Cuba. In the early 1960s Latin America became the focus of large-scale economic aid programs, military training and assistance programs, propaganda efforts, and repeated attention by the President and other high-level American officials. Under the Alliance for Progress, American power was to be used to promote and sustain democratic government and greater social equity in the rest of the Western Hemisphere. This high point in the exercise of United States power in Latin America coincided with the high point of democracy in Latin America. This period witnessed "the Twilight of the Tyrants": it was the age in which at one point all but one of the ten South American countries (Paraguay) had some semblance of democratic government.[31]

Obviously, the greater prevalence of democratic regimes during these years was not exclusively a product of United States policy and power. Yet the latter certainly played a role. The democratic governments that had emerged in Colombia and Venezuela in the late 1950s were carefully nurtured with money and praise. Strenuous efforts were made to head off the attempts of both left-wing guerrillas and right-wing military officers to overthrow Betancourt in Venezuela and to ensure the orderly transition to an elected successor for the first time in the history of that country. After thirty years in which "the U.S. government was less interested and involved in Dominican affairs" than at any other time in history—a period coinciding with Trujillo's domination of the Dominican Republic—American opposition to that dictator slowly mounted in the late 1950s. After his assassination in 1961, "the United States engaged in the most massive intervention in the internal affairs of a Latin American state since the inauguration of the Good Neighbor Policy."[32] The United States prevented a comeback by Trujillo family members, launched programs to promote economic and social welfare, and acted to ensure democratic liberties and competitive elections. The latter, held in December 1962, resulted in the election of Juan Bosch as president. When the military moved against Bosch the following year, American officials first tried to head off the coup, and then, after its success, attempted to induce the junta to return quickly to constitutional procedures. But, by that point, American "leverage and influence [with the new government] were severely limited," and the only concession the United States was able to exact in return for recognition was a promise to hold elections in 1965.[33]

Following the military coup in Peru in July 1962, the United States was able to use its power more effectively to bring about a return to democratic government. The American ambassador was recalled; diplomatic relations were suspended; and 81 million dollars in aid was cancelled. Nine other Latin American countries were induced to break relations with the military junta—an achievement that could only have occurred at a time when the United States seemed to be poised on the brink of dispensing billions of dollars of largesse about the continent.[34] The result was that new elections were held the following year, and Belaunde was freely chosen President. Six years later, however, when Belaunde was overthrown by a coup, the United States was in no position to reverse the coup or even to prevent the military government that came to power from nationalizing major property holdings of American nationals. The power and the will that had been there in the early 1960s had evaporated by the late 1960s, and with it the possibility of holding Peru to a democratic path. Through a somewhat more complex process, a decline in the American role also helped produce similar results in Chile. In the 1964 Chilean elections, the United States exerted all the influence it could on behalf of Eduardo Frei and made a significant and possibly decisive contribution to his defeat of Salvador Allende. In the 1970 election the American government did not make any comparable effort to defeat Allende, who won the popular election by a narrow margin. At that point, the United States tried to induce the Chilean congress to refuse to confirm his victory and to promote a military coup to prevent him from taking office. Both these efforts violated the norms of Chilean politics and American morality, and both were unsuccessful. If, on the other hand, the United States had been as active in the popular election of 1970 as it had been in that of 1964, the destruction of Chilean democracy in 1973 might have been avoided.

All in all, the decline in the role of the United States in Latin America in the late 1960s and early 1970s coincided with the spread of authoritarian regimes in that area. With this decline went a decline in the standards of democratic morality and human rights which the United States could attempt to apply to the governments of the region. In the early 1960s in Latin America (as in the 1910s and 1920s in the Caribbean and Central America), the goal of the United States was democratic competition and free elections. By the mid-1970s, that goal had been lowered from the fostering of democratic government to attempting to induce authoritarian governments not to infringe too blatantly the rights of their citizens.

A similar relationship between American power and democratic government prevailed in Asia. There, too, the peak of American power was reached in the early and mid-1960s, and there, too, the decline in this power was followed by a decline in democracy and liberty. American influence had been most pervasive in the Philippines, which, for a quarter-century after World War II, had the most open, democratic system, apart from Japan, in east and southeast Asia. After the admittedly fraudulent election of 1949 and in the face of the rising threat to the Philippine government posed by the Huk insurgency, American military and economic assistance was greatly increased. Direct American intervention in Philippine politics then played a decisive role not only in promoting Ramon Magsaysay into the presidency but also in assuring that the 1951 congressional elections and 1953 presidential election were open elections "free from fraud and intimidation."[35] In the next three elections the Philippines met the sternest test of democracy: incumbent presidents were defeated for reelection. In subsequent years, however, the American presence and American influence in the Philippines declined, and with it one support for Philippine democracy. When President Marcos instituted his martial law regime in 1972, American influence in southeast Asia was clearly on the wane, and the United States held few effective levers with which to affect the course of Philippine politics. In perhaps even more direct fashion, the high point of democracy and political liberty in Vietnam also coincided with the high point of American influence there. The only free national election in the history of that country took place in 1967, when the American military intervention was at its peak. In Vietnam, as in Latin America, American intervention had a pluralizing effect on politics, limiting the government and encouraging and strengthening its political opposition. The defeat of the United States in Vietnam and the exclusion of American power from Indochina were followed in three countries by the imposition of regimes of almost total repression.

The American relationship with South Korea took a similar course. In the late 1940s, under the sponsorship of the United States, U.N.-observed elections inaugurated the government of the Republic of Korea and brought Syngman Rhee to power. During the Korean War (1950– 1953) and then in the mid-1950s, when American economic assistance was at its peak, a moderately democratic system was maintained, despite the fact that South Korea was almost literally in a state of siege. In 1956, Rhee won reelection by only a close margin and the opposition party won the Vice-Presidency and swept the urban centers.

In the late 1950s, however, as American economic assistance to Korea declined, the Rhee regime swung in an increasingly authoritarian direction. The 1960 vice-presidential election was blatantly fraudulent; students and others protested vigorously; and, as the army sat on the sidelines, Syngman Rhee was forced out of power. A democratic regime under John M. Chang came into office, but found it difficult to exercise authority and to maintain order. In May 1961, this regime was overthrown by a military coup, despite the strong endorsement of the Chang government by the American Embassy and military command. During the next two years, the United States exerted sustained pressure on the military government to hold elections and return power to a civilian regime. A bitter struggle took place within the military over this issue; in the end, President Park, with American backing and support, overcame the opposition within the military junta, and reasonably open elections were held in October 1963, in which Park was elected President with a 43 percent plurality of the vote. In the struggle with the hard-line groups in the military, one reporter observed, "the prestige and word of the United States have been put to a grinding test"; by insisting on the holding of elections, however, the United States "emerged from this stage of the crisis with a sort of stunned respect from South Koreans for its determination—from those who eagerly backed United States pressures on the military regime and even from officers who were vehemently opposed to it."[36] Thirteen years later, however, the United States was no longer in a position to have the same impact on Korean politics. "You can't talk pure Jefferson to these guys," one American official said. "You've got to have a threat of some kind or they won't listen . . . There aren't many levers left to pull around here. We just try to keep the civil rights issue before the eyes of Korean authorities on all levels and hope it has some effect."[37] By 1980, American power in Korea had been reduced to the point where there was no question, as there was in 1961 and 1962, of pressuring a new military leadership to hold prompt and fair elections. The issue was simply whether the United States had enough influence to induce the Korean government not to execute Korea's leading opposition political figure, Kim Dae Jung, and even with respect to that, one Korean official observed, "the United States has no leverage."[38] Over the years, as American influence in Korea went down, repression in Korea went up.

The positive impact of American power on liberty in other societies is in part the result of the conscious choices by Presidents such as Kennedy and Carter to give high priority to the promotion of democracy and human rights. Even without such conscious choice, however, the presence or exercise of American power in a foreign area usually has a similar thrust. The new moralists of the 1970s maintained that the United States has "no alternative" but to act in terms of the moral and political values that define the essence of its being. The new moralists clearly intended this claim to have at least a normative meaning. But in fact, it also describes a historical necessity. Despite the reluctance or inability of those imbued with the myth of American repression to recognize it, the impact of the United States on the world has, in large part, been what the new moralists say it has to be. The nature of the United States has left it little or no choice but to stand out among nations as the proponent of liberty and democracy. Clearly, the impact of no other country in world affairs has been as heavily weighted in favor of liberty and democracy as has that of the United States.

Power tends to corrupt, and absolute power corrupts absolutely. American power is no exception; clearly it has been used for good purposes and bad in terms of liberty, democracy, and human rights. But also in terms of these values, American power is far less likely to be misused or corrupted than the power of any other major government. This is so for two reasons. First, because American leaders and decision makers are, inevitably, the products of their culture, they are themselves generally committed to liberal and democratic values. This does not mean that some leaders may not at times take actions that run counter to those values. Obviously, this happens: sensibilities are dulled, perceived security needs may dictate other actions, expediency prevails, the immediate end justifies setting aside the larger purpose. But American policy makers are more likely than those of any other country to be sensitive to these trade-offs and to be more reluctant to sacrifice liberal-democratic values. Second, the institutional pluralism and dispersion of power in the American political system impose constraints—unmatched in any other society —on the ability of officials to abuse power, and also ensure that those transgressions that do occur will almost inevitably become public knowledge. The American press is extraordinarily free, strong, and vigorous in its exposure of bad policies and corrupt officials. The American Congress has powers of investigation, legislation, and financial control unequaled by any other national legislature. The ability of American officials to violate the values of their society is therefore highly limited, and the extent to which the press is filled with accounts of how officials have violated those values is evidence not that such behavior is more widespread than it is in other societies but that it is less tolerated than in other societies. The belief that the United States can do no wrong in terms of the values of liberty and democracy is clearly as erroneous abroad as it is at home. But so also is the belief—far more prevalent in American intellectual circles in the 1970s—that the United States could never do right in terms of those values. American power is far more likely to be used to support those values than to counter them, and it is far more likely to be employed on behalf of those values than the power of any other major country.

The point is often made that there is a direct relation between the health of liberty in the United States and the health of liberty in other societies. Disease in one is likely to infect the other. Thus, on the one hand, Richard Ullman argued that "the quality of political life in the United States is indeed affected by the quality of political life in other societies. The extinction of political liberties in Chile, or their extension in Portugal or Czechoslovakia, has a subtle but nonetheless important effect on political liberties within the United States." Conversely, he also goes on to say: "just as the level of political freedom in other societies affects our own society, so the quality of our own political life has an important impact abroad."[39] This particular point is often elaborated into what is sometimes referred to as the "clean hands" doctrine—that the United States cannot effectively promote liberty in other countries so long as there are significant violations of liberty within its borders. Let the United States rely on the power of example and "first put our house in order," as Hoffmann phrased it. "Like charity, well-ordered crusades begin at home."[40]

Both these arguments—that of the corrupting environment and that of the shining example—are partial truths. By any observable measure, the state of liberty in countries like Chile or Czechoslovakia has, in itself, no impact on the state of liberty in the United States. Similarly, foreigners usually recognize what Americans tend to forget—that the United States is the most open, free, and democratic society in the world. Hence, any particular improvement in the state of liberty in the United States is unlikely to be seen as having much relevance to their societies. Yet these arguments do have an element of truth in them, when one additional variable is added to the equation. This element is power.

The impact that the state of liberty in other societies has on liberty in the United States depends upon the power of those other societies and their ability to exercise that power with respect to the United States. What happens in Chile or even Czechoslovakia does not affect the state of liberty in the United States because those are small, weak, and distant countries. But the disappearance of liberty in Britain or France or Japan would have consequences for the health of liberty in the United States, because they are large and important countries intimately involved with the United States. Conversely, the impact of the state of liberty in the United States on other societies depends not upon changes in American liberty (which foreigners will, inevitably, view as marginal), but rather upon the power and immediacy of the United States to the country in question. The power of example works only when it is an example of power. If the United States plays a strong, confident, preeminent role on the world stage, other nations will be impressed by its power and will attempt to emulate its liberty in the belief that liberty may be the source of power. This point was made quite persuasively in 1946 by Turkey's future premier, Adnan Menderes, in explaining why his country had to shift to democracy:

> The difficulties encountered during the war years uncovered and showed the weak points created by the one-party system in the structure of the country. The hope in the miracles of [the] one-party system vanished, as the one-party system countries were defeated everywhere. Thus, the one-party mentality was destroyed in the turmoil of blood and fire of the second World War. No country can remain unaffected by the great international events and the contemporary dominating ideological currents. This influence was felt in our country too.[41]

In short, no one copies a loser.

The future of liberty in the world is thus intimately linked to the future of American power. Yet the double thrust of the new moralism was, paradoxically, to advocate the expansion of global liberty, and, simultaneously, to effect a reduction in American power. The relative decline in American power in the 1970s has many sources. One of them assuredly was the democratic surge (of which the new moralism was one element) in the United States in the 1960s and early 1970s. The strong recommitment to democratic, liberal, and populist values that occurred during these years eventually generated efforts to limit, constrain, and reduce American military, political, and economic power abroad. The intense and sustained attacks by the media, by intellectuals, and by congressmen on the military establishment, intelligence agencies, diplomatic officials, and political leadership of the United States inevitably had that effect. The decline in American power abroad weakened the support for liberty and democracy abroad. American democracy and foreign democracy may be inversely related. Due to the mediating effects of power, their relationship appears to be just the opposite of that hypothesized by Ullman.

The promotion of liberty abroad thus requires the expansion of American power; the operation of liberty at home involves the limitation of American power. The need in attempting to achieve democratic goals both abroad and at home is to recognize the existence of this contradiction and to assess the trade-offs between these two goals. There is, for instance, an inherent contradiction between welcoming the end of American hegemony in the Western Hemisphere and, at the same time, deploring the intensification of repression in Latin America. It is also paradoxical that in the 1970s those congressmen who were most insistent on the need to promote human rights abroad were often most active in reducing the American power that could help achieve that result. In key votes in the 94th Congress, for instance, 132 congressmen consistently voted in favor of human rights amendments to foreign aid legislation. Seventy-eight of those 132 representatives also consistently voted against a larger military establishment, and another 28 consistent supporters of human rights split their votes on the military establishment. Only 26 of the 132 congressmen consistently voted in favor of both human rights and the military power whose development could help make those rights a reality.

The new realism of the 1940s and 1950s coincided with the expansion of American power in the world and the resulting expansion of American-sponsored liberty and democracy in the world. The new moralism of the 1970s coincided with the relative decline in American power and the concomitant erosion of liberty and democracy around the globe. By limiting American power, the new moralism promoted that decline. In some measure, too, the new moralism was a consequence of the decline. The new moralism's concern with human rights throughout the world clearly reflected the erosion in global liberty and democratic values. Paradoxically, the United States thus became more preoccupied with ways of defending human rights as its power to defend human rights diminished. Enactment of Title IX to the foreign assistance act in 1966, a major congressional effort to promote democratic values abroad, came at the midpoint in the steady decline in American foreign economic assistance. Similarly, the various restrictions that Congress wrote into the foreign assistance acts in the 1970s coincided with the general replacement of military aid by military sales. When American power was clearly predominant, such legislative provisions and caveats were superfluous: no Harkin amendment was necessary to convey the message of the superiority of liberty. The message was there for all to see in the troop deployments, carrier task forces, foreign aid missions, and intelligence operatives. When these faded from the scene, in order to promote liberty and human rights Congress found it necessary to write more and more explicit conditions and requirements into legislation. These legislative provisions were, in effect, an effort to compensate for the decline of American power. In terms of narrowing the IvI gap abroad, they were no substitute for the presence of American power.

Contrary to the views of both "realists" and "moralists," the contradiction arising from America's role in the world is not primarily that of power and self-interest versus liberty and morality in American foreign policy. It is, rather, the contradiction between enhancing liberty at home by curbing the power of the American government and enhancing liberty abroad by expanding that power.

The Promise of Disappointment

The term "American exceptionalism" has been used to refer to a variety of characteristics that have historically distinguished the United States from European societies—characteristics such as its relative lack of economic suffering, social conflict, political trauma, and military defeat. "The standing armies, the monarchies, the aristocracies, the huge debts, the crushing taxation, the old inveterate abuses, which flourish in Europe," William Clarke argued in 1881, "can take no root in the

New World. The continent of America is consecrated to simple humanity, and its institutions exist for the progress and happiness of the whole people." Yet, as Henry Fairlie pointed out in 1975, "there now *are* standing armies of America; there now *is* something that, from time to time, looks very like a monarchy; there now *is* a permitted degree of inherited wealth that is creating some of the elements of an aristocracy; there now *is* taxation that is crushing."[42] In the same year, Daniel Bell came to a similar conclusion by a different path. The "end of American exceptionalism," he argued, is to be seen in "the end of empire, the weakening of power, the loss of faith in the nation's future . . . Internal tensions have multiplied and there are deep structural crises, political and cultural, that may prove more intractable to solution than the domestic economic problems."[43]

In the late twentieth century, the United States surely seemed to confront many evils and problems that were common to other societies but that it had previously avoided. These developments, however, affected only the incidental elements of American exceptionalism, those of power, wealth, and security. They did not change American political values and they only intensified the gap between political ideals and political institutions that is crucial to American national identity. They thus did not affect the historically most exceptional aspect of the United States, an aspect eloquently summed up and defended by a Yugoslav dissident in the following words:

> The United States is not a state like France, China, England, etc., and it would be a great tragedy if someday the United States became such a state. What is the difference? First of all, the United States is not a national state, but a multinational state. Second, the United States was founded by people who valued individual freedom more highly than their own country.
>
> And so the United States is primarily a state of freedom. And this is what is most important. Whole peoples from other countries can say, Our homeland is Germany, Russia, or whatever; only Americans can say, My homeland is freedom.[44]

Americans have said this throughout their history and have lived throughout their history in the inescapable presence of liberal ideals, semiliberal institutions, and the gap between the two. The United States has no meaning, no identity, no political culture or even history apart from its ideals of liberty and democracy and the continuing efforts of Americans to realize those ideals. Every society has its own distinctive form of tension that characterizes its existence as a society. The tension between liberal ideal and institutional reality is America's distinguishing cleavage. It defines both the agony and the promise of American politics. If that tension disappears, the United States of America, as we have known it, will no longer exist.

The continued existence of the United States means that Americans will continue to suffer from cognitive dissonance. They will continue to attempt to come to terms with that dissonance through some combination of moralism, cynicism, complacency, and hypocrisy. The greatest danger to the IvI gap would come when any substantial portion of the American population carried to an extreme any one of these responses. An excess of moralism, hypocrisy, cynicism, or complacency could do in the American system. A totally complacent toleration of the IvI gap could lead to the corruption and decay of American liberal-democratic institutions. Uncritical hypocrisy, blind to the existence of the gap and fervent in its commitment to American principles, could lead to imperialistic expansion, ending in either military or political disaster abroad or the undermining of democracy at home. Cynical acceptance of the gap could lead to a gradual abandonment of American ideals and their replacement either by a Thrasymachusian might-makes-right morality or by some other set of political beliefs. Finally, intense moralism could lead Americans to destroy the freest institutions on earth because they believed they deserved something better.

To maintain their ideals and institutions, Americans have no recourse but to temper and balance their responses to the IvI gap. The threats to the future of the American condition can be reduced to the extent that Americans:

—continue to believe in their liberal, democratic, and individualistic ideals and also recognize the extent to which their institutions and behavior fall short of these ideals;

—feel guilty about the existence of the gap but take comfort from the fact that American political institutions are more liberal and democratic than those of any other human society past or present;

—attempt to reduce the gap between institutions and ideals but accept the fact that the imperfections of human nature mean the gap can never be eliminated;

—believe in the universal validity of American ideals but also understand their limited applicability to other societies; and

—support the maintenance of American power necessary to protect and promote liberal ideals and institutions in the world arena, but recognize the dangers such power could pose to liberal ideals and institutions at home.

Critics say that America is a lie because its reality falls so far short of its ideals. They are wrong. America is not a lie; it is a disappointment. But it can be a disappointment only because it is also a hope.

NOTES

INDEX

NOTES

1. The Disharmonic Polity

1. *New York Times,* June 13, 1969, p. 30.
2. John Adams, *Works,* ed. Charles Francis Adams (Boston: Little, Brown, 1850–56), 4:401, 6:185, 9:570. Alexander Hamilton, in Max Farrand, ed., *The Records of the Federal Convention* (New Haven: Yale University Press, 1911), 1:299.
3. Quoted in Richard Hofstadter, *The Progressive Historians: Turner, Beard, Parrington* (New York: Knopf, 1968), p. 438.
4. Louis Hartz, *The Liberal Tradition in America* (New York: Harcourt, Brace, 1955), p. 31.
5. Hofstadter, *Progressive Historians,* p. 461.
6. George Santayana, *Character and Opinion in the United States* (Garden City, N.Y.: Doubleday Anchor, 1956), p. 129.
7. Hofstadter, *Progressive Historians,* p. 16.
8. André Béteille, *Inequality and Social Change* (Delhi: Oxford University Press, 1972), p. 15.

2. The American Creed and National Identity

1. See Zbigniew Brzezinski and Samuel P. Huntington, *Political Power: USA/USSR* (New York: Viking, 1964), pp. 17–24.
2. Robert G. McCloskey, "The American Ideology," in Marian D. Irish, ed., *Continuing Crisis in American Politics* (Englewood Cliffs, N.J.: Prentice-Hall, 1963), p. 14. See also John Higham, "Hanging Together: Divergent Unities in American History," *Journal of American History* 61 (June 1974): 16–17. On the unity of and conflicts among American values, see the systematic survey by Kaspar D. Naegele, "From De Tocqueville to Myrdal: A Research Memorandum on Selected Studies of American Values," Com-

parative Study of Values, Working Paper no. 1, October 1949, Laboratory of Social Relations, Harvard University. I am grateful to Daniel Bell for making this study available to me.

3. M. Walzer, "In Defense of Equality," *Dissent* 20 (Fall 1973): 408.

4. See, for example, Milton Rokeach, *The Nature of Human Values* (New York: Free Press, 1973), pp. 191–193.

5. Daniel Bell, "The End of American Exceptionalism," in Nathan Glazer and Irving Kristol, eds., *The American Commonwealth 1976* (New York: Basic Books, 1976), p. 209. Herbert Croly, *The Promise of American Life* (New York: Macmillan, 1909), p. 11.

6. Alexis de Tocqueville, *Democracy in America,* ed. Phillips Bradley (New York: Vintage Books, 1954), 1:409. Gunnar Myrdal, *An American Dilemma* (New York: Harper & Bros , 1944), 1:3.

7. Donald J. Devine, *The Political Culture of the United States* (Boston: Little, Brown, 1972), pp. 33, 116, 151, 362.

8. See James W. Prothro and Charles M. Grigg, "Fundamental Principles of Democracy: Bases of Agreement and Disagreement," *Journal of Politics* 22 (February 1960): 282–286. Herbert McClosky, "Consensus and Ideology in American Politics," *American Political Science Review* 58 (June 1964): 365–368. Devine, *Political Culture,* pp. 179–230. Frank R. Westie, "The American Dilemma: An Empirical Test," *American Sociological Review* 30 (August 1965): 531–532.

9. Prothro and Grigg, "Fundamental Principles," pp. 285–291. Westie, "The American Dilemma," pp. 530–535. McClosky, "Consensus and Ideology," pp. 364–373. Samuel Stouffer, *Communism, Conformity, and Civil Liberties* (Gloucester, Mass.: Peter Smith, 1963), pp. 26–57. Devine, *Political Culture,* pp. 260–265. For testimony verifying the impact of the McClosky and Prothro-Grigg studies, plus a fairly unpersuasive effort to challenge them, see Joseph V. Femia, "Elites, Participation, and the Democratic Creed," *Political Studies* 27 (March 1979): 1–20.

10. Devine, *Political Culture,* p. 33.

11. See Louis Hartz, *The Liberal Tradition in America* (New York: Harcourt, Brace, 1955), ch. 6.

12. For a comprehensive review of the literature on this question, see Seymour Martin Lipset, "Why No Socialism in the United States?" in Seweryn Bialer and Sophia Sluzar, eds., *Sources of Contemporary Radicalism* (Boulder, Colo.: Westview Press, 1977), pp. 31–149.

13. Leon Samson, "Americanism as Surrogate Socialism," in John H. M. Laslett and Seymour Martin Lipset, eds., *Failure of a Dream?* (Garden City: Doubleday Anchor, 1974), pp. 426–442, originally published in *Toward a United Front* (New York: Farrar & Rinehart, 1935).

14. Richard Hofstadter, *The Age of Reform* (New York: Knopf, 1956), p. 9.

15. Edward C. Banfield and James Q. Wilson, *City Politics* (New York: Vintage Books, 1963), pp. 329–330.

16. Tocqueville, *Democracy in America*, 2:271, 275.

17. Clyde Kluckhohn, "Have There Been Discernible Shifts in American Values during the Past Generation?" in Elting E. Morison, ed., *The American Style* (New York: Harper & Bros., 1958), p. 152. Seymour Martin Lipset, *The First New Nation* (New York: Basic Books, 1963), p. 103. Lloyd A. Free and Hadley Cantril, *The Political Beliefs of Americans* (New Brunswick: Rutgers University Press, 1967), pp. 175–177. Devine, *Political Culture*, p. 65.

18. Tocqueville, *Democracy in America*, 1:409.

19. James Bryce, *The American Commonwealth* (London: Macmillan, 1891), 2:417–418. Myrdal, *American Dilemma*, 1:4, 8.

20. David Riesman, *The Lonely Crowd* (New Haven: Yale University Press, 1950), and William F. Whyte, *The Organization Man* (New York: Simon & Schuster, 1956).

21. Lipset, *First New Nation*, pp. 101–139. Carl N. Degler, "The Sociologist as Historian: Riesman's *The Lonely Crowd*," *American Quarterly* 15 (Winter 1963): 483–497.

22. Richard deCharms and Gerald H. Moeller, "Values Expressed in Children's Readers: 1800–1950," *Journal of Abnormal and Social Psychology* 64 (February 1962): 136–142. Fred I. Greenstein, "New Light on Changing American Values: A Forgotten Body of Survey Data," *Social Forces* 42 (May 1964): 441–450.

23. Lee Coleman, "What Is American? A Study of Alleged American Traits," *Social Forces* 19 (May 1941): 492–499.

24. John McDiarmid, "Presidential Inaugural Addresses—A Study in Verbal Symbols," *Public Opinion Quarterly* 1 (July 1937): 79–82.

25. Croly, *Promise of American Life*, p. 3. William R. Brock, "Americanism," in Dennis Welland, ed., *The United States* (London: Methuen, 1974), pp. 59, 68. Myrdal, *American Dilemma*, 1:3.

26. Gabriel A. Almond and Sidney Verba, *The Civic Culture* (Boston: Little, Brown, 1965), pp. 64–65.

27. William T. Bluhm, *Ideologies and Attitudes: Modern Political Culture* (Englewood Cliffs, N.J.: Prentice-Hall, 1974), p. 100.

28. Samson, "Americanism as Surrogate Socialism," p. 426. Richard Hofstadter, quoted in Hans Kohn, *American Nationalism: An Interpretive Essay* (New York: Macmillan, 1957), p. 13.

29. John Higham, "Immigration," and C. Vann Woodward, "The Test of Comparison," in Woodward, ed., *The Comparative Approach to American History* (New York: Basic Books, 1968), pp. 98–99, 93, 351.

30. Bryce, *American Commonwealth*, 2:652.

31. Kohn, *American Nationalism*, p. 8.

32. Carl J. Friedrich et al., *Problems of the American Public Service* (New York: McGraw-Hill, 1935), p. 12.

33. Sidney E. Mead, "The Nation with the Soul of a Church," *Church History* 36 (September 1967): 275.

3. The Gap: The American Creed versus Political Authority

1. *Boston Globe,* October 14, 1971, p. 8.
2. Charles H. Hendel, "An Exploration of the Nature of Authority," in Carl J. Friedrich, ed., *Authority* (Cambridge, Mass.: Harvard University Press, 1958), pp. 4–5.
3. Quoted in Rush Welter, *The Mind of America: 1820–1860* (New York: Columbia University Press, 1975), pp. 165–166, 172.
4. William Schneider, "Public Opinion," *Politics Today* 5 (September-October 1978): 10. Donald J. Devine, *The Political Culture of the United States* (Boston: Little, Brown, 1972), p. 102.
5. William Blackstone, *Commentaries on the Laws of England,* 10th ed. (London: A. Strahan, 1787), 1:48–49. John Bowring, *The Works of Jeremy Bentham* (Edinburgh: n.p., 1843), 1:154n, 10:63, quoted in Chilton Williamson, "Bentham Looks at America," *Political Science Quarterly* 70 (December 1955): 549. On the perpetuation in America of older dispersed forms of government displaced in Europe by the rise of the modern nation-state in the seventeenth century, see Samuel P. Huntington, *Political Order in Changing Societies* (New Haven: Yale University Press, 1968), ch. 2.
6. Henry James, *Hawthorne* (Ithaca, N.Y.: Cornell University Press, 1956; originally published 1879), p. 34. Baron J. A. Graf von Hübner, in Richard L. Rapson, ed., *Individualism and Conformity in the American Character* (Lexington, Mass.: D. C. Heath, 1967), p. 24. James Bryce, *The American Commonwealth* (London: Macmillan, 1891), 2:417–418. H. G. Wells, quoted in Esmond Wright, "The End of Innocence," *Political Quarterly* 43 (January 1972): 35. G. K. Chesterton, *New York Times Magazine,* July 12, 1931, quoted in Leon Samson, *The American Mind* (New York: Jonathan Cape & Harrison Smith, 1932), p. 345n.
7. Seymour Martin Lipset, "Why No Socialism in the United States?" in Seweryn Bialer and Sophia Sluzar, eds., *Sources of Contemporary Radicalism* (Boulder, Colo.: Westview Press, 1977), pp. 94–97. See also Erwin C. Hargrove, "On Canadian and American Political Culture," *Canadian Journal of Economics and Political Science* 33 (February, 1967): 107, and, for a general elaboration of this theme, David DeLeon, *The American as Anarchist: Reflections on Indigenous Radicalism* (Baltimore: Johns Hopkins, 1978).
8. Bryce, *American Commonwealth,* 1:299.
9. Cora Du Bois, "The Dominant Value Profile of American Culture," *American Anthropologist* 57 (December 1955): 1238.
10. John George Cawelti, *Apostles of the Self-Made Man* (Chicago: University of Chicago Press, 1965), p. 2.
11. Alexis de Tocqueville, *Democracy in America,* ed. Phillips Bradley (New York: Vintage Books, 1954), 2:108. Louis Hartz, *The Liberal Tradition in America* (New York: Harcourt, Brace, 1955), pp. 85–86. Huntington, *Political Order,* p. 125.
12. George C. Lodge, *The New American Ideology* (New York: Knopf, 1975), p. 15.

13. The one notable exception to this rule is Judith V. Torney, A. N. Oppenheim, and Russell F. Farnen, *Civic Education in Ten Countries: An Empirical Study* (New York: John Wiley, 1975), which showed teenagers in America to have less commitment to democratic values than those in West Germany, Finland, Ireland, Netherlands, Sweden, Italy, and New Zealand. Only fourteen-year-olds in Israel twere more undemocratic in their outlook than their American counterparts. In these comparisons, a Support for Democratic Values score was calculated by averaging scores for Anti-Authoritarianism, Tolerance and Civil Liberties, Support for Women's Rights, and Support for Equality.

14. Max Beloff, *The Great Powers* (New York: Macmillan, 1959), p. 137.

15. Gabriel A. Almond and Sidney Verba, *The Civic Culture* (Boston: Little, Brown, 1965), pp. 314–315. Devine, *Political Culture,* p. 193.

16. Jack Dennis, Leon Lindberg, Donald McCrone, and Rodney Stiefbold, "Political Socialization to Democratic Orientations in Four Western Systems," *Comparative Political Studies* 1 (April 1968): 94.

17. Fred I. Greenstein and Sidney Tarrow, *Political Orientations of Children: The Use of a Semi-Projective Technique in Three Nations* (Beverly Hills: Sage Publications, 1970), pp. 520–529.

18. Judith Gallatin and Joseph Adelson, "Individual Rights and the Public Good: A Cross-National Study of Adolescents," *Comparative Political Studies* 3 (July 1970): 240–241.

19. See Seymour Martin Lipset, *The First New Nation* (New York: Basic Books, 1963), ch. 7, and Tom Truman, "A Critique of Seymour M. Lipset's Article, "Value Differences, Absolute or Relative: The English-Speaking Democracies,'" *Canadian Journal of Political Science* 4 (December 1971): 497–525. Truman argues (contra Lipset) that Canadian and American values are closer than Australian and American values, but he also stresses the major differences separating American values from Australian, British, and Canadian values.

20. Hargrove, "On Canadian and American Political Culture," p. 107.

21. Edgar Z. Friedenberg, *Deference to Authority: The Case of Canada* (White Plains, N.Y.: M. E. Sharpe, 1980), p. 17.

22. Robert Presthus, *Elites in the Policy Process* (London: Cambridge University Press, 1974), pp. 4–15, 30–39. Lipset, *First New Nation,* pp. 86–89, 250–252.

23. Gad Horowitz, "Conservatism, Liberalism and Socialism in Canada," *Canadian Journal of Economics and Political Science* 32 (May 1966): 150.

24. Edmund Burke, *Reflections on the Revolution in France* (Chicago: Regnery, 1955), pp. 125–126, and idem, "Speech on Moving Resolutions for Conciliation with the Colonies," in Ross J.S. Hoffman and Paul Levack, eds., *Burke's Politics* (New York: Knopf, 1949), pp. 69–71.

25. Lipset, *First New Nation,* pp. 213–234. Eric A. Nordlinger, *The Working-Class Tories* (London: MacGibbon & Kee, 1967), ch. 1. R. D.

Jessop, "Civility and Traditionalism in English Political Culture," *British Journal of Political Science* 1 (January 1971): 1–24.

26. A. P. Thornton, *The Habit of Authority: Paternalism in British History* (London: Allen & Unwin, 1966), p. 386.

27. Maurice L. Farber, "English and Americans: A Study in National Character," *Journal of Psychology* 32 (October 1951): 241–250. Erwin C. Hargrove, "Values and Change: A Comparison of Young *Elites* in England and America," *Political Studies* 17 (September 1969): esp. 343.

28. Edward A. Shils, *The Torment of Secrecy* (Glencoe: Free Press, 1956), pp. 37, 48–49.

29. Alex Inkeles and Daniel Levinson, "National Character: The Study of Modal Personality and Sociocultural Systems," in Gardner Lindzey, ed., *Handbook of Social Psychology* (Cambridge, Mass: Addison-Wesley, 1954), p. 475.

30. Kurt Lewin, "Some Social-Psychological Differences between the United States and Germany," *Character and Personality* 4 (June 1936): 269.

31. Dennis et al., "Political Socialization," p. 95. Edward C. Devereux, Jr., Urie Bronfenbrenner, and George J. Suci, "Patterns of Parent Behavior in the USA and the Federal Republic of Germany: A Cross-National Comparison," *International Social Science Bulletin* 14 (Fall 1962): 488–506. Gallatin and Adelson, "Individual Rights," p. 241. David McClelland, J. F. Sturr, R. H. Knapp, and H. W. Wendt, "Obligations to the Self and Society in the United States and Germany," *Journal of Abnormal and Social Psychology* 56 (March 1958): 245–255.

32. "Subject orientation" and "firmly democratic attitudes": Sidney Verba, "Germany: The Remaking of Political Culture," in Lucian W. Pye and Sidney Verba, eds., *Political Culture and Political Development* (Princeton: Princeton University Press, 1966), p. 169. "Ascriptive elitist values": Lipset, *First New Nation,* p. 238. "Germans fundamentally changed" and "political but not psychological democracy": David C. McClelland, *The Roots of Consciousness* (Princeton, N.J.: Van Nostrand, 1964), p. 89.

33. Kendall L. Baker, Russell J. Dalton, and Kai Hildebrandt, *Germany Transformed: Political Culture and the New Politics* (Cambridge, Mass.: Harvard University Press, 1981), pp. 24–25, 287. David P. Conradt, "Changing German Political Culture," in Gabriel A. Almond and Sidney Verba, eds., *The Civic Culture Revisited* (Boston: Little, Brown, 1980), p. 234.

34. Kurt Sontheimer, *The Government and Politics of West Germany* (London: Hutchinson University Library, 1972), pp. 76, 68–69.

35. Conradt, "Changing German Political Culture," pp. 221, 230. Baker et al., *Germany Transformed,* p. 273.

36. Baker et al., *Germany Transformed,* pp. 69, 288.

37. Lipset, *First New Nation,* p. 228. Fred I. Greenstein and Sidney G. Tarrow, "The Study of French Political Socialization: Toward the Revocation of Paradox," *World Politics* 22 (October 1969): 108.

38. William R. Schonfeld, *Obedience and Revolt: French Behavior toward Authority* (Beverly Hills: Sage Publications, 1976), pp. 137–142.

Stanley Hoffmann, "Paradoxes of the French Political Community," in Hoffmann et al., *In Search of France* (Cambridge, Mass.: Harvard University Press, 1963), p. 8.

39. Mariano Grondona quoted in Peter Krogh and Wenceslao Bunge, eds., *Argentine-American Forum* (Washington, D.C.: Georgetown University School of Foreign Service, 1980), pp. 9–10. Robert F. Peck, "A Comparison of the Value Systems of Mexican and American Youth," *Revista Interamericana de Psicologia* 1 (March 1967): 46–47. Noel McGinn et al., "Dependency Relations with Parents and Affiliative Responses in Michigan and Guadalajara," *Sociometry* 28 (September 1965): 313. See generally Calman Jay Cohen, "Relations to the Polity: A Study of Mexican Fathers and Sons" (diss., Harvard University, 1976), ch. 2.

40. Ivan the Terrible is quoted in B. H. Sumner, *Survey of Russian History*, 2nd ed. (London: Duckworth, 1947), p. 67. Marquis de Custine, *Journey of Our Time*, ed. and tr. Phyllis Penn Kohler (New York: Pellegrini & Cudahy, 1951), p. 73. Henry V. Dicks, "Some Notes on Russian National Character," in Cyril E. Black, ed., *The Transformation of Russian Society* (Cambridge, Mass.: Harvard University Press, 1960), pp. 641–642. Robert C. Tucker, "The Image of Dual Russia," in Black, *The Transformation of Russian Society,* pp. 587–605.

41. Frederick C. Barghoorn, *Politics in the USSR* (Boston: Little, Brown, 1966), pp. 22ff. Urie Bronfenbrenner, *Two Worlds of Childhood* (New York: Russell Sage, 1970), pp. 9–11, 90–91, and "Response to Pressure from Peers versus Adults among Soviet and American School Children," *International Journal of Psychology* 2 (1967): 199–207.

42. Alex Inkeles and Raymond A. Bauer, *The Soviet Citizen* (Cambridge, Mass.: Harvard University Press, 1959), pp. 247–249, 279–280, 392. David K. Shipler, *New York Times*, June 14, 1979, p. 1.

43. See Cyril E. Black et al., *The Modernization of Japan and Russia: A Comparative Study* (New York: Free Press, 1975), passim, esp. pp. 53, 55, 95, 117, 147ff, 154–155, 159, 264–265, 268, 276, 318–319.

44. Lewis Austin, *Saints and Samurai: The Political Culture of the American and Japanese Elites* (New Haven: Yale University Press, 1975), pp. 1, 6, 147.

45. "The social norm": Chie Nakane, *Japanese Society* (Berkeley: University of California Press, 1970), p. 31. "The fact of inequality": Masatake Ushiro and George C. Lodge, "On the Japanese Ideology," in Lodge, *New American Ideology*, p. 344. Ruth Benedict, *The Chrysanthemum and the Sword* (Boston: Houghton Mifflin, 1946), p. 43. "The first element": Hiroshi Kitamura *Psychological Dimensions of U.S.-Japanese Relations,* Harvard University Center for International Affairs, Occasional Paper no. 28 (Cambridge, Mass.: 1971), pp. 10–11.

46. Frank Langdon, *Politics in Japan* (Boston: Little, Brown, 1967), p. 74. Austin, *Saints and Samurai,* pp. 129–130, 139–142.

47. Robert E. Ward, "Japan: The Continuity of Modernization," in Pye and Verba, *Political Culture,* p. 34. Austin, *Saints and Samurai,* p. 59.

48. Nakane, *Japanese Society*, p. 103.

49. Tatsuzo Suzuki, *A Study of Japanese National Character, Part IV* (Tokyo: Institute of Statistical Mathematics, Research Committee on the Study of Japanese National Character, 1969), p. 22. Research Committee on the Study of the Japanese National Character, *A Study of the Japanese National Character: The Fifth Nation-Wide Survey, 1973* (Tokyo: Institute of Statistical Economics, 1974), pp. 80–82. Joji Watanuki, "Japan," in Michel Crozier, Samuel P. Huntington and Joji Watanuki, *The Crisis of Democracy* (New York: New York University Press, 1975), p. 141.

50. Suzuki, *Japanese National Character*, pp. 6–7. Research Committee, *Japanese National Character: Fifth Survey*, pp. 22, 41, 55. Bradley M. Richardson, *The Political Culture of Japan* (Berkeley: University of California Press, 1974), pp. 69–70.

51. Warren M. Tsuneishi, *Japanese Political Style* (New York: Harper & Row, 1966), pp. 17–21.

52. Nakane, *Japanese Society*, p. 63.

53. Tang Tsou, "The Values of the Chinese Revolution," in Michel Oksenberg, ed., *China's Developmental Experience* (New York: Praeger, 1973), pp. 27, 30. Richard W. Wilson, *Learning To Be Chinese: The Political Socialization of Children in Taiwan* (Cambridge, Mass.: MIT Press, 1970), pp. 19, 30, 51.

54. George P. Jan, "Government and Politics of the People's Republic of China" (unpublished manuscript), ch. 1. Lucian W. Pye, *The Spirit of Chinese Politics* (Cambridge, Mass.: MIT Press, 1968), p. 86.

55. John K. Fairbank, quoted in Wilson, *Learning To Be Chinese*, p. 53. Pye, *Spirit of Chinese Politics*, pp. 25–26, 77. Francis L. K. Hsu, *Americans and Chinese* (Garden City, N.Y.: Doubleday Natural History Press, 1972), pp. 177–180.

56. James R. Townsend, *Politics in China* (Boston: Little, Brown, 1974), pp. 30ff. Pye, *Spirit of Chinese Politics*, p. 91. Ch'eng I, quoted in Richard H. Solomon, *Mao's Revolution and the Chinese Political Culture* (Berkeley: University of California Press, 1971), p. 108.

57. Solomon, *Mao's Revolution*, pp. 112–113.

58. Townsend, *Politics in China*, pp. 179–188.

4. Coping with the Gap

1. Alexis de Tocqueville, *Democracy in America*, ed. Phillips Bradley (New York: Vintage Books, 1954), 1:9.

2. Leon Festinger, *A Theory of Cognitive Dissonance* (Evanston, Ill.: Row, Peterson & Co., 1957), p. 3.

3. This has been recognized in passing by some commentators on the American scene, for example, Robin Williams, *American Society* (New York: Knopf, 1951), p. 425. Ethel M. Albert, "Conflict and Change in American Values: A Culture-Historical Approach," *Ethics* 74 (October 1963): 30–31.

4. Ronald Blythe, introduction to *Emma,* by Jane Austen (Harmondsworth: Penguin Books, 1966), p. 16.

5. Louis D. Rubin, Jr., "The Great American Joke," *South Atlantic Quarterly* 72 (Winter 1973), pp. 83–87, where the Robert Penn Warren quote appears. Harold J. Laski, *The American Democracy* (New York: Viking Press, 1948), p. 740. See generally Walter Blair and Hamlin Hill, *America's Humor: From Poor Richard to Doonesbury* (New York: Oxford University Press, 1979).

6. Leon Samson, *The American Mind* (New York: Jonathan Cape and Harrison Smith, 1932), p. 13.

7. Irving Kristol, *On the Democratic Idea in America* (New York: Harper & Row, 1972), p. 130.

8. Judith Shklar, "Let Us Not Be Hypocritical," *Daedalus* 108 (Summer 1979): 11, 14–16, 24.

9. Kristol, *Democratic Idea,* p. 130.

10. *New York Times,* May 4, 1974, p. 1, 24.

11. George Santayana, *Character and Opinion in the United States* (Garden City, N.Y.: Doubleday Anchor, 1956), p. 3.

12. Gunnar Myrdal, *An American Dilemma* (New York: Harper & Bros., 1944), 1:21.

13. Ralph Waldo Emerson, "Lecture on the Times," in Emerson, *Prose Works* (Boston: Fields, Osgood & Co., 1870), 1:149.

14. Robert B. Zajonc, "Thinking: Cognitive Organization and Processes," in David L. Sills, ed., *International Encyclopedia of the Social Sciences* (New York: Macmillan Co. and Free Press, 1968), 15:618.

15. For analyses supporting the conclusions summarized in this paragraph, see: Fred I. Greenstein, *Children and Politics* (New Haven: Yale University Press, 1965), esp. pp. 31–45; David Easton and Jack Dennis, *Children in the Political System* (New York: McGraw-Hill, 1969), esp. pp. 111–143; M. Kent Jennings and Richard G. Niemi, "Patterns of Political Learning," *Harvard Educational Review* 38 (Summer 1968): 463–465; and idem, "The Transmission of Political Values from Parent to Child," *American Political Science Review* 62 (March 1968): 169–184. For the effects of Watergate on children's attitudes toward politics, see F. Christopher Arterton, "Watergate and Children's Attitudes toward Political Authority Revisited," *Political Science Quarterly* 90 (Fall 1975): 477ff.

16. Seymour Martin Lipset, "Youth and Politics," in Robert K. Merton and Robert Nisbet, eds., *Contemporary Social Problems,* 3rd ed. (New York: Harcourt Brace Jovanovich, 1971), pp. 744–745.

17. See, for example, Robert E. Agger, Marshall N. Goldstein, and Stanley A. Pearl, "Political Cynicism: Measurement and Meaning," *Journal of Politics* 23 (August 1961): 487–492, and the data on trust in government for the years 1958–78 collected by the University of Michigan Center for Political Studies, in Warren E. Miller, Arthur H. Miller, and Edward J. Schneider, *American National Election Studies Data Sourcebook, 1952–1978* (Cambridge, Mass.: Harvard University Press, 1980), p. 269.

18. See Donald J. Devine, *The Political Culture of the United States* (Boston: Little, Brown, 1972), pp. 260–265.

19. See James W. Prothro and Charles M. Grigg, "Fundamental Principles of Democracy: Bases of Agreement and Disagreement," *Journal of Politics* 22 (February 1960): 284–291. Samuel A. Stouffer, *Communism, Conformity, and Civil Liberties* (Garden City, N.Y.: Doubleday, 1955), ch. 2.

20. Herbert McClosky, "Consensus and Ideology in American Politics," *American Political Science Review* 58 (June 1964): 371. See also Agger, Goldstein, and Pearl, "Political Cynicism," pp. 477–506.

21. Joan Huber and William H. Form, *Income and Ideology* (New York: Free Press, 1973), pp. 132–133.

22. See Edward S. Greenberg, "Children and the Political Community," *Canadian Journal of Political Science* 2 (December 1969): 471–492, and "Orientations of Black and White Children to Political Authority Figures," *Social Science Quarterly* 51 (December 1970): 561–571. Dean Jarros, Herbert Hirsch, and Frederick J. Fleron, Jr., "The Malevolent Leader: Political Socialization in an American Subculture," *American Political Science Review* 62 (June 1968): 564–575.

23. Henry L. Stimson and McGeorge Bundy, *On Active Service in Peace and War* (New York: Harper & Bros., 1947), p. 672.

24. Richard E. Neustadt, *Presidential Power: The Politics of Leadership* (New York: John Wiley, 1960), pp. vii, 7, 9, 35.

25. Arthur M. Schlesinger, Jr., *The Imperial Presidency* (Boston: Houghton Mifflin, 1973), pp. viii, 377.

26. For the ways in which Eisenhower did in fact use presidential power, see the revisionist analyses of Fred I. Greenstein, "Eisenhower as an Activist President: A Look at New Evidence," *Political Science Quarterly* 94 (Winter 1979–80): 575–599, and George H. Quester, "Was Eisenhower a Genius?" *International Security* 4 (Fall 1979): 159–179.

27. "Passion for publicity": Francis Rourke, *Secrecy and Publicity* (Baltimore: Johns Hopkins Press, 1961), p. ix. "The awe of the press": Edward A. Shils, *The Torment of Secrecy* (Glencoe, Ill.: Free Press, 1956), pp. 51–52.

28. Shils, *Torment of Secrecy*, pp. 53, 57.

29. Seymour Martin Lipset and Earl Raab, *The Politics of Unreason* (New York: Harper & Row, 1970), pp. 13–14.

30. Richard Hofstadter, *The Age of Reform* (New York: Knopf, 1956), p. 72.

31. Bernard Bailyn, *The Ideological Origins of the American Revolution* (Cambridge, Mass.: Harvard University Press, 1967), pp. ix, 153. See also Bernard Bailyn, *The Origins of American Politics* (New York: Vintage Books, 1968), pp. 136–148.

32. Richard Hofstadter, *The Paranoid Style in American Politics and Other Essays* (New York: Vintage Books, 1967), pp. 3–40, and *Age of Reform*, pp. 70–72.

33. Shils, *Torment of Secrecy*, p. 45.

34. Frederick S. Hulse, "Convention and Reality in Japanese Culture," in Bernard S. Silberman, ed., *Japanese Character and Culture* (Tucson: University of Arizona Press, 1962), p. 304. Richard Solomon, *Mao's Revolution and the Chinese Political Culture* (Berkeley: University of California Press, 1971), pp. 110–111. See also Lucian W. Pye, *The Spirit of Chinese Politics* (Cambridge, Mass.: MIT Press, 1968), p. 15.

35. Lionel Trilling, *Sincerity and Authenticity* (Cambridge, Mass.: Harvard University Press, 1972), pp. 57–58.

36. Margaret Mead, *Soviet Attitudes toward Authority* (New York: McGraw-Hill, 1951), pp. 38–39.

37. *Boston Herald-American,* October 7, 1978, p. 14.

5. The Politics of Creedal Passion

1. Benjamin Rush, address delivered July 4, 1787, in Philadelphia, in Richard B. Morris, *The American Revolution Reconsidered* (New York: Harper & Row, 1967), pp. 84–85.

2. Bernard Bailyn, *The Ideological Origins of the American Revolution* (Cambridge, Mass.: Harvard University Press, 1976), p. 21.

3. Irving Kristol, *The American Revolution as a Successful Revolution* (Washington, D.C.: American Enterprise Institute for Public Policy Research, 1973), p. 12.

4. Gordon S. Wood, "Rhetoric and Reality in the American Revolution," in J. R. Howe, Jr., ed., *The Role of Ideology in the American Revolution* (New York: Holt, Rinehart & Winston, 1970), p. 116.

5. Gordon S. Wood, "Republicanism as a Revolutionary Ideology," in Howe, *The Role of Ideology,* p. 83.

6. Hannah Arendt, *On Revolution* (New York: Viking Press, 1963), p. 49.

7. Richard Hofstadter, *The Age of Reform* (New York: Knopf, 1956), pp. 308–312.

8. Ibid., pp. 315–318.

9. R. R. Palmer, *The Age of Democratic Revolution* (Princeton: Princeton University Press, 1959), 1:21. Bernard Bailyn, "Political Experience and Enlightenment Ideas in Eighteenth-Century America," *American Historical Review* 67 (January 1962): 348.

10. Ralph Waldo Emerson, "Man the Reformer" and "New England Reformers," in Emerson, *Prose Works* (Boston: Fields, Osgood & Co., 1870), 1:126, 551.

11. Wood, "Rhetoric and Reality," p. 117. Daniel Webster, quoted in Richard Hofstadter, *The American Political Tradition* (New York: Knopf, 1951), p. 65; Theodore Roosevelt, quoted in Eric Goldman, *Rendezvous with Destiny* (New York: Knopf, 1952), p. 187, from Henry F. Pringle, *Theodore Roosevelt* (New York: Harcourt, Brace, 1931), p. 413.

12. Bailyn, "Political Experience," p. 343. John Adams, letter to H. Niles, February 13, 1818, in *The Works of John Adams* (New York: AMS

Press, 1971), 10:283. Emerson, quoted in Charles A. Madison, *Critics and Crusaders* (New York: Henry Holt, 1947-48), p. 16.

13. Eric Foner, *Tom Paine and Revolutionary America* (New York: Oxford University Press, 1976), p. xv.

14. Bernard Bailyn, "The Central Themes of the Revolution," in Stephen G. Kurtz and James H. Hutson, eds., *Essays on the American Revolution* (Chapel Hill, N.C.: University of North Carolina Press, and New York: W. W. Norton, 1973), p. 17.

15. Marvin Meyers, *The Jacksonian Persuasion* (Stanford: Stanford University Press, 1957), pp. 6, 158. George E. Mowry, *The Era of Theodore Roosevelt, 1900-1912* (New York, Harper & Row, 1958), pp. 100-101, quoted in David Mark Chalmers, ed., *The Social and Political Ideas of the Muckrakers* (New York: Arno Press, 1964), p. 112. Hofstadter, *Age of Reform*, pp. 15-16. Theodore Roosevelt, quoted in Hofstadter, *American Political Tradition*, p. 226.

16. Louis Hartz, *The Liberal Tradition in America* (New York: Harcourt, Brace, 1955), pp. 50-51. See also Clinton Rossiter, *The Political Thought of the American Revolution* (New York: Harcourt, Brace & World, 1963), pp. 42-51.

17. Walter Dean Burnham, "Revitalization and Decay: Looking toward the Third Century of American Electoral Politics," *Journal of Politics* 38 (August 1976): 146-172. On revitalization movements generally, see Anthony F. C. Wallace, *Culture and Personality*, 2nd ed. (New York: Random House, 1970), pp. 178-199.

18. Bailyn, "Central Themes of the Revolution," pp. 26-27, and *Ideological Origins*, p. 56. See also Gordon S. Wood, *The Creation of the American Republic, 1776-1787* (Chapel Hill: University of North Carolina Press, 1969), pp. 18-28.

19. Meyers, *Jacksonian Persuasion*, pp. 16-17. John G. Cawelti, *Apostles of the Self-Made Man* (Chicago: University of Chicago Press, 1965), pp. 44-45.

20. Chalmers, *Muckrakers*, p. 106.

21. Wood, "Rhetoric and Reality," p. 117. Seymour Martin Lipset and Earl Raab, *The Politics of Unreason* (New York: Harper & Row, 1970), p. 41. Hofstadter, *Age of Reform*, pp. 70-81. See generally Richard Hofstadter, *The Paranoid Style in American Politics* (New York, Vintage Books, 1967).

22. Meyers, *Jacksonian Persuasion*, pp. 18-19.

23. Hofstadter, *American Political Tradition*, p. 49.

24. Arthur M. Schlesinger, *New Viewpoints in American History* (New York: Macmillan, 1922), p. 202.

25. Alexis de Tocqueville, *Democracy in America*, ed. Phillips Bradley (New York: Vintage Books, 1955), 2:114.

26. James Russell Lowell, "Thoreau," in *The Writings of James Russell Lowell* (Boston: Houghton Mifflin, 1890), 1:362.

27. Calvin Colton, *Protestant Jesuitism* (New York: Harper and Bros., 1836), pp. 52-53.

28. Arthur M. Schlesinger, *The American as Reformer* (Cambridge, Mass.: Harvard University Press, 1950), p. 52. Howard Zinn, "Abolitionists, Freedom-Riders, and the Tactics of Agitation," in Martin Duberman, ed., *The Anti-Slavery Vanguard* (Princeton: Princeton University Press, 1965), pp. 417–451. James Q. Wilson, *Political Organizations* (New York: Basic Books, 1973), pp. 322–323.

29. Wilson, *Political Organizations*, p. 201.

30. Palmer, *Democratic Revolution*, 1:243.

31. Rossiter, *Political Thought of the American Revolution*, p. 10. Bailyn, *Ideological Origins*, pp. 1–3, 8.

32. Sidney H. Aronson, *Status and Kinship in the Higher Civil Service* (Cambridge, Mass.: Harvard University Press, 1964), pp. 20–21.

33. Tocqueville, *Democracy in America*, 2:119–122.

34. Morton Keller, *Affairs of State: Public Life in Late Nineteenth Century America* (Cambridge, Mass.: Harvard University Press, 1977), p. 566.

35. Chalmers, *Muckrakers*, pp. 10–12. Hofstadter, *Age of Reform*, p. 187.

36. Zbigniew Brzezinski and Samuel P. Huntington, *Political Power: USA/USSR* (New York: Viking Press, 1964), p. 32.

37. Bailyn, "Central Themes," pp. 13–14.

38. Walter Lippmann, *Drift and Mastery* (Englewood Cliffs, N.J.: Prentice-Hall, 1961), p. 31. Hofstadter, *American Political Thought*, p. 66.

39. Bayless Manning, "The Purity Potlatch: Conflict of Interests and Moral Escalation," in Arnold J. Heidenheimer, ed., *Political Corruption: Readings in Comparative Analysis* (New York: Holt, Rinehart & Winston, 1970), pp. 311–313.

40. Ralph Waldo Emerson, "New England Reformers," in Emerson, *Prose Works*, 1:554. Hubert H. Humphrey, statement in 1975.

41. Theodore Roosevelt, "The Man with the Muck-Rake," *Putnam's Monthly* 1 (October 1906): 42–47.

42. Martin Shefter, "Party, Bureaucracy, and Political Change in the United States," in Louis Maisel and Joseph Cooper, eds., *Political Parties: Development and Decay* (Beverly Hills: Sage Publications, 1978), pp. 230ff.

43. James L. Sundquist, *Politics and Policy* (Washington, D.C.: Brookings Institution, 1968), p. 500.

44. Madison, *Critics and Crusaders*, p. 14. Garrison quoted in Schlesinger, *American as Reformer*, p. 109. Ladd quoted in Rush Welter, *The Mind of America: 1820–1860* (New York: Columbia University Press, 1975), p. 334.

45. Schlesinger, *American as Reformer*, pp. 32–33.

46. James Russell Lowell, *The Writings of James Russell Lowell*, 1:362–363. For an excellent brief summary of Jacksonian reform movements and their mutual interaction, see Walter Hugins, *The Reform Impulse 1825–1850* (Columbia: University of South Carolina Press, 1972), pp. 1–22.

278   NOTES TO PAGES 109–122

47. Emerson, "New England Reformers," p. 549. Hofstadter, *American Political Tradition*, p. 141.

48. Alan P. Grimes, *The Puritan Ethic and Women's Suffrage* (New York: Oxford University Press, 1967), pp. 4–5, 100.

49. Hartz, *Liberal Tradition*, pp. 156–157.

50. Lipset and Raab, *Politics of Unreason*, pp. 20–24. Erwin C. Hargrove, "On Canadian and American Political Culture," *Canadian Journal of Economics and Political Science* 33 (February 1967): 107–108.

51. Stanley Elkins, *Slavery: A Problem in American Institutional and Intellectual Life*, 2nd ed. (Chicago: University of Chicago Press, 1968), p. 27.

52. Gerhart B. Ladner, *The Idea of Reform: Its Impact on Christian Thought and Action in the Age of the Fathers* (Cambridge, Mass.: Harvard University Press, 1959), pp. 2, 9, 35.

53. Ibid., pp. 33–34. Michael Walzer, *The Revolution of the Saints* (Cambridge, Mass.: Harvard University Press, 1965), pp. 11–12. Herbert Croly, *The Promise of American Life* (New York: Macmillan, 1909), p. 144.

54. Austin Ranney, *Curing the Mischiefs of Faction: Party Reform in America* (Berkeley: University of California Press, 1975), ch. 1.

55. William J. Crotty, *Political Reform and the American Experiment* (New York: Thomas Y. Crowell, 1977), p. 267.

56. Austin Ranney, " 'The Divine Science': Political Engineering in American Culture," *American Political Science Review* 70 (March 1976): 147.

57. David J. Rothman, *The Discovery of the Asylum* (Boston: Little, Brown, 1971), pp. xiii–xiv, xix.

58. Lawrence Cremin, *The Transformation of the School* (New York: Knopf, 1961), pp. viii, 58–59. See generally David J. Rothman, *Conscience and Convenience: The Asylum and Its Alternatives in Progressive America* (Boston: Little, Brown, 1980).

59. Theodore J. Lowi, *At the Pleasure of the Mayor* (Glencoe, Ill: Free Press, 1964), p. 201.

60. Ranney, *Curing the Mischiefs of Faction*, p. 128.

61. Ibid., p. 191.

62. Richard Olney, letter to Charles E. Perkins, December 28, 1892, quoted in Matthew Josephson, *The Politicos* (New York: Harcourt, Brace, 1938), p. 526. On how accurate Olney's predictions turned out to be, see Samuel P. Huntington, "The 'Marasmus' of the ICC: The Commission, the Railroads, and the Public Interest," *Yale Law Journal* 61 (April 1952): 467–509, and, more generally, Huntington, "Clientelism: A Study in Administrative Politics" (diss., Harvard University, 1951).

63. Rothman, *Discovery of the Asylum*, pp. 240, 295.

64. Lowi, *Pleasure of the Mayor*, pp. 184–186. See also Crotty, *Political Reform*, pp. 267ff.

65. Robert Michels, *Political Parties* (New York: Dover, 1959), p. 408.

66. Walter Dean Burnham, "American Politics in the 1970s: Beyond Party?" in William Nisbet Chambers and Burnham, eds., *The American Party*

Systems: Stages of Political Development, 2nd ed. (New York: Oxford University Press, 1975), pp. 316–317.

67. Walter Dean Burnham, "Revitalization and Decay: Looking toward the Third Century of American Electoral Politics," *Journal of Politics* 38 (August 1976): 147.

68. Charles Pinckney, in Max Farrand, ed., *The Records of the Federal Convention* (New Haven: Yale University Press, 1911), 1:402ff.

69. James Madison, in Alexander Hamilton, John Jay, and Madison, *The Federalist*, no. 51 (New York: Modern Library, 1937), p. 336.

70. Burnham, "Revitalization and Decay," p. 149.

6. The Sources of Creedal Passion

1. John Israel, "Continuities and Discontinuities in the Ideology of the Great Proletarian Cultural Revolution," in Chalmers Johnson, ed., *Ideology and Politics in Contemporary China* (Seattle: University of Washington Press, 1973), p. 25.

2. Ibid.

3. Milton B. Singer, "Shame Cultures and Guilt Cultures," in Gerhart Piers and Milton B. Singer, *Shame and Guilt: A Psychoanalytic and a Cultural Study* (Springfield, Ill.: Charles C. Thomas, 1953), p. 45.

4. See Richard W. Wilson, *The Moral State: A Study of the Political Socialization of Chinese and American Children* (New York: Free Press, 1973), pp. 20ff. Lowell Dittmer, "Thought Reform and Cultural Revolution: An Analysis of the Symbolism of Chinese Politics," *American Political Science Review* 71 (March 1977): 78–79. Lucian W. Pye, *The Spirit of Chinese Politics* (Cambridge, Mass.: MIT Press, 1968), p. 96.

5. Byung-joon Ahn, "The Cultural Revolution and China's Search for Political Order," *China Quarterly* 58 (April-May 1974): 257. Paul J. Hiniker, *Revolutionary Ideology and Chinese Realty: Dissonance under Mao* (Beverly Hills: Sage Publications, 1977).

6. Dai Hsiao-ai, quoted in Lowell Dittmer, *Liu Shao-ch'i and the Chinese Cultural Revolution* (Berkeley: University of California Press, 1974), p. 305. Hong Yung Lee, *The Politics of the Chinese Cultural Revolution* (Berkeley: University of California Press, 1978), pp. 326–328, 340–343.

7. Hiniker, *Revolutionary Ideology*, p. 17. Dittmer, *Liu Shao-ch'i*, pp. 305, 314.

8. Dittmer, "Thought Reform," pp. 75–78, and *Liu Shao-Ch'i*, p. 297.

9. Alan P. L. Liu, *Political Culture and Group Conflict in Communist China* (Santa Barbara: Clio Press, 1976), pp. 24ff.

10. George P. Jan, "Government and Politics of the People's Republic of China" (unpublished manuscript), ch. 9, pp. 26, 29.

11. See Israel, in Johnson, *Ideology and Politics*, pp. 14–15, 22–24.

12. Benjamin Schwartz, "The Reign of Virtue: Some Broad Perspectives on Leader and Party in the Cultural Revolution," in John W. Lewis, ed.,

Party Leadership and Revolutionary Power in China (Cambridge: Cambridge University Press, 1970), pp. 155–156.

13. Ibid., p. 165.

14. James R. Townsend, *Politics in China* (Boston: Little, Brown, 1973), pp. 335–336.

15. Richard M. Pfeffer, "Leaders and Masses," in Michel Oksenberg, ed., *China's Developmental Experience* (New York: Columbia University Academy of Political Science, vol. 31, March 1973), p. 165. Lucian W. Pye, "Mass Participation in Communist China: Its Limitations and the Continuity of Culture," in John M. H. Lindbeck, ed., *China: Management of a Revolutionary Society* (Seattle: University of Washington Press, 1971), p. 30.

16. Michel Oksenberg, "On Learning from China," in Oksenberg, ed., *China's Developmental Experience*, p. 8. Townsend, *Politics in China*, p. 145.

17. For an intricate analysis of political cycles in China, see G. William Skinner and Edwin A. Winckler, "Compliance Succession in Rural Communist China: A Cyclical Theory," in Amitai Etzioni, ed., *Complex Organization: A Sociological Reader*, 2nd ed. (New York: Holt, Rinehart and Winston, 1969), pp. 410–438. They identify eight two-to-three-year cycles between 1949 and 1969.

18. C. P. FitzGerald, "Mao's Tse-Tung's Cultural Revolution," *American Political Science Review* 68 (June 1974): 800.

19. Richard Baum, "Ideology Redivivus," in Baum, ed., *China in Ferment: Perspectives on the Cultural Revolution* (Englewood Cliffs, N.J.: Prentice-Hall, 1971), pp. 70–71. See also Ahn, "The Cultural Revolution," pp. 252–253.

20. Richard M. Pfeffer, "The Pursuit of Purity: Mao's Cultural Revolution," in Baum, ed., *China in Ferment*, p. 207.

21. Marvin Meyers, *The Jacksonian Persuasion* (Stanford: Stanford University Press, 1957), p. 78.

22. See Ted R. Gurr, *Rogues, Rebels, and Reformers: A Political History of Urban Crime and Conflict* (Beverly Hills: Sage Publications, 1976), pp. 171–172, and, for a classic account of how reporters made a crime wave and how Theodore Roosevelt stopped it, Lincoln Steffens, *Autobiography* (New York: Harcourt, Brace, 1931), pt. 2, ch. 14.

23. Theodore J. Lowi, *At the Pleasure of the Mayor* (Glencoe, Ill.: Free Press, 1964), pp. 182–183.

24. Herbert Croly, *The Promise of American Life* (New York: Macmillan, 1909), p. 141.

25. Ronald G. Walters, "The Erotic South: Civilization and Sexuality in American Abolitionism," *American Quarterly* 25 (May 1973): 177.

26. David Donald, *Lincoln Reconsidered: Essays on the Civil War Era* (New York: Knopf, 1959), pp. 22–23.

27. Walter Lippmann, *Drift and Mastery* (Englewood Cliffs, N.J.: Prentice-Hall, 1961), pp. 23–27.

28. For leads into this literature, see John Wilson, *Introduction to Social Movements* (New York: Basic Books, 1973). Michael Useem, *Protest Move-*

ments in America (Indianapolis: Bobbs-Merrill, 1975). Joseph R. Gusfield, ed., Protest, Reform, and Revolt: A Reader in Social Movements (New York: John Wiley, 1970).

29. See Ted R. Gurr, Why Men Rebel (Princeton University Press, 1970), and Samuel P. Huntington, Political Order in Changing Societies (New Haven: Yale University Press, 1968), pp. 32–59.

30. See Donald, Lincoln Reconsidered, pp. 19–36, and Richard Hofstadter, The Age of Reform (New York: Knopf, 1956), pp. 134ff. For critiques of these interpretations, see: Robert A. Skotheim, "A Note on Historical Method: David Donald's 'Toward a Reconsideration of Abolitionists,' " Journal of Southern History 25 (August 1959): 356–365; Richard B. Sherman, "The Status Revolution and Massachusetts Progressive Leadership," Political Science Quarterly 78 (March 1963): 59–65; Jack Tager, "Progressives, Conservatives, and the Theory of the Status Revolution," Mid-America 48 (July 1966): 162–175; and Robert W. Doherty, "Status Anxiety and American Reform: Some Alternatives," American Quarterly 19 (Summer 1967): 329–337. Hofstadter and other scholars also analyzed McCarthyism and other rightist movements of the 1950s and early 1960s in terms of status politics. See Daniel Bell, ed., The Radical Right (Garden City, N.Y.: Doubleday, 1963). For a stimulating and insightful effort to synthesize several theories on the origins of social upheaval in terms of a cognitive dissonance approach, see James A. Geschwender, "Explorations in the Theory of Social Movements and Revolutions," Social Forces 47 (December 1968): 127–135.

31. Hofstadter, in Bell, Radical Right, pp. 98–99.

32. See Herbert Moller, "Youth as a Force in the Modern World," Comparative Studies in Society and History 10 (April 1968): 237–260.

33. See Seymour Martin Lipset, "Youth and Politics," in Robert K. Merton and Robert Nisbet, eds., Contemporary Social Problems, 3rd ed. (New York: Harcourt, Brace, Jovanovich, 1971), pp. 754ff, and Lipset, in Lipset and Gerald M. Schaflander, Passion and Politics (Boston: Little, Brown, 1971), pp. 125, 133–139, 142–149.

34. Anne Foner, "The Polity," in Matilda White Riley, Marilyn Johnson, and Anne Foner, Aging and Society (New York: Russell Sage Foundation, 1972), 3:148.

35. William N. Chambers, "Party Development and the American Mainstream," in William Chambers and Walter Dean Burnham, eds., The American Party Systems, 2nd ed. (New York: Oxford University Press, 1975), pp. 29–30. The cyclical evolution of American party systems has been noted and analyzed in the work of Arthur N. Holcombe, Samuel Lubell, V. O. Key, Jr., Philip Converse, Charles Sellers, and Walter Dean Burnham.

36. Hofstadter, Age of Reform, pp. 16ff. Lowi, At the Pleasure of the Mayor, ch. 8, "The Reform Cycle." William J. Crotty, Political Reform and the American Experiment (New York: Thomas Y. Crowell, 1977), ch. 9, "The Reform Cycle." Arthur M. Schlesinger, The American as Reformer (Cambridge, Mass.: Harvard University Press, 1950), p. 4. Nathan Glazer, "Towards an Imperial Judiciary," in Nathan Glazer and Irving Kristol, eds.,

The American Commonwealth 1976 (New York: Basic Books, 1976), pp. 104–106. Glazer argued that the historical activism-quietism cycle was giving way to a lasting expansion of the judiciary's role.

37. Arthur M. Schlesinger, Sr., *Paths to the Present* (Boston: Houghton Mifflin, 1964), pp. 89–103. James David Barber, *The Pulse of Politics: Electing Presidents in the Media Age* (New York: W. W. Norton, 1980).

38. J. Zvi Namenwirth, "Wheels of Time and the Interdependence of Value Change in America," *Journal of Interdisciplinary History* 3 (Spring 1973): 649–683, and Namenwirth and Richard C. Bibbee, "Change within or of the System: An Example from the History of American Values," *Quality and Quantity* 10 (June 1976): 145–164. Frank L. Klingberg, "The Historical Alternation of Moods in American Foreign Policy," *World Politics* 4 (January 1952): 239–273, and "Cyclical Trends in American Foreign Policy Moods and their Policy Implications," in Charles W. Kegley and Patrick J. McGowan, eds., *Challenges to America: U.S. Foreign Policy in the 1980s* (Sage International Yearbook of Foreign Policy Studies, vol. 4, 1979), pp. 37–55.

39. P. M. G. Harris, "The Social Origins of American Leaders: The Demographic Foundations," in Donald Fleming and Bernard Bailyn, eds., *Perspectives in American History* (Cambridge, Mass.: Warren Center for Studies in American History, 1969) 3: 159–346. David McClelland, *Power: The Inner Experience* (New York: Irvington Press, 1975), pp. 330–359.

40. Schlesinger, *Paths to the Present*, pp. 96–97. Namenwirth, "Wheels of Time," p. 679. Klingberg, "Historical Alternation," pp. 271–273.

41. Clarence L. Ver Steeg, *The Formative Years: 1607–1763* (New York: Hill and Wang, 1964), pp. 129–130.

42. Perry Miller, *The New England Mind: From Colony to Province* (Cambridge, Mass.: Harvard University Press, 1953), pp. 151, 172.

43. Ver Steeg, *Formative Years*, p. 149.

44. Richard Maxwell Brown, "Violence and the American Revolution," in Stephen G. Kurtz and James H. Hutson, eds., *Essays on the American Revolution* (Chapel Hill: University of North Carolina Press, 1973), pp. 86–87. Charles M. Andrews, "General Introduction," in Andrews, ed., *Narratives of the Insurrections, 1675–1690* (New York: Charles Scribner's Sons, 1915), p. 4.

45. David S. Lovejoy, *The Glorious Revolution in America* (New York: Harper and Row, 1972), ch. 16.

46. Brown, "Violence and the American Revolution," p. 87.

47. Michael Walzer, *The Revolution of the Saints* (Cambridge, Mass.: Harvard University Press, 1965), p. 1.

48. Lawrence Stone, *The Causes of the English Revolution, 1529–1642* (London: Routledge & Kegan Paul, 1972), p. 123.

49. Ibid., pp. 110ff.

50. Austin Woolrych, "The English Revolution: An Introduction," and "Puritanism, Politics and Society," in E. W. Ives, ed., *The English Revolution, 1600–1660* (London: Edward Arnold, 1968), pp. 20, 89.

51. Stone, *Causes of the English Revolution*, p. 144.

52. Woolrych, "The English Revolution," p. 87.

53. Stone, *Causes of the English Revolution*, pp. 91, 99.

54. Christopher Hill, *The World Turned Upside Down* (New York: Viking Press, 1972), pp. 12, 14, 294.

55. Ibid., p. 306.

56. Thomas Case, quoted in Walzer, *Revolution of the Saints*, pp. 10–11.

57. Ralph Waldo Emerson, "Man the Reformer," in Emerson, *Prose Works*, rev. ed. (Boston: Fields, Osgood, 1870) 1: 125–126.

58. William Lee Miller, "American Religion and American Political Attitudes," in James Ward Smith and A. Leland Jamison, eds., *Religious Perspectives in American Culture* (Princeton: Princeton University Press, 1961), pp. 84–85. Philip Schaff, *America: A Sketch of Its Political, Social, and Religious Character* (Cambridge, Mass.: Belknap Press of Harvard University Press, 1961), p. 72. Charles L. Sanford, *The Quest for Paradise: Europe and the American Moral Imagination* (Urbana: University of Illinois Press, 1961), p. 74.

59. H. Richard Niebuhr, *The Kingdom of God in America* (Hamden, Conn.: Shoe String Press, 1956), pp. 17ff. Sanford, *Quest for Paradise*, pp. 54–55.

60. H. Richard Niebuhr, "The Protestant Movement and Democracy in the United States," in James Ward Smith and A. Leland Jamison, eds., *The Shaping of American Religion* (Princeton: Princeton University Press, 1961), p. 27.

61. Schaff, *America*, p. 72.

62. Alexis de Tocqueville, *Democracy in America*, ed. Phillips Bradley (New York: Vintage Books, 1954) 1: 314. Seymour Martin Lipset, *The First New Nation* (New York: Basic Books, 1963), pp. 140–150.

63. Tocqueville, *Democracy in America*, 1:46.

64. Quoted in Lipset, *First New Nation*, p. 155.

65. Cushing Strout, *The New Heavens and New Earth: Political Religion in America* (New York: Harper & Row, 1974), pp. 51–52. Krister Stendhal, quoted in William G. McLoughlin and Robert N. Bellah, eds., *Religion in America* (Boston: Houghton Mifflin, 1968), p. xv.

66. John Higham, "Hanging Together: Divergent Unities in American History," *Journal of American History* 61 (June 1974): 13. See also Conrad Cherry, "Two American Sacred Ceremonies: Their Implications for the Study of Religion in America," *American Quarterly* 21 (Winter 1969): 754. Sidney E. Mead, *The Lively Experiment* (New York: Harper & Row, 1963).

67. Tocqueville, *Democracy in America*, 1:311. Miller, in Smith and Jamison, *Religious Perspectives*, pp. 105–113.

68. John Edwin Smylie, "National Ethos and the Church," *Theology Today*, October 1963, pp. 313–318, quoted in Cherry, "Two American Sacred Ceremonies," p. 750. On civil religion in America, see also: Robert N. Bellah, "Civil Religion in America," in McLoughlin and Bellah, *Religion in America*, pp. 3–23; Russell E. Richey and Donald G. Jones, eds., *American Civil Religion* (New York: Harper & Row, 1974), passim; Sidney E. Mead, "The

284   NOTES TO PAGES 159–163

'Nation with the Soul of a Church,' " *Church History* 36 (September 1967): 262–283; and Mead, *Lively Experiment*, pp. 134ff.

69. G. K. Chesterton, *What I Saw in America* (New York: Dodd, Mead, 1923), pp. 11–12. *New York Times,* January 12, 1975, p. 1.

70. D. W. Brogan, *The American Character* (New York: Vintage Books, 1959), p. 164.

71. Mead, "The 'Nation with the Soul of a Church,' " p. 275.

72. Edward M. Burns, *The American Idea of Mission* (New Brunswick, N.J.: Rutgers University Press, 1957), p. 11. On American millennialism, see also Sanford, *Quest for Paradise;* Niebuhr, *Kingdom of God in America;* Strout, *New Heavens and New Earth;* Ernest Lee Tuveson, *Redeemer Nation: The Idea of America's Millennial Role* (Chicago: University of Chicago Press, 1968); Russel B. Nye, *This Almost Chosen People* (Lansing: Michigan State University Press, 1966); and Conrad Cherry, ed., *God's New Israel: Religious Interpretations of American Destiny* (Englewood Cliffs, N.J.: Prentice-Hall, 1971).

73. This dating generally follows that of William G. McLoughlin in *Revivals, Awakenings, and Reform: An Essay on Religion and Social Change in America, 1607–1977*(Chicago: University of Chicago Press, 1978). For slightly different dates, see his earlier writings: *Modern Revivalism: From Charles Grandison Finney to Billy Graham* (New York: Ronald Press, 1959), pp. 7–11, and *Billy Graham: Revivalist in a Secular Age* (New York: Ronald Press, 1960), pp. 7–11.

74. Donald G. Matthews, "The Second Great Awakening as an Organizing Process, 1780–1830: An Hypothesis," *American Quarterly* 21 (Spring 1969): 25.

75. McLoughlin, *Revivals, Awakenings, and Reform,* pp. 2, 10–11, 23.

76. Strout, *New Heavens and New Earth,* pp. 42–43.

77. Alan Heimert, *Religion and the American Mind* (Cambridge, Mass.: Harvard University Press, 1966), pp. 21, 481. William G. McLoughlin, "The American Revolution as a Religious Revival: 'The Millennium in One Country,' " *New England Quarterly* 40 (March 1967): 99ff.

78. Richard L. Bushman, ed., *The Great Awakening* (New York: Atheneum, 1970), p. xi. Sidney E. Ahlstrom, "National Trauma and Changing Religious Values," *Daedalus* 107 (Winter 1978): 19–20.

79. McLoughlin, *Revivals, Awakenings, and Reform,* pp. 52–53.

80. Richard L. Bushman, *From Puritan to Yankee* (Cambridge, Mass.: Harvard University Press, 1967), pp. 189–192. Heimert, *Religion and the American Mind,* p. 32.

81. Whitney R. Cross, *The Burned-Over District* (Ithaca, N.Y.: Cornell University Press, 1950), pp. 75–76. For a detailed study of the causes of the awakening in Rochester, see Paul E. Johnson, *A Shopkeeper's Millennium* (New York: Hill and Wang, 1978).

82. Matthews, "The Second Great Awakening," pp. 27, 32, 34. Heimert, *Religion and the American Mind,* p. 534.

83. Bushman, *From Puritan to Yankee,* p. 192.

84. Strout, *New Heavens and New Earth*, pp. 38–43.
85. Bushman, *Great Awakening*, p. xii. Mead, *Lively Experiment*, pp. 31–34.
86. Heimert, *Religion and the American Mind*, p. 10.
87. William G. McLoughlin, "'Enthusiasm for Liberty': The Great Awakening as the Key to the Revolution," in Jack P. Greene and William McLoughlin, *Preachers and Politicians* (Worcester, Mass.: American Antiquarian Society, 1977), pp. 65–70.
88. Harry S. Stout, "Religion, Communications, and the Ideological Origins of the American Revolution," *William and Mary Quarterly* 34 (October 1977): 519–541.
89. William G. McLoughlin, Jr., *Billy Graham: Revivalist in a Secular Age* (New York: Ronald Press, 1960), pp. 15–18, and *Modern Revivalism: Charles Grandison Finney to Billy Graham* (New York: Ronald Press, 1959), passim.
90. William Warren Sweet, *Revivalism in America: Its Origin, Growth, and Decline* (New York: Scribners, 1944), p. 31. Matthews, "The Second Great Awakening," pp. 36–37. Cross, *Burned-Over District*, p. 356.
91. Niebuhr, "The Protestant Movement," pp. 24, 31–32.
92. McLoughlin, *Modern Revivalism*, p. 526.
93. Alan Heimert, quoted in McLoughlin, "The American Revolution as a Religious Revival," p. 99. McLoughlin, "'Enthusiasm for Liberty,'" p. 48. See also Strout, *New Heavens and New Earth*, ch. 4, and Mead, *Lively Experiment*, pp. 34–35, 52, 61–62.
94. Matthews, "The Second Great Awakening," p. 35. Robert N. Bellah, *The Broken Covenant* (New York: Seabury Press, 1975), p. 44.
95. Sweet, *Revivalism in America*, pp. 152ff. Timothy L. Smith, *Revivalism and Social Reform in Mid-Nineteenth-Century America* (New York: Abingdon Press, 1957). Gilbert Hobbs Barnes, *The Anti-Slavery Impulse, 1830–1844* (New York: D. Appleton Century Co., 1933). John L. Hammond, *The Politics of Benevolence: Revival Religion and American Voting Behavior* (Norwood, N.J.: Ablex, 1979). McClelland also explores the relations among religious revivals, reform, and war in *Power: The Inner Experience*, pp. 346–359.
96. See Alan P. Grimes, *The Puritan Ethic and Woman Suffrage* (New York: Oxford University Press, 1967), esp. p. 71, and, more generally, Paul Boyer, *Urban Masses and Moral Order in America, 1820–1920* (Cambridge, Mass.: Harvard University Press, 1978).

7. The S&S Years, 1960–1975

1. "Eisenhower on the Presidency," interview with Walter Cronkite on CBS television, October 12, 1961, quoted in Emmett John Hughes, *The Ordeal of Power* (New York: Atheneum, 1963), p. 331n.
2. Daniel J. Boorstin, *The Genius of American Politics* (Chicago: University of Chicago Press, 1953), pp. 9, 161.

3. Seymour Martin Lipset, *Political Man* (New York: Doubleday & Co., 1960), p. 414. For representative works rationalizing bigness, see: David E. Lilienthal, *Big Business: A New Era* (New York: Harper & Row, 1953); Adolf A. Berle, *The Twentieth Century Capitalist Revolution* (New York: Harcourt Brace, 1954); and John Kenneth Galbraith, *American Captialism: The Concept of Countervailing Power* (Boston: Houghton Mifflin, 1952). For the roots of this line of thought in the New Deal, see Richard Hofstadter, *The Age of Reform* (New York: Knopf, 1956), pp. 310ff.

4. Philip Converse, "Change in the American Electorate," in Angus Campbell and Converse, eds., *The Human Meaning of Social Change* (New York: Russell Sage Foundation, 1972), pp. 327ff. James S. House and William M. Mason, "Political Alienation in America, 1952–1968," *American Sociological Review* 40 (April 1975): 123ff. See also James D. Wright, *The Dissent of the Governed: Alienation and Democracy in America* (New York: Academic Press, 1976), ch. 7.

5. Lipset, *Political Man*, p. 406. See also Daniel Bell, *The End of Ideology* (Glencoe, Ill.: Free Press, 1960), esp. pp. 369–375.

6. Address, June 1962, Yale University, quoted in Seymour Martin Lipset, "Ideology and No End," *Encounter* 39 (December 1972): 19.

7. Address, May 1962, New York, N.Y., quoted in Lipset, "Ideology and No End," p. 19.

8. Bernard Crick, "The Strange Death of the American Theory of Consensus," *Political Quarterly* 43 (January–March 1972): 59.

9. Henry Fairlie, *The Kennedy Promise* (Garden City, N.Y.: Doubleday & Co., 1973), p. 19.

10. Samuel P. Huntington, "The United States," in Michel Crozier, Samuel P. Huntington, and Joji Watanuki, *The Crisis of Democracy* (New York: New York University Press, 1975), pp. 59–60.

11. Warren E. Miller, Arthur H. Miller, and Edward J. Schneider, *American National Election Studies Data Sourcebook, 1952–1978* (Cambridge, Mass.: Harvard University Press, 1980), pp. 256–260.

12. Louis Harris, "Confidence in Leadership Down Again," press release, Harris Survey, March 22, 1976.

13. These averages are computed from sixty-six Gallup surveys reported in *The Gallup Opinion Index*, 1950–1979, and distributed as follows: 1950–1959, twenty surveys; 1960–1970, nineteen surveys; 1971–1972, seven surveys; 1973–1979, twenty surveys. The question asked was: "What do you think is the most important problem facing this country today?"

14. Everett Carll Ladd, Jr., and Seymour Martin Lipset, "Public Opinion and Public Policy," in Peter Duignan and Alvin Rabushka, eds., *The United States in the 1980s* (Stanford: Hoover Institution, 1980), pp. 72–74.

15. "Revolution": Al Haber, quoted in Edward J. Bacciocco, Jr., *The New Left in America* (Stanford: Hoover Institution Press, 1974), pp. 228–229. "Moral issues": David Horowitz and Michael Rossman, quoted in Lawrence Lader, *Power on the Left* (New York: Norton, 1979), p. 169.

16. "Toward a Theory of Social Change in America, or the Port Au-

thority Statement," position paper released at SDS–REP conference, Princeton University, February 1967, quoted in Bacciocco, *New Left*, p. 229.

17. Norman H. Nie, Sidney Verba, and John R. Petrocik, *The Changing American Voter*, rev. ed. (Cambridge, Mass.: Harvard University Press, 1980), pp. 365–369. The authors of this study attribute these changes largely to the nature and political appeals of the candidates. It seems not unreasonable to assume, however, that the candidates were themselves responding to the temper of the times with the sort of appeal they thought would mobilize support.

18. Quoted in Paul Seabury, "The Moral Purposes and Philosophical Bases of American Foreign Policy," *Orbis* 20 (Spring 1976): 13.

19. The following two paragraphs are from my essay, "The United States," in Crozier, Huntington, and Watanuki, *Crisis of Democracy*, pp. 75–76.

20. See Ladd and Lipset in Duignan and Rabushka, *United States in the 1980s*, pp. 65–67, for a summary of the evidence on public confidence in institutional leadership.

21. Daniel Patrick Moynihan, letter to Richard Nixon, *New York Times*, March 11, 1970, p. 30, quoted in Lawrence Stone, *The Causes of the English Revolution, 1529–1642* (London: Routledge and Kegan Paul, 1972), p. 79.

22. Miller, Miller, and Schneider, *Election Studies Data Sourcebook*, pp. 310, 323. This electoral participation index is a percentage difference index calculated by subtracting the percentage of respondents who neither voted nor engaged in any of five campaign-related activities (talking to people, attending meetings, working for a candidate or party, displaying a bumper sticker or wearing a button, or contributing money) from the percentage of respondents who both voted and engaged in one or more of these activities.

23. Sidney Verba and Norman H. Nie, *Participation in America: Political Democracy and Social Equality* (New York: Harper & Row, 1972), pp. 151–160, 254–255. Anthony M. Orum, "A Reappraisal of the Social and Political Participation of Negroes," *American Journal of Sociology* 72 (July 1966): 32–46. Marvin E. Olsen, "Social and Political Participation of Blacks," *American Sociological Review* 35 (August 1970): 682–697.

24. Verba and Nie, *Participation in America*, ch. 9.

25. Paul Allen Beck and M. Kent Jennings, "Political Periods and Political Participation," *American Political Science Review* 73 (September 1979): 748.

26. Data adapted from Thomas Agnello by Anne Foner, "Age Stratification and Age Conflict in Political Life," *American Sociological Review* 39 (April 1974): 190.

27. Jeffrey M. Berry, *Lobbying for the People* (Princeton: Princeton University Press, 1977), p. 34.

28. *New York Times*, May 18, 1977, pp. A1, B9; Common Cause, 1978 mailing, signed by David Cohen.

29. Beck and Jennings, "Political Periods and Political Participation," p. 739; Miller, Miller, and Schneider, *Election Studies Data Sourcebook,* p. 299.

30. Lader, *Power on the Left,* p. 172.

31. Irwin Unger, *The Movement: A History of the American New Left, 1959–1972* (New York: Dodd, Mead & Co., 1974), p. 88.

32. Frances Fox Piven and Richard A. Cloward, *Poor People's Movements* (New York: Pantheon, 1977), pp. 32–33.

33. Milton Viorst, *Fire in the Streets* (New York: Simon and Schuster, 1979), pp. 347ff, 369, 375–379. James Q. Wilson, *Political Organizations* (New York: Basic Books, 1973), p. 183.

34. Theodore H. White, *Breach of Faith* (New York: Atheneum–Reader's Digest Press, 1975), p. 234.

35. John Chancellor, quoted in *Newsweek* 81 (January 15, 1973): 42.

36. Cord Meyer, *Facing Reality* (New York: Harper & Row, 1980), pp. 86–90.

37. Michael Kinsey and Arthur Lubow, "Alger Hiss and the Smoking Gun Fallacy," *Washington Monthly* 7 (October 1975): 52.

38. Russell Baker, "Ready for Sleep," *New York Times,* February 1, 1977, p. 29.

39. Elliot Zashin, "The Progress of Black Americans in Civil Rights: The Past Two Decades Assessed," *Daedalus* 107 (Winter 1978): 247–250. Miller, Miller, and Schneider, *Election Studies Data Sourcebook, 1952–1978,* p. 317. "Blacks in America: 25 Years of Radical Change," *U.S. News and World Report* 86 (May 14, 1979): 59.

40. Zashin, "The Progress of Black Americans," pp. 250–255, 260. Richard Freeman, "Black Economic Progress since 1964," *The Public Interest* 52 (Summer 1978): 52–68. *Washington Post,* April 2, 1978, pp. A1, A18.

41. Zashin, "The Progress of Black Americans," p. 260.

42. *Time* 110 (August 15, 1977): 67.

43. Anthony King, "Introduction" and "The American Polity in the Late 1970s: Building Coalitions in the Sand," in King, ed., *The New American Political System* (Washington, D.C.: American Enterprise Institute for Public Policy Research, 1978), pp. 2, 388.

44. See: King, *New American Political System;* Nie, Verba, and Petrocik, *Changing American Voter;* Seymour Martin Lipset, ed., *The Third Century* (Chicago: University of Chicago Press, 1979); Huntington, "The United States," in Crozier, Huntington, Watanuki, *Crisis of Democracy;* Nathan Glazer and Irving Kristol, eds., *The American Commonwealth 1976* (New York: Basic Books, 1976); and Everett C. Ladd, Jr., with Charles D. Hadley, *Transformations of the American Party System,* 2nd ed., (New York: Norton, 1978).

45. See *U.S. News and World Report* 76 (April 22, 1974): 34; 78 (April 21, 1975): 34; 80 (April 19, 1976): 30; 82 (April 18, 1977): 36; 84 (April 17, 1978): 38; 86 (April 16, 1979): 40; 88 (April 14, 1980): 41.

46. Louis Harris, "Confidence Climbing," press release, Harris Survey, March 14, 1977.

47. Michael Robinson, "Television and American Politics: 1956–1976," *The Public Interest* 48 (Summer 1977): 12–13.

48. Peter B. Clark, "The Opinion Machine: Intellectuals, the Mass Media, and American Government," in Harry Clor, ed., *Mass Media and Modern Democracy* (Chicago: Rand-McNally, 1974), p. 69.

49. James Reston, quoted in Max Kampelman, "The Media," in Harvey C. Mansfield, Jr., ed., *Congress against the President*, Proceedings of the Academy of Political Science, vol. 32, no. 1 (New York, 1975), p. 95.

50. Benjamin Bradlee, quoted in Kampelman, "The Media," p. 89; and, in general, Max M. Kampelman, "The Power of the Press: A Problem for Our Democracy," *Policy Review* 6 (Fall 1978): 7–39.

51. Austin Ranney, "The Political Parties: Reform and Decline," in King, *New American Political System*, p. 213.

52. Ladd and Hadley, *Transformations*, pp. 320–333. Nie, Verba, and Petrocik, *Changing American Voter*, passim, but esp. chs. 4, 7–10, and Epilogue.

53. Hugh Heclo, "Issues Networks and the Executive Establishment," in King, *New American Political System*, pp. 87ff; and idem, *A Government of Strangers: Executive Politics in Washington* (Washington, D.C.: Brookings Institution, 1977).

54. Harrison W. Fox, Jr., and Susan Webb Hammond, "The Growth of Congressional Staffs," in Mansfield, *Congress against the President*, pp. 112–124.

55. See "When Congress Has the Veto," *National Journal* 8 (May 29, 1976): 745.

56. Fred I. Greenstein, "Change and Continuity in the Modern Presidency," in King, *New American Political System*, pp. 80–82.

57. King, "American Polity," pp. 374–375.

58. Lyndon B. Johnson, quoted in Doris Kearns, *Lyndon Johnson and the American Dream* (New York: Harper & Row, 1976), pp. 177–178. Richard M. Nixon, March 13, 1973, quoted in *New York Times*, May 5, 1974, p. 40. Dwight Chapin, quoted in *New York Times*, August 5, 1973, p. 40. Gerald R. Ford, "Imperiled, Not Imperial," *Time* 116 (November 10, 1980): 30.

59. ABC News–Harris Survey, vol. 2, no. 67 (June 2, 1980).

60. "Opinion Roundup," *Public Opinion* 2 (June–July 1979): 32.

61. "Opinion Roundup," *Public Opinion* 1 (November–December 1978): 29. Nie, Verba, and Petrocik, *Changing American Voter*, pp. 370–371.

62. Quoted in John Cole, "Lament for a Faded Dream," *The Observer*, August 31, 1980, p. 11.

63. Joseph Kraft, *Boston Globe*, March 13, 1975, p. 33, and *Washington Post*, October 25, 1977, p. A19.

64. George F. Will, *Newsweek* 91 (March 6, 1978): 108. High Sidey, *Time* 116 (December 1, 1980): 18.

65. Walter Cronkite, interview, *Playboy*, June 1973, p. 76, quoted in Michael Robinson, "American Political Legitimacy in an Era of Electronic Journalism: Reflections on the Evening News," in Richard Adler, ed., *Television as a Social Force: New Approaches to TV Criticism* (Aspen: Praeger, 1975), p. 123.

66. Roger Mudd, quoted in Kampelman, "The Media," p. 94. Theodore H. White, "America's Two Cultures," *Columbia Journalism Review* 8 (Winter 1969-70):8.

67. Robinson, "American Political Legitimacy," p. 117.

68. Robinson, "Television and American Politics," pp. 18-19, 35.

69. Ibid., p. 35.

70. Stanley Rothman, "The Mass Media in Post-Industrial Society," in Lipset, *Third Century*, p. 383. Samuel P. Huntington, "Postindustrial Politics: How Benign Will It Be?" *Comparative Politics* 6 (January 1974): 182-186.

71. Harry Rosenfeld, metropolitan editor of *The Washington Post*, on BBC television, May 7, 1973.

72. *New York Times*, January 18, 1980, p. A10.

8. The Viability of American Ideals and Institutions

1. Richard Hofstadter, *The American Political Tradition* (New York: Knopf, 1951), pp. 65-66.

2. Marvin Meyers, *The Jacksonian Persuasion: Politics and Belief* (Stanford: Stanford University Press, 1957), p. 8.

3. See Edward Pessen, "The Egalitarian Myth and the American Social Reality: Wealth, Mobility, and Equality in the 'Era of the Common Man,' " *American Historical Review* 76 (October 1971): 989-1034, and *Riches, Class, and Power before the Civil War* (Lexington, Mass.: D. C. Heath, 1973), passim. For critical discussions of Pessen's evidence and argument, see Whitman Ridgway, "Measuring Wealth and Power in Ante-Bellum America: A Review Essay," *Historical Methods Newsletter* 8 (March 1975): 74-78, and Robert E. Gallman, "Professor Pessen on the 'Egalitarian Myth,' " *Social Science History* 2 (Winter 1978): 194-207. For Pessen's response, see his "On a Recent Cliometric Attempt to Resurrect the Myth of Antebellum Egalitarianism," *Social Science History* 3 (Winter 1979): 208-227.

4. Gordon S. Wood, *History Book Club Review*, June 1955, pp. 16-17, commenting on Rush Welter's *The Mind of America: 1820-1860*.

5. Rush Welter, *The Mind of America: 1820-1860* (New York: Columbia University Press, 1975), pp. 7-10.

6. Alexis de Tocqueville, *Democracy in America*, ed. Phillips Bradley (New York: Vintage Books, 1954), 1:6-17.

7. Joseph L. Blau, ed., *Social Theories of Jacksonian Democracy* (New York: Liberal Arts Press, 1954), pp. xxvii-xxviii.

8. Hofstadter, *American Political Tradition*, p. vi.

9. Herbert Croly, *The Promise of American Life* (New York: Mac-

millan, 1909), p. 156. Walter Lippmann, *Drift and Mastery* (Englewood Cliffs, N.J.: Prentice-Hall, 1961), pp. 81–82.

10. Hofstadter, *American Political Tradition*, pp. 223.

11. J. R. Pole, *The Pursuit of Equality in American History* (Berkeley: University of California Press, 1978), p. 326.

12. See Ronald Inglehart, *The Silent Revolution: Changing Values and Political Styles among Western Publics* (Princeton: Princeton University Press, 1977), and George C. Lodge, *The New American Ideology* (New York: Knopf, 1975).

13. Ronald Inglehart, "The Silent Revolution in Europe: Intergenerational Change in Post-Industrial Societies," *American Political Science Review* 65 (December 1971): 991–1017.

14. Samuel P. Huntington, "Postindustrial Politics: How Benign Will It Be?" *Comparative Politics* 6 (January 1974): 188–189.

15. Plato, *The Republic*, tr. Francis MacDonald Cornford (New York: Oxford University Press, 1945), p. 290.

16. Louis Hartz, *The Liberal Tradition in America* (New York: Harcourt, Brace, 1955), p. 181.

17. Samuel P. Huntington, *Political Order in Changing Societies* (New Haven: Yale University Press, 1968), pp. 362–369.

18. See Samuel P. Huntington, *The Soldier and the State: The Theory and Politics of Civil-Military Relations* (Cambridge, Mass.: Harvard University Press, 1957), esp. pp. 143–157.

19. George F. Kennan, *American Diplomacy 1900–1950* (Chicago: University of Chicago Press, 1951), pp. 93–94. Huntington, *The Soldier and the State*, pp. 80–97.

20. Lucian W. Pye, *The Spirit of Chinese Politics* (Cambridge, Mass.: MIT Press, 1968), p. 91.

21. Seymour Martin Lipset, "The Banality of Revolt," *Saturday Review* 53 (July 18, 1970): 26.

22. Peregrine Worsthorne, "America—Conscience or Shield?" *Encounter*, no. 14 (November 1954): 15.

23. Henry Fairlie, "Anti-Americanism at Home and Abroad," *Commentary* 60 (December 1975): 35.

24. See, for example, Hans J. Morgenthau, *In Defense of the National Interest* (New York: Knopf, 1951), and "Another 'Great Debate': The National Interest of the United States," *American Political Science Review* 46 (December 1952): 961–988; Reinhold Niebuhr, *Christian Realism and Political Problems* (New York: Charles Scribner's Sons, 1953), and *The Irony of American History* (New York: Charles Scribners Sons, 1952); Kennan, *American Diplomacy 1900–1950*; Robert E. Osgood, *Ideals and Self-Interest in America's Foreign Relations* (Chicago: University of Chicago Press, 1953); Richard H. Ullman, "Washington versus Wilson," *Foreign Policy*, no. 21 (Winter 1975–76): 97–124.

25. Henry A. Kissinger, quoted in Raymond Gastil, "Affirming Ameri-

can Ideals in Foreign Policy," *Freedom at Issue,* no. 38 (November-December 1976): 12.

26. Jimmy Carter, address, B'nai B'rith convention, Washington, D.C., September 8, 1976.

27. Hans J. Morgenthau, "Repression's Friend," *New York Times,* October 10, 1974, p. 46.

28. See John D. Montgomery, *Forced to be Free: The Artificial Revolution in Germany and Japan* (Chicago: University of Chicago Press, 1957).

29. Theodore P. Wright, *American Support of Free Elections Abroad* (Washington, D.C.: Public Affairs Press, 1964), pp. 137–138.

30. Jorge I. Dominguez, *Cuba: Order and Revolution* (Cambridge, Mass.: Harvard University Press, 1978), p. 13.

31. See Tad Szulc, *The Twilight of the Tyrants* (New York: Henry Holt, 1959).

32. Jerome Slater, *Intervention and Negotiation* (New York: Harper & Row, 1970), p. 7.

33. Abraham F. Lowenthal, *The Dominican Intervention* (Cambridge, Mass.: Harvard University Press, 1972), p. 16.

34. Jerome Levinson and Juan de Onis, *The Alliance that Lost Its Way* (Chicago: Quadrangle Books, 1970), pp. 81–82.

35. H. Bradford Westerfield, *The Instruments of America's Foreign Policy* (New York: Thomas Y. Crowell, 1963), p. 416.

36. A. M. Rosenthal, *New York Times,* April 8, 1963, p. 14.

37. Quoted by Andrew H. Malcolm, *New York Times,* June 11, 1976, p. A2.

38. *The Economist* 275 (August 30, 1980), pp. 27–28.

39. Ullman, "Washington versus Wilson," pp. 117, 123.

40. Stanley Hoffmann, "No Choice, No Illusions," *Foreign Policy,* no. 25 (Winter, 1976–77), p. 127.

41. Adnan Menderes, *Cumhuriyet,* July 18, 1946, quoted in Kemal H. Karpat, *Turkey's Politics* (Princeton: Princeton University Press, 1959), p. 140, n. 10.

42. Fairlie, "Anti-Americanism at Home and Abroad," p. 34, quoting William Clarke, 1881.

43. Daniel Bell, "The End of American Exceptionalism," in Nathan Glazer and Irving Kristol, eds., *The American Commonwealth 1976* (New York: Basic Books, 1976), p. 197.

44. Mihajlo Mihajlov, "Prospects for the Post-Tito Era," *New America* 17 (January 1980): 7.

INDEX

Adams, John, 5, 93, 125
Adams, Samuel, 102
Age: and response to cognitive dissonance, 71; and periods of creedal passion, 146; and political participation, 181–182; and voting behavior, 182–183; and forms of protest, 184
Agnew, Spiro, 189
Alienation, political, in the 1950s, 170
Allende, Salvador, 252–253
Alliance for Progress, 251
Almond, Gabriel, 43
American, The, 101
American Creed, 4, 13–14; sources of, 14–16; conflicts inherent in, 16–18; alternatives to, 18–21; stability of, 21–23; as basis of national identity, 23–30; relation to political institutions, 32; antigovernmental aspects of, 33–38, 216; and socioeconomic status, 73–74; periods of passion over, 85–91; climate of passion over, 91; reformers united by, 107; and reform, 113–114; and Protestantism, 157; in S&S Years, 174; possible lessening of reliance on, 229–231. *See also* Creedal passion
American politics: ideals of, 3–4; structural paradigms of, 5–10; ideals vs. institutions in, 10–12; and IvI gap, 39–41, 51; cycles in, 147–148; relation of religion to, 165–166. *See*

also Political institutions; Political parties
"American's Creed," 159
Angola, 208
Antipower ethic, 38–39, 75; and conspiracy theory, 80; and sincerity, 81–83
Antislavery movement, and creedal passion, 111–112
Antitrust reform, 117
Antiwar movement, and woman suffrage, 110. *See also* Vietnam War
Arendt, Hannah, 89
Argentina, 50–51
Arnold, Thurman, 90–91
Asylums: as symbols of reform, 117; perversion of, 119
Atlantic Monthly, 101
Austria, 249
Authority: American attitude toward, 46, 179; German attitude toward, 47; French attitude toward, 50; Russian attitude toward, 54; Japanese attitude toward, 55; emphasis on, in China, 59–60; reaction to misuse of, 184; misuse vs. erosion of, 211, 213; during S&S Years, 211–220 cynicism and restoration of, 214–220

Bagehot, Walter, 46
Bailyn, Bernard, 33, 92, 93, 107
Baker, Ray Stannard, 103

Baker, Russell, 196–197
Bancroft, George, 11
Bank of the United States, as monopoly, 95, 106, 140, 223
Batista, Fulgencio, 251
Beard, Charles, 163
Belaunde, Fernando, 252
Bell, Daniel, 7, 17, 260
Beloff, Max, 43
Benedict, Ruth, 52, 55
Bentham, Jeremy, 35
Bentley, Arthur F., 8
Bernstein, Carl, 122
Betancourt, Rómolo, 251
Béteille, André, 12
Bible, the, and awakenings, 162–163
Bickel, Alexander, 178
Blacks: political participation of, 181–182; protests of, against discrimination, 184; and black power, 187; gains of, in S&S Years, 198; and the American Creed, 224. *See also* Civil rights movement
Blackstone, William, 35
Blau, Joseph L., 225–226
Bodin, Jean, 35
Boorstin, Daniel, 7, 169
Bosch, Juan, 252
Boudin, Kathy, 187
Bracher, Karl Dietrich, 49
Brandeis brief, 103
Brogan, D. W., 24, 159
Brown, Richard Maxwell, 150
Brown v. Board of Education, 199
Bryan, William Jennings, 226–227
Bryce, James, 22, 24, 29, 34; on concept of state, 35
Budget Control and Impoundment Act, 208–209
Bureaucracy, reform of, 201
Burke, Edmund, 45
Burnham, Walter Dean, 122, 123, 129

Calhoun, John C., 34
Calvin, John, 36
Cambodia, 195, 200
Campaign finance, reform of, 119
Canada, 44–45
Cannon, Joseph, 227

Cantril, Hadley, 21
Carter, Jimmy, 197, 210, 215, 216–217; on morality in foreign affairs, 246–247, 255
Case, Thomas, 153
Castro, Fidel, 251
Central Intelligence Agency (CIA): exposure of operations of, 189, 192; crusades against, 238
Chambers, William, 148
Chancellor, John, 191
Chang, John M., 254
Channing, William Ellery, 108, 111
Charles I, 151
Checks and balances theory, 127–129
Chesterton, G. K., 36, 159
Chile, 252–253, 256
China, 229; political values in, 52, 58–60; emphasis on authority in, 59; sincerity in, 82; and the Cultural Revolution, 131–136; Confucianism in, 132; mobilization and consolidation in, 136–137; modernization in, 137–138; U.S. relations with, 239–240
Christianity, and the idea of reform, 114–115
Civil Rights Acts (1964, 1965), 187
Civil rights movement: and woman suffrage, 110; and religious revival, 165; in Kennedy years, 173, 174; importance of, as issue, 177; mobilization of protest for, 180, 184; reforms accomplished in, 198; for blacks, 198–199; for other minorities, 199; role of media in, 205
Clarke, William, 259–260
Class-conflict theory of American politics, 5–6; and political ideals, 10
Classes: and struggle for wealth and power, 5–6; predominance of middle, 6–7
Climate of creedal passion, 91–104; atmosphere of discontent, 91–93; political ideas and moral passion, 93–94; attack of power and hierarchy, 94–97; political participation and organization, 97–99; political communication, 99–102; muckraking and exposure, 102–104

Cognitive dissonance, 61–75; U.S. problem of, 61–63, 261; responses to, 64–68, 232; dynamics of response, 68–70; group propensities, 70–75
Coke, Sir Edward, 35
Cold War, 7; American influence during, 249–250
Collectivity, Japanese preference for, 56
Colombia, 251
Colonial period, rebellions of, 149–150
Committees of correspondence, 97
Complacency: as response to IvI gap, 64; as failure to perceive dissonance, 69–70; and socioeconomic states, 72, 73; in S&S Years, 169–173; danger of, 261
Confucianism, 132
Congress, U.S.: as agent of exposure, 190; reforms of, 201; increase in power of, 203, 207, 217
Congressional Budget Office, 208
Congressional Research Service, 208
Congress of Racial Equality (CORE), 186, 187–188
Consensus: and instability, 31–41; and antipower ethic, 33–39; and the IvI gap, 39–41; in non-Western societies, 52; and the press, 101; as source of political conflict, 110–111; in Soviet Union, 112; as basic to political change, 131; in the 1950s, 170
Consensus theory of American politics, 6–7, 10
Conservatism, 121; transnationalism of, 28; affinities of, 42; cycles of, 148; shift toward, 216
Conservatives, on equality, 233–234, 235
Conspiracy theories: and cover-up imperative, 78–81; and power, 79–80; and "the smoking gun fallacy," 194
Constituencies, U.S.: of branches of government, 124–126; changes in, 126
Constituent mutability, 124
Constituent plurality, 124
Constitution, American: unique position of, 30; views of human nature reflected in, 37

Constitutional Convention, on theories of government, 124–125
Cover-up imperative, 78–81
Creedal conflict, 105–112; vs. interest group politics, 105
Creedal passion: periods of, 85–91; characteristics of, 86–87; climate of, 91–104; movement vs. establishment, 105–112; source in consensus, 110–111; and reform, 115; and realignment, 129; reasons for, 130; general sources of, 131–138; specific sources of, 138–166; legacies of, 197; changing success of eras of, 222–228. See also Jacksonian era; Progressive era; Revolutionary era; Sixes and Sevens, era of
Cremin, Lawrence, 117
Crèvecoeur, J. Hector St. John, 6, 24
Croly, Herbert, 17, 24, 30, 93; on reform, 115; on reaction to political evils, 142; on progress, 225
Cronkite, Walter, 218
Cuba, 250
Custine, Marquis de, 54
Cycles, 147–149
Cynicism: as response to IvI gap, 64; as toleration of gap, 68–69; and age, 71; and socioeconomic status, 72, 73; and muckraking, 104; and authority, 214–220; danger of, 261
Czechoslovakia, 249, 256

Decatur, Stephen, 241
Declaration of Independence: political ideas in, 14; Bentham on, 35
Deep Throat, 191
Democracy: in Britain, 46; in Germany, 48–50; in France, 50; in Latin America, 51; Japanese attitude toward, 57; in Jacksonian era, 223; in defeated Axis countries, 249
Devine, Donald, 21
Dewey, John, 117
Dickens, Charles, 34
Discontent, atmosphere of, 91–93
Disharmonic society, U.S. as, 12
Dittmer, Lowell, 134
Dominican Republic, 250

Donald, David, 142, 145
Du Bois, Cora, 37–38

Economic interests: importance in politics, 9–10; in S&S Years, 177
Education: progressive movement, 117; gain for blacks in, 199
Edwards, Jonathan, 155
Eisenhower, D. D., 76, 167, 173, 197
Elkins, Stanley, 112
Ellsberg, Daniel, 34, 189, 191, 193, 205
Emerson, Ralph Waldo, 68, 92, 93, 183; on exposure and reform, 102, 103; on reform, 110, 154
Engels, Friedrich, 19
English Revolution, as source of American creedal passion, 150–154
Enlightenment, the, 15
Equality, concept of: and the American Creed, 15; conflict with liberty, 16–18; and social mobility, 37–38; and wealth, 38–39; in periods of creedal passion, 96–97; Tocqueville on, 225; contrived vs. natural, 228; and political beliefs, 233–234
Equal Rights Amendment, 200
Establishment, vs. movement, 108–110, 163
Ethnicity, vs. nationality, 26
Europe: political ideas and nationality in, 28–30; ideological pluralism in, 42–44; political change in, 113; effect of prosperity in, 172; and foreign policy, 236, 240–241; attitude of, toward U.S., 239
Evangelists, role of, in mass mobilization, 163–164
Exogenous events and creedal passion, 143–146; relative prosperity, 144; social and economic change, 144–145; status politics, 145–146; increase in youthful population, 146
Exposure, governmental: investigatory vs. regulatory, 188; dynamics of, 190–191; multiplication of agents of, 192–193; multiplication of targets of, 193–194; decreasing returns of, 194; multiplication of secrets, 194–195
Exposure, politics of, 102–104. See also Muckraking

Fairbank, John K., 58
Fairlie, Henry, 260
Federal Bureau of Investigation (FBI), 238
Federalism, and Progressivism, 5–6
Federalist, The: Madison in, 8, 124; discussions of society in, 37
Federalists, 127
Festinger, Leon, 62
Feudalism, effect of U.S. lack of, 39–40
Filmer, Robert, 19
Finney, Charles Grandison, 163, 164
First Great Awakening, 160, 161; explanations for, 162; polarizations of, 163; and revivalism, 164–165
Ford, Gerald, 192, 210, 246
Foreign policy: increasing role of Congress in, 208; and the IvI gap, 236; institutions of, 236–240; goals of, 240–245; power and liberty, 246–259
Fourth Great Awakening, 160, 162, 165
Fox, George, 109
France: and nationality, 25–26; political culture of, 50
Free, Lloyd, 21
Freedom of Information Acts (1966, 1974), 201
Frei, Eduardo, 252
French Revolution, 89
Friedrich, Carl, 30

Gap between Creed and practice: effect of, in U.S., 32–41; in European societies, 42–51; in non-Western societies, 52–60; coping with, 61–84. See also IvI gap
Garrison, William Lloyd, 84, 98; as reformer, 108, 111, 226
General Accounting Office, 208
George III, 80
Germany: nationality of, 26; attitudes toward authority in, 47–48; democracy in, 249
Government: American suspicion of, 33–38; relative weakness of U.S., 39–41; threatened by consensus, 41; perceptions of in S&S Years, 175–177; public nature of U.S., 188; growing distrust of, 215–219; role of television in legitimacy of, 218

Graham, Billy, 163, 165; use of television, 164
Great awakenings, periods of, 160–166; character of, as revivals, 161–162; causes of, 162; use of means of communication in, 163–164; mass organizing during, 164; relation to political events, 165–166. *See also entries for First, Second, Third, and Fourth Great Awakenings*
Great Britain: ideological pluralism in, 45–46; contrasted with U.S., 46; humor and class structure in, 65; equilibrium among social forces in, 127
Great Leap Forward, 136
Great Proletarian Cultural Revolution: and U.S. creedal passion, 131–135; as period of mobilization, 136–138; and modernization, 138
Greece, 248, 250
Greensboro, N.C., 168
Greenstein, Fred I., 44
Grimes, Alan, 110

Haiti, 250
Hamilton, Alexander, 5, 6
Harper's, 101
Hartz, Louis, 6, 18, 94; and consensus theory, 7, 172; on Constitution, 40; on abolitionists, 111; on conservatives, 121–122
Hawthorne, Nathaniel, 66
Hayakawa, S. I., 83
Hayden, Tom, 187, 202
Hearst, William Randolph, 100
Heimert, Alan, 165
Hendel, Charles, 34
Hierarchy: in Japan, 55; in China, 58
Hill, Christopher, 152
Hiniker, Paul, 134
Hobbes, Thomas, 35, 36, 37
Hoffman, Stanley, 50, 256
Hofstadter, Richard, 7, 8, 11, 25; on immigrants, 20; on conspiracy, 80; on the New Deal, 90; on status anxiety, 145; on looking back, 226; on a new ethic, 230
Hooker, Richard, 35

House of Representative, early conceptions of, 124
Hübner, Baron von, 35
Humphrey, Hubert, 104
Hungary, 249
Huntington, Samuel P., 238
Hutchinson, Gov. Thomas, 102
Hypocrisy: as response to IvI gap, 64, 66–67; as denial of gap, 70; and level of education, 71; and socioeconomic status, 72; at start of S&S Years, 173; danger of, 261

Ideology: vs. nationality, 28, 236–237; and change, in Europe, 113–114; decline of, in 1950s, 171–172; errors in estimating, 172–173; and the Old Left, 177; tension between development and, 229; and foreign-policy institutions, 237; American faith in universality of, 244–245
Immigrants, effect of, on U.S. politics, 20, 230
Immigration, and American identity, 26–27
Independents, political, 206
India, 12
Individualism: opposition to, in non-Western societies, 55; in Jacksonian era, 223; possible displacement of, 230
Industrialization, lack of proletariat of, 19–20
Informants, 193
Inkeles, Alex, 47
Institutions: for contrived congruence of ideal and reality, 228. *See also* IvI gap; Political institutions
Interest groups: politics of, 105; and consensus, 110–111
Italy, 26, 249
Ivan the Terrible, 54
IvI gap (ideals vs. institutions), 39–41; in Europe, 51; in China, 59; U.S. responses to, 64–75; and the power paradox, 75–83; in periods of creedal passion, 88; variations in reaction to, 141–142; impact of reform in S&S Years, 197–202; future of, 221–222; approach to in Middle Period, 223–

IvI gap—*Cont.*
224; possible dilution of ideals of
Creed, 229–231; possible changes in
patterns of response, 231–232; possible destruction of both factors,
232–235; implications for foreign
policy, 236–259; applied to other nations, 242–245; American politics
distinguished by, 259–262

Jacksonian era: as period of creedal
passion, 55, 91; political ideas during, 94; formation of associations in,
97; political communication during,
100; and interest groups, 106, reforms in, 115, 116–117; as rational
response, 139; enigma of outrage
during, 142; relation of, to great
awakening, 165; successes of, 222–
223; as turning point, 224–225;
Tocqueville on, 225
Jacksonians, 34
James, Henry, 35
Japan: political values in, 52, 55–58;
hierarchy in, 55–56; collectivity in,
56; vertical structure and modernization in, 58; sincerity in, 82; U.S. relations with, 239–240; democracy in,
249
Jefferson, Thomas, 6, 128
Johnson, Lyndon B., 76, 149, 192, 194;
on lack of power, 210, 213
Journalists: role of, in exposure, 193;
changing recruitment of, 204. *See
also* Media; Press

Kendall, Willmore, 62–63
Kennan, George, 238, 246
Kennedy, John F., 76, 171, 172, 194;
Presidency of, 173–174; promotion
of democracy by, 255
Kim Dae Jung, 255
King, Anthony, 203
King, Martin Luther, 165
Kinsley, Michael, 194
Kissinger, Henry, 246
Klingberg, Frank L., 148, 149
Kluckhohn, Clyde, 21
Korea, 248. *See also* South Korea

Kraft, Joseph, 217
Kristol, Irving, 66, 88
Kurth, James, 146

Ladd, William, 108
Ladies Home Journal, The, 101
La Follette, Robert, 226
Latin America: political values in, 51;
democracy and U.S. influence in,
250–251
Laud, William, 150
Law, concept of, and American Creed,
14
Leadership: growing need for, 216–
217; basic network necessary to, 219
Lenin, Nikolai, 102
Lerner, Max, 90
Levine, Meldon E., 2–3, 4
Levinson, Daniel, 47
Lewin, Kurt, 47
Liberalism: transnationalism of, 28;
affinities of, 42; and age, 182
Liberals, moralist vs. hypocritical, 233–
234
Liberty: relation to power, 33–34, 258;
during periods of creedal passion, 95;
in Jacksonian era, 223; and the myth
of American repression, 247–259
Lincoln, Abraham, 66
Lippmann, Walter, 103, 143, 144, 226,
246
Lipset, Seymour Martin, 7, 50, 170
Liu Shao-ch'i, 134
Locke, John, 6, 15, 19, 21, 94; possible
displacement of, 230
Lodge, George, 229–230
Lowi, Theodore J., 118, 120
Lowell, James Russell, 98, 109
Lubow, Arthur, 194

Machiavelli, Niccolo, 35
Madison, James, 8, 21, 34, 95, 124; on
concentration of power, 211
Magazines, growth of, 101
Magsaysay, Ramon, 253
Main Currents of American Thought
(Parrington), 5
Mann, Horace, 117
Mao Tse-tung, 133, 134, 135

Marcos, Ferdinand, 253
Marshall, Stephen, 152
Marx, Karl, 19, 163, 171
Marxism, 28; of Hartz, 7; affinities of, 42; in U.S., 111; of the Old Left, 177; and the New Left, 187; in U.S. vs. Western Europe, 234–235
Marxism-Leninism, 241; domination of party, 53; and perceptions of equality, 234
McCarthy, Joseph, 80, 169, 170
McClelland, David, 148
McCloskey, Robert, 16
McClosky, Herbert, 72
McClure's, 101, 102
Mead, Margaret, 83
Mead, Sidney, 30, 159
Media: use of, in periods of creedal passion, 99–102, 190; newspapers and magazines, 100–101, 190; television, 101, 190; in the Colonial period, 152; role of evangelists in, 163–164; in the S&S Years, 190, 203; decline of, in the 1980s, 210; national vs. local, 217–218
Menderes, Adnan, 257
Mexico, 51
Michels, Robert, 122
Middle class: predominance in American society, 6; and failure of socialism, 19
Mihajlov, Mihajlo, 260
Military, power of, 76–77
Mills, C. Wright, 6, 170
Monopolies, 38
Moody, Dwight, 164
Moralism: as response to IvI gap, 64, 67–68, 74; as response to eliminate gap, 68; and age, 71; in periods of creedal passion, 93–94; during S&S Years, 174; effect of on authority, 214; and foreign policy, 241, 246; danger of, 261
Moral issues, and American politics, 11
Morgenthau, Hans, 246, 247
Morris, Gouverneur, 125
Movement and reform vs. establishment, 108, 163
Moynihan, Daniel Patrick, 180
Muckraking, 102–104

Mudd, Roger, 218
Muskegon, Mich., 72
Myrdal, Gunnar, 16, 17, 24, 199; on stability of American Creed, 22; on IvI gap, 39, 224; on American moralism, 67, 69
Myth of American repression, 247–259; democracy and authoritarianism in Latin America, 250–253; in Asia, 253–255; relation of power to, 257–259

Nader, Ralph, 98, 110, 122, 166
Nakane, Chie, 56
Namenworth, J. Zvi, 148–149
National identity: based on political ideas, 23–30, 63; U.S. contrasted with British, 25–26; and ethnicity, 26; effect of immigration on, 26–27; in Europe, 28–30, 237; Creed less essential to, 230
National Student Association, 192
Neustadt, Richard, 75
New Deal: and consensus theory, 7; not a creedal passion period, 87, 90–91
New Left, 177; vs. Old Left, 178; shifts in, over time, 186–187
Newspapers, growth of, 100–101
Newsweek, 101
New York City, reform in, 118, 120
New York Times, 101; Watergate story in, 189; on the CIA, 192; on the bombing of Cambodia, 195; national scope of, 204; and the Pentagon Papers, 205
Nicaragua, 250
Niebuhr, H. Richard, 164
Niebuhr, Reinhold, 155, 246
Nineteen-fifties: complacency during, 169–170; decline of ideology in, 171–172
Nineteen-sixties; summarized by Levine, 3; American Creed in, 4–5
Nixon, Richard M., 67, 76, 180; tapes of, 189; Presidency of, 191–192, 195, 200, 210, 213

Office of Technology Assessment, 208
Oksenberg, Michel, 136

Old Left, 177
Olney, Richard, 119
Organizations: proliferation of in S&S Years, 183; radical reform vs. radical revolutionary, 187
Osgood, Robert, 246

Packwood, Senator Bob, 67
Paine, Thomas, 93, 100
Palmer, R. R., 92
Palmerston, Viscount, 240
Pamphlets, 99–100
Paradigms of American politics: class-conflict theory, 5–6; consensus theory, 6–7; pluralist theory, 7–8; limitations of, 8–9; implications of, 9–10
Paraguay, 251
Park Chung Hee, 254
Parrington, Vernon, 5–6
Parsons, Talcott, 7
Participant orientation in U.S., 43
Parties, political, in U.S., 5–6; reform of, 201
Pentagon Papers, 102, 189, 205
People's Republic of China, monism of, 25. See also China
Periods of U.S. creedal passion, 85–91; Jacksonian, 85; Progressive, 85; 1960s and early 1970s (S&S Years), 85; characteristics of, 86–87; Revolutionary, 87–89; repetition between, 109. See also American Creed; Creedal passion
Peru, 252
Phillippines, 253
Phillips, David Graham, 103
Phillips, Wendell, 110, 111
Pinckney, Charles, 124
Plato, 232–233
Pluralism, ideological, in Europe vs. U.S., 45–51
Pluralist theory of American politics, 7–8; in works of James Madison, 8; and political ideals, 10
Poland, 249
Political ideals, American, 3–4; in periods of creedal passion, 93–94. See also IvI gap
Political institutions: challenged by consensus on ideals, 32–33; and IvI

gap, 39–41; and social forces, 125–129; continuity of, 126–127; perception of, in S&S Years, 175
Political participation, 97–99; of blacks, 181–182; and age, 182
Political parties: decline in power of, 203, 210; earlier functions of, 205–207; factors influencing decline of, 207
Political values: U.S. vs. other Western countries, 45–51; in non-Western societies, 52–60; and cognitive dissonance, 63
Populists, on power, 96
Port Huron statement, 186–187
Portugal, 248, 256
Potter, David, 7
Power: relation of, to liberty, 33–34, 247, 258; American attitudes toward, 36–37, 78; and success, 38; and wealth, 38–39; paradox of, 75–78; and cover-up, 78–83; attacked in periods of creedal passion, 94–97, 139–140; balance of, 126–127; as explicit goal, 188
Power paradox, and the IvI gap, 75–78
Presidency: impact of 1960s on, 135; evaluation of candidates for, 178–179; decline in power of, 203, 217; Congressional curbs on, 208–209
President: power of, 75–78; Nixon's weakness as, 191–192; limits on, 200
Press: power of, 78–79, 205; as agent of exposure, 190; emergence of national, 203–204; as adversary, 204, 218; reduction in influence of, 219
Primaries, reform of, 118
Progress: in accord with history, 222–224; at cross-purposes with history, 222, 225; consequences of divorce of history and, 226–228, 232
Progressive era: as period of creedal passion, 85, 91; political ideas during, 94; formation of associations in, 97–98; political communication during, 100–101; and interest groups, 106; reforms in, 115, 117; reform of primaries in, 118–119; enigma of public reaction in, 143; the past as ideal of, 226–227

Progressive theory (class-conflict): historic perspective on, 5–6; elements of, 6; vs. consensus theory, 6–7
Protest: mobilization of, 180–188; demonstrations and riots, 184–185
Protestantism: and the American Creed, 14–15, 229; intermingling of religion and politics, 154–159; and plurality of religious organizations, 156–157; great awakenings of, 160–166
Publicity, in periods of creedal passion, 99, 189
Public opinion polls, 174–177
Pulitzer, Joseph, 100
Puritanism, 151; and the Bible, 152; after the English Revolution, 153; legacy of, 154
Pusey, Nathan, 2
Pye, Lucian, 58, 59, 136
Pym, John, 150

Radicalism, in U.S., 36, 186
Ramparts, 192
Ranney, Austin, 205
Reagan, Ronald, 216
Realignment of institutions, 122–129; vs. reform, 112–113, 114; and critical elections, 122–123; party vs. political, 123–125; social forces and, 125–129; as surrogate for revolution, 129; during S&S Years, 203–210
Rebellions, in Colonial period, 149–150
Red Guards, 134–135
Reform of political institutions; use of American Creed by, 107–108; movement vs. establishment, 108; limits of, 112–122; European vs. U.S., 113; periods of, 115–118; perversion of, 119–120; and realignment, 122; of S&S Years, 197–202; changing nature of, 228; liberal vs. Marxist, 234–235
Republican Party, comeback of, 210
Reston, James, 205
Revolutionary era: as period of creedal passion, 85, 87–89; political ideas in, 93–94; opposition to power during, 95; formation of associations during, 97; political communication during, 99–100; and interest groups, 105–106; as period of reform, 115–116; as rational response, 139; relation to great awakenings, 165; successes of, 222
Rhee, Syngman, 254
Riots, 185
Robinson, Michael, 205
Rockefeller, Nelson, 189
Roosevelt, Franklin D., 66, 194
Roosevelt, Theodore, 92, 94; on muckraking, 102, 103, 104; as pragmatist, 227
Rothman, David, 109, 117
Rothman, Stanley, 218
Rousseau, Jean Jacques, 37, 135
Rubashov, Nicolas, 82
Rubin, Louis D., Jr., 65
Rush, Benjamin, 88
Russell, Richard, 208

Saint-Simon, Claude Henri, 135
Samson, Leon, 25
Santayana, George, 11
Saturday Evening Post, The, 101
Schaff, Philip, 154
Schlesinger, Arthur, Sr., 98, 148
Schlesinger, Arthur, Jr., on presidential power, 75–76
Schonfeld, William, 50
School desegregation, 199
Schurtz, Carl, 241
Schwartz, Benjamin, 135
Scripps, Edward, 100
Second Great Awakening, 160; explanations of, 162; and revivalism, 164, 165
Secrecy, privacy, and publicity, 79
Security institutions, relation of, to ideology, 237–238
Senate, early conceptions of, 124
Shils, Edward, 46, 78; on publicity and privacy, 79; on conspiracy, 81
Sihanouk, Prince, 195
Sincerity: role of, in politics, 81–84; in U.S., 83–84
Sinclair, Upton, 103, 110, 122
Sixes and Sevens, era of (S&S Years, 1960–1975): as period of creedal passion, 85, 91; voluntary associa-

Sixes and Sevens, era of—*Cont.*
   tions in, 98; interest groups in, 106;
   reforms in, 115; primaries in, 118–
   119; compared to Cultural Revolution, 135; enigma of reactions in,
   143; changing pattern of response in,
   167–169; complacency preceding,
   169–173; interlude of hypocrisy,
   173–174; surge of moralism, 174–
   180; mobilization of protest, 180–
   188; dynamics of exposure, 188–196;
   legacies of, 196–197; civil rights reforms of, 198–200; reforms of foreign and military policy, 200–201;
   reforms of political processes, 201–
   202; institutional realignment in,
   203–210; misuse and erosion of authority, 211–214; cynicism and restoration of authority, 214–220; lack
   of success in reforms of, 227–228
Slavery, and the American Creed, 111–
   112, 224
Smith, Ian, 83
Smith, Sir Thomas, 35
"Smoking gun fallacy," 194
Social class, and European ideologies,
   28
Social forces: relation of, to institutions
   and political parties, 125–129; and
   revivalism, 165
Socialism: failure of, in U.S., 19;
   transnationalism of, 28; affinities of,
   42
Social settlements, 117
Socioeconomic status: and response to
   cognitive dissonance, 71–75; and political participation, 181
Solomon, Richard H., 52
Somoza, Anastasio, 251
Sources of creedal passion, 131–166;
   general, 131–138; specific, 138–166;
   rational response to changes in
   power, 139–143; exogenous events,
   139, 143–146; recurring cycle of
   change, 139; consciousness cycle,
   147–149; original, in English Revolution, 149–154; and Protestantism,
   154–166
South, the, alternative set of political
   values in, 18–19

Southern Christian Leadership Conference, 187
South Korea, 249; democracy in, 254–
   255
Soviet Union: nationality and ideology
   in, 26; political values in, 52–55;
   consensus politics in, 112; attitude
   toward in 1950s, 171; perceived
   threat of, 173; U.S. relations with,
   239–240; foreign policy of, 241
Spain, 248
Stalin, Josef, 241
State, the: lack of U.S. concept of, 34–
   36, 78; and church, 36
Status anxiety: as source of creedal
   passion, 145; in English colonies, 149
Steffens, Lincoln, 102, 103, 122
Steinbeck, John, 174
Stimson, Henry, 74–75
Stone, Lawrence, 152
Strauss, Robert, 67
Student Nonviolent Coordinating Com-
   mittee (SNCC), 186, 187
Students for a Democratic Society
   (SDS), 1, 177–178, 186; changes in,
   187
Sunday, Billy, 163
Supreme Court, shifts in, 128

Tarbell, Ida, 103
Tarrow, Sidney, 44
Television: use of, by evangelists, 164;
   in the 1960s, 190; increased influence of, on news, 204–205; adversarial role of, 218
Third Great Awakening, 160, 162, 165
Thornton, A. P., 46
Time, 101
Title IX, 259
Tocqueville, Alexis de, 6, 11, 17, 21,
   24, 27; on stability of American
   values, 22, 43; on lack of democratic
   revolution, 40; on competitive elements of U.S. culture, 46; unaware
   of gap, 51; on authority, 52; on
   power, 61; on associations, 97, 101;
   on religion, 155, 157
Townsend, James, 60
Trilling, Lionel, 82
Trotsky, Leon, 241

Trujillo, Rafael, 251–252
Turkey, 208, 250, 257
Twain, Mark, 65

Ullman, Richard, 256, 258
Un-Americanism, unique concept of, 25
United Kingdom, concept of nationality in, 25–26

Verba, Sidney, 43
Vietnam, democracy in, 253–254
Vietnam War: opposition to, 174, 177, 187, 246; mobilization of protest against, 180, 184; publicity over conduct of, 189; withdrawal from, 200; role of television in, 205
Voluntary associations, 97
Voting: during S&S Years, 182, 198; abstention from, as protest, 182; reforms in, 201; decline in, 202
Voting Rights Act (1965), 198

Wall Street Journal, 204
Walters, Ronald, 142
Walzer, Michael, 17, 150
War, American attitude toward, 242.
   See also Vietnam War
War Powers Act, 200, 208
Warren, Robert Penn, 65, 221
Washington, civil rights march on, 187
Washington Post, 101, 198; national

scope of, 204; and Watergate, 205;
   and antigovernment feeling, 218–219
Watergate, 189, 193, 205; reactions to, 143, 246
Wealth, "gospel of," 33; American ambivalence toward, 38–39
Weathermen, 187
Webster, Daniel, 92
Wells, H. G., 35–36
West Germany, democratic values in, 48–49. *See also* Germany
White, Theodore H., 218
Whitefield, George, 163
Whites, political participation of, 181, 188
Wilson, James Q., 98–99
Wilson, Woodrow, 35, 226, 246
Winstanley, Gerrard, 153
Woman suffrage, 110
Wood, Gordon, 92, 223–224
Woodward, Bob, 122
Woolrych, Austin, 151
Working-class, U.S., lack of Marxism in, 19–20
World War II, 242
Wright, Theodore, 250
Wu Han, 133

Yao Wen-yuan, 133
Yugoslavia, nationality and ideology in, 26